Interdisciplinary Perspectives on Socioecological Challenges

This book explores interdisciplinary perspectives on socioecological challenges and offers innovative solutions at both a European and global level.

This book critically reflects on the latest scientific knowledge regarding the increasing instability of the Earth System caused by human activities during the Anthropocene and the Great Acceleration. It focuses on the global and European challenges regarding climate, resources, bio-integrity, and environment. The authors assess the obstacles to overcoming these challenges and examine the risks posed by path dependencies, lock-ins, and trade-offs between global and regional goals. They also drill down into the complexities of the European Green Deal, specifically the similarities and differences between the scientific analyses and recommendations from the European Environment Agency and the content of the Deal. Finally, the book looks at the Just Transition put forward by the European Green Deal. The authors discuss this in a context of global and European ecological and socioecological challenges and put the question of equality, recognition, and democratization at the center.

Outlining new pathways to broaden the scope of scientific collaboration between the natural and technical sciences and the social sciences and the humanities, this volume will be of great interest to students and scholars of sustainable development, environmental policy and governance, and environmental justice.

Anders Siig Andersen is an Associate Professor at Roskilde University, Department of People and Technology. He holds a PhD in educational studies, is special advisor for the Rector of Roskilde University on socioecological sustainability issues, and is Study Director of the Master's in Education and Learning at Roskilde University.

Henrik Hauggaard-Nielsen is a Professor at Roskilde University, Department of People and Technology. He is an agronomist with a PhD in agroecology. He works on demand-driven transitions within urgent climate and environmental problems, primarily focusing on agri-food systems.

Thomas Budde Christensen is an Associate Professor at Roskilde University, Department of People and Technology. He works in the field of circular economy with special emphasis on research in sustainable consumption and production systems. His current research focuses on policy, strategies, and planning activities associated with recycling industrial waste, plastics waste, bio waste, and construction and demolition waste.

Lars Hulgaard is a Professor at Roskilde University, Department of People and Technology. He is a sociologist and holds a PhD in public administration. He works on issues related to social change, social innovation, solidarity economy, and sustainability. He collaborates with scholars globally to understand better how social innovation, solidarity economy, and epistemologies of the South can inspire social change in the North.

Routledge Studies in Sustainable Development

This series uniquely brings together original and cutting-edge research on sustainable development. The books in this series tackle difficult and important issues in sustainable development including: values and ethics; sustainability in higher education; climate compatible development; resilience; capitalism and de-growth; sustainable urban development; gender and participation; and well-being.

Drawing on a wide range of disciplines, the series promotes interdisciplinary research for an international readership. The series was recommended in the *Guardian*'s suggested reads on development and the environment.

The Politics of the Sustainable Development Goals
Legitimacy, Responsibility, and Accountability
Magdalena Bexell and Kristina Jönsson

Ecological Limits of Development
Living with the Sustainable Development Goals
Kaitlin Kish and Stephen Quilley

Learning Strategies for Sustainable Organisations
Bryan Hopkins

Social Progress and the Authoritarian Challenge to Democracy
Donald G. Reid

Decentralization, Local Governance, and Localizing the Sustainable Development Goals in Asia and the Pacific
Edited by Bruno Carrasco, Hanif A. Rahemtulla, and Rainer Rohdewohld

The Sustainable Development Goals
Diffusion and Contestation in Asia and Europe
Edited by Paul Bacon, Mina Chiba and Frederik Ponjaert

Interdisciplinary Perspectives on Socioecological Challenges
Sustainable Transformations Globally and in the EU
Edited by Anders Siig Andersen, Henrik Hauggaard-Nielsen, Thomas Budde Christensen, and Lars Hulgaard

For more information about this series, please visit: www.routledge.com/Routledge-Studies-in-Sustainable-Development/book-series/RSSD

Interdisciplinary Perspectives on Socioecological Challenges

Sustainable Transformations Globally and in the EU

Edited by
Anders Siig Andersen,
Henrik Hauggaard-Nielsen,
Thomas Budde Christensen,
and Lars Hulgaard

Cover image: Kjartan Siig Søderberg

First published 2023
by Routledge
4 Park Square, Milton Park, Abingdon, Oxon OX14 4RN

and by Routledge
605 Third Avenue, New York, NY 10158

Routledge is an imprint of the Taylor & Francis Group, an informa business

© 2023 selection and editorial matter, Anders Siig Andersen, Henrik Hauggaard-Nielsen, Thomas Budde Christensen, and Lars Hulgaard; individual chapters, the contributors

The right of Anders Siig Andersen, Henrik Hauggaard-Nielsen, Thomas Budde Christensen, and Lars Hulgaard to be identified as the authors of the editorial material, and of the authors for their individual chapters, has been asserted in accordance with sections 77 and 78 of the Copyright, Designs and Patents Act 1988.

All rights reserved. No part of this book may be reprinted or reproduced or utilised in any form or by any electronic, mechanical, or other means, now known or hereafter invented, including photocopying and recording, or in any information storage or retrieval system, without permission in writing from the publishers.

Trademark notice: Product or corporate names may be trademarks or registered trademarks, and are used only for identification and explanation without intent to infringe.

British Library Cataloguing-in-Publication Data
A catalogue record for this book is available from the British Library

ISBN: 978-1-032-33437-0 (hbk)
ISBN: 978-1-032-33438-7 (pbk)
ISBN: 978-1-003-31967-2 (ebk)

DOI: 10.4324/9781003319672

Typeset in Bembo
by codeMantra

Contents

List of contributors   vii

Introduction   1
ANDERS SIIG ANDERSEN, HENRIK HAUGGAARD-NIELSEN,
THOMAS BUDDE CHRISTENSEN, AND LARS HULGAARD

PART I
Global ecological and socioecological challenges and UN solutions   15

1 **Global ecological risks**   16
ANDERS SIIG ANDERSEN, HENRIK HAUGGAARD-NIELSEN,
THOMAS BUDDE CHRISTENSEN, AND LARS HULGAARD

2 **UN ecological risk governance**   32
ANDERS SIIG ANDERSEN, HENRIK HAUGGAARD-NIELSEN,
THOMAS BUDDE CHRISTENSEN, AND LARS HULGAARD

3 **Socioecological challenges and UN policies**   59
ANDERS SIIG ANDERSEN AND LARS HULGAARD

4 **Affirmative and critical perspectives on the 2030 Agenda of sustainable development and the sustainable development goals**   93
ANDERS SIIG ANDERSEN AND LARS HULGAARD

PART II
European ecological and socioecological challenges, and EU solutions 115

5 The European Green Deal and the state of the European environment 116
ANDERS SIIG ANDERSEN, HENRIK HAUGGAARD-NIELSEN, THOMAS BUDDE CHRISTENSEN, AND LARS HULGAARD

6 Climate change-motivated development of EU's energy production and use systems 146
THOMAS BUDDE CHRISTENSEN AND TOBIAS PAPE THOMSEN

7 Resources and the circular economy 174
THOMAS BUDDE CHRISTENSEN

8 The food system and agriculture 194
HENRIK HAUGGAARD-NIELSEN AND NIELS HEINE KRISTENSEN

9 Biodiversity and nature's contributions to people 218
THORKIL CASSE AND HENRIK HAUGGAARD-NIELSEN

10 Just Transition and the EU 239
LARS HULGAARD AND ANDERS SIIG ANDERSEN

PART III
Cross-cutting issues: governance, the "Anthropocene", and interdisciplinary research 263

11 Ecological and socioecological governance in the UN and the EU 264
ANDERS SIIG ANDERSEN, THOMAS BUDDE CHRISTENSEN, AND LARS HULGAARD

12 Decentering humanity: the Anthropocene and the perils of Anthropocentricity 301
ANDERS SIIG ANDERSEN AND LARS HULGAARD

13 Interdisciplinary research and knowledge creation 320
ANDERS SIIG ANDERSEN, HENRIK HAUGGAARD-NIELSEN, THOMAS BUDDE CHRISTEN, AND LARS HULGAARD

Index 355

List of contributors

Thorkil Casse is an Associate Professor in the Department of Social Sciences and Business at Roskilde University, he holds a candidate's degree in economics and a PhD in development economics. His research focuses on the relationship between nature and people, looking for synergies in a world where other scholars emphasize the existence of trade-offs. The research examines new forms of the environmental state in Asia, specifically with reference to how governance models address the dual crisis of social and environmental protections in fringe areas. Recent fieldwork in Vietnam raises issues beyond synergies or trade-offs. Can societies develop and strive without any protection of biodiversity?

Niels Heine Kristensen is a Professor in the Department of People and Technology at Roskilde University, and he is a civil engineer (environment) with a PhD in socio-technology. His research focuses primarily on food studies, food systems, and food policies, especially modern practices within the complex and linked systems of actors and artifacts in agriculture, food, meals, and gastronomy. His special emphasis is the understanding of and how to explain which mechanisms and dynamics are at play in connection with the major societal challenges of converting these systems to more sustainable, ecological, and climate-friendly practices. Visible and invisible food system practices in several organizations and networks have been characterized over the years through comprehensive national and international collaborations and his work has attracted competitive funding, including from the EU research funds, the Nordic and Danish research councils, and private research funds.

Tobias Pape Thomsen is an Associate Professor in the Department of People and Technology at Roskilde University, and he has a background in chemical and biochemical engineering and a PhD in sustainable energy engineering. Today, his research has a broad scope encompassing technical, socio-technical, and techno-environmental aspects of value chain innovation and system assessment related to the development of a more circular and bio-based economy. Most of his work revolves around the food-energy-material nexus and relates to the production and use of biomass and secondary resources, and he has a particular interest and expertise in development, analysis, and assessment related to the production and use of biochar. While he does undertake some laboratory and workshop activities, most of his present research is within quantitative sustainability assessment studies, including material- and energy flow analysis, footprint accountings, and life-cycle assessments, as well as stakeholder- and incentives analysis, sector integration, and innovative resource management.

Introduction

Anders Siig Andersen, Henrik Hauggaard-Nielsen, Thomas Budde Christensen, and Lars Hulgaard

> Half of humanity is in the danger zone, from floods, droughts, extreme storms, and wildfires. No nation is immune. Yet we continue to feed our fossil fuel addiction. We have a choice. Collective action or collective suicide. It is in our hands.
>
> Antònio Guterres, General-Secretary of the UN, 2022

The incremental governance approaches that have been implemented during the last decades seem insufficient to respond effectively to the "super-wicked" and intertwined challenges of climate change, biodiversity loss, resource depletion, and social injustices and inequalities. Illustrating the urgency of the matter, in August 2022, prominent Earth System, climate, and environment scientists published a paper in *Proceedings of the National Academy of Sciences* titled "Climate endgame: Exploring catastrophic climate change scenarios" (Kemp et al., 2022). The authors argue that there are "ample reasons to suspect that climate change could result in a global catastrophe." They underscore risks created by tipping cascades "in which multiple tipping elements interact in such a way that tipping one threshold increases the likelihood of tipping another." They, further, highlight that the global aggregate impacts from warming of above 3°C are underexamined and that the Intergovernmental Panel on Climate Change (IPCC) has focused on lower-end warming and simple risk analysis. They point at three reasons to this fact: (1) the Paris Agreement focuses on the goal of limiting warming to well below 2°C and preferably below 1.5°C; (2) the dominant culture within climate science tends to stay on the side of "least drama"; and (3) full IPCC reports are the result of consensus processes performed by nationally appointed scientists, and the reports' summaries for policy makers are based on consensus between scientists and politicians (Kemp et al., 2022: 2). Against this background, the authors propose further research into the possible mechanisms governing extreme ecological and socioecological consequences of a worldwide societal collapse, along with possible trajectories regarding human extinction.

DOI: 10.4324/9781003319672-1

Despite accumulating scientific evidence on ecological and socioecological challenges, the world continues to face several intertwined global, regional, and local crises. The urgency of solving the problems increases year by year, despite political intentions and international agreements to change the trajectory. In the area of climate change, the frequency of heat waves is increasing; the ice melts, water levels rise, and more floods occur; droughts cause forest fires and food shortages; and hurricanes and typhoons claim more and more human lives. In the area of biodiversity, animal and plant species are endangered; agricultural land is exhausted; wild nature is increasingly cultivated; monocultures are spreading; coral reefs are dying; and fish stocks and other species in the oceans are declining. In the area of resources, evidence reveals that resources on which we are existentially dependent are at risk of being depleted within the next 25–50 years. Furthermore, social inequalities and injustices are rising within and between nations; minorities are misrecognized; peoples—particularly in the global South—are driven off their land; and the world is facing democratic backlashes and state-sanctioned violence against climate and environmental activists. Daily, we are exposed to the dire climate and environmental state of the world. At the same time, we encounter serious pandemics, economic crises, food crises, energy crises, and armed conflicts. These crises are fueling each other in interrelated manners that further add to the complexity of challenges ahead.

Human reactions to the escalating and interconnected climate and environmental crises are diverse. Some accept that life as we know it cannot be saved and put their trust in technological solutions. Some deny the existence of the crises and resort to notions of "ethnically pure" nation-states as safe havens for continuing a "harmonious" way of life. Some acknowledge the crises but argue that those who have created the problems should also be the ones who must bring about the solutions. Others recognize the problems but do not feel that they have the power to influence the solutions. However, many people are taking action—whether in organizational form, from the local to the global, or in private forms, changing patterns of consumption or adopting other types of sustainable practices.

Globally, scientific knowledge providers paint a clear picture of the nature and scope of challenges. However, when such providers question which solutions will be most appropriate and what fundamentally creates the problems, scientific views become divided. Some attribute the causes to market failures, arguing that market-based solutions should be applied. Others attribute the causes to complicated historically and institutionally developed economic, political, and technological structures, path-dependencies, and lock-ins, and argue for a transition toward green growth using the diverse array of management tools available to advanced societies. Still others point to fundamental mechanisms that drive the capitalist system's instrumental and oppressive relationship with nature and people and argue for degrowth and organized resistance.

The knowledge gap and the aim of the book

We present this book on account of the lack of (1) comprehensive analysis of the intertwined character of ecological, economic, social, and even epistemological challenges related to climate change, biodiversity loss, and resource depletion and different political responses; (2) critical overviews of different paradigms pertaining to ecological and socioecological sustainable solutions; and (3) broader knowledge on the array of different interdisciplinary contributions to the field.

Overviewing academic publications, many contributions are relevant to the topics of ecological and socioecological challenges. Several publications present varied, but less integrated, contributions pertaining to the different areas of challenges and solutions. Some focus on single countries, single research areas, single environment and climate change challenges, and single academic subjects. Together, these publications contribute immensely to enhancing our knowledge and understandings. However, broader and more integrated accounts are sparse, especially regarding interplays between the following topics:

- The increasing erosion of the Earth system, caused by human activities and the need to combat challenges regarding climate change, biodiversity loss, and resource depletion;
- The profound social inequalities regarding contributions to ecological challenges and the risk of rising inequalities as a result of different institutional responses to these challenges, between the Global North and the Global South and within countries;
- Different strategies, policies, and plans targeting ecological and combined ecological, economic, and social challenges;
- Different views on obstacles to ecological and socioecological development and the risks posited by path-dependencies, lock-ins, and trade-offs between economic, social, and ecological goals and responses;
- Varying paradigms regarding conceptualizations of government/governance, development strategies, and the fundamental drivers of ecological and socioecological challenges;
- Differing conceptualizations of the notion of the Anthropocene as well as diverse theoretical conceptualizations of human–nature and time-space relations and the drivers of unsustainable development;
- New pathways in interdisciplinary research seeking to enhance scientific collaboration between the natural and social sciences and the humanities and, furthermore, new combinations of scientific and non-scientific forms of knowledge that seek to broaden the scope and relevance of knowledge creation relevant to ecological and socioecological drivers, challenges, and solutions.

In this book, we present interdisciplinary scientific knowledge about ecological challenges and critically assess some major political initiatives within the context of the UN and the EU. Furthermore, we present a critical overview of different paradigms regarding ecological and socioecological drivers and sustainable solutions. We have chosen to focus on analyzing (1) global ecological and socioecological challenges and UN policies; (2) European ecological and socioecological challenges and EU policies; and (3) three cross-cutting themes—governance and different paradigms pertaining to the understanding of indirect drivers of challenges and responses; different philosophical and scientific views on the "Anthropocene"; and different interdisciplinary scientific paradigms and combinations of research and other forms of knowledge creation. Pertaining to solutions, we aim to discuss (1) whether political goals are sufficiently precise and comprehensive in their scope to respond adequately to the challenges; (2) whether adopted measures and types of intervention are sufficiently effective to achieve the stated objectives; and (3) whether the implementation of policies and other levers of change may succeed in fulfilling political intentions.

Scientists and politicians know much about what the future will bring if efforts to deal with the ecological and socioecological challenges are handled insufficiently. What they do not know for sure is whether existing crises will worsen and whether completely new crises will arise. This points to the importance of continuously upgrading and developing disciplinary as well as interdisciplinary knowledge. Knowledge alone, however, will not solve the problems. In responding to the intertwined known as well as unknown crises, constantly revised and flexible action is crucial. The needed actions comprise top-down initiatives such as the formulation of common goals and internationally, regionally, and nationally binding agreements. However, without engaging a range of non-state and local actors in bottom-up initiatives based upon an understanding of and respect for the historic trajectories of the world regions and creating an influential democratic interplay between local and centralized action levels, there is a risk that solutions will not be effective, flexible, feasible, or sustainable in the long run.

Overview

In Figure I.1, we present the overarching concept underlying the structure and content of the book.

The center of the model (Figure I.1) depicts intertwined social and ecological changes. In the book, acknowledging that not all ecological changes are social and that not all social changes are directly intertwined with ecological change, we outline some of the general ecological and social drivers, changes, and solutions. Regarding ecological changes, we narrow our focus to climate change, biodiversity loss, and resource depletion and to the climate change–biodiversity–resource nexus. Pertaining to social changes, we discuss drivers and consequences of social development such as general inequalities. Our main focus, however, is on socioecological changes—that is, the drivers, structures, and differentiated contributions to the intertwined ecological

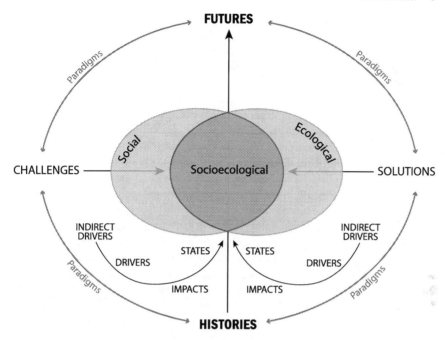

Figure I.1 Overarching concept underlying the structure and content of the book

and socioecological changes and the stratified impact of these changes, with special focus on the notions of freedom, security, equality, recognition, participation, and intergenerational justice. We also focus on the intertwined relations between ecological, social, and economic changes.

In Figure I.1, "states" refers to the social, ecological, and socioecological situation. "Impacts" are defined as the changes in states caused by drivers, understood as any human-induced factors that directly or indirectly cause changes in social, ecological, or socioecological systems. "Direct drivers"— as, for example, climate change, land degradation, and resource extraction— directly influence ecological and socioecological systems and are altered by "indirect drivers" such as demographic, economic, sociopolitical, scientific, technological, cultural, and religious factors. In the book, we presuppose that the realms of ecology and socioecology are changing states because of human impacts and human-created drivers of change. However, for people to react to changes, they need to conceive them as human challenges. This happens through contested processes in discursive landscapes characterized by unequal power relations and many competing interests. For people to start elaborating and deciding on solutions, even more complicated social processes are at play. In the outer circle of the model, we have depicted the social, cultural, and political construction of challenges and solutions in terms of different paradigms. As we will account for in the book, there is neither clear agreement on how challenges should be conceived nor agreement on which solutions will need to be implemented. This disagreement also pertains to the question of how we should understand history and which futures we want.

Viewed against the corpus of scientific evidence, it generates hope that most governments in the world have come to agree on the scientific basis of climate change, biodiversity loss, and resource depletion, and that—at least in some areas—global agreements have been adopted. Furthermore, by adopting the 2030 Agenda for Sustainable Development and the Sustainable Development Goals, many governments have agreed to focus and act on socioecological issues. Broadly accepted scientific assessments, however, have concluded that we are not on track to meet the most important ecological and socioecological goals and to secure a socially sustainable world within the planetary boundaries. For some scientists, the main problem is that we are not currently acknowledging the deep-seated historical dynamics and indirect drivers that are conceived as steering the world in the completely wrong direction. History itself is contested and so are human ideas and visions of the future: can we maintain the global social order by shifting from the present trajectory of unsustainable development to green growth while repairing social injustices and inequalities, or must we recognize that degrowth, regeneration of the biosphere, and redistribution by design is the answer? Is it sufficient to reform the present structural condition and power relations to tame the drivers of development, or do we have to completely transform the drivers and deeply ingrained structures of the entangled human and natural world as well as people's everyday behavior? These, and several similar, questions remain unresolved.

Contents of the book

The book consists of an introduction, three parts, and thirteen individual chapters. In the following we will outline the content of the parts and the chapters.

Part I: Global ecological and socioecological challenges and UN solutions

The first part of the book highlights global ecological and socioecological challenges and UN agreements directed at promoting concerted global action as well as several types of critical assessments of the outcomes of international agreements aimed at resolving pressing ecological and socioecological issues.

Chapter 1, "Global Ecological Risks," aims to provide an overall scientific understanding of how human activities create risks to life on Earth. It explains the development and functions of the biosphere from the "Great Oxidation Event" to the present and the history of the human species from being hunters, fishers, and gatherers to the "Great Acceleration" during the last 70 years. According to some scientists, these years represent a transition from the geological period called the Holocene to the Anthropocene. The chapter describes major challenges to humanity, including climate change, biodiversity loss, and resource depletion. At a more general level, it presents the planetary boundary framework that Earth-system scientists have developed to assess the most challenging global ecological risks to humanity. The chapter is primarily based on scientific reports from the UN that review and synthesize state-of-the-art scientific knowledge from all over the world and furthermore, on interdisciplinary scientific contributions in the tradition of Earth-system science. This body of scientific knowledge on climate change, biodiversity, and resources serves as an overall context for the other chapters in this book.

Chapter 2, "UN Ecological Risk Governance," focuses on the field of global ecological policy and governance. During more than five decades, scientists have warned of serious anthropogenic environmental and climate change challenges, expressing increasing alarm and calling for dramatic transformations in response. Politically, there has been a growing recognition of the severe and complex challenges at the global, regional, and national, as well as the local level. It remains, however, an open question whether the current policy decisions and efforts are sufficiently comprehensive, well-considered, and effective? This chapter highlights general actions and solutions that have been proposed by the Intergovernmental Panel on Climate Change (IPCC), the Intergovernmental Science-Policy Platform on Biodiversity and Ecosystem Services (IPBES), the International Resource Panel (IRP), and the United Nations Development Program (UNDP). Furthermore, it presents UN attempts to govern climate change, biological diversity, and the use of natural resources. For each of these areas, the chapter highlights scientific assessments of the gaps between the adopted and implemented plans. Focusing on the complexities, the chapter highlights important knowledge, intervention, and governance aspects pertaining to the climate change–biodiversity nexus.

Chapter 3, "Socioecological Challenges and UN Policies," focuses on the interdependence between, on the one hand, contemporary socioecological challenges and, on the other, UN policies and their efficiency in implementing solutions. First, core notions are defined regarding socioecological transformation focusing on freedom, safety, and different forms of equality. Second, the chapter focuses on inequalities pertaining to unequal contributions to the erosion of the Earth system, the unequal consequences of environment and climate challenges for different nations and groups of people, and the unequally distributed consequences of environment and climate interventions. Third, attention is directed at UN governance, briefly covering socioecological aspects of the forms of governance that are predominantly oriented toward climate change, biodiversity, and resources. Mainly, however, the chapter focuses on the UN 2030 Agenda for Sustainable Development and the Sustainable Development Goals (SDGs). The chapter critically discusses the relations between the SDGs and socioecological issues, as well as the type of goal-based governance and Nationally Determined Contributions that characterize the 2030 Agenda and the SDGs. Fourth, the chapter critically reflects on an attempt by the Stockholm Resilience Center and the Norwegian Business School to combine a small number of targets and indicators pertaining to the SDGs as well as the Planetary Boundaries to indicate solutions to the intertwined ecological, economical, and social challenges. Following up on the SDGs, the chapter draws on the first Global Sustainability Report that was published in 2019 highlighting state-of-the-art knowledge for transformations toward socioecological sustainable development and identifying possible areas of transformational change.

Chapter 4, "Affirmative and Critical Perspectives on the 2030 Agenda of Sustainable Development and the Sustainable Development Goals," shifts the perspective from system-internal to system-external critical assessments, and especially the types of assessments that are directed at the relations between goals, responses, and the fundamental drivers underlying global socioecological challenges. It is an important aspect of the creation of the 2030 Agenda and the sustainable development goals (SDGs) that various popular movements, non-governmental organizations (NGOs), and trade unions had the opportunity to be significantly more active and influential than was the case in relation to the millennium development goals (MDGs). This means that many different perspectives—other than the perspectives of nations—have been merged during negotiations, including environmental and climate, human rights, Global South, and labor market/workers' perspectives. First, this chapter highlights some affirmative assessments of the negotiation process and the outcomes of the 2030 Agenda on Sustainable Development and the SDGs. Second, it thematizes substantial points of critique—from grassroots movements and scholars critically assessing goals and drivers of ecological, social, and economic development. Finally, the chapter discusses which driving forces, pressures, states, impacts, and responses the 2030 Agenda and the SDG targets are addressing and which they are not, and, furthermore, elaborates on the multiple structures, power relations, and drivers that would have to be considered in order to fully realize the intentions of the Agenda and the SDGs.

Part II: European ecological and socioecological challenges, and EU solutions

Focusing on climate change, biodiversity, resources, and Just Transition, the second part of the book turns its attention to the European Green Deal strategy and to selected areas covered by the strategy: climate change and energy; resources and circular economy; agriculture and food-systems; biodiversity and Nature's contribution to people; and Just Transition.

Chapter 5, "The European Green Deal and the State of the European Environment," presents an overview of the European Green Deal and the scientific knowledge and recommendations provided by the European

Environmental Agency (EEA). The European Green Deal covers many different areas: (1) overall climate ambition; (2) sector- and system-oriented strategies regarding energy, building and construction, industry and resources, biodiversity and eco-services, food, agriculture and fisheries, mobility, and pollution; (3) levers in the sustainable transition, such as global cooperation, finance and investments, regulation and governance, innovation, and research; and (4) measures to support a just and fair transition and the participation of stakeholders and citizens. The first part of the chapter presents the background to the Green Deal and gives an overall characterization of the different areas covered by the strategy. The second part describes the state of the environment in Europe and the policy recommendations proposed by the EEA. The third part analyzes the European Green Deal in the light of these recommendations.

Chapter 6, "Climate Change-Motivated Development of EU's Energy Production and Use Systems," discusses historic and current climate and energy policies in the European Union in light of the climate crisis. In the international arena, the European Union has been one of the most coherent groups of countries advocating for global climate action under the United Nations Framework Convention on Climate Change (UNFCCC). The European Union has recently set a climate target that includes greenhouse gas emission reductions of 55 percent by 2030 (as compared to 1990) and a goal of climate neutrality by 2050. These goals should deliver the required reduction in the union's climate impact to assist the world in achieving an emission trajectory consistent with the UN Paris Agreement goals, set in the attempt to prevent a global temperature increase beyond irreversible tipping points. However, the achievement of these targets is associated with huge disagreements among European Union member states and from the beginning, it has been clear that there are economic, technical, and social difficulties associated with the new strategy's practical implementation. The challenges are diverse and complex, relating both to the transition of the energy sector toward 2030 and to emission reductions outside the energy sector post-2030 (e.g., in transport and agriculture). This chapter lays out the parallel historical development of EU's energy systems and climate policies, utilizing established knowledge for a critical discussion of the actions agreed upon in the European Union toward 2050. It further explores whether these commitments will be sufficient to deliver the needed reductions and if the agreements and actions planned are fair and just from local, regional, and global perspectives.

Chapter 7, "Resources and the Circular Economy," discusses the relation between resource consumption and economic development in the context of the European economy and European Union policies. The discussion is framed by the concept of the circular economy, which has been used by the European Union (and many other countries, companies, and organizations) as a policy strategy to decouple resource consumption from economic growth. Over the last 100 years, there has been a very close link between economic growth and increased resource consumption. The achieved global prosperity has been based on a constantly growing consumption of energy resources, building materials, metals, and biomass. By 2050, global waste production is expected to increase by 70 percent, and most of this waste is expected to end up incinerated or dumped in landfills. To deal with this problem, the European Commission has proposed a set of policies and strategies under the umbrella concept of the "circular economy." The first circular economy action plan was adopted by the European Union in 2015, and it was followed up by a revised plan 2020 as a part of the European Green Deal. The action plan aims to reduce resource consumption and secure vital raw materials for the European economy while, at the same time, creating sustainable economic growth and jobs. The chapter discusses the philosophy behind the plans and critically evaluates whether the implemented and proposed policies already have or will enable a decoupling of resource consumption from economic growth.

Chapter 8, "The Food System and Agriculture," presents major trends in modern food systems initiated from the ruins of World War II (WWII) to a situation failing to sustain farmer livelihoods and to address food quality and health, with critical negative impacts of industrial food production and consumption on the environment and climate change. Special attention is directed toward the strategies developed and applied by the European Common Agricultural Policy (CAP) to meet the EU Green Deal's objectives and to ensure a transition to a more sustainable food system that engages actors in the supply chains—short or complex—following the Farm-to-Fork strategy. Specific attention is focused on regulatory scopes and interventions and the ways in which this regime has influenced and transformed the food system. The need for new policies and their theoretical and analytical foundation is discussed with reference to recent findings from studies mapping actor needs for methods, tools, and competences to support a green transition of the agri-food regime. Major lock-ins at the structural, as well as at the practical level, are presented and applied as a common frame of understanding for the development and implementation of pathways for the generation of global concentrations, as well as decentralized agri-food systems. Analogies between the rise of the organic farmers and foods movements since the 1980s and current plant-based food movements are applied to identify radical game changing agents to power agri-food system transitions. It is argued that farmers and other agri-food actors cannot make the required changes at their own risk and that they must demand political and not solely technical resolutions to challenge the agri-food sector and climate change linkages. It is concluded that agents with the power of transformative decision-making can especially support the development of conditions for farming that integrate societal, environmental, and ethical needs with market conditions for agri-food chain actors.

Chapter 9, "Biodiversity and Nature's Contribution to People," focuses on strategies to put Europe's terrestrial biodiversity crises on the path to recovery in line with the European Green Deal and Farm-to-Fork strategies that propose ambitious EU actions and commitments. From this perspective, this chapter is influenced by EU support for the Intergovernmental Science-

Policy Platform on Biodiversity and Ecosystem Services (IPBES), an international independent body qualifying EU policies beyond continental priorities when addressing the science-policy interface. Present protected areas are not sufficiently large to safeguard biodiversity at the EU level, requiring improved governance with, for example, EU intentions to enlarge existing Natura 2000 areas for protection, maintenance, and restoration. However, environmental planners continue to declare new protected areas in isolated sites as a possible result of governments supporting agricultural production by rewarding output or lowering input prices, not necessarily in the favor of local support and regional development. A more reflective understanding is required to link biological richness and cultural diversity on both geopolitical and biogeographic terms to provide access to many of the same resources as agricultural producers. Furthermore, little biodiversity improvement from such protection activities has been reported until now, indicating the need for a more ambitious and holistic approach to engaging institutions to play a role.

Chapter 10, "Just Transition and the EU," addresses Just Transition from the European perspective. The notion of Just Transition is an important pillar of the European Green Deal. In the EU, in the aftermath of the financial crises and then increased by the Covid-19 crises, income and wealth inequality, social mobility, poverty, and precarious work conditions have followed a downward trajectory. At the same time, measures to deal with environment and climate change challenges could put even more Europeans at risk. This is evident when focusing on regions dependent on fossil fuels extraction. Vulnerabilities, however, may also arise because of increasing energy prices and the general transition from "brown" to "green" jobs. Without targeted actions, there will be winners and losers, and many types of inequality in Europe may rise to new levels. In this chapter, we first describe inequalities in Europe, emphasizing socioecological inequalities. Second, we highlight how the distributive and procedural aspects of environmental and climate justice are dealt with in the European Green Deal and its follow up interventions, as well as how the different elements regarding these interventions have been criticized. Third, we present alternative ideas for a Just Transition proposed by the Green New Deal for Europe Coalition in the Blueprint for Europe's Just Transition. Fourth, we introduce a Global South perspective, viewing EU policies regarding Just Transition as Eurocentric and taking too limited responsibility for global socioecological justice.

Part III: Cross-cutting issues: governance, the "Anthropocene," and interdisciplinary research

The third part of the book focuses on three main themes: ecological and socioecological government and governance in the UN and the EU as well as theoretical and political paradigms underlying or confronting dominant political responses; different conceptualizations of the "Anthropocene" and its drivers; and different types of interdisciplinary research and knowledge creation.

Chapter 11, "Ecological and Socioecological Governance in the UN and the EU," critically compares and reflects on structural and procedural aspects of governance in the UN and the EU and, furthermore, on differing paradigms regarding solutions pertaining to climate change, environment, and socioecological issues. First, the chapter presents different ideal types of structural and procedural government and governance, before analyzing UN and EU government/governance by applying this typology as a theoretical lens. Second, it highlights the compositions of different paradigms for strategies and solutions that are underlying policies, responses, and governance in the UN and the EU: market-based technological and socioecological modernization. Third, it presents paradigms that are situated at the margin of and conflicting with hegemonic paradigms: technological escapist and quick fix, nationalist, and socioecological transformative.

Chapter 12, "Decentering Humanity: the Anthropocene and the Perils of Anthropocentricity," focuses on different philosophical and social science paradigms for understanding the fundamental character of the contemporary human and planetary condition. The point of departure is the notion of the "Anthropocene." Loosely but quite radically, the term defines a new conceptualization of the relationship between humanity and nature. It suggests that we have entered a new geological epoch in which the human species is now the dominant Earth-shaping force. Hereby, it unsettles the philosophical, epistemological, and ontological ground on which the natural sciences as well as the social sciences/humanities have traditionally stood. The notion of the Anthropocene, however, is differently defined within scientific paradigms and, furthermore, questioned and criticized by several scholars as well as activists. Natural scientists regard the Anthropocene as a period in which people and nature are dynamically intertwined and embedded in the biosphere, placing shocks and extreme events as part of this dynamic. Social scientists and humanists generally accept that the human–nature relationship and the relation between time and space have changed, and most of these scholars also agree that human actions have caused unprecedented ecological and socioecological challenges. However, they also disagree on several issues. First, the chapter presents core characteristic of the Anthropocene concept as proposed by natural scientists. It then turns to conceptualizations of the notion within the social sciences and the humanities. The aim is to critically reflect important differences between positions and to analyze how they may legitimize different political paradigms. The chapter focuses on three selected themes: (1) the human–nature relationship; (2) the unified notion of the "Anthropos"; and (3) alternative understandings of what is driving the Anthropocene. By presenting these themes the chapter covers different notions of the epoch such as "Multiple Anthropocenes," the "Capitalocene," and the "Plantationocene," and different scholarly paradigms such as neo-materialist, post-human, post-modern, critical reflexive, eco-Marxist, and degrowth.

Chapter 13, "Interdisciplinary Research and Knowledge Creation," focuses on interdisciplinary research and combinations of academic research and other forms of knowledge creation. The recognition that the Anthropocene confronts humanity with unprecedented ecological and socioecological challenges has questioned several taken-for-granted viewpoints in science and academic scholarship and initiated a multifaceted endeavor to understand and find solutions to new and wicked problems. One reaction has been a call for increased interdisciplinarity. The chapter starts by presenting the background for this call and continues by defining interdisciplinarity and by highlighting some of the barriers to implementing the concept. Focusing on ecological and socioecological challenges, the chapter outlines some aspects of the history of interdisciplinarity within the natural and social sciences and the humanities, to consider how each of these has adapted to the call. Looking across these areas, it reflects on possible pathways to lead science and academic scholarship forwards. The chapter concludes with some examples of multi-actor and participatory action research funded by the EU. These examples cover the areas "urban circularity," "agroecological food systems," and "nature-based solutions."

About the writing of this book

When, in 2016, Thomas Piketty published a small volume of essays reporting on world affairs, there was no mention of a series of events that have reshaped the world in less than a decade. Writing in the wake of the financial crisis, he asked the question,

> Will Europe manage to take sovereignty, that we'll need to take control of a globalized capitalism gone mad? Or will it once again be no more than a technocratic instrument of deregulation, intensified competition, and the subjection of governments to the markets?
>
> (Piketty, 2016: 1)

Piketty writes on most subjects and day-to-day events that relate to issues of democracy, economy, and inequality, and his outlook is the aftermath of the financial crisis. However, the years since he published his essays has revealed how, in today's world, one crisis does not replace another; instead, they appear simultaneously, and when they mix, they lead to new and unpredictable consequences. The European security crisis in 2022 fueled the global food crisis that fueled the migration crisis toward a situation still marked by economic hardship and a global health crisis.

Focusing on ecological and socioecological issues, we have been writing this book from summer 2021 to summer 2022 in a continuous stream of critical events accompanied by an increasing number of new reports and scientific publications. In trying to accommodate to this stream of events, predominantly, we have selected knowledge sources that are relatively new—that is, from the period 2016 to 2022. To meet the deadline for the book, the final material collected was a 3675-page IPCC report from spring 2022 and the article mentioned at the start of this introduction.

As scholars and authors, we do not presume that we can analyze all aspects of the complicated contexts that constitute ecological and socioecological challenges, nor do we presume that we can identify the best solutions. Therefore, our aim in writing this book has not been to reach unequivocal conclusions, but rather, to allow many voices to be contrasted and heard. Regarding theory-of-science, scientific theory, and methodology, our personal backgrounds differ. When preparing and writing the book, we have embraced these different starting points as a strength. We have offered each other in-depth accounts of our positions and provided mutual feedback from different points of view covering the natural sciences, planning sciences, sociology, and the humanities. A draft of each chapter has been written by the first author. Co-authors have read, commented on, revised, and added content to the chapter. All chapters have been discussed thoroughly in the editorial group of authors. At the same time, we recognize that our interdisciplinary range of viewpoints is limited when compared to the variety of scientific knowledge areas and paradigmatic positions between and within the individual branches of science. Although we represent different academic backgrounds and present different voices in the book, we acknowledge that we cannot fully escape our blind spots, for example, regarding the influence of nationality, gender, race, and class on the synthesis of existing knowledge, and the selected conceptualizations and analysis of drivers, challenges, and solutions.

References

Kemp, L., Xu, C., Depledge, J., Ebi, K. L., Gibbins, G., Kohler, T. A., Rockström, J., Scheffer, M., Schellnhuber, H. J., Steffen, W. and Lenton, T. M. (2022). Climate endgame: Exploring catastrophic climate change scenarios. *Proceedings National Academy Science U S A*, 119(34), 1–9. DOI: 10.1073/pnas.2108146119.

Piketty, T. (2016). *Chronicles on our troubled times*. Milton Keynes: Penguin Books.

Part I

Global ecological and socioecological challenges and UN solutions

The first part of this book highlights global ecological and socioecological challenges and UN agreements directed at promoting concerted global action as well as several types of critical assessments of the outcomes of international agreements aimed at resolving pressing ecological and socioecological issues.

Part I consists of four chapters:

Chapter 1: Global Ecological Risks
Chapter 2: UN Ecological Risk Governance
Chapter 3: Socioecological Challenges and UN Policies
Chapter 4: Affirmative and Critical Perspectives on the 2030 Agenda of Sustainable Development and the Sustainable Development Goals

1 Global ecological risks

Anders Siig Andersen, Henrik Hauggaard-Nielsen, Thomas Budde Christensen, and Lars Hulgaard

> One can see from space how the human race has changed the Earth. Nearly all of the available land has been cleared of forest and is now used for agriculture or urban development. The polar icecaps are shrinking and the desert areas are increasing. At night, the Earth is no longer dark, but large areas are lit up. All of this is evidence that human exploitation of the planet is reaching a critical limit. But human demands and expectations are ever-increasing. We cannot continue to pollute the atmosphere, poison the ocean, and exhaust the land. There isn't any more available.
>
> Stephen Hawking, Physicist & Author

Introduction

This chapter aims to provide an overall scientific understanding of how human activities create risks to life on Earth. We start by explaining the development and functions of the biosphere from the "Great Oxidation Event" to the present and the history of the human species from being hunters, fishers, and gatherers to the "Great Acceleration" of the last 70 years. Some scientists claim that these years represent a transition from the geological period known as the Holocene to the Anthropocene (for a critical discussion, see Chapter 12). We next describe some major challenges to humanity, including climate change, biodiversity loss, and resource depletion. At a more general level, we present the planetary boundary framework that Earth-system scientists have developed to assess the most challenging global ecological risks to humanity. The chapter is primarily based on scientific reports from the United Nations (UN) that review and synthesize state-of-the-art scientific knowledge from all over the world and furthermore, on scientific contributions in the tradition of Earth-system science. This body of scientific knowledge on climate change, biodiversity, and resources serves as an overall context for the other chapters in this book.

Natural evolution and human development

Around 3 billion years ago, the first cyanobacterial cells evolved, producing the most abundant waste product of life, oxygen. This led to a transition around 2.4 billion years ago known as the "Great Oxygenation Event." Oxygen levels rose abruptly so that it became the chemically dominant gas in the atmosphere. Once enough oxygen had been created, the ozone layer started to form. This layer shields the atmosphere below it. According to the United Nations Development Program (UNDP, 2020: 100f), this event established an environment suitable for the evolution of complex cells. About 400 million years ago, complex plants and fungi colonized the land and pushed oxygen up to modern levels, which lead to a cooling of the climate. The Great Oxygenation Event also triggered an explosive growth in the diversity of minerals, as many elements near the Earth's surface became oxidized. These changes were crucial for the further evolution of complex life, including us, *Homo sapiens*. Evolution depends on interactions between the ever-changing biosphere and its use and recycling of materials. Through these interactions, new forms of life evolve, the chemical composition of the atmosphere changes, and energy and material consumption increase. Eventually, the Earth system began efficiently recycling nutrients.

Complex human societies developed during the geological period called the Holocene, which spans the last 11,700 years. This is generally regarded as the only geological period that we know has been able to support the continuing development of human societies (UNDP, 2020: 739). Scientists argue that this stable period could have continued for at least 20,000 years if not for the interference of humans. Other scientists, however, claim that the Holocene is a rather unstable period, characterized by progressively deeper and stronger glacial-to-interglacial oscillations, and that actually human activity has prevented the world from entering a new glacial period (UNDP, 2020: 101).

Homo sapiens evolved between 200,000 and 300,000 years ago. The first humans were nomadic hunters, fishers, and gatherers. The intentional use of fire allowed for humans to spread further. Semi-permanent settlements became the building blocks of established communities and led to the development of agriculture. The transition to agricultural communities represented a fundamentally new stage in human development. The energy value of food consumed by each person could now increase by three orders of magnitude. This helped humans to develop the social complexity found in cities. It also resulted in the specialization and division of labor, the exchange of goods and trade, and productive innovations such as writing (UNDP, 2020: 31).

However, human development was limited by a reliance on recent photosynthesis, which was overcome by using fossil energy that had accumulated over millions of years. Human society then industrialized. As a result, the amount of energy consumed globally rose tenfold from 1850 to 2000. The world population grew by a factor of 4.6 and GDP per person by a factor of

8.3 (UNDP, 2020: 31). Folke et al. (2021: 836) state that the human population reached 1 billion around 1800. It doubled to 2 billion around 1930 and doubled again to 4 billion around 1974. In 2022, the global population is approaching 8 billion and is expected to stabilize around 9–11 billion toward the end of this century.

On the one hand, humans are a deeply integrated part of the biosphere. On the other hand, they are unlike other living creatures. According to the UNDP (2020):

> Humans pass a whole suite of cultural information through societies and down the generations: It is our collective culture, even more than individual intelligence, that makes us smarter than the other animals, and it is this that creates the extraordinary nature of us: a species with the ability to be not simple objects of a transformative cosmos, but agents of our own transformation.
>
> (UNDP, 2020: 119)

Thus, the UNDP regards the ability of humans to create, store, retrieve, communicate, negotiate, and process information as one of the most important preconditions for the accumulative process of collective learning.

Many natural scientists argue that there has been a transition from the geological period of the Holocene to a completely different period that is termed the Anthropocene. This implies that the human imprint on the Earth system has itself become a geophysical force, equaling some of the great forces of Nature in terms of the functioning of the Earth system, and that the human enterprise is now a fully coupled, interacting component of the Earth system itself (Steffen et al., 2011:739 and 743; for a critical discussion, see Chapter 12). Human influence on the Earth system has been accelerating, especially over the last 70 years. Population growth, economic activity, and the extraction of resources have speeded up significantly since the 1950s. Some researchers call this period the Great Acceleration (Steffen et al., 2011: 743). The Anthropocene is characterized by a tightly interconnected world with dimensions operating at accelerating speeds. These dimensions include the global food production and distribution system, the extensive trade and transport systems, the strong connectivity of financial and capital markets, the international supply and value chains, the widespread movement of people, social innovation, the development and exchange of technology, and widespread communication (Folke et al., 2021: 837).

Climate change, biodiversity, and resource challenges

Different UN reports document serious and increasing challenges to the ecological systems on Earth, such as climate change, biodiversity loss, and resource depletion. In the following, we will explain the basic features of these three issues, describe the most important ecological challenges that have been highlighted in UN reports from the Intergovernmental Panel on Climate Change (IPCC), the World Meteorological Organization (WMO), the Intergovernmental Science-Policy Platform on Biodiversity and Ecosystem Services (IPBES), and the International Resource Panel (IRP), and indicate some features of the risk horizon for inadequate actions.

Climate change

The climate system is affected by the amount, distribution, and net balance of energy at the Earth's surface. The total amount of energy sets the overall conditions for life. Ice and water vapor play a critical role in the physical feedback mechanisms of the climate system. The distribution of energy over the land and sea surfaces and within the oceans play a major role in the circulation of the two great fluids, the oceans, and the atmosphere. These systemic physical characteristics are key spatial determinants in the distribution of the biota and the structure and functioning of ecosystems and are the main controllers of biochemical flows (Steffen et al., 2015: 8).

With its 193 member states and territories, the WMO is a specialized agency of the UN. It is the UN System's authoritative voice on the state and behavior of the Earth's atmosphere, its interaction with the land and oceans, the weather and climate it produces, and the resulting distribution of water resources. In 1988, the WMO and the United Nations Environment Program (UNEP) created the IPCC, which is an international body for assessing the science related to climate change. The IPCC provides policy makers with regular assessments of the scientific basis of climate change, its impacts and future risks, and possible options for adaptation and mitigation. The IPCC membership comprises governments that are members of the UN or the WMO. The IPCC currently has 195 members. Open and transparent reviews by experts and governments around the world are an essential part of the IPCC's process. These reviews ensure that assessments are complete and reflect a diverse range of views and expertise. Through its assessments, the IPCC identifies the strength of scientific agreement in different areas and where further research is needed. IPCC assessments underlie negotiations at the UN Climate Conferences (COPs). The assessments are relevant for policy but are not prescriptive. They present projections of future climate change based on different scenarios of the risks that climate change poses and discuss the implications of response options (see also Chapter 13).

For the first time, in its 2021 report, the IPCC stated: "It is unequivocal that human influence has warmed the atmosphere, ocean and land" (IPCC, 2021: 5). This IPCC report highlights that human influence has warmed the climate at a rate that is unprecedented in at least the last 2,000 years. In 2019, atmospheric CO_2 concentrations were higher than at any time in at least 2 million years, and concentrations of methane and nitrous oxide were higher than at any time in the last 800,000 years. Temperatures during the most recent decade (2011–2020) exceed those of the most recent multi-century warm period, around 6,500 years ago (IPCC, 2021: 9).

From pre-industrial levels, greenhouse gas (GHG) concentrations have increased by 148 percent (carbon dioxide), 260 percent (methane), and 123 percent (nitrous oxide) (WMO, 2020: 8). GHG emissions of different GHGs are expressed in the common unit of CO_2-equivalent. According to the IPCC, in 2019, approximately 34 percent of total net anthropogenic GHG emissions came from the energy sector, 24 percent from industry, 22 percent from agriculture and other land use, 15 percent from transport, and 6 percent from buildings (IPCC, 2022: 7). The average global temperature was 1.09°C higher in 2011–2020 than in 1850–1900, with a larger increase over land (1.59°C) than over the oceans (0.88°C) (WMO, 2021). The average global temperature in 2020 is set to be about 1.2°C above the pre-industrial levels (1850–1900). In 2022, in its update of the global climate for the decade, the WMO states that there is a 93 percent chance that at least one of the years between 2022 and 2026 will be the warmest on record and that the possibility of temporarily transcending 1.5°C for at least one of the five years to come is 50 percent (WMO, 2022).

By extracting and analyzing deep cores from glaciers, it has become possible to determine in detail the composition of 800,000 years of Antarctic ice. This analysis has revealed a repeated pattern of falls in atmospheric CO_2 of 100 ppm (parts per million) from an interglacial value of 280 to 300 ppm to a floor of 180 ppm and then a rapid recovery to the interglacial value. This suggests that there is a tightly governed control system. This regular planetary metabolic pattern has been equated with a rhythmic "breathing" (Angus, 2016: 62). Today's CO_2 in the atmosphere (421 ppm in May 2022) stands more than 100 ppm above the previous maximum of 280–300 ppm. According to Angus (2016: 69), each of the temperature jumps took only a few decades.

The WMO (2020: 5) states that all analyses of the different data sets agree that the rate of ocean warming has been particularly strong during the past two decades. The energy that accumulates in the Earth system due to increasing concentrations of GHGs is taken up by the oceans. This affects ocean chemistry through acidification. As the acidity of the oceans increases, their capacity to absorb CO_2 from the atmosphere decreases, which hampers their role in moderating climate change. The Arctic has undergone drastic changes since the mid-1980s. Arctic surface temperatures have warmed twice as fast as the global average. The amount of sea ice has decreased, and permafrost temperatures have increased (WMO, 2020: 14).

The WMO's State of the Climate Report (2020:5) highlights the following scientific observations:

- Concentrations of the major GHGs – carbon dioxide (CO_2), methane (CH_4), and nitrous oxide (N_2O) – continued to increase in 2020 despite the temporary reduction in emissions in 2020 due to measures taken in response to COVID-19.

- 2020 was one of the three warmest years on record. The past six years, including 2020, have been the six warmest years on record.
- The rise in sea levels is accelerating. In addition, the amount of heat stored in the oceans and the acidification of the oceans are both increasing, diminishing their capacity to moderate climate change.
- The minimum extent of Arctic sea ice in September 2020 was the second lowest on record.
- The loss of ice from the Antarctic accelerated from around 2005. Currently, Antarctica is losing approximately 175 to 225 Gt of ice per year.
- The 2020 North Atlantic hurricane season was exceptionally active.
- Some 9.8 million people were displaced during the first half of 2020, largely due to hydrometeorological hazards and disasters.
- Disruptions to agriculture by COVID-19 exacerbated weather impacts along the entire food supply chain, elevating levels of food insecurity.

For all the emissions scenarios considered, the IPCC (2021: 17) projects that global surface temperatures will continue to increase until at least mid-century and that global warming will exceed both 1.5°C and 2°C during the 21st century unless there are deep reductions in GHG emissions in the coming decade. The IPCC report also notes that hot extremes, heavy precipitation, and drought impact different regions of the world very differently (IPCC, 2021: 12).

In the longer term, climate change is a threat to human well-being and life on Earth. In 2018, the IPCC (2021: 16) concluded that a 1.5°C world would be substantially better for societies than 2°C (IPCC, 2018). Going beyond 2°C could potentially trigger natural processes to drive uncontrollable warming and pushing the planet toward a Hothouse Earth state (illustrated by Khanna, 2016). A so-called tipping point occurs when critical thresholds are exceeded, causing significant changes in the state of the system. According to the IPCC, there is strong evidence to suggest that such positive feedback mechanisms are unlikely to be triggered if the temperature rise remains below 2°C (Falk et al., 2020).

Without drastic reductions in emissions over the coming two to three decades, a 2–3°C scenario of continued global warming will increase the likelihood of severe, pervasive, and irreversible consequences, such as the collapse of the Arctic ice sheet, the Greenland ice sheet, the Arctic summer sea ice, Alpine glaciers, and coral reefs. Global temperatures may rise even higher if mitigation approaches are insufficient, so that transgressing many more tipping points might turn the globe into a hothouse state. A scenario with 4°C of global warming indicates that large parts of Asia, Africa, South America, Australia, Southern Asia, and the majority of the US will turn into inhabitable deserts. This scenario contains devastating consequences for life on Earth and human civilization as we know it.

Long before this state happens, climate change will have had an increasing effect on the living conditions of humans and other forms of life by impacting health, food, water security, biodiversity, and ecosystem services as well as human security, equality, livelihoods, economies, and infrastructures. As mentioned already, climate change is causing many high impact events: heat waves, cold waves, fires, droughts, flooding, marine heat waves, tropical cyclones, and coastal erosion (WMO, 2020: 30). In total, worldwide, the number of disasters linked to natural hazards has increased by 75 percent over the past 20 years.

Biodiversity

From the early days of biodiversity governance, the scientific community has wanted to actively participate in multilateral discussions (Arjjumend et al., 2016: 12). During the international conference on biodiversity ("Biodiversity, Science, and Governance") held in 2005 in Paris (France), the concept for an international expert panel on biodiversity was developed. In 2008, in Bonn (Germany), the Conference of the Parties (COP9) to the Convention of Biological Diversity voted to establish an ad hoc expert group (Arjjumend et al., 2016: 14). In 2010, delegates to a meeting on biodiversity, held under the auspices of the UNEP, agreed to establish a scientific body akin to the IPCC with a focus on biodiversity. This body is the IPBES. In 2012, the IPBES was established as an independent nongovernmental body by 94 governments. Currently the IPBES has 137 member states. The IPBES seeks to focus attention on and help member states develop plans to protect biodiversity and the ecosystem services on which people depend (Arjjumend et al., 2016: 14). Thus, the organization functions as a clearing house that guarantees the global availability of biodiversity knowledge that has been standardized and scientifically validated (Arjjumend et al., 2016: 15).

As mentioned, biosphere integrity is crucial to the normal functioning of the Earth system. The biosphere is defined as the totality of all ecosystems on Earth and their biota, i.e., the animal and plant life of a particular region, habitat, or geological period. Ecosystems and biota play a critical role in determining the state of the Earth system and in regulating its material and energy flows and its responses to abrupt and gradual change. Diversity in the biosphere makes terrestrial and marine ecosystems more resilient. On average, communities with a greater diversity of species and functional types – both terrestrial and marine – are less affected by and recover sooner from climate variability and extremes. This diversity/stability relationship also applies to entire ecosystems. Ecosystem integrity, which is the ability of an ecosystem to maintain its structure and functions, is facilitated by greater biodiversity (Pörtner et al., 2021: 31). The ultimate basis for the many roles of the biosphere is the genetic code of the biota, the basic information bank that defines the biosphere's functional role and its capacity to innovate and persist over time (Steffen et al., 2015: 8).

Living organisms are a crucial part of the Earth system, which acts to keep the local, regional, and global climate sufficiently stable and suitable for life.

Living organisms control the climate system by regulating the reflectivity of the land surface, altering the concentration of GHGs in the atmosphere, and by influencing the formation of clouds and atmospheric dust. Living organisms are also the main actors in the global carbon cycle and play a central role in the dynamics of all the major GHGs. It is not only the abundance of living organisms but also their variety that matters. On land and in the oceans, the variety and specific types of soil and sediment biota influence the biogeochemical cycling of nutrients and carbon, while the composition, variety, and abundance of both plants and animals impact carbon storage and the carbon cycle (Pörtner et al., 2021: 27f).

To understand the dependency between people and nature, IPBES (2019) proposed the concepts "Nature's contributions to people" and "Nature-based solutions." These are active strategies for protecting, sustainably managing, and restoring natural and modified ecosystems (see Chapter 9 for a further discussion of these concepts). The concept of Nature's contributions to people was developed to embrace diverse actors and worldviews and the knowledge base produced by the natural and social sciences, the humanities, as well as the knowledge held by practitioners and indigenous and local communities.

Over the past 50 years, the negative impacts of environmental change have reduced Nature's vital contributions to people in several categories. IPBES (2019: 23) distinguishes between the following types of contribution:

- *Materials and assistance*: Energy; food and feed; and medicinal, biochemical, and genetic resources.
- *Regulation of environmental processes*: Habitat creation and maintenance; pollination and dispersal of seeds and other propagules; regulation of air quality; regulation of climate change; regulation of ocean acidification; regulation of freshwater quantity and coastal water quality; formation, protection, and decontamination of soils and sediments; regulation of hazards and extreme events; and regulation of detrimental organisms and biological processes.
- *Non-material*: Learning and inspiration; physical and psychological experiences: and supporting identities and maintaining options.

According to Folke et al. (2021: 869), we know from science that human society needs to be viewed as part of the biosphere and as dependent on Nature's contributions to people. Furthermore, these authors indicate that there is a dynamic connection between the living biosphere and the broader Earth system, which includes the atmosphere, the hydrosphere, the lithosphere, the cryosphere, and the climate system. Folke et al. (2021: 837) state that the complex adaptive interplay between living organisms, the climate, and broader Earth-system processes has led to the evolution of a resilient biosphere. However, the human dimension has become a dominant force in shaping the evolution of all species on Earth. Through artificial selection, by controlling the reproduction of crops, livestock, trees, and microorganisms, through altering the degree of harvest pressure and selection, through producing the chemicals and pollution that alter the life histories of species, and by sculpting the new habitats that blanket the planet, humans, directly and indirectly, are choosing which species succeed or fail. Folke et al. (2021: 834) further argue that, depending on the collective actions of humanity, future conditions could be either beneficial or hostile for human life and well-being.

In its 2019 report, the IPBES considered that it was well established that humanity has an increasingly negative influence on the biosphere. Humans have caused natural terrestrial, freshwater, and marine ecosystems to decline (IPBES, 2019: 24). Biodiversity is declining to an unparalleled degree and faster than at any time in human history (IPBES, 2019: 10). Increasing the fragmentation of habitats by expanding infrastructure is a key risk. This includes the development of mines, cities, roads, and railways and the transformation of coastlines into ports. These changes affect coastal protection, aquaculture, and energy facilities (Pörtner et al., 2021: 41). Less than a quarter (23 percent) of the Earth's terrestrial area (excluding Antarctica) and 13 percent of the ocean remains free from substantial human impacts. 77 percent of land (excluding Antarctica) and 87 percent of the area of the ocean has been modified by the direct effects of human activities. Globally, around 75 percent of terrestrial environments and 40 percent of the marine environment have been severely altered (EEA, 2019: 10). In coastal zones, increasing nutrient and chemical inputs to coastal waters combined with climate drivers such as higher temperatures and hypoxia have resulted in an expansion of coastal dead zones and compounded stress and mortality. Approximately, half the area of coral reefs and over 85 percent of global wetland by area has been lost.

Human activities over millennia have resulted in an estimated 83 percent reduction in wild mammal biomass (both terrestrial and marine) and a 50 percent reduction in the biomass of plants, relative to pre-human times. The total weight of everything made by humans is about to exceed the mass of all living things on Earth (Folke et al., 2021: 837). Livestock and humans now account for nearly 96 percent of all mammal biomass on Earth. By mass, only 4 percent of the mammals on Earth are wild mammals (Pörtner et al., 2021: 14f). The biomass of domestic poultry is nearly threefold that of wild birds. Although humans have evolved to eat more than 7,000 plants, just three, however (wheat, rice, and maize), now provide more than half of our calories. Just 12 plant crops and 5 animal species account for 75 percent of our entire planetary food system (UNDP, 2020: 194). Over the last few centuries, terrestrial vertebrates have become extinct at rates that are up to 100 times higher than previous (background) levels (Pörtner et al., 2021: 28). Human impacts are causing species loss at a greater than normal rate and the processes of evolution (speciation) cannot keep up with this loss (Cowie et al., 2022).

Some researchers claim that the world is on the brink of the sixth mass species extinction (UNDP, 2020: 3). However, unlike previous mass species extinctions in geological time, this one will be caused by humans. A mass extinction would have an extreme negative impact on human life, as the loss of biodiversity could possibly push the Earth to a completely new and uninhabitable state for humans as well as many other species (EEA, 2019: 38; see also Chapter 9).

Resources

The International Resource Panel (IRP) was launched by the UNEP in 2007 to build and share the knowledge needed to improve our use of resources worldwide. The IRP consists of scientists with expertise in resource management. It fosters connections among policy makers, industry, and communities and provides advice to these stakeholders about how they can better manage global and local resources. The IRP makes scientific assessments of policy relevant to the sustainable use of natural resources. The IRP also aims to increase our understanding of how we can decouple economic growth from environmental degradation. Scientifically, the types of tasks carried out by the IRP are very similar to those performed by the IPCC and IPBES. Unlike the reports published by the IPCC and IPBES, however, IRP reports are not orientated toward any UN convention.

According to the IRP, natural resources include biomass (wood and crops, including food, fuel, feed, and plant-based materials), fossil fuels (coal, gas, and oil), metals (such as iron, aluminum, and cooper), non-metallic minerals (including sand, gravel, and limestone), water, and land. The IRP regards population growth and economic activity (GDP) as the most important drivers of natural resource use. However, there are huge regional differences in consumption and production patterns and growth rates. Overall, since the 1970s, the global population has doubled and global GDP has grown fourfold. Measured in constant 2010 prices, GDP expanded at a yearly rate of 3 percent from US$18.9 trillion in 1970 to US$76.5 trillion in 2016 (IRP, 2019: 42). These trends have required large amounts of natural resources, and there has been no stability or decline in global demand for material during the last 50 years. Rather, global resource extraction has grown rapidly and continuously. Extraction reached 92 billion tonnes in 2017, compared with 27 billion tonnes in 1970 (IRP, 1919: 7). The use of synthetic fertilizers (which increased eightfold between 1960 and 2000) and the combustion of fossil fuels have produced the largest disturbance to the biogeochemical cycle of nitrogen since it emerged 2.5 billion years ago (UNDP, 2020: 23).

Regarding the country-based use of resources, domestic material consumption is a direct measure of the materials that are consumed in a national economy. This consumption is calculated as domestic extraction plus the physical trade balance. As such, it directly measures the physical quantity of materials that are extracted from or imported into a nation's territory (minus any physical exports). It is a direct indicator of the total amount of material that must be directly managed and disposed of in a nation's territory. However, using domestic material consumption to assess the environmental load of a specific territory has a major weakness when attributing responsibility for the mobilization of resources and emissions. An individual nation that outsources the most material- and energy-intensive processes in its production chains will score well on measures based on domestic material consumption. Measurements of the material footprint complement domestic material consumption by ensuring that the total amount of raw material extracted to meet final consumption demands, but which largely take place in other countries' territories and impose their environmental costs there, are attributed to an end consumer's account (IRP, 2019: 51f). The IRP has highlighted that the global material footprint is increasing at a faster rate than both population and economic output. In other words, at the global level, there has been no decoupling of resource growth from either population or GDP growth.

Overall, the extraction and processing of natural resources account for more than 90 percent of global biodiversity loss and water stress impacts and for approximately half of global GHG emissions (IRP, 2019: 5). According to the IRP, unless a fundamental change drives natural resource use in another direction, this use will continue to grow to 190 billion tonnes and to over 18 tonnes per capita by 2060. This would cause substantial stress to many resource-supply systems, increase the risk of resource depletion, and lead to unprecedented environmental pressure and impact (IRP, 2019: 99).

The IRP has noted that, globally, economic policies have focused on improvements in labor productivity at the cost of material and energy productivity. We are now in a world where natural resources and environmental sinks have become the limiting factor of production (IRP, 2019: 53). Material productivity – US$ of GDP per kilogram of material use – has had the slowest growth rate compared to other forms of productivity factors and started to decline around 2000, being stagnant in recent years. The IRP has argued that this is particularly discouraging from an environmental point of view, as increasing material productivity is a necessary (but not sufficient) condition to enable the continuation of growth while reducing environmental impacts (IRP, 2019: 53). One of the reasons why material productivity has not improved globally is that there has been a shift in the share of global production, from economies with high material productivity to economies with much lower material productivity. This is partly the result of the outsourcing of material- and energy-intensive processes by many of the wealthiest countries (IRP, 2019: 53; see also Chapter 2).

Planetary boundaries

The overall environmental and climate risks to Nature's contributions to people and to biology and human lives may also be understood from the perspective of planetary boundaries. Different UN reports have applied this methodology (e.g., UNDP, 2020; IPBES, 2019; IRP, 2019). As developed by the Stockholm Resilience Center, the planetary boundaries framework defines a safe operating space for humanity based on the intrinsic biophysical processes that regulate the stability of the Earth system (Steffen et al., 2015: 1).

The main idea is that natural systems operate within stability landscapes that may be forced by anthropogenic or natural perturbations to transform into contracting states of stability (stability regimes or basins of attraction) as the systems pass a critical threshold (Steffen et al., 2011: 756). A scientific analysis of planetary boundaries suggests that climate change and biosphere integrity are highly integrated, emergent, system-level phenomena that are connected to other planetary boundaries. This means that large changes in the climate or biosphere integrity might change important balances within the Earth system, making it uninhabitable for humans as well as many other forms of life. The crossing of one or more of the seven other boundaries may also seriously affect human well-being. These boundaries are land-system change, freshwater use, biochemical flows (especially phosphorus and nitrogen), ocean acidification, atmospheric aerosol loading, stratospheric ozone depletion, and novel entities (IPBES, 2019: 22f; Steffen et al., 2015: 8; UNDP, 2020 note 66: 275).

As originally defined, a planetary boundary is not equivalent to a global threshold or tipping point. Even when there is a threshold in an Earth-system process, the proposed planetary boundary is not placed at the position of the biophysical threshold but well before this threshold. According to Steffen et al. (2015: 736f), this buffer between the boundary (the end of the safe operating space) and the threshold not only accounts for scientific uncertainty in the precise position of the threshold but also gives society time to react to early warning signs that it may be approaching a threshold.

The current values (2015) of the control variables for biosphere integrity and biochemical flows are transgressing the planetary boundaries, creating a high risk of destabilizing the Earth system. The values for climate change, land-system change, and ocean acidification are within the zone of uncertainty, whereas the current values of stratospheric ozone depletion and freshwater use are still within the safe operating space. No planetary boundaries are defined for atmospheric aerosol loading and novel entities. The latter include new substances as, for example, chemicals, new forms of existing substances, and modified life forms that have potential for unwanted geophysical or biological effects (Steffen et al., 2015: 739ff).

Summary

The Earth formed approximately 4.5 billion years ago. It is the only place in the universe where we know that life has evolved. From its beginning, the Holocene has been a safe period for humans and other life forms. During the latest 200,000 years, *Homo sapiens* has orchestrated an increasingly sophisticated use of Earth's resources that has made it possible to establish hyper-complex societies. However, science unequivocally documents that, especially over the past 70 years, humans' excessive exploitation of nature has reached a level and scale that threaten to degrade ecosystems and harm biological life because of climate change, biodiversity loss, and the depletion of available natural resources. With the advent of the Great Acceleration and the Anthropocene, the fundamental conditions for human life have been put at risk. Environmental erosion and climate change are negatively affecting ecosystems across the globe with severe negative effects on human populations, especially in the Global South. Much damage has already been done.

Over the years, the WMO and IPCC have published several reports on climate change that document how GHG emissions are continuing to increase. According to the IPCC, potentially, if the temperature rises more than 2°C above the mean level for the period from 1850 to 1900, there is a risk of catastrophic consequences. The IPCC strongly recommends that we limit the temperature rise to no more than 1.5°C above this level. In its 2022 report, WMO predicted that there is a 50 percent chance that the temperature rise will temporarily exceed 1.5°C during the period from 2023 to 2028. The serious consequences of climate change are already being observed in an increasing number of high impact events, which are causing extensive loss and damage, especially but not only in the Global South.

The "sister organization" of the IPCC, the IPBES has highlighted that the human impact on biodiversity has led to a degradation of natural terrestrial, freshwater, and marine ecosystems to a hitherto unparalleled degree. Some researchers even claim that the world is on the brink of the sixth mass species extinction, with climate change playing a key role. The same goes for habitat fragmentation due to the accelerating activities of the globally increasing human population. The loss of biodiversity threatens the supply of food and water, human health, and livelihoods. At the same time, there is a great risk that the loss of biodiversity will increase the extent and speed of climate change, leading to a negative spiral of higher temperatures and reduced biodiversity.

Economic growth has required ever more natural resources in the form of biomass, fossil fuels, metals, non-metallic minerals, water, and land. The IRP predicts that the total consumption of natural resources will increase from 97 tonnes to 190 million tonnes per year by 2060. According to the IRP, current resource consumption is already responsible for a very large part of the global biodiversity loss and GHG emissions. The present challenges will only become increasingly serious in the coming years.

The planetary boundary framework, developed by Earth-system science offers a holistic perspective on environmental challenges. When tipping points are exceeded, climate change and environmental trends will no longer be linear and are expected to accelerate the ecological challenges in unpredictable ways. Scientists warn that there is an urgent need to change the course, while leaving it to politicians to decide which risks they are willing to take on behalf of planetary life.

To assess global political actions, their adequacy, and efficiency, in the next chapter of this book (Chapter 2) we will focus on the UN organizations that have been assigned the primary responsibility for counteracting the intertwined challenges of climate change, biodiversity loss, and resource depletion.

References

Angus, I. (2016). *Facing the Anthropocene: Fossil capitalism and the crisis of the Earth system*. New York: Monthly Review Press.

Arjjumend, J. H., Islamia, J. M. and Koutouki, K. (2016). IPAN research brief No. 01. Published in *Journal of Global Resources*, 3(Print), (Online). Retrieved from: http://www.ipan.in/wpcontent/themes/ipan/ebooks/57581305699ef_Evolution percent 20of percent20International percent20Biodiversity percent20Governance_IPAN.pdf.

Cowie, R. H., Bouchet, P., and Fontaine, B. (2022). The sixth mass extinction: Fact, fiction, or speculation? *Biol Rev*, 97, 640–663. DOI: 10.1111/brv.12816

EEA (2019). *The European environment - state and outlook 2020. Knowledge for transition to a sustainable Europe*. European Environment Agency. Luxembourg: Publication Office of the European Union. DOI: 10.2800/96749

Falk, J., Gaffney, O., Bhowmik, A. K., Bergmark, P., Galaz, V., Gaskell, N., Henningsson, S., Höjer, M., Jacobson, L., Jónás, K., Kåberger, T., Klinngenfeld, D., Lenhart, J., Loken, B., Lundén, D., Malmodin, J., Malmquist, T., Olausson, V., Otto, I., Pearce, A., Pihl, E., and Shalit. T. (2020). Exponential roadmap 1.5.1. Future Earth, Sweden. Retrieved from: https://exponentialroadmap.org/wp-content/uploads/2020/03/ExponentialRoadmap_1.5.1_216x279_08_AW_Download_Singles_Small.pdf

Folke, C., Polasky, S., Rockström, J., Galaz, V., Westley, F., Lamont, M., Scheffer, M., Österblom, H., Carpenter, S. R., Chapin III, F. S., Seto, K. C., Weber, E. U., Crona, B. I., Daily, G. C., Dasgupta, P., Gaffney, O., Gordon, L. J., Hoff, H., Levin, S. A., Lubchenco, J., Steffen, W. and Walker B. H. (2021). Our future in the Anthropocene biosphere. *Springer, the Royal Swedish Academy of Science, Ambio*, 50, 834–869. DOI: 10.1007/s13280-021-01544-8

IPBES (2019). *Summary for policymakers of the global assessment report on biodiversity and ecosystem services of the intergovernmental science-policy platform on biodiversity and ecosystem services*. S. Díaz, J. Settele, E. S. Brondízio, H. T. Ngo, M. Guèze, J. Agard, A. Arneth, P. Balvanera, K. A. Brauman, S. H. M. Butchart, K. M. A. Chan, L. A. Garibaldi, K. Ichii, J. Liu, S. M. Subramanian, G. F. Midgley, P. Miloslavich, Z. Molnár, D. Obura, A. Pfaff, S. Polasky, A. Purvis, J. Razzaque, B. Reyers, R. Chowdhury, Y. J. Shin, I. J. Visseren-Hamakers, K. J. Willis & C. N. Zayas (eds.). Bonn, Germany: IPBES secretariat, 56 pages. Retrieved from: https://www.ipbes.net/sites/default/files/202002/ipbes_global_assessment_report_summary_for_policymakers_en.pdf.

IPCC (2018). Summary for policymakers. In: V. Masson-Delmotte, P. Zhai, H.-O. Pörtner, D. Roberts, J. Skea, P.R. Shukla, A. Pirani, W. Moufouma-Okia, C. Péan, R. Pidcock, S. Connors, J. B. R. Matthews, Y. Chen, X. Zhou, M. I. Gomis, E. Lonnoy, T. Maycock, M. Tignor & T. Waterfield (eds.), *Global warming of 1.5 °C: An IPCC special report on the impacts of global warming of 1.5°C above pre-industrial levels and related global greenhouse gas emission pathways, in the context of strengthening the global response to the threat of climate change, sustainable development, and efforts to eradicate poverty*. Geneva, Switzerland: World Meteorological Organization, 3–24. Retrieved from: https://www.ipcc.ch/site/assets/uploads/sites/2/2022/06/SR15_Full_Report_LR.pdf

IPCC (2021). Summary for policymakers. In: V. Masson-Delmotte, P. Zhai, A. Pirani, S. L. Connors, C. Péan, S. Berger, N. Caud, Y. Chen, L. Goldfarb, M. I.

Gomis, M. Huang, K. Leitzell, E. Lonnoy, J. B. R. Matthews, T. K. Maycock, T. Waterfield, O. Yelekçi, R. Y. and B. Zhou (eds.), *Climate change 2021: The physical science basis. Contribution of working group I to the sixth assessment report of the intergovernmental panel on climate change.* Cambridge, United Kingdom and New York: Cambridge University Press, 3–32. DOI:10.1017/9781009157896.001.

IPCC (2022). Summary for policymakers. In: H.-O. Pörtner, D. C. Roberts, E. S. Poloczanska, K. Mintenbeck, M. Tignor, A. Alegría, M. Craig, S. Langsdorf, S. Löschke, V. Möller, & A. Okem (eds.). *Climate change 2022: Impacts, adaptation, and vulnerability.* Contribution of Working Group II to the Sixth Assessment Report of the Intergovernmental Panel on Climate Change. Cambridge University Press. Retrieved from: https://www.ipcc.ch/report/ar6/wg2/downloads/report/IPCC_AR6_WGII_SummaryForPolicymakers.pdf

IRP (2019). Global resources outlook 2019: Natural resources for the future we want. In: B. Oberle, S. Bringezu, S. Hatfield-Dodds, S. Hellweg, H. Schandl, J. Clement, L. Cabernard, N. Che, D. Chen, H. Droz-Georget, P. Ekins, M. Fischer-Kowalski, M. Flörke, S. Frank, A. Froemelt, A. Geschke, M. Haupt, P. Havlik, R. Hüfner, M. Lenzen, M. Lieber, B. Liu, Y. Lu, S. Lutter, J. Mehr, A. Miatto, D. Newth, C. Oberschelp, M. Obersteiner, S. Pfister, E. Piccoli, R. Schaldach, J. Schüngel, T. Sonderegger, A. Sudheshwar, H. Tanikawa, E. van der Voet, C. Walker, J. West, Z. Wang & B. Zhu (eds.), *A report of the international resource panel.* Nairobi, Kenya: United Nations Environment Programme, 162 pages. Retrieved from: https://www.resourcepanel.org/reports/global-resources-outlook.

Khanna, P. (2016). The world four degrees warmer. Retrieved from: https://www.paragkhanna.com/2016-3-9-the-world-4-degrees-warmer/

Pörtner, H. O., Scholes, R. J., Agard, J., Archer, E., Arneth, A., Bai, X., Barnes, D., Burrows, M., Chan, L., Cheung, W. L., Diamond, S., Donatti, C., Duarte, C., Eisenhauer, N., Foden, W., Gasalla, M. A., Handa, C., Hickler, T., Hoegh-Guldberg, O., Ichii, K., Jacob, U., Insarov, G., Kiessling, W., Leadley, P., Leemans, R., Levin, L., Lim, M., Maharaj, S., Managi, S., Marquet, P. A., McElwee, P., Midgley, G., Oberdorff, T., Obura, D., Osman, E., Pandit, R., Pascual, U., Pires, A. P. F., Popp, A., Reyes-García, V., Sankaran, M., Settele, J., Shin, Y. J., Sintayehu, D. W., Smith, P., Steiner, N., Strassburg, B., Sukumar, R., Trisos, C., Val, A. L., Wu, J., Aldrian, E., Parmesan, C., Pichs-Madruga, R., Roberts, D. C., Rogers, A. D., Díaz, S., Fischer, M., Hashimoto, S., Lavorel, S., Wu, N., and Ngo, H. T. (2021). IPBES-IPCC co-sponsored workshop report on biodiversity and climate change, IPBES and IPCC. DOI:10.5281/zenodo.4782538

Steffen, W., Persson, Å., Deutsch, L., Zalasiewicz, J., Williams, M., Richardson, K., Crumley, C., Crutzen, P., Folke, C., Gordon, L., Molina, M., Ramanathan, V., Rockström, J., Scheffer, M., Schellnhuber, H. J. and Svedin, U. (2011). The anthropocene: From global change to planetary stewardship. *Ambio,* 40, 739–761. DOI 10.1007/s13280-0011-0185-x.

Steffen, W., Richardson, K., Rockström, J., Cornell, S. E., Fetzer, I., Bennett, E. M., Biggs, R., Carpenter, S. R., de Vries, W., de Wit, C. A., Folke, C., Gierten, D., Heinke, J., Mace, G. M., Persson, L. M., Ramanathan, V., Reyers, B. and Sörlin, S. (2015). Planetary boundaries: Guiding human development on a changing planet. *Science,* 347(6223), 12. http://dx.doi.org/10.1126/.

UNDP (2020). The Next Frontier—Human development and the Anthropocene, 412 pages. Retrieved from: http://hdr.undp.org/sites/default/files/hdr2020.pdf

WMO (2020). State of the Global Climate 2020, WMO No. 1264, 56 pages Retrieved from: https://library.wmo.int/doc_num.php?explnum_id=10618
WMO (2021). United in Science 2021: A multi-organization high-level compilation of the latest climate science information. Retrieved from: http://public.wmo.int/en/resources/united_in_science
WMO (2022). State of the Global Climate 2021, WMO No. 1290, 57 pages. Retrieved from: https://library.wmo.int/doc_num.php?explnum_id=11178

2 UN ecological risk governance

Anders Siig Andersen, Henrik Hauggaard-Nielsen, Thomas Budde Christensen, and Lars Hulgaard

> We can't solve problems by using the same kind of thinking we used when we created them.
>
> Albert Einstein

Introduction

During more than five decades (see Chapter 1), scientists have been documenting negative anthropogenic environmental change, expressing increasing alarm, and calling for dramatic transformations in response. Early on, such documentation included the Club of Rome's study of the Limits to Growth (Meadows et al., 1972). In 1987, the United Nations (UN) commissioned Our Common Future, commonly called the Brundtland Report, which focused on sustainable development (Brundtland, 1987). The "Earth Summit" in 1992 (UN Conference on Environment and Development in Rio de Janeiro) agreed to define sustainable development as an overarching objective. The principles of the Rio Declaration on Environment and Development and the global action plan, Agenda 21, included many goals and targets, some of which informed the Millennium Development Goals (MDGs) eight years later (UN, 2000). Now, the 2030 Agenda for Sustainable Development, adopted by all United Nations Member States in 2015, provides a shared blueprint for peace and prosperity for people and the planet, now and into the future (UN, 2015, see also Chapter 3). This journey underlines the move from pollution control to ecological and socioecological responsibility in a period when science documents as a fact that human exploitation of nature is eroding the ecological basis of life on Earth and that this erosion is accelerating. Politically, there is a growing recognition of the severe and complex challenges at the global, regional, and national, as well as the local level. It remains, however, an open question whether the current policy decisions and efforts are sufficiently comprehensive, well-considered, and effective?

To try to answer these questions, we turn our attention to the field of global ecological politics and governance. We highlight some general actions and solutions that have been proposed by the Intergovernmental Panel on Climate Change (IPCC), the Intergovernmental Science-Policy Platform on Biodiversity and Ecosystem Services (IPBES), the International Resource Panel (IRP), and the United Nations Development Program (UNDP). Furthermore, we present UN attempts to govern climate change, biological diversity, and the use of natural resources. For each of these areas, we present scientific assessments of the gaps between the adopted and implemented plans. Focusing on the complexities, we highlight important knowledge, intervention, and governance aspects pertaining to the climate change–biodiversity nexus.

Like many other providers of scientific knowledge to the UN, the IPCC applies the core concept of ecological "risk" to understand the kind of challenges that the world is facing (IPCC, 2022: 4). By applying the terms "loss and damage", the IPCC (2022: 6) refers to adverse observed impacts and/or projected risks that can be economic and/or non-economic. The IPCC (-2022: 5) defines "exposure" as the presence of people, livelihoods, species or ecosystems, environmental functions, services and resources, infrastructure, or economic, social, and cultural assets in places and settings that could be adversely affected. The IPCC defines "vulnerability" as the predisposition of exposed human and natural systems to be adversely affected as a component of risk. Vulnerability is understood to differ within communities and across societies, regions, and countries, as well as changing through time. "Adaptation" plays a key role in reducing the exposure and vulnerability to ecological challenges. In ecological systems, adaption includes autonomous adjustments through ecological and evolutionary processes. In human systems, adaptation can be anticipatory or reactive, as well as incremental and/or transformational. The IPCC applies the term "maladaptation" when referring to actions that may lead to increasing the risks. For the IPCC, "resilience" describes not just the ability to maintain persistent essential functioning through mitigation and adaption, but also the human capacity for transformation (IPCC, 2022: 6).

Overall UN governance structure regarding climate change, biodiversity, and resources

Discovery of the beginning depletion of the ozone layer was the first reminder that human activities may cause disasters on Earth. The thin layer of ozone surrounding the Earth is a shield against dangerous radiation. Scientists discovered that the depletion was caused by a new refrigerant called Freon (chlorofluorocarbons, CFCs). In response, during the late 1970s a ban of most CFC-based aerosol products was initiated in the United States, Canada, and Scandinavia. However, these products remained on the market elsewhere, and within just eight years the total CFC production was higher than it was before the aerosol ban (Angus, 2016: 83). In 1979, what had been a gradual, linear process crossed a tipping point for the depletion to become nonlinear, which caused the hole in the ozone layer to increase rapidly (Angus, 2016: 85). In September 1987, 27 countries and the European Union signed the Montreal Protocol on Substances that Deplete the Ozone Layer. Dupont, the main supplier of CFCs and one of the world's largest chemical companies in terms of sales, now agreed to stop CFC production by the century's end, and the rest of the chemical industry followed (Angus, 2016: 85f). There are, however, important differences between, on the one hand, our ability to stop the hole in the ozone layer from expanding and, on the other, the climate change, biodiversity, and resource crisis. While the ozone crisis could be overcome by a few companies and industries, the elimination of fossil fuels and greenhouse gas emissions, the preservation of the biosphere, and significant reductions in resource consumption will require a decades-long transformation of the economy, technology, culture, and regulation to be resolved.

Two binding agreements, the United Nations Framework Convention on Climate Change (UNFCCC), which targets industrial and other emissions of greenhouse gases, such as carbon dioxide (CO_2), and the Convention on Biological Diversity (CBD), the first global agreement on the conservation and sustainable use of biological diversity, were included in the 1992 "Earth Summit" agreement. However, the resource area was not included and is not governed by a convention. Instead, in 2012, the United Nations General Assembly adopted a 10-Year Framework of Programs on Sustainable Consumption and Production (10YFP) allocating the responsibility for implementation to the One Planet Network (see below).

UN climate change governance

During the 1970s and 1980s, scientists increasingly warned politicians and the public that the Earth was becoming warmer, and that the warm-up was caused by CO_2 and other greenhouse gases (GHGs). In the following, we present the United Nations Framework Convention on Climate Change (UNFCCC) and the most important UN agreements pertaining to the climate area. We follow up by presenting different assessments of the outcomes (see also Chapter 6 on climate and energy governance in the EU and its connection to global climate governance).

The United Nations Framework Convention on climate change

At the Rio meeting, 195 parties signed the United Nations Framework Convention on Climate Change (UN, 1992a) with follow-up ratification in 1994. The objective of the Convention was to "stabilize greenhouse gas concentrations in the atmosphere at a level that would prevent dangerous anthropogenic interference with the climate system", stating that, "such a level should be achieved within a time frame sufficient to allow ecosystems to adapt naturally to climate change, to ensure that food production is not threatened, and to enable economic development to proceed in a sustainable manner" (UN, 1992a). Inspired by the Montreal Protocol (1987), Member States were bound to act in the interests of human safety even in the face of scientific uncertainty.

The Convention assigns common but different responsibilities to different groups of countries, classed as: (1) developed countries; (2) developed countries with special financial responsibilities; and (3) developing countries. Industrialized countries, which are equivalent to developed countries, are the main source of accumulated GHGs in the atmosphere. They are therefore expected to take a leading role in the efforts to cut GHG emissions. Thus, industrialized nations agreed to support climate change activities in developing countries by providing financial support for action on climate change – above and beyond any financial assistance they may have already provided to those countries. A system of grants and loans was set up under the Convention and managed by the Global Environment Facility (GEF), which operates outside the UNFCCC. The aim was for the fund to be replenished every fourth year by 40 developed donor countries. Industrialized countries also agreed to share technologies with developing countries. Developing countries should report their annual reporting of GHG emissions, including data for their base-year (1990) and all the years since, climate change policies, and related measures. Further, developing countries should report in more general terms on their actions both to address climate change and to adapt to its impacts. Their reporting, however, was contingent on them getting funding for the preparation of the reports, particularly in the case of the Least Developed Countries (LDCs), which are highly vulnerable to economic and environmental shocks.

The UNFCCC was formulated as a framework convention. It did not set any specific limits on GHG emissions for individual countries and contained no enforcement mechanisms. Instead, it established a framework for international negotiations of future agreements or protocols. Participating countries should meet at a Conference of the Parties (COP) to assess their progress and continue talks on how to tackle climate change.

The Kyoto Protocol

The Kyoto Protocol was signed in 1997 at COP3 in Japan (UNFCCC, 1997). It was the first international treaty to establish legally binding GHG emission reduction targets. It set targets for 37 industrialized countries, including countries in the European Union and economies in transition. However, some of the countries responsible for the biggest emissions of GHGs did not ratify the Protocol (most notably, the United States) or did not have any reduction obligations under the protocol (like China, India, Brazil, and South Africa). This meant that the targets of the Protocol covered a relatively limited amount of the total global emissions. However, some individual reduction targets were negotiated and once set, the parties were legally obliged to meet their commitments (Held & Roger, 2019: 7). The targets for those parties that had emission reduction obligations under the Kyoto Protocol added up to an average 5 percent emission reduction compared to 1990 levels over the first five-year reduction period, i.e., 2008 to 2012. In the second eight-year reduction period, i.e., 2013 to 2020, the target was to reduce GHG emissions by an average of 18 percent. The Kyoto Protocol improved the UNFCCC monitoring, reviewing, and verifying systems. In the Kyoto Protocol, non-state actors played a limited role (Held & Roger, 2019: 8)

According to the Kyoto Protocol, countries must meet their targets primarily through national measures. However, if domestic efforts were insufficient, they could also meet their targets by way of market-based mechanisms. Emissions trading, for instance, allows countries that have emissions permitted but not used to sell their excess capacity to countries that are over their targets. Thus, the Kyoto Protocol created a new commodity and a new notion: the "Carbon Market". This market works by applying three mechanisms: (1) emission trading; (2) the Clean Development Mechanism (CDM) – allowing industrialized countries with a greenhouse gas reduction commitment to invest in projects that reduce emissions in developing countries as an alternative to more expensive emissions reductions in their own countries; and (3) Joint Implementation (JI) – allowing industrialized countries to meet part of their required cuts in greenhouse gas emissions by paying for projects that reduce emissions in other industrialized countries. The CDM provided for the creation of certified emission reductions (CERs), whereas JI provided for the creation of emission reduction units (ERUs). By introducing the concept of Voluntary Carbon Offsets (VCOs), the CDM also allowed for the participation of private companies and other entities to earn carbon credits by investing in emission reduction activities in developing countries (for a critical discussion, see Chapter 11).

The Copenhagen accord and the Paris agreement

At COP15 in Copenhagen, it seemed as if very little progress had been made. However, in the final days of the COP, the Copenhagen Accord was formulated (UNFCCC, 2009), which was largely incorporated into the Cancun governance decision on the bottom-up voluntary actions of states. Intentionally, the Copenhagen Accord set a long-term target of limiting global temperatures to 2°C (Held & Roger, 2019: 13f). Initially, 114 states agreed to its terms. Later, the total was brought up to 144. Based on the Copenhagen Accord, in advance of COP21 in Paris, states agreed to develop "Nationally Determined Contributions" (NDCs) (Held & Roger, 2019: 17). Non-party actors played essentially no role in this system (Held & Roger, 2019: 15).

This new direction in climate change governance formed an important inspirational input to the COP21 Paris meeting conducted in 2015. The Paris Agreement was signed as a legally binding international agreement on climate change under the UNFCCC (UN, 1992a). By 2022, 197 countries had ratified the Agreement. The goal of the Agreement is to limit global warming to well below 2°C and preferably 1.5°C, compared to pre-industrial levels (UNFCCC, 2015). To achieve this long-term temperature goal, countries should aim to reach a global peaking of greenhouse gas emissions as soon as possible and to achieve a climate neutral world by 2050.

Primarily, the Paris Agreement works through countries' delivery of National Determined Contributions (NDCs). In their NDCs, countries communicate the actions they will take to reduce their greenhouse gas emissions to reach the long-term goals of the Paris Agreement and the UNFCCC. In the NDCs, countries also communicate the actions they will take to build resilience to adapt to the impacts of rising temperatures. Unlike the Kyoto Protocol, all countries – rich, poor, developed, and developing – are required to do their part in reducing greenhouse gas emissions. Thus, the Paris Agreement is based on the principle of common but differentiated responsibilities and the respective capabilities between countries of the Global North and the Global South.

The NDCs deliver quantifiable information, including on the time frame, scope, and coverage, planning processes, assumptions, and methodological approaches, how the party consider that its NDC is fair, and how the NDC will contribute toward achieving the objective of the Agreement. However, substantial freedom is given to the parties to design their NDC and the NDCs therefore differ significantly in these essential parameters. To better frame the efforts toward the long-term goal, the Paris Agreement invited countries to formulate and submit by 2020 their long-term low GHG emission development strategies providing their vision and direction for future development. However, unlike the NDCs, these are not mandatory.

With the Paris Agreement, the UN established an Enhanced Transparency Framework (ETF) in three stages: plan, implement, and review. This includes a series of mandatory measures for the monitoring, verification, and public reporting of progress toward a country's emission-reduction targets. The aim of enhanced transparency was operationalized by the adoption of the Katowice package in 2018 at the UN climate conference (COP24), which contains common and detailed rules, procedures, and guidelines. The information gathered through the ETF feeds into the five-year global stocktake, which assesses the collective progress toward the long-term climate goals. Countries are expected to revisit their pledges in their NDCs, following a predesigned schedule that aligns stocktaking, NDC revisions, and COP meetings, and to put forward progressively stronger targets every five years, with the goal of further driving down emissions. This is the so-called ambition mechanism. Under the ETF, biannual reports are subjected to technical review and each party is to take part in a "facilitative, multilateral consideration" regarding implementation.

Opposite to the Kyoto Protocol and the Copenhagen Accord, the decision adopting the Paris Agreement promoted the action of non-party stakeholders, confirming that they should register their climate-related actions at the

Non-State Actor Zone for Climate Action (NAZCA) platform, that these actors should meet at "high-level events", and that two "high-level champions" should be responsible for engaging stakeholders on the behalf of the UNFCCC (Held & Roger, 2018: 24).

The Paris Agreement also provides a framework for financial, technical, and capacity-building support aiming at fully realizing technology development and its transfer for both improving resilience to climate change and reducing GHG emissions. The Agreement reaffirms that developed countries should take the lead in providing financial assistance to countries that are less endowed and more vulnerable, while also encouraging voluntary contributions by other parties. The Agreement also states that climate finance is needed for mitigation because large-scale investments are required to significantly reduce emissions. Furthermore, it states that climate finance is equally important for adaptation, as significant financial resources are needed to adapt to the adverse effects and reduce the impacts of a changing climate. The Paris Agreement affirms the financial commitments of the 2009 Copenhagen Accord, which aimed to scale up public and private climate finance for developing nations to $100 billion a year by 2020.

Finally, the Paris Agreement aimed at improving the market mechanisms that were initiated in the Kyoto Protocol. Article 6 provides for accounting rules that require parties to apply robust accounting frameworks to approaches that involve the use of "internationally transferred mitigation outcomes" toward NDCs. It also provides for a mitigation mechanism to replace existing mechanisms (such as CDM and JI) and provides for the certification of emission reductions for use toward NDCs. However, disagreements between the parties under the Convention have delayed the efforts to agree on new common rules for the market mechanism.

Climate change, the 2030 Agenda, and the SDGs

The 2030 Agenda for Sustainable Development and the Sustainable Development Goals (SDGs) that were adopted in 2015 (UN, 2015: 8f) acknowledge that the UNFCCC is the primary international, intergovernmental forum for negotiating the global response to climate change and for holding the increase in global average temperature to well below 2°C and for pursuing efforts to limit the temperature increase to 1.5°C above pre-industrial levels (see also Chapter 3). With the formulation of five targets, SDG 13 specifically addresses climate adaption, mitigation, and finance: resilience and adaption (target13.1), integration of climate change measures into national policies, strategies, and planning (target 13.2), improving education, awareness, and human and institutional capacity (target 13.3), mobilizing $100 billion annually by 2020 to address the needs of developing countries for fully operationalizing the Green Climate Fund (target 13.a), and promoting mechanisms for raising the capacity for effective climate change-related planning and management in the Least Developed Countries (LDCs) and small island developing states, including focusing on women, youth, and local and marginalized communities (target 13.b) (UN, 2015).

Global stocktaking of national climate change plans and actions

Studies evaluating the national pledges show that the cumulative effect of the currently implemented emissions reductions will not be large enough to meet the temperature goal. In 2021, Antonio Guterres, Secretary-General of the United Nations, expressed this challenge directly:

> We are still significantly off-schedule to meet the goals of the Paris Agreement. This year (2021) has seen fossil fuel emissions bounce back, greenhouse gas concentrations continuing to rise, and severe human-enhanced weather events that have affected health, lives, and livelihoods on every continent.
>
> (WMO, 2021: 3)

The WMO 2021 report concludes that as of mid-November 2020, the National Determined Contributions remained "blatantly inadequate" to achieve the climate change goals of the Paris Agreement and would lead to a temperature rise of at least 3°C by the end of the century (WMO, 2021: 27). Limiting warming to below 2°C would then rely on a rapid acceleration of the mitigation efforts after 2030. Furthermore, policies implemented by the end of 2020 are projected to result in higher global GHG emissions than those implied by the NDCs. The IPCC (2022: 21) assessed that without a strengthening of the policies beyond those that were implemented by the end of 2020, GHG emissions could be projected to rise beyond 2025, leading to a median global warming of 3.2°C by 2100. The WMO report (2021: 28) also points out that the COVID-19-related fiscal spending of G20 members has primarily supported the global status quo of high-carbon economic production or have even fostered new high-carbon investments.

The Production Gap Report 2021 (SEI et al., 2021) tracks the discrepancy between governments' planned fossil fuel production and global production levels consistent with limiting warming. The report also tracks how governments worldwide continue to support fossil fuel production. The Paris Agreement set no specific requirements about how or how much countries should cut emissions. According to the report, however, there have been political expectations about the type and stringency of targets by various countries based on the latest science (SEI et al., 2021: 2).

The key findings of the 2021 gap assessment are that governments plan to produce more than twice the amount of fossil fuels in 2030 than would be consistent with the temperature targets. Most major oil and gas producers are planning on increasing production to 2030 or beyond, and equivalently, several major coal producers are planning on continuing or even increasing production (SEI et al., 2021: 15). Over the next two decades, governments are collectively projecting an increase in global oil and gas production, and only a modest decrease in coal production. China is the primary producer of coal (49 percent). The United States is the primary producer of oil (17 percent) and gas (23 percent) followed by Russia (13 percent and 18 percent) (SEI et al., 2021: 37). The G20, or Group of Twenty, countries have directed nearly USD 300 billion in new public funds toward fossil fuel activities since the beginning of the COVID-19 pandemic (March 2020), which is more than for clean energy investments (SEI et al., 2021: 28). Indeed, governments' production plans and projections would lead to around 240 percent more coal, 57 percent more oil, and 71 percent more gas than would be consistent with limiting global warming to 1.5°C (SEI et al., 2021: 16). This is despite Multilateral Development Banks (MDBs) and G20 Development Finance Institutions (DFIs) holding a total of over USD 2 trillion in assets having adopted policies that exclude fossil fuel production activities from future finance. The Gap report states that while existing transparency initiatives have shed some light on fossil fuel production, the available information is incomplete, inconsistent, and scattered (SEI et al., 2021: 5).

In addition to strengthening measures to reduce the demand for fossil fuels, the report recommends that governments should take actions to ensure a managed and equitable decline in production, such as the following (SEI et al., 2021: 6):

- Acknowledging in their energy and climate change plans that there is a need to wind down global fossil fuel production in line with the Paris Agreement's temperature limits;
- Charting the course toward a rapid, just, and equitable winding down of fossil fuel production as part of overall decarbonization plans;
- Placing restrictions on fossil fuel exploration and extraction to avoid locking in levels of fossil fuel supply that are inconsistent with climate change goals;
- Phasing out government support for fossil fuel production and directing greater support toward low-carbon development; and
- Leveraging international cooperation to ensure a more effective and equitable global winding down of production.

UN biodiversity governance

In the following, we turn our attention from climate change to the regulation of biodiversity by presenting the Convention on Biological Diversity (CBD) and an overview of the different UN protocols, plans, and strategies that have been directed at safeguarding and restoring bio-integrity and biodiversity. Furthermore, we present a global stocktaking on the action plans and actions within this area (see also Chapter 9 on biodiversity governance in the EU and its UN governance interplays).

The Convention on Biological Diversity (CBD) was opened for signature in 1992 at the Rio de Janeiro meeting (UN, 1992b), and then came into force at the end of 1993 and was ratified by most countries (Arjjumend et al., 2016: 8). The Convention recognizes that human health and livelihoods ultimately depend on genetic differences, leading to differences in the associated community composition and ecosystem functions and services processes. The Convention recognizes that the conservation of biological diversity is "a common concern of humankind" and an integral part of the development process for avoiding the long-term decline of biological diversity. The agreement links traditional conservation efforts to the economic goal of using biological resources sustainably, acknowledging the need for substantial investments to conserve biological diversity. According to the Convention, the Global Environment Facility (GEF) must help forge international cooperation and finance actions to address four critical threats to the global environment: biodiversity loss, climate change, depletion of the ozone layer, and the degradation of international waters. The Convention sets principles for the fair and equitable sharing of the benefits arising from the use of genetic resources, notably those destined for commercial use. It also covers the field of biotechnology, addressing technology development and transfer, benefit-sharing, and biosafety (UN, 1992b).

The Convention offers decision-makers guidance based on the precautionary principle that, where there is a threat of a significant reduction or loss of biological diversity, lack of full scientific certainty should not be used as a reason for postponing measures to avoid or minimize such a threat. Important issues include (UN, 1992b):

- Measures and incentives for the conservation and sustainable use of biological diversity;
- Regulated access to genetic resources;
- Access to and the transfer of technology, including biotechnology;
- Technical and scientific cooperation;
- Impact assessment;
- Education and public awareness;
- Provision of financial resources; and
- National reporting on efforts to implement treaty commitments.

The responsibility for achieving the goals of the Convention rests largely with the individual countries. Under the Convention, governments are required to develop National Biodiversity Strategies and Action Plans (NBSAPs), and to integrate these into broader national plans for the environment and development. Promoting that everyone benefits from biodiversity goods and services provided in an equitable way, the treaty commitments include (UN, 1992b):

- Identifying and monitoring the important components of biological diversity that need to be conserved and used sustainably;

- Establishing protected areas to conserve biological diversity while promoting environmentally sound development around these areas;
- Rehabilitating and restoring degraded ecosystems and promoting the recovery of threatened species in collaboration with local residents;
- Preventing the introduction of, controlling, and eradicating alien species that could threaten ecosystems, habitats, or species;
- Controlling the risks posed by organisms modified by biotechnology;
- Promoting public participation, particularly when it comes to assessing the environmental impacts of development projects that threaten biological diversity;
- Educating people and raising awareness about the importance of biological diversity and the need to conserve it; and
- Reporting on how each country is meeting its biodiversity goals.

The Convention also recognizes the close and traditional dependence of indigenous and local communities on biological resources and the need to ensure that these communities share the benefits arising from the use of their traditional knowledge and practices relating to the conservation and sustainable use of biodiversity. Member governments have undertaken "to respect, preserve, and maintain" such knowledge and practices, to promote their wider application with the approval and involvement of the communities concerned, and to encourage the equitable sharing of the benefits derived from their utilization.

The Convention's ultimate authority is the Conference of the Parties (COP), consisting of all governments (and regional economic integration organizations) that have ratified the treaty. This governing body reviews progress under the Convention, identifies new priorities, and sets workplans for members. The COP can also make amendments to the Convention, create expert advisory bodies, review progress reports by member nations, and collaborate with other international organizations and agreements. Since the adoption of the Convention, COPs have been held regularly to coordinate efforts pertaining to biodiversity (Taylor et al., 2020: 1090).

The Cartagena Protocol

Aiming at regulating living modified organisms (LMOs), a special protocol, the Cartagena Protocol on Biosafety to the Convention on Biological Diversity, entered into force in 2003 (CBD, 2000). This is an international agreement that aims to ensure the safe handling, transport, and use of LMOs resulting from modern biotechnology that may have adverse effects on biological diversity, also taking into account risks to human health. The Protocol requires that products developed through new technologies must be based on the "precautionary principle" while calling for a balance between public health and economic benefits. For example, it allows countries to ban imports of a genetically modified organism (GMO), if they consider that there is not enough scientific evidence of product safety (Arjjumend et al., 2016: 10).

The strategic plan for biodiversity 2011–2020, the Aichi targets, and the Nagoya Protocol

At a meeting in Nagoya in 2010, the Strategic Plan for Biodiversity 2011–2020 and the Aichi Biodiversity Targets (SPB) were adopted (Futhazar, 2016: 2f). The strategic plan introduced a shared vision, a mission, five strategic goals, and 20 targets known as the Aichi Targets. The Strategic Plan serves as a flexible framework for the establishment of national and regional targets. The five strategic goals are (CBD, 2010):

A   Address the underlying causes of biodiversity loss by mainstreaming biodiversity across government and society;
B   Reduce the direct pressures on biodiversity and promote sustainable use;
C   Improve the status of biodiversity by safeguarding ecosystems, species, and genetic diversity;
D   Enhance the benefits to all from biodiversity and ecosystem services;
E   Enhance implementation through participatory planning, knowledge management, and capacity-building.

At the national level, National Biodiversity Strategies and Action Plans (NBSAPs) are the principal instruments for implementing the Convention. The Convention requires countries to prepare NBSABs or an equivalent instrument, and to ensure that their strategy is mainstreamed into the planning and activities of all those sectors whose activities can have an impact on biodiversity. The aim of the NBSAPs is to provide important information on national targets and commitments and on the activities planned to achieve them.

The participants in the meeting in Nagoya also adopted the Nagoya Protocol that entered into force in 2014 (CBD, 2011). This is a supplementary agreement to the Convention on Biological Diversity regarding Access to Genetic Resources and the Fair and Equitable Sharing of Benefits Arising from their Utilization (Arjjumend et al., 2016: 10).

Biodiversity, the 2030 Agenda, and the SDGs

Relevant Sustainable Developments Goals (SDGs) are aligned with many of the Aichi Targets. In the 2030 Agenda, determination is expressed to conserve and sustainably use the oceans and seas, freshwater resources, as well as forests, mountains, and drylands and to protect biodiversity, ecosystems, and wildlife (UN, 2015; see also Chapter 3). SDG 14, "Life below water", deals with the conservation and sustainable use of the oceans, seas, and marine resources and targets 10 different although overlapping areas: marine pollution (target 14.1); protection, restoration, and conservation of coastal and marine ecosystems (targets 14.2 and 14.5); reduce ocean acidification (target 14.3); sustainable fishing and use of marine resources (targets 14.4, 14.6, 14.7, and 14.9); increase scientific knowledge, research, and technology for ocean health (target 14.8); and enforce international sea law (14.c). SDG 15, "Life on land", is about the sustainable management of forests, combating desertification, halting and reversing land degradation, and halting biodiversity loss. It consists of 12 partly overlapping targets: end deforestation and desertification, conserve and restore terrestrial and freshwater ecosystems, protect biodiversity and natural habitats, and ensure the conservation of mountain ecosystems (targets 15.1–15.5); protect access to genetic resources and a fair sharing of the benefits (target 15.6); eliminate the poaching and trafficking of protected species (targets 15.7 and 15.C); prevent invasive alien species on land and in water ecosystems (target 15.8); integrate ecosystems and biodiversity in governmental planning (target 15.9); and increase financial resources to conserve and sustainably use and manage ecosystems and biodiversity (targets 15.A and 15.B).

Global stocktaking of biodiversity plans and actions

Published by the Secretariat of the Convention of Biological Diversity, "The Outlook 5" report (Secretariat of the Convention on Biological Diversity, 2020) demonstrates that very few of the Aichi Biodiversity Targets have been fully met and that the world is not on track to reach the 2050 Vision for Biodiversity. Examining the 60 specific elements of the Aichi Biodiversity Targets, it reports that seven have been achieved and 38 show different degrees of progress. Thirteen elements show no progress or indicate a move away from the target, while for two elements, the level of progress is unknown (Secretariat of the Convention of Biological Diversity, 2020: 10).

Some progress, however, has been reported. Almost 100 countries (50 percent of CBD parties) have incorporated biodiversity values into their national accounting system. The rate of deforestation has fallen globally by about a third compared to the previous decade; where good fisheries management policies have been introduced, the abundance of marine fish stocks has been maintained or rebuilt; and there have been an increasing number of successful cases of the eradication of invasive alien species from islands. In addition, there has been significant expansion of the protected area estate, increasing over the 2000–2020 period from about 10 percent to at least 15 percent terrestrially, and from about 3 percent to at least 7 percent in marine areas. Also, the protection of areas of particular importance for biodiversity (key biodiversity areas) has increased from 29 percent to 44 percent over the same period. Recent conservation actions have reduced the number of extinctions through a range of measures. According to the Outlook 5 report, without such actions, the extinctions of birds and mammals in the past decade would likely have been two to four times higher. The Nagoya Protocol on Access to Genetic Resources and the Fair and Equitable Sharing of Benefits Arising from their Utilization has come into force and is now fully operational in at least 87 countries (43 percent of CBD parties) and internationally. National Biodiversity Strategies and Action Plans (NBSAPs) have been updated by

170 countries (85 percent of CBD parties). Also, there has been a substantial increase in the data and information on biodiversity available to citizens, researchers, and policymakers, including through the efforts of citizen science, while the financial resources available for biodiversity through international flows have doubled.

The Outlook 5 report states that the overall picture from the national reports provided by countries is one of progress, but at levels generally insufficient to achieve the Aichi Biodiversity Targets. The information from the national reports suggests that there are gaps in both the level of ambition of the commitments of countries as well as in the actions to reach these commitments (Secretariat of the Convention on Biological Diversity, 2020: 10). According to Outlook 5, the information in the national reports is broadly consistent with an indicator-based analysis at the global level. While the indicators relating to policies and actions in support of biodiversity show positive trends, those relating to the drivers of biodiversity loss and to the current state of biodiversity itself mostly show significantly worsening trends (Secretariat of the Convention on Biological Diversity, 2020: 10).

UN resource governance

As opposed to the areas of climate change and biodiversity, the resource area is not governed by a convention. Instead, it is governed by a 10-Year Framework of Programs on Sustainable Consumption and Production (10YFP) and the One Planet Network (see also Chapter 7 on resources and circular economy governance in the EU and its relation to the UN context). According to the IRP:

> Natural resources are inextricably linked to combatting climate change, biodiversity loss, and desertification, as well as the achievement of the SDGs. The use of resources has consequences, and the uptake in natural resource use has contributed to the situation where four out of nine planetary boundaries are surpassing their recommended limits.
> (IRP, 2019: 31)

The IRP (2019: 7) focuses on the principles of sustainable consumption and production, which address the entire life cycle of economic activities from the extraction of natural resources, through the production and use phase of products and goods, and finally, to the disposal of resources. The IRP promotes the concept of the circular economy as a central mechanism for decoupling (IRP, 2019: 125 and 138; for critical discussions, see Chapters 4, 7, and 11). According to the IRP, decoupling occurs when resource use or a pressure on the environment grows at a slower rate than the activity causing it (relative decoupling) or declines while the economic activity continues to grow (absolute decoupling). The IRP argues that absolute decoupling in high-income countries can lower the average resource consumption. The IRP indicates that relative decoupling in developing economies and economies in transition can raise the average income levels and eliminate poverty, while still increasing the levels of natural resource consumption. In general, following the IRP, the concept of decoupling is about maintaining economic growth, resource safety, and human well-being in all countries of the world by means of technology development, incentives, and innovative organization secured by co-ordinated sustainability actions – particularly, resource efficiency, sustainable consumption and production, and circular economy policies (IRP, 2019: 29). While the linear economy is based on a simple, linear process: extract, produce, consume, and trash, with little regard for ecological concerns, the circular economy is one in which the value of products, materials, and resources is maintained in the economy for as long as possible, and the generation of waste is minimized. The circular economy aims to decouple prosperity from resource consumption (IRP, 2019: 23), reconciling the problem of how to increase productivity while considering the externalities of the production process, the consumption of the products, and the end-of-life impacts (see also Sauvé et al., 2015: 53) to ensure the long-term material basis of societies without surpassing the thresholds of a safe operating space (IRP, 2019: 25).

The IRP also proposes the concept of "leapfrogging" based on the idea that industrializing countries can bypass the resource-intensive conventional pathway of development paved by high-income, already industrialized countries and can "leap" forward to use the most advanced sustainable technologies (IRP, 2019: 140).

IRP reports formed part of the scientific background for the UN adoption of the 10YFP – a global commitment made by 193 Member States targeting a transformation of the ways societies produce and consume in order to achieve social and economic development (UN, 2012: 2). The 10YFP covers six areas: (1) Consumer Information for sustainable consumption and production; (2) Sustainable Lifestyles and Education; (3) Sustainable Public Procurement; (4) Sustainable Buildings and Construction; (5) Sustainable Tourism, including ecotourism; and (6) Sustainable Food-Systems (UN, 2012: 9). The main aims of the 10YFP are to

> Promote social and economic development within the carrying capacity of ecosystems by addressing and, where appropriate, decoupling economic growth from environmental degradation by improving efficiency and sustainability in the use of resources and production processes and reducing resource degradation, pollution, and waste.
>
> (UN, 2012: 2)

In general, the 10YFP is oriented toward global growth combined with the ecological and resource aims to:

- Conserve, protect, and restore the health and integrity of the Earth's ecosystems;

- Reduce the use of hazardous materials and toxic chemicals, the generation of wastes, and the emission of pollutants;
- Promote a more efficient use of natural resources, products, and recovered materials; and
- Promote life cycle approaches, including resource efficiency and the sustainable use of resources, as well as science-based and traditional knowledge-based approaches, cradle to cradle, and the Reduce, Reuse, and Recycle concept (UN, 2012: 2f).

The UN appointed the One Planet Network the task of being the main implementation agency of the 10YFP (One Planet Network). The One Planet Network is a global community of practitioners, policymakers, and experts that supports collaboration, cooperation, and coordination between participants to increase the combined knowledge, effectiveness, and impact. The United Nations Environment Program facilitates the activities of the network.

Resources, the 2030 agenda, and the sustainable development goals

In the 2030 Agenda and the SDGs (UN 2015), the 10YFP is referred to as a key implantation mechanism for SDGs 12.1 and 12.2 on Sustainable Consumption and Production and SDG 8.4 on Decent Work and Economic Growth (UN, 2015: 8; see also Chapters 3 and 4). In the SDGs, decoupling resource use from well-being and adverse social and environmental impacts is regarded as key to achieving sustainable development. Target 12.1 mentions that the 10YFP should be implemented with developed countries taking the lead, considering the development and capabilities of developing countries. The indicator of target 12.1 is: "Number of countries developing, adopting, or implementing policy instruments aimed at supporting the shift to sustainable consumption and production". Target 12.2 states that by 2030 the world should achieve a sustainable management and efficient use of natural resources. In accordance with the 10YFP, target 8.4 mentions that global resource efficiency in consumption and production must improve progressively through to 2030 and that the parties must endeavor to decouple economic growth from environmental degradation. Targets 12.2 and 8.4 share both their indicators: (a) the material footprint as the quantity of all material resources that must be mobilized globally to meet the consumption in a country, material footprint per capita, and material footprint per GDP, and (b) the domestic material consumption per capita, and domestic material consumption per GDP. Pertaining to sustainable consumption and production, it is noteworthy that the SDGs are more specific than the goals of the 10YFP. For example, SDG 12 contains the following targets that should be achieved in 2030: achieve the sustainable management and efficient use of natural resources, halve per capita global food waste at the retail and consumer levels, and reduce food losses along the production and supply chains, including post-harvest losses; substantially reduce waste generation through prevention, reduction, recycling, and reuse; and ensure that people everywhere have the relevant information and awareness for achieving sustainable development and lifestyles in harmony with nature.

Stocktaking

A report published in 2018 on the progress of the 10YFP quotes the Secretary-General of the UN for having highlighted significant gaps in ensuring sustainable consumption and production patterns. According to the Secretary-General, the scale and pace of concerted actions by all actors of society, including government, business, and civil society, need to be embraced and dramatically stepped up (UN, 2018: 2). The report underlines:

- While cost-effective and high-impact solutions exist, reporting results indicate that effecting concrete changes in practices and impacts remains a challenge (UN, 2018: 2);
- There is a clear gap between the development of policies and tools and their implementation (UN, 2018: 5); and
- An independent external review identified the 10-year framework as dramatically resource-constrained (UN, 2018: 25).

The IRP points at severe societal and human challenges caused by the present use of resources and highlights the likelihood of even more pressing challenges if the use of resources continue to rise as predicted. Furthermore, the IRP highlights global solutions regarding resource productivity, the circular economy, and leapfrogging. In general, however, it is noteworthy that the UN governance of the resource area seems to be much weaker than its governance of climate change and biodiversity. In the words of the IRP: "Until now, the importance of natural resources has not been in the implementation domain of (…) internationally agreed-upon conventions" (IRP, 2019: 31). Indeed, there are no targets concerning the use of resources in the 10YFP, there is no convention or conferences of the parties (COPs) dedicated to this area, the programs of the 10YFP omit important areas, such as industry and technology, and the One Planet Network has restricted authority to only support collaboration and the dissemination of practical and scientific knowledge.

The climate change–biodiversity nexus

In his foreword to the Global Biodiversity Outlook 5 (2020), António Guterres, Secretary-General of the United Nations, acknowledges a dual challenge between climate change and biodiversity loss:

> Part of this new agenda must be to tackle the twin global challenges of climate change and biodiversity loss in a more coordinated manner, with

the understanding that climate change threatens to undermine all efforts to conserve and sustainably manage biodiversity and that nature itself offers some of the most effective solutions to avert the worst impacts of a warming planet.

(Pörtner et al., 2021: 4)

However, in practice, the two areas have largely been addressed separately to date, creating the risk that actions to combat climate change can harm biodiversity as well as natural and managed habitats, while measures to protect biodiversity can impair climate mitigation (Pörtner et al., 2021: 32). Each issue has its own international convention, and each has an intergovernmental body (IPCC and IPBES) that assesses the available knowledge

In 2021, for the first time, the IPBES and IPCC collaboratively conducted a workshop that resulted in the publication of a joint report. The report states that the individual parts cannot be managed in isolation from one another, and the workshop set out to explore these complex and multiple connections, challenges, and solutions (Pörtner et al., 2021: 3). Some examples of synergy include actions taken to protect biodiversity that simultaneously contribute to the mitigation of climate change; or an action increasing the capacity of species or ecosystems to adapt to those climate changes that cannot be avoided. In contrast, negative trade-offs can result, for instance, if an action taken to mitigate climate change by using the land or ocean to absorb greenhouse gases results in a loss of biodiversity or the supply of other nature-linked benefits. As stated by the UN Secretary-General, it is only by considering climate change and biodiversity as parts of the same complex problem that solutions can be developed that avoid maladaptation and maximize beneficial outcomes. The IPBES and IPCC argue that simultaneously meeting these agreements relies on immediate and sustained efforts for transformative change, which encompass both technological and environmental policies as well as changes to economic structures and profound shifts in society (Pörtner et al., 2021: 14).

Biodiversity protection and climate change mitigation

Potentially useful approaches to bridge climate change and biodiversity actions include nature-based solutions and solutions that create technological–ecological synergies, or integrated systems – approaches that recognize the potential co-benefits that exist in combining technological and nature-based solutions (Pörtner et al., 2021: 33). Nature-based solutions are active strategies to protect, sustainably manage, and restore natural and modified ecosystems. The concept embraces a wide range of descriptions of human–nature interactions, including through the concept of ecosystem services and the concept of biodiversity (Pörtner et al., 2021: 10). By focusing on maintaining genetic and species diversity and creating healthy ecosystems, nature-based solutions can play a powerful role in reducing temperatures in the long term (Pörtner et al., 2021: 14ff).

However, achieving synergistic benefits and positive trade-offs between biodiversity conservation, ecosystem service enhancement, and climate change mitigation is strongly dependent on which ecosystem uses and sectoral interactions are under consideration (Pörtner et al., 2021: 20). Increasingly, biodiversity conservation actions are being considered across the whole gradient of the state of nature from intact to completely altered. At the one end is "intact wilderness" (comprising about 25 percent of land and 3 percent of the ocean), while at the other extreme are "anthromes", i.e., completely transformed spaces (about 21 percent of land, 1 percent of the ocean). In between are "shared spaces", which comprise about 55 percent of land and likely >95 percent of the ocean (Pörtner et al., 2021: 45). On a broader scale are multifunctional "scapes" embedded in ecosystem and regional scale processes, which often require transboundary approaches for conservation (Pörtner et al., 2021: 46). The IPBES and IPCC argue that achieving multiple sustainable outcomes becomes progressively more feasible at the larger scale of a "scape" (Pörtner et al., 2021: 20).

Although nature-based solutions are important and must be promoted, faster-acting mitigation efforts needs to come from rapid, ambitious emissions reductions in fossil fuel emissions (Pörtner et al., 2021: 52). Ecosystems can aid change mitigation over time, but only when complementing rapid emission reduction in the energy production, transportation, agriculture, building, and industrial sectors (Pörtner et al., 2021: 16). The combination of nature-based and technology-based climate change solutions on land and at sea may provide co-benefits for climate mitigation, adaptation, and biodiversity. For example, grazing and cropping underneath solar panels can enhance soil carbon stocks, provide food, and deliver pollinator habitats (Pörtner et al., 2021: 18).

Critical assessment of the reciprocity between biodiversity protection and climate change mitigation

The IPBES and the IPCC express major concerns about nature-based solutions developed for single purposes that do not consider the dual challenge of biodiversity protection and climate change mitigation. For example, mitigating climate change by devoting vast land areas globally to reforestation for carbon sequestration may be efficient, but at the same time can harm biodiversity. Equivalently, afforestation that focuses solely on replanting species with large carbon sequestration and storage potential may result in degradation of the ecosystem and community structure and function and the loss of distinctive species (Pörtner et al., 2021: 47). Likewise, planting crops for bioenergy purposes to substitute fossil energy use can be detrimental to ecosystems and reduce the supply of many of nature's other contributions to people arising from the competition for space and through fertilizer and pesticide use or by increasing water withdrawals (Pörtner et al., 2021: 18).

UN *ecological risk governance* 51

The IPBES and IPCC also note that numerous technology-based climate change mitigation actions raise concerns and risks for biodiversity actions (Pörtner et al., 2021: 55f):

- Renewable energies in the transport and energy sector rely on mining for minerals on land and in the ocean. This has the potential to have a large detrimental environmental impact. For example, the lifecycle of material resources required for lithium batteries can exceed the weight of the battery itself by nearly 200 times, the demand for lithium will likely surpass the production output by as soon as the end of the 2020s, and 1 kWh Li-ion batteries cost more than 400 kWh to manufacture;
- Enhanced ocean uptake of CO_2 can occur through (a) creating and restoring "blue carbon" biological sinks, (b) ocean fertilization, and (c) increasing the alkalinity of seawater. The IPBES and IPCC state that, while options under (a) have a sound footing in biological processes, the actions under (b) and (c) are generally theoretical and the fate of the extra captured carbon is unknown, but may include potentially harmful disruption in the marine food web;
- Accelerated mineral weathering, i.e., the chemical breakdown of minerals in mountains and soils, may remove carbon dioxide from the atmosphere and transform it into stable minerals on the planet's surface and in ocean sediments. Enhanced rock weathering involves: (a) the mining of rocks containing minerals that naturally react with CO_2 from the atmosphere over geological timescales; (b) the crushing of these rocks to increase their surface area; and (c) the spreading of these crushed rocks on soils (or in the ocean) so that they may absorb atmospheric CO_2. The IPBES and IPCC argue that the biodiversity impacts of such interventions are largely unquantified;
- Biochar is produced by the pyrolysis of biomass, with the resulting product applied to soils. According to the IPBES and IPCC, the production of biomass for the pyrolysis products required to provide CO_2 removal may have potential negative impacts on biodiversity.

The IPBES and IPCC argue that on- and offshore windfarms, solar plants, and dams for creating hydropower may represent minor or major challenges to habitats and biodiversity, but that, in general, technological solutions are at hand that can limit the damages.

The two organizations are critical of the practice of mitigating the negative impacts of developments on biodiversity by restoring biodiversity, or by setting aside areas for protection elsewhere at remote sites (Pörtner et al., 2021: 19f). Allowing businesses to fund nature-based solutions in return for continued fossil fuel emissions or biodiversity-damaging activities elsewhere diminishes the impact of the nature-based solutions. Also, there are risks that fast-track approaches, such as the planting of billions of trees, may emphasize monocultures and exotic species. Another obstacle that needs to be looked at with a critical eye is the double counting of any offsets, whether for climate change or biodiversity (Pörtner et al., 2021: 153).

Wicked problems and flexible solutions

Biodiversity and climate change can be considered as wicked problems with high uncertainty, contested values, and unclear policy pathways, and prompt a high urgency to act to preserve nature's benefits for future generations (Pörtner et al., 2021: 145).

While clear quantitative targets, such as net zero emissions by 2050, have been pledged by an increasing number of countries, biodiversity is not easily reduced to single indicators (see also Chapter 9). While scenarios and pathways for climate change mitigation choices can be analyzed through integrated modeling, trade-off analyses for biodiversity are considerably more difficult given the different roles of species, the multifaceted nature of ecosystems and their contributions to people, and the absence of clear metrics to measure policy impacts (Pörtner et al., 2021: 145). Furthermore, while biodiversity–climate change interactions can be placed into co-beneficial, trade-off, or co-detrimental categories, these categorizations are subject to change by virtue of the fact that they are often dependent on a specific spatiotemporal context. Thus, the same policy measures taken in different spatiotemporal contexts could have positive effects on biodiversity or climate change in one context and negative effects in another.

Biodiversity and climate change challenges are tightly intertwined phenomena and share some of the underlying direct drivers and many of the indirect drivers (Pörtner et al., 2021: 28). The direct drivers of biodiversity decline include land/sea use intensity and change, the direct exploitation of organisms, pollution, climate change, and invasive species. Some direct anthropogenic drivers, such as deforestation and land-use changes associated with agriculture and pollution, can strongly drive both climate change and biodiversity decline, whereas other drivers primarily impact one or the other (Pörtner et al., 2021: 28f). The indirect drivers include key institutions (formal and informal) and governance (policy, law, international agreements) in addition to human demographic drivers, economic drivers (supply, production and consumption, affluence, inequality, and poverty), technological drivers, and sociocultural drivers (values, norms, beliefs, education). These drivers interact across multiple scales and varying degrees of proximity to the location in question, from global to regional, national, and local scales (Pörtner et al., 2021: 28f). The possibilities of short-term economic gains by the primary actors, fragmented decision-making, limited communication among stakeholders, short-term visions, and a severe lack of financial resources, time, and knowledge present further challenges to governance (Pörtner et al., 2021: 157). The lack of political will, complexity of the issues for any specific level of jurisdiction to grapple with, scale mismatches (temporal, spatial, and institutional), lack of transparency and accountability, and institutional inertia tend to complicate the solution space (Pörtner et al., 2021: 157). Furthermore, there can be questions around the uncertainties within scenarios (known unknowns); uncertainties prevailing around the climate system and biodiversity responses to stressors and pressures (unknown unknowns); and uncertainties existing around the scale of impacts (Pörtner et al., 2021: 165).

The IPBES and IPCC argue that decisions following an iterative and flexible procedure that accounts for the complexity and uneven power dynamics among actors and scales are likely to be more successful. This implicates arguments in favor of approaches to biodiversity loss and climate change adaptation that put a strong emphasis on risk management and the capacity to evolve over time, as opposed to implementing strategies that focus on managing for a specific future scenario and that lack flexibility once implemented (Pörtner et al., 2021: 175). Both at sea and on land, adopting dynamic approaches to conservation, rather than static goals, will allow flexible responses and leverage biodiversity's capacity to contribute to climate-change mitigation and adaptation. In the face of climate change, conservation will be about managing the change since a return to the historical state will be impossible to achieve (Pörtner et al., 2021: 65). However challenging, the IPBES and IPCC argue that system approaches could help address the increasingly tele-coupled nature of global systems, and that designing climate change and biodiversity resilient pathways should build on an understanding of the interconnections between climate change and biodiversity and the roles of faraway actors (Pörtner et al., 2021: 160).

Goal-based governance

Goal-based governance is the norm for climate change, biodiversity, and sustainable development, but can cause challenges for implementation (see also Chapter 3). For example, in the biodiversity domain, goal-setting that relies on achieving area-based protected area targets alone is unlikely to be successful, given the climate change pressures in the biodiversity domain (Pörtner et al., 2021: 23). A key difference in the goal-setting approach from the rulemaking approach of previous decades is that goals focus on an aspiration to motivate behavioral drivers for both biodiversity and climate change, while rulemaking generally includes behavioral prescriptions, such as requirements and prohibitions. The former tends toward generating global interest by establishing priorities and motivating efforts, while the latter emphasizes compliance and enforcement (Pörtner et al., 2021: 158).

The IPBES and IPCC conclude that there are weak enforcement mechanisms of most global and local policies. While there have been attempts to remedy this, such as through the "ambition" or "ratchet" mechanism that exist in the Paris Agreement requiring stronger pledges over time, this does not yet have an equivalent corollary for biodiversity policies. Similarly, some key areas related to climate change and biodiversity are still missing goals and targets, such as, for example, the lack of global goals for climate change adaptation (Pörtner et al., 2021: 158). The IPBES and IPCC argue that one important factor in future governance will be understanding the impacts and challenges of the move toward goals-based approaches. At the same time, the IPBES and IPCC hold the view that goal-setting and binding legal instruments should be seen as complementary tools in the contemporary governance toolbox (Pörtner et al., 2021: 158).

Summary

In this chapter, we have outlined and discussed different UN conventions, protocols, and strategies framing global actions regarding climate change, biodiversity, and resources. For each of these areas, we have presented UN-commissioned assessments of their efficiency regarding the stated goals (global stocktaking). Over the last 30 years, the knowledgebase underlying negotiations, agreements, and evaluations at the global and national levels has been strengthened. Scientific research, scientific reviews by the IPCC, IPBES, and IRP, voluntary national contributions, and global stocktaking have provided increasing knowledge on climate change, biodiversity loss, and resource depletion, as well as assessments of national and global actions and their efficiency in reaching negotiated goals and targets. The picture provided by this knowledgebase is not promising. We have followed up by looking into questions raised jointly by the IPBES and IPCC critically reflecting on the predominantly separate dealing with the issues of climate change and biodiversity.

The area of climate change is governed by the United Nations Framework Convention on Climate Change (UNFCCC) that was adopted in 1992. Within this framework, in 1997, the Kyoto Protocol set negotiated legally binding GHG emission reduction targets for industrialized countries and adopted market-based emission trading mechanisms. However, rather few countries signed the protocol and some countries responsible for major emissions left the protocol. In 2015, the Paris Agreement introduced a new governance model by setting an overall temperature goal of 2°C and preferably 1.5°C and by shifting from legally binding GHG emission goals to Nationally Determined Contributions (NDCs) covering all countries, but with varying commitments. At the same time, the Paris Agreement included mitigation as well as adaption, it created the Enhanced Transparency Framework (ETF); provided a framework for financial, technical, and capacity-building efforts; confirmed the decision by COP15 in Copenhagen to scale up public and private finance to developing nations; and it promoted the actions of non-party stakeholders.

The area of biodiversity is governed by the CBD, which was adopted in 1992. It covers a broad variety of issues, such as conservation and protected areas, controlling alien species, access to genetic resources, transfer of technology and scientific cooperation, provision of financial resources, strengthening education, public awareness, the maintenance of traditional and indigenous knowledge, and public participation. In 2000, the Cartagena Protocol was adopted focusing especially on biosafety. In 2010, the adoption of the Strategic Plan for Biodiversity 2011–2020, the Aichi Targets, and the Nagoya Protocol (genetic resources) aimed at strengthening the governance of the biodiversity area by introducing National Biodiversity Strategies and Action Plans (NDSAPs). In some respects, this governance model anticipates as well as parallels the NDCs under the Paris Agreement.

The resource area is governed by the 10YFP on sustainable consumption and production and the One Planet Network. When compared to the areas of climate change and biodiversity, this is a very different governance model: there is no convention, the 10YFP contains no concise negotiated targets, and countries are not supposed to deliver national determined contributions.

Regarding the areas of climate change and biodiversity, the SDGs reiterate the goals, targets, and indicators from the global agreements. Within the area of resources, the SDGs contain more specific goals, targets, and indicators than the 10YFP itself.

Current global stocktaking is generally pessimistic, and suggests the world is not on track to reaching the negotiated goals within the areas of climate change, biodiversity loss, and resource depletion. According to the Secretary-General of the UN, within the area of climate change, "we are still significantly off-schedule". As stated by the secretariat of the CBD, developments related to the drivers of biodiversity loss and the current state of biodiversity "mostly show significantly worsening trends". In the area of resources, the Secretary-General of the UN warns that the scale of concerted actions "needs to be embraced and dramatically stepped up". According to the global-stocktaking reports, this is not only because countries are missing out in fulfilling their obligations, but also because the goals and obligations are not strong enough and do not cover all the relevant areas of intervention. For example, within the area of climate change, the global-stocktaking report recommends that there is a need to wind down global fossil fuel production and to phase out government support for fossil fuel exploration and extraction. Within the area of biodiversity, the stocktaking report indicates that the global regulation of the drivers of biodiversity loss is "far too weak". Within the area of resources, the stocktaking underlines that "the importance of natural resources has not been in the implementation domain (…) of internationally agreed-upon conventions".

Regarding the areas of climate change and biodiversity, the challenges are aggravated by the fact that the two areas are deeply intertwined. Climate change represents a threat to biodiversity, and the loss of biodiversity can increase climate change. Moreover, solutions to mitigate or adapt to climate change may result in biodiversity loss, and, in some cases, solutions to counteract biodiversity loss may speed up climate change. This picture becomes further complicated if one considers the complete climate change–biodiversity–resource nexus. An increasing number of politicians as well as scientists conceive of climate change, biodiversity loss, and resource depletion as a truly intertwined and wicked set of problems that are presenting global and national governance with hitherto unprecedented challenges.

These challenges become even more "wicked" when focusing not only on ecological sustainability and the climate change–biodiversity–resource nexus but also on the interrelations between the ecological, social, and economic aspects of sustainable development and governance. These questions will be in focus of the next chapter of this book.

References

Angus, I. (2016). *Facing the Anthropocene: Fossil capitalism and the crisis of the Earth system.* New York: Monthly Review Press.

Arjjumend, J. H., Islamia, J. M. and Koutouki, K. (2016). IPAN research brief No.01. *Journal of Global Resources*, 3, July (Print), 2455–2445 (Online). Retrieved from: http://www.ipan.in/wpcontent/themes/ipan/ebooks/57581305699ef_Evolution%20of%20International%20Biodiversity%20Governance_IPAN.pdf

Brundtland, G. (1987). *Report of the world commission on environment and development: Our common future.* New York: United Nations General Assembly document A/42/427.

CBD (2000). *Cartagena Protocol on biosafety to the convention on biological diversity: Text and annexes.* Montreal: Secretariat of the Convention on Biological Diversity. Retrieved from: https://www.cbd.int/doc/legal/cartagena-protocol-en.pdf

CBD (2010). *Strategic plan for biodiversity 2011–2020 and the Aichi Targets "living in harmony with nature".* Secretariat of the Convention on Biological Diversity. Retrieved from: https://www.cbd.int/sp/

CBD (2011). *Nagoya Protocol an access to genetic resources and the fair and equitable sharing of benefits arising from their utilization to the Convention of Biological Diversity.* Secretariat of the Convention on Biological Diversity. Retrieved from: https://www.cbd.int/abs/doc/protocol/nagoya-protocol-en.pdf

Futhazar, G. 2016). The diffusion of the strategic plan for biodiversity and its Aichi biodiversity targets within the biodiversity cluster: An illustration of current trends in the global governance of biodiversity and ecosystems. *Yearbook of International Environmental Law*, 25, 133–166. DOI: 10.1093/yiel/yvv061. halshs-01477899.

Held, D. and Roger, C. (2019). Three models of global climate governance: From Kyoto to Paris and beyond. *Global Policy*, 9(4), 1–39.

IRP (2019). Global resources outlook 2019: Natural resources for the future we want. In: B. Oberle, S. Bringezu, S. Hatfield-Dodds, S. Hellweg, H. Schandl, J. Clement, L. Cabernard, N. Che, D. Chen, H. Droz-Georget, P. Ekins, M. Fischer-Kowalski, M. Flörke, S. Frank, A. Froemelt, A. Geschke, M. Haupt, P. Havlik, R. Hüfner, M. Lenzen, M. Lieber, B. Liu, Y. Lu, S. Lutter, J. Mehr, A. Miatto, D. Newth, C. Oberschelp, M. Obersteiner, S. Pfister, E. Piccoli, R. Schaldach, J. Schüngel, T. Sonderegger, A. Sudheshwar, H. Tanikawa, E. van der Voet, C. Walker, J. West, Z. Wang & B. Zhu (eds.), *A report of the international resource panel.* Nairobi, Kenya: United Nations Environment Programme, 162 pages. Retrieved from: https://www.resourcepanel.org/reports/global-resources-outlook

Meadows, D. H., Meadows, D. L., Randers, J., and Behrens III, W. W. (1972). *Limits to growth. A report for the Club of Rome's Project of the predicament of mankind.* New

York: Potomac, 211 pages. Retrieved from: https://www.donellameadows.org/wp-content/userfiles/Limits-to-Growth-digital-scan-version.pdf

Pörtner, H. O., Scholes, R. J., Agard, J., Archer, E., Arneth, A., Bai, X., Barnes, D., Burrows, M., Chan, L., Cheung, W. L., Diamond, S., Donatti, C., Duarte, C., Eisenhauer, N., Foden, W., Gasalla, M. A., Handa, C., Hickler, T., Hoegh-Guldberg, O., Ichii, K., Jacob, U., Insarov, G., Kiessling, W., Leadley, P., Leemans, R., Levin, L., Lim, M., Maharaj, S., Managi, S., Marquet, P. A., McElwee, P., Midgley, G., Oberdorff, T., Obura, D., Osman, E., Pandit, R., Pascual, U., Pires, A. P. F., Popp, A., Reyes-García, V., Sankaran, M., Settele, J., Shin, Y. J., Sintayehu, D. W., Smith, P., Steiner, N., Strassburg, B., Sukumar, R., Trisos, C., Val, A. L., Wu, J., Aldrian, E., Parmesan, C., Pichs-Madruga, R., Roberts, D. C., Rogers, A. D., Díaz, S., Fischer, M., Hashimoto, S., Lavorel, S., Wu, N., and Ngo, H. T. (2021). IPBES-IPCC co-sponsored workshop report on biodiversity and climate change, IPBES and IPCC. DOI: 10.5281/zenodo.4782538

Sauvé, S., Sloan, P., and Bernard, S. (2015). Environmental sciences, sustainable development and circular economy: Alternative concepts for transdisciplinary research. *Environmental Development,* 17, 48–56. DOI:10.1016/j.envdev.2015.09.002

Secretariat of the Convention on Biological Diversity (2020). Global Biodiversity Outlook 5. Montreal. Retrieved from: https://www.cbd.int/gbo/gbo5/publication/gbo-5-en.pdf.

SEI, IISD, ODI, E3G, and UNEP (2021). The production gap report 2021. Retrieved from: http://productiongap.org/2021report

Taylor, B., Chapron, G., Kopnina, H., Orlikowska, E., Gray, J. and Piccolo, J. J. (2020). The need for ecocentrism in biodiversity conservation. *Conservation Biology,* 34(5), 1089–1096. DOI: 10.1111/cobi.13541

UN (1992a). United Nations framework convention on climate change. Retrieved from: https://unfccc.int/resource/docs/convkp/conveng.pdf

UN (1992b). Convention on Biological Diversity (CBD). Retrieved from: https://www.cbd.int/doc/legal/cbd-en.pdf

UN (2000). United Nations millennium declaration. Retrieved from: https://www.un.org/en/development/desa/population/migration/generalassembly/docs/globalcompact/A_RES_55_2.pdf

UN (2012). A 10-year framework of programs on sustainable consumption and production patterns. Annex to the letter dated 18 June 2012 from the permanent representative of Brazil to the United Nations addressed to the Secretary-General of the United Nations Conference on Sustainable Development. Retrieved from: https://sdgs.un.org/documents/aconf2165-10-year-framework-programmes-o-19090

UN (2015). General Assembly, Transforming our world: The 2030 Agenda for sustainable development, 21 October, A/RES/70/1. Retrieved from: https://www.refworld.org/docid/57b6e3e44.html

UN (2018). Progress report on the 10-year framework of programs on sustainable consumption and production patterns. High-level political forum on sustainable development, convened under the auspices of the economic and social council. Retrieved from: https://digitallibrary.un.org/record/1627351

UNFCCC (1997). Kyoto Protocol to the United Nations framework convention on climate change. Retrieved from: https://unfccc.int/resource/docs/convkp/kpeng.pdf

UNFCCC (2009). The Copenhagen Accord, United Nations Framework convention on climate change. Retrieved from: http://unfccc.int/meetings/copenhagen_dec_2009/items/5262.php

UNFCCC (2015). Paris agreement. Retrieved from: https://unfccc.int/sites/default/files/english_paris_agreement.pdf

WMO (2021). United in science – A multi-organization high-level compilation of the latest climate science information. Retrieved from: http://public.wmo.int/en/resources/united_in_science

3 Socioecological challenges and UN policies

Anders Siig Andersen and Lars Hulgaard

> We are resolved to free the human race from the tyranny of poverty and want and to heal and secure our planet. We are determined to take the bold and transformative steps which are urgently needed to shift the world on to a sustainable and resilient path. As we embark on this collective journey, we pledge that no one will be left behind.
>
> (UN, 2015)

Introduction

In the first chapter of this book, we focused on global ecological challenges regarding climate change, biodiversity loss, and resource depletion. In the second chapter, we highlighted UN policies, gaps between the policies and outcomes, and the complexities pertaining to the climate change–biodiversity nexus. In this third chapter, we shift our focus to the interdependence between contemporary social and ecological challenges and, furthermore, to UN policies and their efficiency in implementing solutions. As Kate Raworth proposed in her book on "Doughnut Economics", promoting socioecological sustainable transformation is fundamentally about creating a more free, safe, just, and equal world for all people on Earth, while, at the same time, regenerating nature and securing the Earth as a safe space for humanity to live in (Raworth, 2017). Similarly, Leach et al. (2018: 1) highlight two defining challenges of our age: (1) addressing rising inequalities and inequities and (2) maintaining a stable and resilient planet. Combined, these intertwining challenges raise questions of how to secure sustainable human futures in the Anthropocene within our planetary life support system in a way that is also fair and just. The United Nations Development Program (UNDP) further states that the goal of socioecological sustainable transformation should be to go beyond sustaining the present to creating a future that is better than the present (UNDP, 2020: 41).

First, in this chapter, we define core notions regarding socioecological transformation focusing on freedom, safety, and different forms of equality. Second, we focus on inequalities pertaining to the unequal contributions to the erosion of the Earth system, the unequal consequences of the environment

DOI: 10.4324/9781003319672-5

and climate challenges for different nations and groups of people, and the unequally distributed consequences of the environment and climate interventions. Third, we turn our attention to UN governance, briefly covering the socioecological aspects of the forms of governance that are predominantly directed at climate change, biodiversity, and resources. Mainly, however, we focus on the UN 2030 Agenda for Sustainable Development and the Sustainable Development Goals (SDGs). We discuss the relation between the SDGs and socioecological issues and critically discuss the type of goal-based governance and Nationally Determined Contributions that characterize the agenda and the SDGs. Then, we turn our attention to and critically reflect on an attempt by the Stockholm Resilience Center and the Norwegian Business School to combine a small number of targets and indicators pertaining to the SDGs as well as the planetary boundaries (see also Chapter 1) to suggest solutions to the combined ecological, economical, and social challenges. Following up on the SDGs, highlighting state-of-the-art knowledge for transformations toward socioecological sustainable development and identifying possible areas of transformational change, we draw on the first Global Sustainability Report that was published in 2019 (Independent Group of Scientists, 2019).

Key concepts about socioecological sustainable transformation

Shifting from the ecological to the socioecological perspective, we focus on the interlinkage between, on the one hand, the environment and climate challenges, and, on the other, questions regarding social justice and socioecological sustainability. We understand socioecological sustainability through the intertwined drivers and outcomes of coupled natural and social dynamics. Over time, such dynamics become part of pathways that may move outside or potentially be steered within a desirable zone of socioecological sustainability (Leach et al., 2018: 1). This view is consistent with the view expressed in the 2022 Summary for Policymakers report from the Intergovernmental Panel on Climate Change (IPCC, 2022: 3), in which the IPCC recognizes the interdependence among climate, ecosystems, biodiversity, and human societies by applying an interdisciplinary perspective that integrates knowledge across the natural, ecological, social, and economic sciences (see also Chapter 13).

The notions of freedom and safety

Fundamentally, the understanding of socioecological sustainability in different UN reports on climate change, biodiversity, and resources and in the 2030 Agenda for Sustainable Development builds on the Universal Declaration of Human Rights (UN, 1948). Countries voting in favor of this Declaration have acknowledged that all human beings are born free and equal in dignity and rights and that they should act toward one another in a spirit of brotherhood (UN, 1948). This means that dignity and freedom belong to everyone without distinction of any kind, such as race, color, sex, language, religion, political or other opinion, national or social origin, property, birth, or other status (UN, 1948). The notion of human rights is about the right to life and to live in freedom and safety. The notion of freedom covers phenomena such as the freedom to move in and out of one's own country; freedom of thought, conscience, and religion; freedom of opinion and expression; freedom to peacefully assembly and associate; and free choice of employment (UN, 1948). The notion of safety encompasses the protection of the family, of one's own things, and from attacks upon one's reputation; the right to a safe place to live; the right to a standard of living adequate for health and wellbeing; labor market protection against unemployment; social protection against lack of livelihood, food, and shelter; and the right to a fair and free world with a proper order so all can enjoy their rights and freedoms in their own country and all over the world (UN, 1948).

Concerning the "socio" in socioecological, the United Nations Development Program (UNDP) argues for the importance of human freedom: "Human development is about expanding human freedoms and opening more choices for people to chart their own development paths according to their diverse values" (UNDP, 2020: 6). However, combined with the notion of ecological sustainability, the notion of freedom does not denote absolute freedom, but only freedom that respects the continuous need of regenerating nature as a necessary condition for human life. The UNDP (2020: 10) argues for nesting human development and freedom – including social and economic systems – into ecosystems and the biosphere. In a socioecological context, an important aspect of safety is about humans' right to be protected and secured against situations of vulnerability when experiencing ecological or climate change challenges by taking action now, by securing the future, or by preparative actions in case an event occurs (Eizenberg & Jabareen, 2017: 8).

The notions of equity and justice

According to the UNDP (2020); IPCC (2022), and Newell et al. (2020), the notions of equity and justice cover crucial aspects of socioecological sustainability. They apply a distinction between four forms of equity and justice linked to the key aspects of empowerment and democratic participation:

- Distributional equity and justice, which refers to the distribution of resources, burdens, and benefits among individuals, communities, and nations. Newell et al. (2020: 31) argue that there are three main aspects of that distribution: (1) what: identifying the resources that are being distributed (e.g., economic, social, cultural, political, spatial, environment, and knowledge); (2) between whom: identifying the entities between which they are to be distributed (e.g., the members of certain communities or stakeholders, certain generations, all of humankind); and (3) based on which criteria: identifying which criteria the distribution is based on (e.g., status, need, merit, rights, or ascriptive and social identities). According to the UNDP (2020: 64), access to different kind of resources enhances an individual's ability to choose, so those resources are channels to exercise empowerment, agency, and freedom.

- Procedural equity and justice relate to how decisions are made in reference to institutions, governance, and participation, i.e., who decides and participates in the decision-making? This is fundamentally about the processes for making decisions on the impacts of and responses to the environment and climate change and ensuring that they are fair, accountable, and transparent. Representation, power, and voice are linked directly to empowerment – they shape communities and individuals' ability to influence and participate in decision-making to achieve their desired outcomes and goals (Newell et al., 2020: 30: UNDP, 2020: 64).
- Recognitional equity and justice are closely related to procedural as well as to distributional justice but focus on the recognition of differences, referring to the recognition of interest holders and respect for their identity, values, cultures, perspectives, and associated rights. Newell et al. (2020: 33) quoted Nancy Frazer, who argues that recognition designates an ideal reciprocal relation between subjects, in which each sees the other as their equal. Recognitional justice centers on showing which groups encounter intolerance and discrimination and supports the idea that all groups should be guaranteed a fair representation of their views without distortion or fears of reprisal. Empowerment is positively associated with the recognition of human rights and the principles of non-discrimination (UNDP, 2020: 64). In many contexts, the recognition of the rights of nature (i.e., justice for the environment) is also gaining ground. This notion aims to respect and protect the living environment and to change how human society relates to its own supporting biosphere (Newell et al., 2020: 35; see also IPCC, 2022: 5; and Chapter 12).
- Intergenerational equity and justice encompass distributional, recognitional, and procedural justice and lie at the heart of sustainable transformation, being about the ability of current generations to meet their needs without compromising the ability of future generations to meet their needs, as well as protecting future generations from harm. The focus is on preserving resources, biodiversity, and nature's contribution to people for the generations to come (UNDP, 2020: 75).

In the socioecological context, on the one hand, the notions of equity and justice focus on how exposure and vulnerability to environment and climate change reflect various structural injustices and inequalities in society, such as the exclusion of marginalized groups from decision-making and from environment and climate resilient livelihoods. On the other hand, they focus on how environment and climate change provide an opportunity to reinforce democratic governance at all scales, and to promote equity and social inclusion. The different forms of equity and justice may be applied to loss and damage, mitigation, and adaption, as well as to resilience.

Different UN reports also apply more detailed notions of "a good quality of life" or "wellbeing", acknowledging the challenge, however, that notions of a good quality of life are highly dependent on place, time, and culture. Different societies espouse different views of the relationships with nature and place, and different levels of importance on the collective versus individual rights, the material versus the spiritual domain, intrinsic versus instrumental values, and the present time versus the past or the future. The concept of human wellbeing is used in many Western societies and its variants. In other parts of the world, there are more holistic concepts that focus on human's embeddedness in nature. Concepts such as, for example, "Living in harmony with nature", "Living well in balance and harmony with Mother Earth", and "Buen Vivir" are examples of different perspectives of a good quality of life (IPBES, 2019: 52f; see also Chapter 12).

Leach et al. (2018: 1) note that there is remarkably little scientific work in the literature on the interlinkages between sustainability and equity. They argue that these twin sets of issues have largely been addressed in separate literature fields, not least reflecting the separation between the natural sciences, social sciences, and the humanities (Leach et al., 2018: 10). To Leach et al., a shift is needed from perceiving people and nature as separate parts that occasionally interact, to seeing them as intertwined socioecological systems (Leach et al., 2018: 10; see also Chapter 13).

Socioecological challenges and differentiated human consequences

As highlighted in several UN reports, the pathways to development followed by today's wealthy countries after WWII were built on plentiful, cheap fossil energy resources, an abundance of other material resources, and large expanses of productive land to be developed. These pathways can no longer be continued in the wealthy countries or be followed by the 75 percent to 80 percent of the human population that is now at various stages in its own trajectory out of poverty and is beginning to compete with today's wealthy countries for increasingly scarce resources (Steffen et al., 2011: 739). In the following, we outline some of the main distributive and procedural inequalities in the world, with a special focus on socioecological inequality. Whereas in Chapter 1, we emphasized the global significance of the ecological challenges for humanity, in this chapter, we emphasize the differentiated significance of the socioecological challenges for different groups and nations. Summing up, regarding the distributive inequalities: (1) The general inequalities in the world and within many countries are increasing; (2) the contributions to the erosion of the Earth system follow patterns of the existing inequalities; (3) the poorest people and nations on Earth are suffering the most from the impacts of climate change, resource depletion, and the loss of biodiversity; and (4) these groups are at risk of experiencing the most negative consequences of the mitigation and adaption interventions.

The increase in general inequality

In the post-war period, the world has experienced an increase in prosperity, which in some ways has positively impacted poorer countries and populations. In recent years, however, inequality in the world has increased tremendously. The global development model in this period has been based on the limitless utilization of the world's resources. This model has been proven to primarily benefit the richest nations and people. Today's global inequality is at record levels, with 40 percent of the total wealth in the hands of billionaires and nearly half of humanity living on less than $5.50/day. Applying the World Bank definition of extreme poverty as living on less than $1.90/day, in 2015, about 10 percent of the world population or some 740 million people are living in extreme poverty (Folke et al., 2021: 846; see also Piketty, 2020). Since 2015, the eight richest people in the world own the same amount of wealth as the poorest half, and the 1,810 dollars billionaires on the 2016 Forbes list own as much wealth as the bottom 70 percent of humanity. In the US, over the last 30 years, the growth in the incomes of the bottom 50 percent of people has been zero, whereas the incomes of the top 1 percent have grown 300 percent (Ahmed et al., 2022: 7; Harndon, 2017: 2). Further, the COVID epidemic actually increased global inequalities. From the beginning of 2020 to the end of 2021, the wealth of the ten richest persons doubled, while the incomes of 99 percent of humanity decreased and the world's small elite of billionaires saw its fortunes grow more during COVID-19 than they had during the last 14 years (Ahmed et al., 2022: 7).

Socially differentiated contributions to the ecological challenges

The general economic inequalities between people and nations on Earth are mirrored in their different contributions to the erosion of the Earth system. Some of the indicators of inequality concerning carbon emissions and material consumption clearly show this fact:

Carbon emissions: The richest 10 percent of the world's population are responsible for half of the world's carbon emissions, while the poorest 50 percent are responsible for just 10 percent. Indeed, the wealthiest 1 percent of the world's population have been responsible for more than twice as much carbon pollution as the poorest half of humanity collectively, and the top ten emitting countries account for three quarters of global GHG emissions, while the bottom 100 countries account for only 3.5 percent (Folke et al., 2021: 840; UNDP, 2020: 121).

Material consumption: The billion richest individuals account for 72 percent of the consumption of global resources, while the poorest 1.2 billion consume only 1 percent (IRP, 2019: 125). Further, the material footprint per capita of high-income nations was reported to be approximately 27 tonnes, while the material footprint per capita was around 17 tonnes for upper-middle income countries, almost five tonnes for lower-middle income countries, and only two tonnes per capita for low-income countries (IRP, 2019: 126). In absolute terms, materials extraction is dominated by the fast developing upper-middle income countries (especially China). Per capital levels of extraction are also higher for this group, and almost 15 percent higher than for the high-income group. This reflects two major dynamics: the first is the demand for materials to build up the infrastructure required for newly industrializing countries, while the second is likely to be the outsourcing of the material and energy-intensive stages of production chains by higher-income countries to lower-income transition countries (IRP, 2019: 4). The second dynamic delivers the main reason why the material footprint per capita is more than 60 percent higher in high-income nations than in upper-middle income countries.

Socially differentiated consequences of ecological challenges

In the current situation, where significant limits are set on the utilization of the world's resources, equality issues are exacerbated. Natural scientists acknowledge that the transgression of planetary boundaries is unevenly caused by different human societies and different social groups, and that global ecological perspectives do not account for the regional distribution of the impact and its historical patterns (Steffen et al., 2011: 8). The "Anthropo" (human in general) in the Anthropocene masks deep inequalities with respect to the question of which groups in the world are contributing most to the erosion of the Earth systems and the environment (see also Chapter 12). One common line of criticism is that the notion of the Anthropocene, especially the more natural science-based formulations, does not strike at the heart of the problem, which is seen as the current dominant mode of production (UNDP, 2020: 54). The UNDP (2020: 31) argues that the historical origins and initial diffusions of industrialization were concentrated geographically, leading to the "Great Divergence" between early industrializing countries and the rest of the world. This divergence was exacerbated in some cases by colonialism and the intercontinental slave trade, whose impacts persists to this day (see also Piketty, 2020).

UNDP (2020: 121) states that the distributional inequalities of the world matter because the richest people in the world are doing the most damage to the environment; yet they experience few consequences and the least danger and loss and damage. Numerous research projects have documented that climate change injustices and injustices concerning ecosystem services and the distribution of resources occur along ethnic, gender, class, and racial lines. Distant areas of the world are increasingly connected (teleconnected), as consumption, production, and governance decisions increasingly influence materials, waste, energy, and information flows in other countries, generating aggregate economic gains while shifting economic and environmental costs (IPBES, 2019: 32). This can lead to conflicts and "poverty traps", where path dependencies and political and economic goals and institutional structures create situations characterized by a loss of opportunities to deal with change for those nations and communities exposed to poverty.

Focusing on climate changes, the World Meteorological Organization (WMO, 2020) stated that:

> Rising temperatures are leading to the loss of species and ecosystems, which can reduce agricultural and fishing yields – contributing to food insecurity and affecting livelihoods. Extreme weather and climate events can cause health risks, damage infrastructure, and lead to water scarcity. These threats, together with others, are interrelated with conflict and stability. It is critical to highlight that these risks will not impact all populations or regions equally and can therefore reinforce or worsen existing inequalities.
> (WMO, 2020: 22)

According to the IPCC (2022: 11), the vulnerability of ecosystems and people to climate change differs substantially among and within regions, driven by patterns of intersecting socioeconomic development, unsustainable ocean and land use, inequity, marginalization, and historical and ongoing patterns of inequity. This means that regions and people with considerable development constraints have a high vulnerability to climatic hazards, and that vulnerability is higher in locations with poverty, governance challenges, limited access to basic services and resources, violent conflict, and high levels of climate-sensitive livelihoods (e.g., smallholder farmers, pastoralists, fishing communities). Furthermore, vulnerability is exacerbated by inequity and marginalization linked to gender, ethnicity, and low income, none the least for many Indigenous Peoples and local communities (IPCC, 2022: 12).

Especially in areas where climate hazards interact with high ecological and social vulnerability, climate change is contributing to humanitarian crises. Climate and weather extremes are increasingly driving displacement in all regions, with small island states disproportionately affected. Flood and drought-related acute food insecurity and malnutrition have increased in Africa and Central and South America. In urban settings, the observed impacts of climate change are often concentrated among the most economically and socially marginalized urban residents, for example, in informal settlements (IPCC, 2022: 11).

There is also increasing evidence that the degradation and destruction of ecosystems by humans increases the vulnerability of people. Unsustainable land-use and land-cover change, the unsustainable use of natural resources, deforestation, loss of biodiversity, pollution, and their interactions adversely affect the capacities of ecosystems, societies, communities, and individuals to adapt to climate change. The loss of ecosystems and their services has cascading and long-term impacts on people globally, especially for Indigenous

Peoples and local communities who are directly dependent on the ecosystems to meet their basic needs (IPCC, 2022: 12).

Unequal consequences of mitigation and adaption

In the view of IPBES and IPCC, the prevention of climate challenges could in some cases impact the prevention of biodiversity challenges negatively, and *vice versa* (see also Chapter 2). Similarly, the prevention of environmental and climate challenges may pose a risk for the development of socioecological sustainability. There are concerns that some climate mitigation interventions may have unintended negative consequences in terms of human rights, land use, and other implications for livelihoods that may affect the vulnerability to environment and climate-related shocks and stressors. In addition, environment and climate action may reinforce conflicts or introduce new forms of injustices regarding the exploration, extraction, and distribution of resources, and there are concerns regarding the just access to nature's contributions to people. In the following, we exemplify a range of potentially disfavoring global social consequences of climate mitigation and adaption.

Low-carbon transitions are often assumed to be positive phenomena because they reduce carbon emissions. Yet, there is evidence that they can in fact create new injustices and vulnerabilities, while also failing to address pre-existing structural drivers of injustice in energy markets and the wider socio-economy (Newell et al., 2020: 71). For example, carbon tax increases or the abolition of fuel subsidies have regressive income effects, because low-income households then spend a higher proportion of their income on fuel or transportation expenses (IPCC, 2022: 60). Furthermore, there is a risk that new economic opportunities to produce clean energy technology will be concentrated in countries with larger, existing industrial capacity (concentrated around manufacture and assembly in China and India, for example) while the dirty parts of the supply chains (mining and extraction) will be situated in lower-income countries (Newell et al., 2020: 73).

Because most renewable energy needs large amounts of land due to its low power density, large-scale renewable transitions often take place in rural areas. This transition can put pressure on rural populations and may compete with or displace existing land uses and dynamics. Newell et al. (2020: 74) argue that there is a risk (and clear examples) that the environmental and socioeconomic impacts of new approaches to energy supply will be mediated by the existing power of different groups over resources previously not highly valued by the energy industry. According to the IPCC (2022: 13), in many countries, especially those with limited institutional capacities, several adverse side-effects have been observed because of the diffusion of low-emission technology, for example, low-value employment, and dependency on foreign knowledge and suppliers.

Technologies such as electric vehicles, wind turbines, and solar panels all depend on a "mineral foundation" of raw materials, such as lithium and cobalt.

The increasing reliance on electric vehicles has set in motion a land grab for territories with newfound value, such as the Altiplano in Bolivia or the Sonora desert in Mexico, where there are vast deposits of lithium (Newell et al., 2020: 74). The Democratic Republic of the Congo (DRC) is the largest producer of cobalt, responsible for roughly 60 percent of global supply. Many injustices are associated with mining cobalt. These include the fact that once cobalt is discovered, homes and the land are often torn up to get at it, which has resulted in some cases of major landslides that have killed dozens of people. Other constant dangers to artisanal or small-scale mining include chemical poisoning from mercury and cyanide, methane and coal dust explosions, electrocution, and even death through the inappropriate use of underground explosives and the resulting fires and explosions. Cobalt mining also brings severe environmental impacts: the pollution of rivers, soil, and food systems, and even of people through dust and air. Indigenous people may also be displaced and there are negative effects on community stability, including food security (Newell et al., 2020: 72).

Shifting the focus to solar PV modules, their manufacturing may reproduce unequal occupational health and environmental pollution burdens. Solar PV technologies rely on semiconductor technologies that are fabricated using hazardous industrial chemicals through complex global supply chains and contract manufacturing (Newell et al., 2020: 73).

Likewise, the history of biofuels development provides many examples of how attempts to address energy insecurity have produced patterns of injustice. For instance, while Brazil has been able to transform itself from an oil importer to an exporter and is self-reliant in fuel for passenger cars from sugarcane ethanol, the industry is confronted with accusations of slave and child labor operating in poor working conditions (Newell et al., 2020: 74). In 2008, the demand for biofuels contributed to rising prices for corn, leading to "tortilla riots" by campesino groups in Mexico, for whom the crop is a food staple. Here, there is also a series of issues around land acquisition, as the push for agricultural investments for clean energy places pressures on land rights (Newell et al., 2020: 75; see also Chapter 11).

There may also be social risks related to the distribution of energy harvested by wind farms. In Mexico, private–private or public–private partners have set up societies for the generation and commercialization of wind energy by paying a fee to the Mexican government. The implication of this generation scheme has been that local communities do not benefit from the energy generation taking place in their territories. Rather, energy is transmitted to industrial plants in Mexico City or Monterrey (Newell et al., 2020: 78).

Similarly, the advent of climate-smart agriculture has been used to exploit opportunities to consolidate and advance the control of private actors over land at the expense of local farmers and Indigenous People (Newell et al., 2020: 85). Climate-smart agriculture has become a focal point for the attempted resolution of the need for finance to find something to invest in, extending control over land; for governments and neo-liberal global institutions to shore up flagging carbon markets by expanding into agriculture; for biotechnology firms to re-invent GMOs as "climate-smart"; and for global agricultural institutions to raise their profile and diversify their funding streams by taking on mandates for tackling and responding to climate change (Newell et al., 2020: 86; see also Chapter 11).

Digital technologies can contribute to the mitigation of climate change. However, the IPCC (2022: 13) states that digitalization can also involve trade-offs, for example, increasing electronic waste, negative impacts on labor markets, and exacerbating the existing digital divide.

Adaptation and resilience benefits may affect people differently. Indeed, adaptation and resilience interventions may in themselves be neither just nor have just outcomes and may in some cases lead to maladaptation. For example, ecosystem restoration and reforestation can displace food production and livelihoods (IPCC, 2022: 53). Likewise, the building of flood defenses in one risk area may increase the flood risk for downstream populations (Newell et al., 2020: 79). Menton et al. (2019: 1627) refer to the story of the Tuxá of Northeastern Brazil who suffered numerous injustices linked to the Itaparica dam, built along the São Francisco River in Bahia, Brazil in the 1980s. The construction of the dam aimed to create both hydroelectricity and supply water for irrigation in semi-arid areas of Brazil's northeast. The dam flooded 834 km^2 of land and displaced thousands of families, including the Tuxá Indigenous Peoples who lived on the islands in the river and whose ancestral lands, burial grounds, and sacred sites were suddenly submerged. Despite this, similar dams are currently being proposed and justified, in part, for their contribution to sustainable development.

Procedural inequalities

A key concern pertaining to socioecological sustainable transformation is the extent to which processes and interventions are participatory and inclusive, recognizing the different burdens, costs, and the potentials for benefits among different social groups. There is evidence that procedural injustice and inequality follow the same lines of divisions as distributive injustice and inequality. Newell et al. (2020: 26ff) argue that injustice and inequality are a root cause of environment and climate challenges, at the heart of its impacts, and vital to whether and how effective policies can be devised and implemented to mitigate the associated risks. The authors list the following risks and challenges concerning equal and just participation in solving environment and climate challenges:

- Participation in international policy processes: A core concern, from the Global South in particular, is the ability to participate equally in international negotiation processes. Major challenges remain in this area.
- Participation of different social groups at the national levels: Beyond the global level, at the national and sub-national level, decision-making

processes are vulnerable to capture and abuse by stronger political and economic actors.
- Ability to make claims for resource access: A necessary focus is the proactive agency of marginalized groups in asserting and defending their rights, and making their voices heard. This concerns climate-related interventions, but equally important, the policies and decisions that underpin adaptive capacity, such as land and water rights. Landgrabbing is occurring in many places, especially in the Global South.
- Recognition and integration of plural knowledges: There is growing attention paid to local knowledge and its importance in understanding challenges as well as to devising solutions. However, there is limited progress on actually integrating knowledge other than scientific or formal knowledge into the decision-making processes.
- Legal empowerment and use of rights: This concerns the legal recognition of the rights of vulnerable groups and their ability to realize those rights. For example, integrating women in environment and climate-related interventions is necessary, but not sufficient, if the underlying conditions mean that women are disadvantaged.
- Accountability in government and non-government/private sector climate action: This concerns to what extent processes that are meant to serve poor and marginalized populations are transparent in their goals as well as processes. Severe challenges persist in this area.

Socioecological governance within the UN

In the following, we shift our focus to deal with how the governance aspects of socioecological sustainable development are treated within the UN system. Addressing socioecological issues is a consistent feature of UN conventions, protocols, strategies, and action plans on climate change, biodiversity, and resources. In the second chapter of the book, we dealt with these documents from an ecological perspective. In this chapter, we briefly elaborate on some of their socioecological dimensions. As we highlight, directly or indirectly, socioecological issues are at the core of the 2030 Agenda of Sustainable Development and the Sustainable Development Goals (SDGs). First, however, we define some of the core notions regarding governance as proposed by the IPCC.

In Chapter 2, we drew on the main concepts proposed by the IPCC regarding ecological challenges, actions, and solutions. Further inspired by the IPCC, in this chapter, we turn to the concepts related to governance. The IPCC defines "governance" as

> The structures, processes, and actions through which private and public actors interact to address societal goals. This includes formal and informal institutions and the associated norms, rules, laws, and procedures for

deciding, managing, implementing, and monitoring policies and measures at any geographic or political scale, from global to local.

(IPCC, 2022: 11)

According to the IPCC (2022: 28), "enabling conditions" are key for implementing, accelerating, and sustaining adaptation in human systems and ecosystems. These include political commitment and follow-through; institutional frameworks, policies, and instruments with goals and priorities; enhanced knowledge on the impacts and solutions; the mobilization of and access to adequate financial resources; monitoring and evaluation; and inclusive governance processes. By using the term "effectiveness", the IPCC (2022: 6) refers to the extent to which an action reduces vulnerability and climate-related risk, increases resilience, and avoids maladaptation. In the report (2022: 23), "feasibility" refers to the potential for a mitigation or adaptation option to be implemented. The factors influencing the feasibility are context-dependent, temporally dynamic, and may vary between different groups and actors. According to the IPCC, feasibility depends on the geophysical, environmental–ecological, technological, economic, sociocultural, and institutional factors that enable or constrain the implementation of an option (see also Chapter 11 on government and governance).

Socioecological sustainability aspects of the UN decisions on ecological sustainability

In the early 1990s, the objectives of socioecological equity were given high priority in the Rio Declaration on the Environment and Development (UN, 1992). This Declaration contained several principles, which, since then, have been integrated in various conventions, protocols, strategies, plans, and goals on climate change, biodiversity, and resources. Regarding the different forms of equity, some of the most important principles of the Rio Declaration were as follows (UN, 1992):

- Eradication of poverty, decreasing disparities in the standard of living, and priority for developing countries, particularly the least developed and the most environmentally vulnerable countries.
- Special responsibilities for developed countries in view of the pressures they place on the global environment and their capabilities regarding technologies and financial resources ("common but differentiated responsibilities").
- Development that equitably meets the developmental and environmental needs of the present and future generations.
- Recognition and support of the identity, culture, and interests of Indigenous People and their knowledge and traditional practices.
- Access for all to information concerning the environment, the opportunity to participate in decision-making processes, and access to judicial and administrative proceedings, including for redress and remedy.

- Full participation of women in environmental management and development, and the participation of Indigenous People in the achievement of sustainable development.

The Paris Agreement reiterates many of these principles, emphasizing the intrinsic relationship that climate change actions, responses, and impacts have with equitable access to sustainable development and the eradication of poverty. In line with the Universal Declaration of Human Rights, the Paris Agreement acknowledges that all parties should respect, promote, and consider their respective obligations on human rights, the right to health, and the rights of Indigenous Peoples, local communities, migrants, children, persons with disabilities, and people in vulnerable situations. It also acknowledges gender equality, the empowerment of women, and intergenerational equity (UNFCCC, 2015). The Paris Agreement especially notes the importance for some of the concept of "climate justice", when taking action to address climate change, and, furthermore, the importance of the concept of "Just Transition" (for critical discussions, see Chapter 4). In the Strategic Plan for Biodiversity 2011–2020 and the Aichi targets, specific emphasis is put on the sharing of benefits to all from biodiversity, ecosystem services, and from the use of biotechnologies based on genetic resources. In addition to the Rio principles, the 10-Year Framework Program on Sustainable Consumption and Production promotes a competitive, inclusive economy delivering full and productive employment and decent work for all and fostering efficient social protection systems. The ten-year program also mentions the root causes of the current consumption and production patterns, and the cost and benefits related to the implementation of sustainable consumption and production, particularly regarding the impact on employment and poverty (UN, 2012). Within these three areas, i.e., climate change, biodiversity, and resources, the signatories want to support developing countries and especially the least developed countries and small island states in capacity-building by providing financial resources and access to relevant technologies, education, and information (UN, 2012).

Socioecological goals, targets, and indicators in the 2030 Agenda for Sustainable Development

As mentioned in Chapter 2, the 2030 Agenda for Sustainable Development (UN, 2015) refers to and reiterates many of the ecological aims and goals of the United Nations Framework Convention on Climate Change, the Convention on Biological Diversity, and the 10-Year Framework Program on Sustainable Consumption and Production. However, the main principle of the 2030 Agenda and the Sustainable Development Goals and targets is to balance three "integrated and indivisible dimensions of sustainable development": the economic, the social, and the environmental (UN, 2015). This is expressed in the overarching aims of the Agenda (UN, 2015):

- "People: End poverty and hunger and ensure that all human beings can fulfill their potential in dignity and equality and in a healthy environment.
- Planet: Protect the planet from degradation, including through sustainable consumption and production, sustainably managing its natural resources, and taking urgent action on climate change, so that it can support the needs of the present and future generations.
- Prosperity: Ensure that all human beings can enjoy prosperous and fulfilling lives and that economic, social, and technological progress occurs in harmony with nature.
- Peace: Foster peaceful, just, and inclusive societies that are free from fear and violence. There can be no sustainable development without peace and no peace without sustainable development.
- Partnership: Mobilize the means required to implement the Agenda through a revitalized Global Partnership for Sustainable Development, based on a spirit of strengthened global solidarity, focusing in particular on the needs of the poorest and most vulnerable and with the participation of all countries, all stakeholders, and all people".

The 17 SDG Goals themselves were formulated in a much more separated way (UN, 2015):

1. End poverty in all its forms everywhere.
2. End hunger, achieve food security and improved nutrition, and promote sustainable agriculture.
3. Ensure healthy lives and promote wellbeing for all at all ages.
4. Ensure inclusive and equitable quality education and promote lifelong learning opportunities for all.
5. Achieve gender equality and empower all women and girls.
6. Ensure the availability and sustainable management of water and sanitation for all.
7. Ensure access to affordable, reliable, sustainable, and modern energy for all.
8. Promote sustained, inclusive, and sustainable economic growth, full and productive employment, and decent work for all.
9. Build resilient infrastructure, promote inclusive and sustainable industrialization, and foster innovation.
10. Reduce inequality within and among countries.
11. Make cities and human settlements inclusive, safe, resilient, and sustainable.
12. Ensure sustainable consumption and production patterns.
13. Take urgent action to combat climate change and its impacts.
14. Conserve and sustainably use the oceans, seas, and marine resources for sustainable development.
15. Protect, restore, and promote the sustainable use of terrestrial ecosystems, combat desertification, halt and reverse land degradation, and halt biodiversity loss.

16 Promote peaceful and inclusive societies for sustainable development, provide access to justice for all, and build effective, accountable, and inclusive institutions at all levels.
17 Strengthen the means of implementation and revitalize the global partnership for sustainable development.

The SDGs build on the UN Millennium Development Goals (MDGs) that were in place during 2000–2015. In contrast to the MDGs, however, the SDGs apply to all types of countries. In addition to the social and economic goals of the MDGs, the SDGs also address ecological sustainability challenges through the "triple bottom line approach to human wellbeing". And, while the MDGs were developed at a technocratic level, the SDGs were formulated and decided through the participation of a multitude of stakeholders, including many NGOs (Winkler & Willams, 2017: 1023).

Looking at the SDGs from a socioecological point of view, it turns out that only rather few of the goals relate directly to combined socioecological issues. Goals 1.5 and 11.5 aim to build the resilience of the poor and those in vulnerable situations and to increase their safety by reducing their exposure to climate-related extreme events and other economic, social, and environmental shocks and disasters. Goals 4.7 and 13.3 are about education as an awareness-raising and capacity-developing measure with respect to mitigation, adaption, impact reduction, and early warning. Goal 17.4 focuses on enhancing policy coherence across the SDGs, which includes the socioecological goals. Also, the objective of Goal 17.14 is to increase the availability of reliable data in developing countries disaggregated by income, gender, age, race, ethnicity, migratory status, disability, geographic location, and other characteristics relevant in national contexts, which will potentially make it possible to evaluate socioecological issues (UN, 2015).

However, many goals and targets address how developed countries should support developing countries in introducing ecologically sustainable solutions through economic and technological support. A range of other goals and targets focus on how to ensure that the populations of developing countries can access economic growth, money, energy, water, sanitation, food, housing, mobility, health, social security, education, technology development, IT services, employment, and decent jobs. While these goals and targets do not directly address the ecological challenges, they are greatly dependent on them. Therefore, they are important in the socioecological context. In addition, many targets pay attention to inequality in particular countries, especially the least developed developing countries, such as small island developing states and landlocked developing countries, that are especially threatened by the ecological challenges, and, furthermore, to inequality pertaining to particular groups, especially women, young people, migrants, persons with disabilities, and Indigenous People. Yet, other targets focus on equal rights to the ownership and control of land and property and access rights for small-scale fishers. With dramatically increasing inequalities, and a situation where ecological challenges are predicted to increase inequality even more, several of the SDGs are about reducing the general inequality between countries and between groups within countries. The notion of inequality and similar notions – equitable sharing, equal access, and equal rights – are used in some of the SDGs and their targets. Furthermore, the aim of increasing equality is formulated in many other ways, such as, for example, "universal access", "pro-poor and gender sensitive politics", and "increased resources and possibilities available for the developing countries". Some of these statements refer to equality in absolute terms. Other statements refer to "upward convergence", i.e., that the developing countries and poorer groups within societies must have greater access to increase their share of the available resources than the developed countries and the richer groups within these societies (UN, 2015).

Regarding recognitional equity, the SDGs and their targets contain general objectives as well as objectives aimed at the recognition of specific groups. The general targets aim at eliminating discriminatory laws, policies, and practices and implementing non-discriminatory laws and policies for sustainable development. In relation to specific groups, the concepts of recognition and discrimination are used primarily about women and girls everywhere and about unpaid care and domestic work (UN, 2015).

In the SDGs, procedural equity covers several different aspects, such as representation, inclusion in participatory decision-making, transparency, and empowerment. At a general level, the SDGs are human rights oriented and aim at empowering and promoting the social, economic, and political inclusion of all people irrespective of age, sex, disability, race, ethnicity, origin, religion, or economic or other status. Furthermore, the SDGs aim to support responsive, inclusive, participatory, and representative decision-making at all levels. At a more specific level, the SDGs aim at strengthening the participation of developing countries in global governance and international economic and financial institutions, at ensuring women's full and active participation at all levels, at empowering all women and girls, and at strengthening the participation of local communities in sustainable local planning and human settlement planning (UN, 2015).

Critical views on goal-based governance and the Nationally Determined Contributions

The 17 Sustainable Development Goals are specified in 169 targets and 246 indicators; albeit some of the indicators are repeated in relation to more than one target, which brings the actual number of different indicators down to 232. The indicators are classified into three tiers depending on their level of methodological development and the availability of data. Tier I indicators are well defined with sufficient data regularly collected, while tier II indicators are well defined, but data are not regularly collected at the country level, and tier III indicators are those for which definitions, methodologies, or standards are under development (Independent Group of Scientists, 2019: 9). In the

2030 Agenda for Sustainable Development, it is recognized that the baseline data for several targets remain unavailable. Therefore, the UN is committed to addressing this gap in data collection, in particular for those targets that do not have a clear numerical value (UN, 2015). The targets and indicators were revised by the Statistical Commission after five years in 2020 and will be revised again every fifth year.

The targets are defined as aspirational and global, with each government setting its own national targets through its Nationally Determined Contribution (NDC). Each government will also decide how these targets should be incorporated into its planning processes, policies, and strategies, and how they should be reviewed and followed up by the state. A high-level political forum has a central role in overseeing follow-up and review at the global level. This activity is informed by an Annual Progress Report based on the global indicator framework and quadrennially Global Sustainable Development Reports (UN, 2015). Fundamentally, this goal-based governance process is comparable to the governance process pertaining to the areas of climate change and biodiversity, and it is very different from government through legally binding agreements (see also Chapters 2 and 11).

This raises the question of how adequate and effective this form of goal-based governance is?

According to Mair et al. (2018: 2), indicators are central to many sustainability initiatives because they are a useful way to generate knowledge of complex issues and to measure otherwise immeasurable entities. However, the authors view indicators as reductionist analytical tools. This means that their use risks oversimplification, particularly in highly complex and contested contexts ("wicked problems"). They argue that this can be especially problematic because indicators are often assumed to be objective and complete descriptions of the concepts they measure. In reality, however, they are often value-laden and incomplete. Furthermore, Mair et al., state that the use of indicators may also lead to policies and strategies that focus on what is measurable rather than addressing less tangible or measurable issues (Mair et al., 2018: 2f).

Mair et al., point at GDP as a particularly pertinent example of the dangers of indicators. First, they argue that it is an inadequate measure of societal progress because it misses important factors that contribute to broader conceptions of progress. Second, GDP growth is strongly correlated with negative environmental impacts. Third, the impact of using GDP has wide ranging consequences because policymakers use this measurement as the principal objective of most government policy (Mair et al., 2018: 3).

To Mair et al. (2018: 4), contested concepts are characterized by multiple, conflicting ideas about how a system works, and an indicator set is only able to represent a subset of these understandings. Moreover, the differences in system understanding result in different indicators. Therefore, the authors, argue that an indicator of a contested system should not be understood as a piece of information about a system, but rather as a piece of information reflecting how an individual or group conceptualizes that system. This means that the act of measuring is not passive; rather, it shapes and defines what it is that is measured, highlighting the aspects considered to be important and, by omission, defining those aspects that are not important. As a result, indicators that ignore important elements of a concept may lead to policies that either overlook or actively conflict with the original concept as it is more broadly understood (Mair et al., 2018: 10).

Challenges associated with goal-based governance in relation to the SDGs may be illustrated with an example concerning Goal 9, Target 9.1, and Indicators 9.1.1 and 9.1.2.

Goal 9. Build resilient infrastructure, promote inclusive and sustainable industrialization, and foster innovation

Target	Indicator	Tier
9.1 Develop quality, reliable sustainable, and resilient infrastructure to support economic development and human wellbeing, with a focus on affordable and equitable access for all	9.1.1 Proportion of rural population who live within 2 km of an all-season road	III
	9.1.2 Passenger and freight volumes by mode of transport	I

Reading this target and its associated indicators, it is quite clear that the indicators do not very precisely represent the target. What the indicators are suitable for measuring is partly the proximity to transport in rural areas and partly the transport volume distributed on different means of transport. This says very little about whether the infrastructures are resilient and sustainable and to what degree they support human wellbeing. Furthermore, the measuring of Indicator 9.1.2 is considered "reliable", whereas the methods for measuring Indicator 9.1 are "under development". Note, this example does not cover all the targets and indicators, and it was chosen only to clarify a couple of fundamental issues in relation to goal-based governance.

In other SDGs, the relationship between the targets and indicators is significantly more accurate. This applies, for example, to Goal 1: End poverty in all its forms everywhere.

Goal 1. End poverty in all its forms everywhere

Target	Indicator	Tier
1.1 By 2030, eradicate extreme poverty for all people everywhere, currently measured as people living on less than $1.25 a day	1.1.1 Proportion of the population living below the international poverty line by sex, age, employment status, and geographic location (urban/rural)	I

In many SDGs, the accuracy of the relationship between the targets and indicators can be located between these two examples, either because the measurement method is insufficiently developed and uncertain or/and because the indicators insufficiently represent the target.

Criticism has also been directed at the principle of voluntariness in the implementation of the SDGs via the Nationally Determined Contributions. The SDGs are non-binding and aspirational. According to Schleicher et al., this is especially a problem regarding some of the more challenging, or difficult to measure, goals. In addition, governments may not be held accountable for missing the targets. Moreover, the authors argue that if past priorities are an indication of future ones, the possibility to select only a subset of the SDGs will likely result in less attention being paid to environmental issues, even if their direct relationship to the prioritized SDGs is known. Furthermore, the burden of reporting on all the SDGs may reduce the efforts going into each of the goals. Schleicher et al. (2018: 44) indicate that which SDGs will be taken forward may depend not only on national priorities, but at least in the short term also on what can be measured, and for which SDGs data already exist or can be obtained relatively readily. This means that the voluntary principle contains a risk of countries delivering contributions that are not very ambitious and/or are very selective regarding which goals they address. This principle also carries the risk that there could be important discrepancies between the plans put forward by countries and which parts of the plans will actually be implemented and to what extent.

The Earth3 model: Reaching the SDGs within planetary boundaries

Elaborating on the connection between the SDGs and the planetary boundary framework, some researchers have worked with computer-based models with an aim to combine a small number of targets and indicators to indicate solutions to the combined ecological and social challenges. Based on a collaboration between the Stockholm Resilience Center and the Norwegian Business School, in a report to the Club of Rome, Randers et al. (2018: 1) focused on calculating the effects of the policy actions needed for meeting the globally agreed aspirational goals for human development within the safe operating space of a stable planet. In doing so, they used the Earth3 model.

The Earth3 model calculates socioeconomic development, environmental effects, indicators for the achievement of the 17 SDGs, and indicators for the pressure on the nine planetary boundaries. The model assigns one threshold value to each of the planetary boundaries and, furthermore, selects one threshold value for each of the 17 SDGs. The number of SDGs achieved every year is defined as the "SDG success score". Thus, the SDG success score goes from 0 to 17. This is calculated for each region in the world as well as for the whole world. Earth's safety margin goes from 0 to 9; whereby, if all the planetary boundaries are in the safe zone, the safety margin is nine, while if all the planetary boundaries are violated, the safety margin is zero (Randers,

2018: 11). Based on this, the Earth3 model was used for calculating the SDG success score for each region and the Earth's common safety margin based on the state of the planetary boundaries (Randers et al., 2018: 12).

Through modeling four scenarios, the research group tested different answers to their overarching question: "How can the world achieve the Sustainable Development Goals within Planetary Boundaries?" The first answer came from modeling how far the world will get by following a "business as usual" scenario to 2050; the second from simulating how far the world could get with faster economic growth; the third by pushing existing policies harder toward sustainability; and the fourth by calculating the scale of key transformational actions needed to reach the goals (Randers et al., 2018: 13). According to Randers et al. (2018: 14), only the fourth scenario offers the potential to reach the combined goals. The model showed that, in 1980, the world was in a relatively safe space pertaining to the planetary boundaries, but it was far removed from reaching the SDGs. The model also indicated that the fourth scenario can lead the world in a direction where most of the SDGs can be met within planetary boundaries.

This fourth scenario explored five possible transformations in our societies and economies to see whether these can bring the human world to a desired future (Randers et al., 2018: 31ff).

1 *Energy: Accelerated renewables growth*
    A worldwide rapid electrification in power and transport, as well as heating and cooling is rolled out. This happens by scaling up mainly solar and wind power, distributed energy storage, electric vehicles, heat pumps, and the necessary distribution infrastructure, all digitized and integrated in smart grids to replace fossil fuels. Nearly all investments in fossil fuels are shifted to renewables and power infrastructure during the 2020s. Most regions halve their carbon emissions every decade, starting in 2020. This rapidly reduces global carbon emissions and at the same time eliminates human suffering by spreading affordable electricity to cities, slums, and remote areas.

2 *Food: Accelerated shift to sustainable food chains*
    The world accelerates the transformation to sustainable agriculture, linking production to better logistics, which drives down food waste, as well as nutrient and pesticide overuse. People shift their diets to more plant-rich foods (particularly in richer countries). The food system gets more direct links between food producers and consumers. This brings down food waste. New technology makes real-time big data available to monitor the state of each field, river, crop, and shop. Through better water management, total water use is brought within planetary boundaries. Biogas and composting replace landfills and surface run-off to the oceans, creating the capacity to recapture nitrogen and phosphorus and to circulate these nutrients within bioregions. Climate-smart agriculture becomes a net carbon sink and draws down 1 billion tons of carbon into the soil each year from 2040.

3   **Growth: Rolling out new development models in poor countries**
    A higher growth rate is achieved in the world's poorest countries by increasing investment, strengthening institutions, and allowing favorable trade arrangements in the early stages of industrial development. During the 2020s, many of the world's poorer countries roll out forward-looking protectionist policies to raise standards of living by allowing their economies to catch up, and protect infant industries, to ensure they are without full immediate exposure to competition with advanced global industries in their home market in the beginning stages. The effect in these countries is more rapid economic growth, which lifts many millions out of poverty and also delivers on hunger, jobs growth, clean water, better health, education, and infrastructure.

4   *Active inequality reduction*
    Increasingly, both rich and poor countries reduce growing unemployment and inequity. Fairer wages and more progressive taxation succeed in redistributing the total output. Many developing countries intensify their domestic resource mobilization by improving their tax systems. As a result, there are funds for better service delivery, and development for the majority. By shortening the work-year for everyone, it becomes possible to create and share more jobs, even in regions and sectors where there is low or no per capita GDP growth. The 10 percent richest take no more than 40 percent of the total income.

5   *Investment in education for all, gender equality, health, family planning*
    Global funds that focus on education, especially for women, are strengthened. In addition, better family planning and urbanization give women more freedom to choose the kind of life they want. In many countries, five factors (education, urbanization, job opportunities, family planning, and reproductive health) combine to support better wellbeing for both women and children.

According to Randers et al. (2018: 30), these five transformations hold the promise of achieving (nearly) all the 17 SDGs within (nearly all) the nine planetary boundaries by 2050, although it will take some time before the Earth's safety margin is back to acceptable levels, from its low of 4.5 in 2015. The world SDG success score goes up to 13 in 2030 and 15 in 2050. By 2050, the Earth's safety margin is moving in a safer direction.

The authors argue that humanity's material footprint growth is the most important problem for the environment, climate, and wellbeing, not the growth in GDP per person. However, related studies indicate that, at most, the costs of implementing these five actions would result in the global GDP in 2051 being at the same level as the global GDP would have been in 2050. This equals the postponing of economic gains for 12 months (Randers et al., 2018: 8).

As stated by the authors, the Earth3 model suggests actions to achieve the Sustainable Development Goals within planetary boundaries. The authors, however, admit that the model has to be improved (Randers et al., 2018: 7). Going into more detail, the indicators chosen from the SDGs were very few, and some of the chosen indicators seem to be questionable, when viewed standing alone.

- SDG 9: Build resilient infrastructure, promote inclusive and sustainable industrialization, and foster innovation. In the model, the indicator was industrial output measured as GDP per person in manufacturing and construction. Yet, this indicator is about economic efficiency and not necessarily about resilience, inclusiveness, and sustainability.
- SDG 16: Promote peaceful and inclusive societies for sustainable development, provide access to justice for all, and build effective, accountable, and inclusive institutions at all levels. The indicator here is governance spending per person. However, this indicator is about general public spending and not about how money is distributed by governments to different groups. Although government spending indicates a country's ability to raise taxes and distribute revenues, there is no necessary link between, on the one hand, public spending, and, on the other, the development of peaceful and inclusive societies, access to justice, and accountable and inclusive institutions.
- SDG 17: Strengthen the means of implementation and revitalize the global partnership for sustainable development. The indicator here is export as a fraction of GDP. Again, there is no necessary logical connection between the share of exports and global partnerships for sustainable development.

Regarding these SDGs, the model prioritizes economic indicators and avoids questioning if these indicators are sufficient to measure the multifaceted aims of the SDGs. The Earth3 model shares its ambition as well as some of its challenges with different ideas of extending the globally applied GDP measure with indicators pertaining to socioecological transformation, such as, for example, the Human Development Index (HDI) (UNDP, 2020). In assessing whether the model's results are convincing, the limited indicator base poses a challenge to its validity. At the same time, there are not clearly documented connections between the indicators and the proposed solutions. In relation to the combined indicators, similar goal fulfillment could probably be achieved via other solutions (for further discussions, see Chapter 13).

Assessing the SDG outcomes and proposing ways forward: The first Global Sustainability Report

In 2012, at the Rio+ Conference, United Nations Member States decided to form a High-Level Political Forum on Sustainable Development. This forum would be informed by the Global Sustainability Report produced quadrennially by an independent group of scientists, providing a state-of-the-art evidence-based instrument to support policymakers with knowledge and recommendations on how to implement the necessary transformations to reach the SDGs. The Future is Now: Science for Achieving Sustainable Development is the first Global Sustainability Report (Independent Group of Scientists, 2019: II). In the introduction to the report, the authors explain that the report is distinct from, and complementary to, the annual Sustainable Development Goals progress report prepared by the Secretary-General. As is the case in reports from the IPCC and IPBES, the Global Sustainability Report does not produce new evidence. Instead, it highlights state-of-the-art knowledge for transformations toward socioecological sustainable development and identifies concrete areas where transformational change is possible (Independent Group of Scientists, 2019: XIX). In the political context of the UN, the report is important, as, for the first time, the SDGs' goal fulfillment and possible future actions to realize the SDGs are dealt with in a comprehensive scientific analysis.

In his foreword to the report, António Guterres expresses that the world is "not on track to achieve the Sustainable Development Goals by 2030", and that all nations "must dramatically step up the pace of implementation as we enter a decisive decade for people and the planet" (Independent Group of Scientists, 2019: XI). In her prologue to the report, Gro Harlem Brundtland states that it is "important to tackle the underlying causes of the problems that the Goals seek to address, such as poverty, discrimination, conflict, and inequality" (Independent Group of Scientists, 2019: XVI). Brundtland argues that the world is doomed to failure if we do not put inequality at the heart of the global development agenda.

The report indicates that the world is not on track to achieving most of the 169 targets that comprise the Sustainable Development Goals. According to the report, some of those negative trends presage a move toward the crossing of negative tipping points, and under current trends, the world's social and natural biophysical systems cannot support the aspirations for universal human wellbeing embedded in the Sustainable Development Goals (Independent Group of Scientists, 2019: XX).

Acknowledging that achieving the individual goals and targets of the SDGs separately may lead to negative trade-offs, the report states that the most efficient way to make progress on a given target is to take advantage of positive synergies with other targets while resolving or ameliorating the negative trade-offs with yet others (Independent Group of Scientists, 2019: XXI). This statement can be interpreted as an implicit critique of the fragmented SDGs with their isolated targets and indicators and as a call for national governments to plan and act more holistically. The report argues that in an increasingly globalized and hyper-connected world, any intervention on behalf of just one goal can lead to unintended consequences for the achievement of other goals nearby or faraway, today, or tomorrow. Conversely, the chances of progress on one goal in a specific part of the world will depend on the interventions made in sometimes distant places. These interactions often imply trade-offs, but also give rise to possible co-benefits and a significant potential for transformations toward sustainable development (Independent Group of Scientists, 2019: 4).

The Global Sustainable Development Report identifies six entry points into underlying systems for achieving the desired transformations at the necessary scale and speed (Independent Group of Scientists, 2019: XXI).

The selected entry points are:

- Human wellbeing and capabilities
- Sustainable and just economies
- Food systems and nutrition patterns
- Energy decarbonization with universal access
- Urban and peri-urban development
- Global environmental commons.

The report also identifies four levers, which can be deployed through each entry point to bring about the necessary transformations (Independent Group of Scientists, 2019: XXI):

- Governance
- Economy and finance
- Individual and collective action
- Science and technology.

According to the report, true transformation is possible only when the levers are deployed together in an integrated and intentional manner. The authors argue that the central innovation needed to advance the implementation of the 2030 Agenda must therefore come from novel combinations of different levers and the novel collaboration of the respective actors in governance, economy and finance, individual and collective action, and science and technology (Independent Group of Scientists, 2019: 27).

In the following, first, we present some of the main features regarding the report's analyses and proposals for action regarding the six entry points and then briefly explain the mechanisms of the four proposed levers.

Entry points

1 Human wellbeing and capabilities
   Under this heading, the relation between poverty and wellbeing is addressed. The focus is especially on the many vulnerable groups in the world. This concerns those who have just moved out of extreme poverty and the 4 billion people who do not have any form of social protection and who remain highly vulnerable to shocks that threaten to push them into extreme poverty. The report recommends that actions must be taken to eliminate deprivations and build resilience, especially through targeted

interventions in areas where poverty and vulnerability are concentrated or where millions are at risk of being left behind. It emphasizes that the deprivations that people experience are not only due to a lack of technical or financial resources but are often linked to deeply rooted structures of social and political inequality and discriminatory laws and social norms. The most deprived often experience intersecting deprivations – poor, older or younger age, ethnic group, gender (Independent Group of Scientists, 2019: 41). The report argues that human wellbeing and capabilities are key to the overarching mission of eradicating poverty in all its forms and manifestations, reducing inequalities, and leaving no one behind. It underscores that advancing human wellbeing – including material wellbeing, health, education, voice, access to a clean and safe environment and resilience – is at the core of the transformations toward socioecological sustainable development (Independent Group of Scientists, 2019: XXII).

2   Sustainable and just economies

The report states that, in recent times, economic growth has been deeply unequal, increasing disparities in wealth and income and generating expectations that they will continue to be exacerbated into the future. Furthermore, it states that current modes of production and consumption may be unsustainable if trade-offs related to human wellbeing, equality, and environmental protection are not addressed. Regarding this background, the report argues that there is an urgent need to address those aspects of economic growth and production that perpetuate deprivations, generate socioeconomic and gender inequalities, deplete the global environmental commons (the biodiversity, land, the atmosphere, and the oceans), and threaten to cause irreversible damage. According to the report, this presupposes that economic activity should be seen not as an end in itself, but rather as a means for sustainably advancing human potential (Independent Group of Scientists, 2019: 50f).

The report criticizes the use of gross domestic product (GDP) – the market value of goods and services produced over a year – as the sole predominant metric for guiding economic policy for human development (Independent Group of Scientists, 2019: XXIIIf), stating, for example, that it fails to include the value of activities that contribute positively to society but that take place outside of the market. Also, it cannot capture economic inequality, which can increase along with growth in GDP, but which is ultimately inimical to societal wellbeing. Nor does it factor environmental impacts into economic decision-making (Independent Group of Scientists, 2019: 52f). According to the report, a significant part of the transformation will come from changing the volumes and patterns of investment, both public and private. The report estimates that the magnitude of the needed investment is generally in the order of trillions of dollars annually.

3   Food systems and nutrition patterns

The report warns that upscaling current food production practices to meet the projected food demand of the world's population in 2050 would be completely incompatible with meeting the Paris Agreement, as well as many of the Sustainable Development Goals. It adds that pests and crop diseases put global food supplies at risk, but that managing them with the increased use of chemical inputs could jeopardize many environment-related goals (Independent Group of Scientists, 2019: XXV). It suggests that, in transitioning toward sustainable food systems, the focus must be on enabling more equitable global access to nutritional foods, reducing food loss and waste, and maximizing the nutritional value of produce while, at the same time, minimizing the climate and environmental impacts of production and increasing the resilience of food systems. In the report, technological innovation is viewed as a prerequisite for the transition to sustainable food systems, but on its own, the report states, it cannot deliver the transition without changes in governance, behavior, and economic incentives (Independent Group of Scientists, 2019: 64).

4 Energy decarbonization with universal access
   According to the report, 840 million people currently lack access to electricity, predominantly in sub-Saharan Africa, and more than 3 billion people rely on polluting solid fuels for cooking, which causes an estimated 3.8 million premature deaths each year. It points to cheaper renewable energy technologies and the rising role of electricity and digital applications as critical factors for change in providing various energy services. Furthermore, it suggests that fossil fuels should be replaced through resilient, effective, and context-specific energy mixes and with scaled-up efforts directed toward energy efficiency and the promotion of renewables. It elicits some challenges regarding energy decarbonization, such as, for example, the slow progress in smart-grid management and long-term electricity storage, the currently inadequate alternative energy sources for some transport modes, and the lack of policies to ensure that biomass use does not reduce the free-standing biomass in nature. The report takes a critical stance toward the fact that direct and indirect government support for fossil fuels reaches $5 trillion per year, while global public subsidies for renewables are in the range of $150 billion to $200 billion (Independent Group of Scientists, 2019: 5). Furthermore, it states that there is strong evidence of funding from the fossil fuel industry directed toward undermining the scientifically documented link between CO_2 emissions emanating from the use of fossil fuels and climate change (Independent Group of Scientists, 2019: 78).

5 Urban and peri-urban development
   The fifth entry point is urban and peri-urban development. The report argues that sustainable cities are central to achieving all 17 Sustainable Development Goals, because if current trends continue, by 2050 cities will contain approximately 70 percent of the world's population and produce 85 percent of the global economic output. This means that the policy and investment decisions made today will have deep and long-lasting impacts, based on the increasing concentration of people and economic

activities, and the "locked in", long-term nature of urban systems and infrastructure. The report suggest that urban development should proceed in a well-planned, integrated, and inclusive manner, with city governments working together with businesses, civil society organizations, academia, individuals, and with national governments, as well as the authorities in neighboring peri-urban towns and rural areas, and peer cities around the world. It especially suggests that urban and peri-urban decision-makers should prioritize pro-poor development and access to decent jobs, high-quality public services, health care and education, sustainable transport, and safe and attractive public spaces for all, regardless of gender, age, ability, and ethnicity. The report states that innovative governments can create livable cities, where livable cities are defined by the delivery of high-quality services and increased "naturbanity" (Independent Group of Scientists, 2019: 83). By promoting the ideas of naturbanity and urban metabolism, the report conceptualizes cities as regenerative ecosystems (Independent Group of Scientists, 2019: 91).

6   Global environmental commons
The global environmental commons include biodiversity, land, the atmosphere, and the oceans. According to the report, the Earth system's recovery and resilience imply anticipating the feedback effects between commons to maximize co-benefits and minimize trade-offs at the global and local levels. It states that the management of global commons must explicitly address environmental injustice by avoiding the unequal use of resources and by repairing the damage already caused, through a combination of technical, financial, and political interventions. It argues that there is an urgent need to manage how natural resources are extracted from global commons and how the resulting waste is managed. It proposes that policies to protect global environmental commons should address hard-to-change behaviors in economies and lifestyles through incentives, taxation, and regulation. It highlights that transnational agreements are key to the protection of the commons and that adaptive governance involving a wide range of institutions and stakeholders can help ensure their sustainable management (Independent Group of Scientists, 2019: 94). Further, it notes some prominent examples of movements in support of the global commons including those promoting divestment, agroecology, and the environmental justice movement. It argues that such movements can raise awareness, catalyze innovation, build social capital, harness local knowledge, and diffuse knowledge about sociotechnical alternatives. At the same time, they can influence local and global political agendas in favor of the global commons (Independent Group of Scientists, 2019: 104).

Levers

The report divides the possible levers of transformation into four categories. The mechanisms of the levers are put actively into play in relation to the description of possible actions for each of the six entry points (see above). However, they are also described as independent mechanisms. In the following, we briefly explain these mechanisms.

1 Governance
   Governance is an essential lever of the systemic transformations needed to achieve all 17 Sustainable Development Goals. In a continuation of the reports holistic view on socioecological challenges, it argues that governments will need to prioritize policy coherence, overcome sectoral silos, and align existing rules and regulations toward achieving the goals that are interlinked across sectors. This means that new integrated approaches are needed that take into account systemic interactions and the causal relationships between goals and policies. The report highlights that there are several points of agreement in global sustainable development governance: (1) involving grassroots actors in processes toward inclusive, multi-scale politics; (2) identifying and supporting regimes and transformative alliances between traditional and new actors (governments, academia, science, citizens, cities, private sector) toward greater dynamism in transformative governance; and (3) improving the ability to manage hard choices, build coordination and consensus, and channel the necessary resources. The report argues that effective and transparent institutions can fight against corruption and make policy and perform budget planning in a transparent and rigorous manner, with citizen participation where possible. It suggests that effective institutions must also protect the rule of law and access to justice and guarantee a safe and productive space in which civil society organizations can operate. The report warns that recent trends in that regard are troubling, with countries around the world seeing increased numbers of killings of civil rights activists, journalists, and trade union leaders (Independent Group of Scientists, 2019: 29).

2 Economy and finance
   According to the report, economic policy typically encompasses fiscal, monetary, and trade policy, while financial flows include flows from public and private sources, within and across national borders. It argues that policies that encourage trade in sustainably produced goods and services with fair prices, decent labor conditions and wages, and environmentally friendly production techniques can significantly boost progress toward the Sustainable Development Goals. Similarly, it indicates that the ways in which finance flows within countries and across borders significantly shape the Sustainable Development Goals outcomes. This means that attracting private capital and encouraging official development assistance (ODA) toward sectors and activities that enhance human wellbeing and reduce environmental externalities is critical. The report states that fiscal policy is another key mechanism. Effective tax policies can not only generate resources for public expenditures and investments, but also support the reduction of inequalities. In particular, predictable

and transparent tax rules can reduce illicit financial flows and increase investment in sustainable goods and services (Independent Group of Scientists, 2019: 32f).

3 Individual and collective action

The report argues that engaged citizenry is an essential force for advancing sustainable development. This includes enabling people to participate in setting development priorities, monitoring results, and holding decision-makers accountable, because this can help ensure that policies are tailored to the needs of the population and increases the sustainability of their impact (Independent Group of Scientists, 2019: 33). Transformative change is a key notion in the report, and means harnessing bottom-up social, technological, and institutional innovation, including indigenous knowledge and creativity at the grassroots level and in the informal sector. Transformative change also requires the reconfiguration of social practices, social norms, values, and laws that promote unsustainable or discriminatory behavior and choices. The report indicates that behavior is culturally embedded and linked to power hierarchies and the dynamics of influence that strongly condition individual choices as well as collective action. It argues that the political and legal marginalization of some groups and the inequalities between men and women must be eliminated in order for all people to be equally able to participate fully in society. The report mentions a variety of mechanisms for empowering people, changing behaviors, and expanding the space for collective action, such as laws and regulations, taxes, fines, education, advertising, and public information campaigns. The report also argues that the existence of unions, political parties, women's groups, and other collectives provide the means for forming shared goals and pursuing them jointly (Independent Group of Scientists, 2019: 35f).

4 Science and technology

The report highlights that realizing the full potential of science and technology in all parts of the world depends on a host of actors, including scientists and engineers in both the public and private sectors, entrepreneurs, financiers, policymakers, and educators. It places special emphasis on digitalization by stating that our entire future – the way we work, move, interact, and experience the world – will be shaped in countless ways by digitalization. According to the report, there is a critical need to ensure that the digital development is shaped in a comprehensive and far-sighted manner that prioritizes equity, accessibility, inclusion, human dignity, international collaboration, and sustainability (Independent Group of Scientists, 2019: 36f).

Summary

In this chapter, we have broadened the scope of the book from ecological challenges to the interrelations between the social and ecological challenges,

UN policies and governance targeting this complex area, and a global stocktaking of the SDG outcomes commissioned by the UN. By doing so, we have focused on the dual challenge of addressing rising social inequalities and injustices while at the same time regenerating nature and securing the Earth as a safe space for humanity. Whereas in the first two chapters of the book, we concentrated on global challenges, in this chapter, we have focused on the differentiated significance of the various challenges for different groups and populations. In order to distinguish between different aspects of socioecological sustainability, we introduced key concepts about socioecological transformation that are widely applied in different UN reports: freedom, safety, distributional, procedural and recognitional equity and justice, and intergenerational equity and justice.

In recent years, general inequality in the world has been characterized by a growing divide between the rich and the poor, the Global North and the Global South. Furthermore, rich countries, people, and companies are contributing the most to increasing the challenges pertaining to climate change, biodiversity loss, and resource depletion; while injustices and inequalities regarding these issues occur along ethnic, gender, class, and racial lines. At the same time, interventions are often deepening injustices and inequalities along the same lines of social division. Not surprisingly, recognitional and procedural inequalities follow the same patterns.

The Rio Declaration gave socioecological issues high priority. The Paris Agreement, the Strategic Plan for Biodiversity 2011–2020, and the Aichi targets as well as the 10-Year Framework Program on Sustainable Consumption and Production reiterate this concern for the social aspects of an ecological sustainable transformation. At the UN level, however, comprehensive socioecological goals, targets, and indicators are most prominent in the 2020 Agenda for Sustainable Development and the Sustainable Development Goals (SDGs), which explicitly aim at targeting three integrated and indivisible dimensions of sustainable development: the economic, the social, and the environmental.

In this chapter, we presented the goals, targets, and indicators of the SDGs, with a special focus on the connections between the environmental and social aspects. We also criticized some of the goals, targets, and indicators as well as the governance model based on Nationally Determined Contributions. As highlighted, this paradigm of multilevel goal-based governance seems to be the "new normal" within the UN system (see also Chapter 11). One aspect of criticism regarding goal-based governance has been that the isolated goals, targets, and indicators are exposed to the risks of promoting siloed and fragmented interventions. To highlight the possibilities of applying goal-based governance in a more integrated manner, we presented an attempt to use the goal-based Earth3 model to investigate if and how it would be possible to reach the SDGs within the planetary boundaries (see Chapter 1). We concluded that this model appears reductionist and primarily orientated toward the measurement of economic and ecological factors rather than all the relevant factors related to socioecological issues. Although spurred by good intentions and containing constructive proposals, this implies that the proposed solutions seem to be more or less detached from the actual measurements of the model's indicators.

In the final part of the chapter, we highlighted some of the results from the first Global Sustainability Report that assesses how far the world has come in implementing the SDGs. Having read the report, the General- Secretary of the UN concluded that the world "is not on track to achieve the SDGs before 2030", and that all nations must "dramatically step up the pace and implementation". Apart from assessing countries lack of success in implementing the SDGs, the report also underlines that the chosen governance model with separated goals and Nationally Determined Contributions may not be the most efficient way to steer the world in a socioecological sustainable direction. The report argues that the goals and interventions should target systems instead of isolated phenomena. As highlighted in the chapter, the report proposes targeting six systems: human wellbeing and capabilities, economies, food systems and nutrients patterns, energy decarbonization with universal access, urban and peri-urban development, and the global environmental commons. Furthermore, it proposes the application of four levers in combination with each of these systems: governance, economy and finance, individual and collective action, and science and technology.

No doubt, the world is in dire need of ecological and socioecological transformation. No doubt also, the governance models applied at the global level are in dire need of improvement. The question then is, which way to go on from here? In the next chapter, we highlight some fundamental differing views regarding this question, especially pertaining to which structures, power relations, and driving forces should be addressed to reach the commonly stated goal of saving the planet and promoting just and inclusive societies.

References

Ahmed, N., Marriot A., Dabi, N., Lowthers, M., Lawson M., and Mugehera, L. (2022). *Inequality kills. The unparalleled action needed to combat unprecedented inequality in the wake of COVID-19*. Oxfam GB for Oxfam International. DOI: 10.21201/2022.8465

Eizenberg, E. and Jabareen, J. (2017). Social sustainability: A new conceptual framework. *Sustainability*, 9, 68, 16 pages. DOI:10.3390/su9010068

Folke, C., Polasky, S., Rockströme, J., Galaz, V., Westley, F., Lamont, M., Scheffer, M., Österblom, H., Carpenter, S. R., Chapin III, F. S., Seto, K. C., Weber, E. U., Crona, B.I., Daily, G. C., Dasgupta, P., Gaffney, O., Gordon, L. J., Hoff, H., Levin, S. A., Lubchenco, J., Steffen, W. and Walker B. H. (2021). Our future in the Anthropocene biosphere. *Springer, the Royal Swedish Academy of Science Ambio*, 50, 834–869. Retrieved from: https://doi.org/10.1007/s13280-021-01544-8.

Harndon, D. (2017). *An economy for the 99 percent. It's time to build a human economy that benefits everyone, not just the privileged few*. Oxfam GB for Oxfam International, Oxfam Briefing Paper. DOI: 10.21201/2017.8616

Independent Group of Scientists (2019). *Global sustainable development report: The future is now – science for achieving sustainable development*. New York: United Nations, 252 pages. Retrieved from: https://sdgs.un.org/sites/default/files/2020-07/24797GSDR_report_2019.pdf

IPBES (2019). Summary for policymakers of the global assessment report on biodiversity and ecosystem services of the intergovernmental science-policy platform on biodiversity and ecosystem services. In: S. Díaz, J. Settele, E. S. Brondízio, H. T. Ngo, M. Guèze, J. Agard, A. Arneth, P. Balvanera, K. A. Brauman, S. H. M. Butchart, K. M. A. Chan, L. A. Garibaldi, K. Ichii, J. Liu, S. M. Subramanian, G. F. Midgley, P. Miloslavich, Z. Molnár, D. Obura, A. Pfaff, S. Polasky, A. Purvis, J. Razzaque, B. Reyers, R. Chowdhury, Y. J. Shin, I. J. Visseren-Hamakers, K. J. Willis, & C. N. Zayas (eds.), Bonn, Germany: IPBES Secretariat, 56 pages. Retrieved from: https://www.ipbes.net/sites/default/files/202002/ipbes_global_assessment_report_summary_for_policymakers_en.pdf.

IPCC (2022). Summary for policymakers. In: H.-O. Pörtner, D. C. Roberts, E.S. Poloczanska, K. Mintenbeck, M. Tignor, A. Alegría, M. Craig, S. Langsdorf, S. Löschke, V. Möller & A. Okem (eds.), *Climate change 2022: Impacts, adaptation, and vulnerability*. Contribution of Working Group II to the Sixth Assessment Report of the Intergovernmental Panel on Climate Change, 40 pages. Retrieved from: https://www.ipcc.ch/report/ar6/wg2/downloads/report/IPCC_AR6_WGII_SummaryForPolicymakers.pdf.

IRP (2019). Global resources outlook 2019: Natural resources for the future we want. In: B. Oberle, S. Bringezu, S. Hatfield-Dodds, S. Hellweg, H. Schandl, J. Clement, L. Cabernard, N. Che, D. Chen, H. Droz-Georget, P. Ekins, M. Fischer-Kowalski, M. Flörke, S. Frank, A. Froemelt, A. Geschke, M. Haupt, P. Havlik, R. Hüfner, M. Lenzen, M. Lieber, B. Liu, Y. Lu, S. Lutter, J. Mehr, A. Miatto, D. Newth, C. Oberschelp, M. Obersteiner, S. Pfister, E. Piccoli, R. Schaldach, J. Schüngel, T. Sonderegger, A. Sudheshwar, H. Tanikawa, E. van der Voet, C. Walker, J. West, Z. Wang & B. Zhu (eds.), *A Report of the International Resource Panel*. Nairobi, Kenya: United Nations Environment Programme, 162 pages. Retrieved from: https://www.resourcepanel.org/reports/global-resources-outlook.

Leach, M., Reyers, B., Bai, X., Brondizio, E. S., Cook, C., Díaz, S., Espindola, G., Scobie, M., Stafford-Smith, M., and Subramanian S. M. (2018). Equity and sustainability in the Anthropocene: A social–ecological systems perspective on their intertwined futures. *Global Sustainability*, 1, e13, 1–13. Retrieved from: https://doi.org/10.1017/sus.2018.12

Mair, S., Jones, A., Ward, J., Christie, I., Druckman, A., and Lyon, F. (2018). A critical review of the role of indicators in implementing the sustainable development goals. In: L. Filho W. (ed.), *Handbook of sustainability science and research*. World Sustainability Series. Cham: Springer, 41–56. Retrieved from: http://hdl.handle.net/10454/18258.

Menton, M., Larrea, C., Latorre, S., Martinez-Alier, J., Peck, M., Temper, L. and Walter, M. (2019). Environmental justice and the SDGs: From synergies to gaps and contradictions. *Sustainability Science*, 15, 1621–1636. Retrieved from: https://doi.org/10.1007/s11625-020-00789-8.

Newell, P., Srivastava, S., Naess, L. O., Contreras, G. A. T., and Price, R. (2020). Towards transformative climate justice: Key challenges and future directions for research. Working Paper Volume 2020, Number 540. The Institute of Development Studies, 151 pages. Retrieved from: https://opendocs.ids.ac.uk/opendocs/bitstream/

handle/20.500.12413/15497/Wp540_Towards_Transformative_Climate_Justice. pdf?sequence=1&isAllowed=y

Piketty (2020). *Capital and ideology*. Cambridge, MA: Harvard University Press, 1104 pages

Raworth, K. (2017). *Doughnut economics: Seven ways to think like a 21st-century economist*. London: Cornerstone.

Randers, J., Rockström, J., Stoknes, P. E., Golüke, U., Collste, D., and Cornell, S. (2018). Transformation is feasible. How to achieve the Sustainable Development Goals within Planetary Boundaries. A report to the Club of Rome, for its 50 years anniversary 17 October 2018. Stockholm Resilience Centre, 60 pages. Retrieved from: https://www.stockholmresilience.org/download/18.51d83659166367a9a16353/1539675518425/Report_Achieving percent20the percent20Sustainable percent20Development percent20Goals_WEB.pdf.

Schleicher, J., Schaafsma, M., and Bhaskar, V. (2018). Will the Sutainable Development Goals address the links between poverty and the natural environment? *Current Opinion in Environmental Sustainability*, 34, 43–47. Retrieved from: https://doi.org/10.1016/j.cosust.2018.09.004

Steffen, W., Persson, Å., Deutsch, L., Zalasiewicz, J., Williams, M., Richardson, K., Crumley, C., Crutzen, P., Folke, C., Gordon, L., Molina, M., Ramanathan, V., Rockström, J., Scheffer, M., Schellnhuber, H. J. and Svedin, U. (2011). The Anthropocene: From global change to planetary stewardship. *Ambio*, 40, 739–761. DOI: 10.1007/s13280-0011-0185-x.

UN (1948). Universal declaration of human rights. Retrieved from: https://www.un.org/en/about-us/universal-declaration-of-human-rights

UN (1992). Rio Declaration on environment and development. Retrieved from: https://www.un.org/en/development/desa/population/migration/generalassembly/docs/globalcompact/A_CONF.151_26_Vol.I_Declaration.pdf

UN (2012). A 10-year framework of programs on sustainable consumption and production patterns. Annex to the letter dated 18 June 2012 from the Permanent Representative of Brazil to the United Nations addressed to the Secretary-General of the United Nations Conference on Sustainable Development. Retrieved from: https://sdgs.un.org/documents/aconf2165-10-year-framework-programmes-o-19090

UN (2015). General assembly, Transforming our world: The 2030 Agenda for sustainable development, 21 October, A/RES/70/1. Retrieved from: https://www.refworld.org/docid/57b6e3e44.html

UNDP (2020). Human Development Report 2020, the Next Frontier - Human development and the Anthropocene, 412 pages. Retrieved from: http://hdr.undp.org/sites/default/files/hdr2020.pdf

UNFCCC (2015). Paris agreement. Retrieved from: https://unfccc.int/sites/default/files/english_paris_agreement.pdf

Winkler, I. T. and Williams, C. (2017). The sustainable development goals and human rights: A critical early review. *The International Journal of Human Rights*, 21(8), 1023–1028. DOI: 10.1080/13642987.2017.1348695

WMO (2020). State of the climate. *World Meteorological Organization*, WMO-No. 1264, 56 pages. Retrieved from: https://library.wmo.int/doc_num.php?explnum_id=10618

4 Affirmative and critical perspectives on the 2030 Agenda of sustainable development and the sustainable development goals

Anders Siig Andersen and Lars Hulgaard

> By comparison to what it could have been, it's a miracle. But by comparison to what it should have been, it's a disaster.
>
> George Monbiot, writer, journalist, and political activist

Introduction

In the first three chapters of this book, we have highlighted global ecological and socioecological challenges and UN agreements directed at promoting concerted global action. Furthermore, we have highlighted several critical assessments of the outcomes of international agreements in relation to resolving the pressing ecological and socioecological issues. Primarily, these assessments have been based on the UN system's own monitoring activities, review of academic work, and UN-commissioned assessment reports. In this chapter, we shift our perspective from system-internal to system-external critical assessments, and especially the types of assessments that are directed at the relations between goals, responses, and the fundamental drivers underlying socioecological challenges.

It is an important aspect of the creation of the 2030 Agenda and the sustainable development goals (SDGs) that various popular movements, non-governmental organizations (NGOs), and trade unions had the opportunity to be significantly more active and influential than was the case in relation to the millennium development goals (MDGs) (see also Chapter 3). This means that many different perspectives – other than the perspectives of nations – have been merged during negotiations, including environmental and climate, human rights, Global South, and labor market/workers' perspectives. In this chapter, first, we highlight some affirmative assessments of the negotiation process and the outcomes of the 2030 Agenda on Sustainable Development and the SDGs as expressed from these perspectives, and second, we thematize substantial points of critique – from grassroots movements and scholars critically assessing single goals and the drivers of ecological, social, and economic development. We finalize the chapter by discussing which driving forces, pressures, states, impacts, and responses the 2030 Agenda and the SDG targets are addressing

DOI: 10.4324/9781003319672-6

and which they are not, and, furthermore, by elaborating on the multiple structures, power relations, and drivers that would have to be considered in order to fully realize the intentions of the 2030 Agenda and the SDGs.

Affirmative views on the 2030 Agenda and the SDGs

Assessing the 2030 Agenda and the SDGs, the most visible innovation and departure from the MDGs is that the 2030 Agenda has integrated its goals pertaining to economic and social development with those of the environment. After the conclusion in 2012 of the Rio+ 20 Conference on Sustainable Development, it was not clear whether the UN and the intergovernmental system would succeed in merging the discussions around a successor agenda to the MDGs with the Rio process (Koehler, 2016: 1f). The decision to merge the processes of developing SDGs and the follow-up on the MDGs was introduced later (Spangenberg, 2016: 312). Many actors regarded the adoption of the 2030 Agenda and the SDGs as a victory for environmental as well as social sustainability. As outlined in Chapter 2, regarding environmental and climate change issues, the 2030 Agenda and the SDGs adopt and reiterate important parts of the UN Conventions on Climate Change and Biodiversity and the 10-Year Framework of Programmes on Sustainable Consumption and Production (10YFP). Pertaining to the resource area, some of the targets and indicators have even been strengthened. In the following, we will shortly present some affirmative views on the parts of the 2030 Agenda and the SDGs that are attempting to tackle the combined socioecological challenges.

Human rights perspectives

According to Winkler and Williams (2017: 1023), human rights advocates were generally satisfied with the 2030 Agenda its goals, targets, and monitoring mechanisms. The authors state that human rights advocates achieved a lot in SDG negotiations – from the overall promise of "leaving no one behind," to references to human rights, to many of the targets that reflect human rights language (Winkler & Williams, 2017: 1026f). Winkler and Williams argue that this resulted from the opportunity of the human rights community, along with civil society more generally, to engage in the negotiations for the new development agenda during a broad and lengthy process including early thematic and country consultations, the Rio+ 20 negotiations, and the Open Working Group (OWG) on the SDGs. Against this background, the authors state that because the world adopted the SDGs, they offer one of the best contemporary global opportunities to oppose social injustices that human rights advocates can use as a tool (Winkler & Williams, 2017: 1023). Although Koehler (2016: 2) is predominantly critical in her assessment of the 2030 Agenda and the SDGs, she acknowledges that the 2030 Agenda commits to transformation, to human rights, and to universalism in the sense that it applies to all countries, and that all UN member states have committed to follow the agreement in light of the immense persistence of poverty, accelerating inequities, and the degradation of the environment. She also acknowledges that the 2030 Agenda presents a rights-oriented preamble and that it offers an encompassing set of goals spanning many areas of public and personal life. Therefore, from Koehler's standpoint, the 2030 Agenda should be regarded as an anchor by which to claim rights and to move societies toward transforming global relations for economic, social, and environmental justice (Koehler, 2016: 10).

The Global South

In an article from 2020, Fukuda-Parr and Muchhala (2020) examine the agency of the Global South in the emergence of sustainable development as the consensus framework laying behind the adoption of the 2030 Agenda for Sustainable Development and the SDGs. These authors state that the reconceptualizing of development from a donor aid framework for meeting basic needs to a universal agenda for socially inclusive, economically equitable, and environmentally sustainable development would not have happened without the active participation of representatives of the Global South. They highlight three main areas within the SDGs where southern intellectuals, NGOs, and governments have succeeded in promoting their views: (1) structural change and industrialization; (2) international trade and finance; and (3) inequality (Fukuda-Parr & Muchhala, 2020: 9).

According to Fukuda-Parr and Muchhala (2020: 7), the inclusion of industrialization and structural change in the SDGs was promoted by African countries. These countries viewed structural change – particularly diversification into manufacturing and technological upgrading – as an integrated strategy of sustainable economic development that could foster social inclusion and environmental conservation. Their core idea was that sustainable improvements in living standards cannot be achieved when the economy depends on primary commodity exports that are subject to fluctuating international market prices and low-productivity agriculture (Fukuda-Parr & Muchhala, 2020: 6). The authors highlight that the agreement on infrastructure, industrial development, and domestic technology development in SDG 8 and 9 and targets 8.2, 9.2, 9.b, & 17.7 reflects a legitimization of the subject (Fukuda-Parr & Muchhala, 2020: 7).

Reforms in the international financial, trade, and economic architecture includes policies related to, for example, trade, financial regulation, lending, debt, aid, international tax cooperation, and illicit financial flows. According to Fukuda-Parr and Muchhala (2020: 7), representatives of the Global South argued that global reforms within these areas are indispensable to rendering development sustainable. They point out that the wish for reforms to the policies and frameworks in the international financial and trade architecture is reflected through various SDG target – as, for example, target 16.4 on illicit financial and arms flows; target 17.4 on supporting debt financing, debt relief, and debt restructuring; target 17.12 on market access for least-developed countries; target 10.5 on the regulation and monitoring of global financial markets; target 10.6 on the participation of developing countries in decision-making in global international economic and financial institutions; and targets 10.a and 10.b on aid and financial flows to the least-developed countries, African countries, and small-island developing countries. The framework also addresses trade and investment rules that could obstruct the achievement of other SDGs, such as target 3.b on intellectual property relevant for access to medicines and public health more broadly, and 2.b on agricultural export subsidies important for food security (Fukuda-Parr & Muchhala, 2020: 8).

Fukuda-Parr and Muchhala (2020:8) point out that the inclusion of inequality in the SDG framework can be widely attributed to the insistence of developing countries and the persistent advocacy of international civil society networks. The authors state that during the final stage of negotiations, the stand-alone inequality goal was one of the most difficult to reach agreement on, as powerful bilaterals, philanthropies, and influential academics opposed this goal.

Just transition and decent work

In 2013, the UN tripartite International Labor Organization (ILO) adopted a resolution concerning sustainable development, decent work, and green jobs, which refers to Just Transition (Heyen et al., 2020: 10). In 2015, following up on the resolution, the ILO published "Guidelines for a just transition towards environmentally sustainable economies and societies for all" (Heyen et al., 2020: 10). In these guidelines, the ILO formulates a concern for securing green and decent jobs in a post-carbon transition, emphasizing the role of governments in integrating Just Transition visions through nine aspects: (1) macroeconomic and (green) growth policies; (2) industrial and sectoral policies; (3) enterprise policies; (4) skills development for technological change; (5) health and safety at work; (6) social protection; (7) active labor market policies; (8) workers' rights; and (9) social dialog (Kreinin, 2020: 7). In 2015, the notions of Just Transition and Decent Work became part of the SDGs. Against this background, the ILO expressed great satisfaction that significant components of the organization's Decent Work Agenda have been included in the framework of the 2030 Agenda. To the ILO, decent jobs are productive, deliver a fair income, and provide social protection and the freedom for people to express their opinion and organize, along with assuring equality of opportunity and treatment for all women and men (ILO, 2017: 1). In the socioecological context, the greening of jobs may occur in different ways as new jobs will be created, certain jobs will be eliminated, other jobs will be substituted, and most jobs will be transformed (ILO, 2020:13).

The ILO fully supports the 2030 Agenda and the SDGs both politically and practically. As a specialized agency under UN, the ILO is a custodian agency of several targets and has been assigned important tasks in terms of implementing the SDGs at national as well as international levels. The ILO emphasizes that Decent Work features prominently in the Agenda – not only mainstreamed across the goals and targets, but also as a part of the stated vision of the Agenda: "We resolve, between now and 2030 (...) to create conditions for sustainable, inclusive, and sustained economic growth, shared prosperity, and decent work for all, taking into account different levels of national development and capacities" (ILO, 2016: 2). In particular, the ILO highlights the organization's interest in SDG 8, which focuses on promoting sustained, inclusive, and sustainable economic growth. References to ILO areas of competence, however, are found in several other targets. The ILO highlights the following: the importance of social protection, including national floors (target 1.3); wage and fiscal policies as an important means of reducing inequality (target 10.4); eradication of extreme poverty (target 1.1); reduction of poverty (1.2); technical and vocational skills (targets 4.3–4.5); and ending all forms of discrimination against all women and girls everywhere (target 5.1) (ILO, 2016: 4).

Critical views on the 2030 Agenda and the SDGs

In this part of the chapter, we shift our perspective from affirmative assessments covering most aspects of the SDGs to presenting critical academic views. To provide a context for understanding the main themes of this criticism, first, we will briefly present the background and standpoints of three broad international movements concerned with environmental justice, climate justice, and energy justice, respectively.

The environmental justice movement

In the 1980s, the term "environmental justice" began to be used in struggles against the disproportionate dumping of toxic waste in urban or peri-urban African-American areas in the United States (Martinez-Alier et al., 2016: 2). According to Newell et al. (2020), most of the now globally organized environmental justice movements and intellectual debates converge around three key ideas or themes: (1) the anti-racist environmentalism that characterized the 1980s and 1990s, linking demands of social justice and fairness vis-à-vis ecological problems and environmental harms such as pollution; (2) demands in the 1990s to recognize the "ecological debt" owed by the Global North to the Global South, made by groups such as Acción Ecológica, leading up to the Kyoto Protocol negotiations; and (3) the Global Justice Movement, which came to the fore in the 1999 World Trade Organization (WTO) protests in Seattle. The theory of environmental justice argues for respect for the dignity of communities and their capabilities, recognition of the legitimacy of other identities and values, and the importance of participation and representation of all affected parties in decision-making regarding socio-environmental policies (Velicu & Barca, 2020: 264f.). During recent years, the Environmental Justice Movement has expanded its focus to include the commons, seeing the commons as a crucial sector of the economy, which must be defended to preserve de-commodified access to food, water, forests, and clean air. Influenced by Karl Polanyi, the movement fights against old and new enclosures (Martinez-Alier et al., 2016: 15). Newell et al. (2020: 27) argue that environmental justice activists are as interested in changing the prevailing power relations as they are in environmental questions with a typical focus on structural root causes. Thus, some activists' readings of environmental justice have defined themselves against the more mainstream environmental activism and the UN processes, which are frequently depicted as technocentric, bureaucratic, and co-opted by corporate actors, pushing "false" market solutions and overriding the rights of poor and marginalized groups.

The climate justice movement

While the Environmental Justice Movement originated from the socially unjust location of environmentally polluting companies in poor areas, the Climate Justice Movement has its origins in the fight against climate change. This movement focuses specifically on issues of loss and damages, mitigation, and adaption concerning the disproportionate impacts of climate change on the most vulnerable and marginalized human populations, and the need for structural solutions (see also Chapter 3). Advocates for climate justice have emerged as a critical voice in climate diplomacy and have challenged various technological and market-oriented approaches to the climate crisis as well as political interests linked to the fossil fuel industry in many countries (Tokar, 2019: 1). According to Schlosberg and Collins (2014: 367), the Climate Justice Movement focuses on four basic issues: (1) abandoning fossil fuels and leaving them in the ground; (2) financial transfers from the Global North to the Global South for payment of ecological debt based on historical responsibility; (3) food and land sovereignty for vulnerable communities, including a transition to renewable and sustainable practices; and (4) a critique of purely market-based policies to address climate change. The authors state that these themes focus on changing the nature of production systems that are creating risks, compensating for those risks, and providing for procedural justice and autonomy. The two authors argue that the idea of the historical responsibility approach is a basic "polluter pays" principle, which ties responsibility for addressing the issue with those who have created the problem. This approach is one way to operationalize the "common but differentiated responsibilities and respective capacities," agreed on in the United Nations Framework Convention on Climate Change (UNFCCC) (Schlosberg & Collins, 2014: 364). The Climate Justice Movement emphasizes the values of self-determination through grassroots control over the use of resources, food sovereignty, energy democracy, and respect for indigenous and peasant rights (Velicu & Barca, 2020: 263). With a climate justice approach, carbon markets are generally seen as giveaways to polluters at the expense of poor communities. A simple cap-and-trade system, where the original credits are given to polluters, is contrasted with preferred cap-and-dividend or fee-and-dividend policy, where permits would be auctioned to polluters and the revenue returned to poor and vulnerable communities (see also Chapters 6 and 11). Tokar (2019: 10ff) attributes the following type of actions to the Climate Justice Movement:

- Climate justice campaigners continue to highlight the disproportionate impacts of climate disruptions on the lives and livelihoods of the most vulnerable and politically marginalized populations.
- Climate justice advocates bring an understanding that the institutions and economic policies responsible for climate destabilization are also underlying causes of poverty and economic inequality.
- Climate justice brings a broadly intersectional outlook into the climate movement as a means to address the many common threads that link environmental abuses to patterns of discrimination by race, class, gender, sexual orientation, and other social factors.
- Climate justice campaigners strive to link efforts to challenge climate-damaging practices to an alternative vision of a future without fossil fuels.
- Climate justice advocates believe that policy changes need to be substantively driven by the priorities and agendas that emerge from grassroots campaigns.

Specifically aiming at abandoning fossil fuels and leaving them in the ground, the Divestment Movement revolves around undermining the "social legitimacy" of the carbon socio-energy system, thus directing attention to issues such as political economy, power, equity, and ideology (Healy & Barry, 2017: 453). The Divestment Movement links demands to "keep it in the ground" to proposals concerning the reorientation of an energy system currently dominated by fossil fuels. Ultimately, this necessitates leaving approximately 33 percent of oil reserves, 50 percent of gas reserves, and over 80 percent of current coal reserves in the ground by 2050 (Healy & Barry, 2017: 453). Healy and Barry (2017: 453f) argue that while most analyses of low-carbon transitions focus on green energy niche innovations, the fossil fuel Divestment Movement shifts attention to the resistance by the fossil fuel regime as the most significant obstacle to fundamental changes in energy systems. According to these authors, many of the divestment campaigns incorporate a "divest to reinvest" element.

The energy justice movement

While the Climate Justice Movement centers on the causes of climate change and the unequal distribution of the negative impacts of climate change, the Energy Justice Movement also places an emphasis on the provision of safe, affordable, and sustainable energy for all (Healy & Barry, 2017: 452). However, the focus of the Energy Justice Movement is also on the multiple injustices of petro-violence and human rights abuses by so-called petrostates, and the geopolitical instability caused by illegal wars and invasions for fossil fuels. Aligned with the Energy Justice Movement, indigenous peoples' movements, NGOs, and trade unions have mobilized to demand both procedural justice and distributional justice in defense of land and ways of living free from fossil fuel exploration and extraction (Healy & Barry, 2017: 454; see also Chapter 11).

Main themes in the critical discussion of the 2030 Agenda and the SDGs

The academic criticism of the 2030 Agenda and the SDGs reflects various aspects of the fundamental views of the grassroots movements and the NGOs. In the following, based on our reading of academic articles, we have chosen to focus on six themes that highlight some main aspects of this criticism: (1) poverty reduction; (2) justice; (3) the growth paradigm, decoupling, and leapfrogging; (4) financing, free trade, and the multinationals; (5) ecological depth and loss & damages; and (6) Decent Work and Just Transition (see also Chapter 10).

Theme 1: Poverty reduction

Koehler (2016: 2) criticizes the ambition of the 2030 Agenda regarding income poverty and the redistribution of income and wealth, arguing that the Agenda fails to face up to the reasons underlying hunger and acute poverty and the destruction of the environment. Menton et al. (2019: 1631) explain that the targets and the related indicators address neither the accumulation of wealth by rich countries and the impacts of this wealth accumulation on financial systems nor well-being indicators within lower- or middle-income countries. They argue strongly that the primary goal of inequality, SDG 1, does not address any of the driving underlying structural factors that cause poverty, such as exploitation, dispossession, and disenfranchisement.

Menton et al. (2019: 1631) further highlight that GDP statistics obscure the real livelihood basis of many poor sectors of the world population, and fail to consider injustices caused by pollution, enclosure, and environmental degradation. They point to the fact that many communities depend on ecosystem services and goods outside the market (clean water, fertile soil, and locally adaptable seeds), and that this can make up between 50 percent and 90 percent of the total source of livelihoods among poor rural and forest-dwelling households. This means that improvements in one poverty dimension cannot always compensate for the deterioration of other dimensions.

Theme 2: Justice

Justice is a main pillar of the SDGs. Menton et al. (2019: 1626) refer to SDG 16, which emphasizes the "rule of law," with a reference to international human rights and an approach to accountability and transparency that prioritizes the eradication of state-based corruption. They argue, however, that this focus largely bypasses the question of how state definitions of justice inevitably privilege some actors and some conceptions of justice over others and that, accordingly, it fails to address the power dynamics and structural conditions that impede environmental and social justice – and constrains its ability to support environmental justice.

Menton et al. (2019) also indicate that although part of SDG 16 frames its focus on peace and physical violence, it does not take into account other forms of violence. They refer to reports on killings of human rights defenders that have identified 321 murders in 2018, 77 percent of which involved individuals defending environmental and/or land rights. In some cases, the state is complicit in the violence against environmental justice activists. According to Menton et al. (2019: 1626), these killings only represent the tip of an iceberg of violence linked to resource extraction and economic growth, as many more people suffer from slow violence, structural violence, and psychological violence through threats and other forms of intimidation. The authors highlight that the Environmental Justice Atlas is documenting over 3,000 ecological distribution conflicts globally, which point to slow violence via environmental degradation, changes in social metabolism, and effects on local livelihoods. They argue that these types of conflicts, violence, and environmental injustices are not addressed directly by the SDGs.

At a more specific level of justice, Menton et al. (2019: 1627ff) summarize a number of inadequate understandings and measures linked to the SDGs, described below:

- *No mentioning of the right to food:* The right to food and nutrition is not explicitly included in the language of the SDGs. Instead, it is assumed that market mechanisms will lead to food security.
- *Agriculture-related goals fail to recognize power relations and structures:* Target 2.4 calls attention to the environmental impacts of agriculture but fails to recognize the power relations and structures within the agricultural sector that exclude the poor from equitable benefit from that production.
- *The energy question is reduced to the problem of decarbonization:* The overall SDG framework acknowledges that energy and climate are necessary conditions for the achievement of social justice and other developmental goals. However, the energy question is reduced to a problem of decarbonization of energy sources and energy poverty, not including structural drivers.
- *Vulnerable groups' exposure to risk is not contested:* What is considered as climate risks and the identification and prioritization of adaptation measures in the SDGs is derived from states' priorities; this specific view on adaptation is linked to the fact that the unequal exposure to climate risks within states is not directly contested.

- *Renewable energy affects rural areas the most and is often privatized:* Because renewable energies are more spatially extensive than fossil fuels, production space is needed that disproportionately affects rural areas where land values are lowest and fewer formal land rights exist. SDG 7 focuses on the material domain of the current socio-technological energy system but mainly remains silent on the unequal structures of ownership and control of energy.
- *Drivers affecting wildlife and ecosystems are not covered:* Many of the drivers affecting wildlife and ecosystems can be attributed to growth in social metabolism that supports economic growth. Disproportionate burdens of the negative consequences of degradation are shouldered by marginalized communities, which impacts their access to clean water, health, land for agriculture, and, therefore, loss of livelihoods. These types of challenges are not covered sufficiently by the SDGs.
- *There is a conservation risk for vulnerable groups:* Conservation tends to be located in lower-income countries and often displaces already marginalized families from their lands and/or limits their access to their traditional hunting grounds. Resulting environmental injustices have included cultural destruction, forced relocation, impoverishment, and the undermining of traditional systems of natural resource management. Pertaining to these challenges, the SDGs remain silent (see also Chapter 11).

Theme 3: The growth paradigm, decoupling, and degrowth

Economic and political thinking has shifted in the period after WWII – from Keynesianism with an active fiscal and monetary mixed-policy approach emphasizing social equality and protections, to neoliberalism with a market-first policy approach prioritizing tax cuts for the rich, the undermining of trade unions, deregulation, privatization, outsourcing, and competition in public services (see also Chapter 11). Gilbert (2004) talks about a "silent surrender of public responsibility for welfare," and Jessop (2002) describes a transition from the postwar Keynesian welfare state to a Schumpeterian workfare state. However, within both paradigms, a core value has been the ever-increasing material wealth generated by a growth-oriented economy that has been the global driver of the Great Acceleration. The Great Acceleration has delivered important improvement in living standards. However, it has also caused dramatic negative impact on climate, environment, and equality (see also Chapter 3). Growth as society's main value has been supported by "modern" Cartesian scientific and industrial cultures that distinguish sharply between the human and the nonhuman (see also Chapter 12). This disconnection of humans from nature underpins seeing nature as generalized "environment," "biodiversity," and "natural capital," and legitimizes that nature can be commodified, priced, and exploited (UNDP, 2020: 89). This stands in contrast to contextualized approaches, which emphasize the uniqueness of place, reliance on local resources, and the involvement of people (Egmose et al., 2021).

In this context, much criticism of the SDGs has been directed at the underlying growth paradigm and prescription to technological solutions that are aimed at decoupling resource use from GDP growth and leapfrogging (see also Chapter 2). Different scholars have criticized the aim of increasing GDP, arguing that growth in developed countries will need to substantially decrease to have any chance of meeting the climate targets of the Paris Agreement (Adelman, 2017: 18).

The growth concept is clearly articulated in SDG 8 of the 2030 Agenda on "promoting sustained, inclusive, and sustainable economic growth, full and productive employment, and decent work for all." The indicators of SDG 8 are directed at measuring informal employment, hourly earnings, youth employment, education and training, child labor, occupational injuries, compliance of labor rights, access to financial services, aid for trade, and the existence of youth employment strategies. SDG 8, however, also contains three targets that lie very much at the heart of the economic side of the SDGs. These targets are as follows:

- Target 8.1 Sustain per capita economic growth in accordance with national circumstances and, in particular, at least 7 percent GDP growth per annum in the least developed countries.
- Target 8.2 Achieve higher levels of economic productivity through diversification and technological upgrading & and innovation, including through a focus on high-value-added and labor-intensive sectors.
- Target 8.4 Improve progressively, through 2030, global resource efficiency in consumption and production and endeavor to decouple economic growth from environmental degradation, in accordance with the 10-Year Framework of Programmes on Sustainable Consumption and Production, with developed countries taking the lead.

Thus, important targets under SDG 8 call for increased annual GDP growth, especially – but not only – in least-developed countries, along with higher levels of economic and resource productivity everywhere.

According to Menton et al. (2019: 1632), the introduction of economic growth was probably a sine qua non in the international negotiations. The growth paradigm, however, is also at the center of much criticism directed at the SDGs. For example, Robra and Heikkurinen (2019: 6) state that the 17 SDGs do not mention the need to reduce consumption and production, and that economic growth is encouraged throughout the framework, as explicitly shown in SDG 8, which targets sustainable economic growth and full employment for all. In both SDG 8 and SDG 12, economic growth is seen as the main driver providing employment for a growing global population. Similarly, SDG 7 (Affordable and Clean Energy) mainly focuses on efficiency and increasing sustainable energy practices but does not mention the need for reduced energy consumption to help reduce throughput. Robra and Heikkurinen (2019: 6) conclude that the SDGs contain no mention of a need for reduction in either consumption or production, and that technology is considered the solution to continue economic growth while, at the same time, promoting a healthy ecosystem.

Kagan and Burton (2018: 287) criticize the take on economic growth, arguing that it is conflating growth in GDP with societal progress. They critically highlight that industrialization is still seen as the main driver of growth, that countries are supposed to significantly raise industry's share of employment and GDP, and that economic growth is the first and foremost generator of domestic resources needed to achieve the SDGs. To Koehler (2016: 3f), this poses a problem for two reasons. First, statistical evidence from many countries suggests that decades of high GDP growth did not necessarily result in an increase in formal-sector employment. Many economies witnessed jobless growth and growth that led to an increase in informal employment, with jobs parceled out under conditions that were highly unfavorable to the workers concerned, in many cases denying their human, labor, and social rights. Second, Koehler (2016: 4) argues that per capita economic growth on a finite planet is the essence of un-sustainability. She argues that only a combination of post-growth in the Global North and economic growth – albeit low in resource intensity – in the Global South will be compatible with re-stabilizing the planet's ecosystems. To Koehler, while appearing progressive, the 2030 Agenda remains in the logic of the capitalist rationale. It does not question hierarchical, and ultimately oppressive, power relations and the logic of the system. Hence, it may reinforce and stabilize the inherently exploitative and ecologically destructive economic and political dynamics (Koehler, 2016: 9; see also Chapter 11).

As mentioned in Chapter 1, according to the International Resource Panel (IRP), decoupling occurs when resource use or a pressure on the environment grows at a slower rate than the activity causing it (relative decoupling) or declines while the economic activity continues to grow (absolute decoupling) (IRP, 2019: 7). The concept of decoupling is about maintaining economic growth and human well-being by means of technology development, incentives, and innovative organization. Leapfrogging embodies the idea that industrializing countries can bypass the resource-intensive conventional pathway of development paved by high-income, industrialized countries to "leap" to the most advanced and sustainable technologies (IRP, 2019: 140).

Wennersten and Qie (2018) state that the world economy today uses around 30 percent fewer resources to produce one euro or dollar of GDP than was the case 30 years ago. At the same time, overall resource use continues to increase. As we consume ever growing amounts of products and services, this positive trend is more than outweighed by the overall growth of our economies. Robra and Heikkurinen (2019: 5) argue that decoupling is based on the idea of eco-efficiency – i.e., the notion of using less energy and fewer resources per unit produced. They state, however, that eco-efficiency is known to lead to rebound effects. Rebound effect describes the phenomenon of an unintended increase in the overall resource use or emissions. This is because greater eco-efficiency often leads to lower prices, which, in turn, lead to higher demand, or because the reduction in cost enables the use of funds for other production or consumption using other resources. In these cases, the actual measure intended to reduce resource use ultimate leads to a higher overall resource use in the end (see also Chapters 5 and 11).

According to Adelman (2017) historical data and modeled projections demonstrate how difficult it is to decouple GDP growth from increases in material and energy. He argues that it is therefore misleading to develop growth-oriented policy around the expectation that decoupling is possible (Adelman, 2017: 19). Robra and Heikkurinen (2019) argue that the idea that the economy can continue to grow while emissions decrease implies that economic growth should be absolutely decoupled from emissions. They refer to Jackson (2011), who calculated that with the economic and population growth predictions current at the time of his publication, carbon intensity would have to decrease 130 times by 2050 to reach the Intergovernmental Panel on Climate Change (IPCC) 2007) target, making the pursuit of absolute decoupling not a viable option (Robra & Heikkurinen, 2019: 5).

Wennersten and Qie (2018: 325f) criticize the concept of "leapfrogging," which may accelerate development in developing economies by skipping inferior, less efficient, more expensive, or more polluting technologies and industries and move directly to more advanced ones based more on service industries than manufacturing. They argue that the basic assumptions of the SDGs promote the idea of leapfrogging by aiming at an economic growth of around 7 percent in the developing countries and that the price for this will be an increasing use of resources and environmental degradation. They argue that it seems increasingly likely that decoupling does not have pure technical solutions, but rather, places more focus on developing socio-economic systems and institutions that do not depend on continued material growth in consumption (Wennersten & Qie, 2018: 334f).

Theme 4: Financing, free trade, and the multinationals

Koehler (2016: 4) argues that it is a systematic flaw in the 2030 Agenda that it is oblivious to the international structures in trade, investment, finance, intellectual property rights, and the monopolistic economic predominance of large firms and large nations. Similarly, Menton et al. (2019: 1631) state that while SDG 1 calls for mobilization of aid and development resources from rich to poor countries, it does not address world system dynamics such as trade rules, structural adjustment, debt burdens, and so on.

In an article from 2021, Perry (2021: 7) indicates that the post-2015 development agenda has sought additional overseas aid in order to initiate a greater thrust for attracting private foreign investment. He asserts that the 2030 Agenda, and its financial framework, represents an evolution in the process toward increasing forms of financial intervention and extraction – with particular attention on new financing arrangements and enclosures that move away from public finance and domestic resource mobilization and toward a greater emphasis on bonds, derivatives, blended finance, and debt. He argues that the intentional and uneven integration of developing countries in the global financial system has resulted in increasing debt and financial speculation in developing countries, which, in turn, contributes to vulnerabilities (see also Chapter 11). He asserts that financial crises in many developing countries have an adverse impact at the macro-level on governments' ability to pursue the SDGs and at the micro-level on households' resilience. In addition, debt accumulation constitutes obstacles to achieving the SDGs and identifying appropriate financing mechanisms that support development (Perry, 2021: 8).

Schleicher et al. (2018: 46) highlight that the SDGs have been argued to promote a highly contested neoliberal capitalist approach to development through the promotion of an open trading system under the World Trade Organization (WTO) (target 17.10). Supiot (2020: 122) states that in 1994, the WTO was created outside the UN system to generalize competition between nations, which are individually encouraged to maximize their comparative advantage. Unlike for different branches of the UN system, the WTO has a tribunal that allows it to enforce its trade standards across its 164 member states. This has led to a conflict of legal logics at the international level, juxtaposing the principles and rules of international trade and finance, which treat work, medicines, culture, and natural resources as mere economic assets in competition on an open market, with the principles and standards of the UN. Supiot (2020: 122) argues that no institution is currently capable of harmonizing the private law rules governing the global market (regulations on property, free competition, free movement of capital and goods) with the non-market dimensions of labor, health, culture, and the environment. According to Supiot, this has contributed to the rise in inequality, the social and environmental race to the bottom, and the mass emigration from countries that have no future to offer their youth (see also Chapter 11).

Looking at enterprises, Supiot states that they have undergone two major structural changes over the past 40 years. The first was their financialization, subjecting their executives to the short-term financial interests of their shareholders. The second was their fragmentation across international production networks. The Fordist model of the enterprise was thus replaced by networks of global supply and production chains. This new model was made possible by IT instruments that allow certain tasks to be outsourced to contractors, while continuing to monitor them. This mode of organization encourages "law shopping," or the transfer of activities to countries with looser social, fiscal, and environmental rules. Economic power in these production or distribution networks relies less on the material ownership of the means of production than on the intellectual property of their information systems (Supiot, 2020: 123). In this context, Supiot criticizes multinational businesses of doing in the developing countries what they would never do in developed countries. Quoting Pope Francis, Menton et al. (2019: 1632) state that after

Affirmative and critical perspectives on the 2030 Agenda 107

ceasing their activity and withdrawing, multinationals leave behind great human and environmental liabilities, such as unemployment, abandoned towns, the depletion of natural reserves, deforestation, the impoverishment of agriculture and local stock breeding, open pits, riven hills, and polluted rivers that are no longer sustainable.

Theme 5: Ecological depth and loss & damages

Perry (2021: 11) points to the fact that the onset of ever more ferocious typhoons, storms, longer droughts, and flooding has placed climate adaptation, loss, and damage as central concerns for lesser-industrialized countries, which have limited fiscal capacity to recover and rebuild. However, according to Perry (2021: 12), loss and damage concerns are relegated in the political economy of climate finance owing to the lack of interest especially in the United States, despite the most marginalized countries and populations making claims on the international community to meet these costs in the spirit of "common and differentiated responsibilities." In addition, Menton et al. (2019: 1632) observed that the Paris COP (Conference of Parties) agreement of 2015 explicitly excluded "environmental liability" for climate change. This means that there is no recognition of those who claim that environmental liabilities (or, equivalently, ecological debts) should be faced. According to Menton et al. (2019: 1632), however, a true ecological debt exists, particularly between the Global North and South, connected to commercial imbalances with effects on the climate and the environment, and the disproportionate use of natural resources by certain countries over long periods of time (see also Chapter 3).

Perry (2021: 1f) argues that current development financing arrangements under the SDGs would increase the cost burdens and compromise the Global South's capacities to democratically manage and meet their developmental needs, owing to accumulating loss and damage from major extreme climate-induced events. He states that there are no specific and targeted international funding mechanisms to meet these massive losses and damages, and that finance operates as an entanglement of power relations accruing rent from climate devastation, returning the world close to the period of colonialization under new guises and spatial orientations. According to Perry (2021: 20), climate devastation should constitute an area for reparations based on current or future incidents/needs at a global level.

Theme 6: Decent work and just transition

The notion of Just Transition has been criticized for its vagueness, and its inoperability in practice, and for being used to fight for various conceptualizations of justice (Kreinin, 2020: 1). Winkler and Williams (2017:1026) refer to two conflicting visions of Just Transition: the market-centered business approach, informing the economic growth side of the goal, and the rights-based approach, which focuses on decent work for all. They argue that, rather than resolving the conflict between these visions, the SDGs have merged them and made the realization of SDG 8 dependent on economic growth. At the same time, they acknowledge that SDG 8 includes important levers by which human rights advocates can demand accountability for realizing decent work for all. Oxfam (2022: 46) argues that the undermining of trade unions and workers' rights – for example, to strike or to collectively bargain – has been central to the increase in inequality and counterproductive to a Just Transition. The organization proposes that governments should set legal standards to protect the rights of workers to unionize and to strike, and that they should rescind laws that undermine these rights, which protect freedom of speech and association and civic and political rights for all.

To Velicu and Barca (2020: 270), despite its welcoming attempts to support workers in gaining more rights within future green politics, the version of Just Transition in the SDGs that focus on supporting workers as fixed identities neglects its own contribution to the reproduction of the system's privileges and inequalities by not engaging the possibilities of change implied in the idea (and practice) of transforming labor relations and social metabolism away from capitalism. The authors want to call attention to the fact that the position of being a waged worker, no matter how valuable and entitled to benefits, serves to reproduce alienation and reification of workers as proletarians, depending on a wage relation to survive. They argue that such naturalized hierarchies end up embracing an exclusively redistributive vision of justice intended as benefits-recognition and compensations for harms upon "minority groups" from a system that in fact thrives on creating such groups themselves, and not just the harms they suffer (Velicu & Barca, 2020: 265). Velicu and Barca (2020: 270) argue that an alternative, equality-based theory of Just Transition could be an opportunity for workers to redesign the productive system on equal terms with capital, or even away from it, according to their autonomous needs, creativity, and abilities in self-management of the commons (see also Chapters 10 and 11).

General framings of critical views

As presented above, from different perspectives, the same goals and targets of the 2030 Agenda have been assessed with very different conclusions regarding their outcomes – positive and negative, respectively. One reason for this may be that the assessments concentrate on different levels of the SDGs. The Drivers-Pressures-States-Impacts-Responses (DPSIR) framework used by the European Environment Agency (EEA) can help in classifying the SDG targets. "State" in this terminology refers to the socio-ecological situation – be it the current one or a desired future one. "Impacts" are the changes of the state caused by "pressures," which are, in turn, caused and directed by "driving forces." "Responses" are policy actions that can address each of the states but with different intentions and effects (Spangenberg, 2016: 313).

By applying this framework on the SDGs, Spangenberg (2016: 313) reaches the following conclusion: targets addressing states and impact are multiple, targets for pressures are largely missing, and targets referring to driving forces are mentioned (sustained growth, unconditioned free markets, free trade, and globalization) as the continuing basis of societal and environmental development – but not problematized – and there are no targets referring to responses. While SDG targets should address unsustainable trends, Spangenberg (2016: 314) argues that they focus on changing unsustainable states and impacts, neglecting the need to change pressures, and supporting counter-productive drivers such as sustained GDP growth, modernization-led development concepts, free trade, and deregulation (see also Chapter 11).

The DPSIR framework analysis implies that many actors may value the description of aims, states, and impacts of the 2030 Agenda and the SDGs, whereas other actors concentrate on the missing parts related to pressures, drivers, and responses. As demonstrated in this chapter, it may also imply that many actors agree with the presentation of driving forces while other actors strongly disagree. In this last part of the chapter, drawing on an article by Kagan and Burton (2018), we will turn our focus to a critical understanding of some of the mutual enforcing drivers that contribute to the fundamental shaping of socioecological challenges.

Kagan and Burton (2018: 288f) argue that the world is in an unprecedented time of turmoil and crisis. They outline six different, although mutually enforcing crises, pertaining to: (1) ecology; (2) energy; (3) demography; (4) economy; (5) work; and (6) social and cultural conditions. They further state that these crises tend to erode the promise of the SDGs by sharing the following characteristics: they have a systemic nature; they are complex and nonlinear; they differently affect different nations and groups within nations; they lead to a succession of misery, conflicts, and migration; their nature is not transparent; and they present the global society with wicked problems and unprecedented challenges (Kagan & Burton, 2018: 289). In addition to these crises, other crises might be added pertaining to health, security, and food.

To understand the drivers of the different crises, Kagan and Burton (2018: 289f) apply the theoretical framework of ideology-action-structure complexes. Ideology, here, refers not just to ideas but also to socially embedded and embodied systems of thought about the way things are and how they should be. Ideologies reflect structure but not in a simple manner. They shape and constrain actions without fully determining them. Structure refers to the organization of power, institutions, and ordered systems (e.g., economic arrangements). Action refers to socially structured practices and everyday activities: conversations, interactions, and behaviors that people engage with collectively and that produce, reproduce, resist, and potentially transform both ideology and structure.

The authors cluster Western ideology-action-structure complexes in terms of some key interconnected dimensions deriving from critical sociology, psychology, and political economy. They suggest seven preliminary core complexes (Kagan & Burton, 2018: 290ff):

1 Linear progress: Progress is a culturally located idea, absent in some languages. It implies a linear path from the primitive to the modern, with no detours and no end. It is authoritarian since it defines other paths as "out of scope";
2 The primacy of exploitation: The system depends on exploitation. The high levels of consumption of the few (globally), mostly living in the core capitalist countries, depend on labor exploitation and to varying degrees on the ruthless exploitation of the planet's living and mineral resources;
3 Mono-culturality and the suppression of other cultural systems: Particular cultural forms dominate. Here, culture means the ordinary ways people live and pass on and share their way of life through traditions, crafts, arts, rituals, and the material trappings of everyday life;
4 Assumed superiority: Western civilization is perceived as the primary goal to reach. It follows then that other cultures (and hence peoples) are inferior. This is deeply ingrained in Western education, culture, and foreign and domestic policies;
5 The rational administration of complexity: This denotes the administrative impulse to order and simplify, rather than describing the dimensions and layers of complexity and working with the flow. By reducing complexity to a few elements and controlling them, the hope is to manage the complex system itself;
6 Taming natures: The wild, the natural, is to be controlled – to be mastered, enclosed, and channeled, or suppressed. It is seen as, or turned into, natural resources. It is viewed as separate from humanity, and humanity as separate from it. When valued, it is appreciated in a distorted version of itself. The ideology of man's dominion over nature is upheld by actions creating environmental degradation and artificial means of controlling the elements and the structures of technological solutions; and
7 The dominance of exchange and possession: What was once free is subject to exchange relations. That which was once common is now owned, in private hands, for the purposes of shareholder profit rather than the common good (see also Chapters 11 and 12).

What becomes clear from this presentation of ideology-action-structure complexes is that although the adoption of the SDGs has been a major effort by the UN system, its member states, and the participating NGOs and grassroots organizations, assessments of the SDGs are subject to deeply divided interests and socio-cultural worldviews that effect positions and values regarding possible solutions to the multitude of interwoven crises. Further, we may ask ourselves whether we get the fullest picture of a crisis, when looking at its particularities, or whether we should try instead to understand the interdependencies between simultaneously occurring crises. Some argue for a reformist transition of the existing societal structures and institutions. This is what is predominantly expressed by the 2030 Agenda and the SDGs. Others argue that we need a complete transformation of existing structures regarding economy, power, institutions, and culture if we want to create a freer, saver, and more equal world that keeps all of us within the safety margins of the planetary boundaries (see also Chapters 11 and 12). Here, we have highlighted examples of both views.

Summary

In this chapter, we have turned our attention from UN perspectives of challenges and regulations pertaining to climate change, biodiversity loss, resource depletion, and socioecological unsustainable development to external perspectives dealing with the same issues.

The 2030 Agenda of Sustainable Development and the SDGs have been welcomed by proponents of human rights and Global South perspectives, as well as by the International Labor Organization (ILO). Positive assessments from these perspectives are based on the experience of real involvement in the preparation and adoption of the Agenda and the SDGs, along with a recognition of the fact that the perspectives have left significant imprints in the documents regarding visions, goals, targets, and indicators. Some of the major movements working with environmental justice, climate justice, and energy justice voice significantly more critical views on the ability of the 2030 Agenda and the SDGs to promote socioecological sustainable development. For example, these movements call for a global defense of the commons, the changing of global power relations, the keeping of fossil fuels in the ground, the payment of historical debts from the Global North to the Global South, food and land sovereignty for vulnerable communities, the prevention of injustices stemming from land-grabbing and extraction, and reinvestment and socially stratified redistribution to support populations that are most at risk of suffering not only from environmental and climate change but also from mitigation and adaption measures.

Critical voices in the academic community reiterate many of the views expressed by social movements. We have chosen to focus on six themes in which this academic criticism is expressed with particular emphasis: poverty reduction; justice; growth; finance, businesses, and economy; ecological depth; and labor conditions. Following Spangenberg (2016) and his application of the DPSIR framework, the different types of criticism generally reflect that only to a very limited degree do the SDGs address global as well as regional and national societal structures, power relations, and driving forces of climate change, biodiversity loss, resource depletion, inequality, misrecognition, and a lack of participation.

To better understand structures, power relations, and driving forces, we have presented the concept of ideology-action-structure complexes that focus on the interrelations between, on the one hand, mutually enforcing crises that the world is encountering, and on the other, core ideology-action-structure complexes.

We shall return to, and deepen, our critical discussion especially in Chapter 11, on governance, and Chapter 12, on the Anthropocene. First, however, in the next part of the book, we shall turn our attention to the question of how ecological and socioecological issues are understood and governed in the EU. The EU is a union of some of the wealthiest nations in the world. It has a reputation of being at the forefront in dealing with environmental and climate change issues at a regional as well as a global level. We will look at the EU's overall green growth strategy, the European Green Deal, and take a closer look at some of the more specific areas relating to climate change: energy, resources, agriculture, biodiversity, and Just Transition. Our overall guiding questions will be: what is the EU doing, and to which extent do the actions of the EU support the aim of creating a just and fair world within the confines of the Planet's ecological boundaries?

References

Adelman, S. (2017). *The sustainable development goals, Anthropocentrism and neoliberalism.* Draft chapter that has been accepted for publication by Edward Elgar Publishing in the forthcoming book Global Goals: Law, Theory & Implementation edited by French, D. and Kotze, L. due to be published in 2018. Retrieved from: https://wrap.warwick.ac.uk/90232/3/WRAP-sustainable-development-goals-Anthropocentrism-Adelman-2017.pdf

Egmose, J., Jacobsen, S. G., Hauggaard-Nielsen, H. and Hulgård, L. (2021). The regenerative turn: on the re-emergence of reciprocity embedded in living ecologies. *Globalizations*, 18(7), 1271–1276. DOI: 10.1080/14747731.2021.1911508

Fukuda-Parr, S. and Muchhala, B. (2020). The Southern origins of sustainable development goals: ideas, actors, aspirations. *World Development*, 126(C), 1–11. DOI: 10.1016/j.worlddev.2019.104706

Gilbert, N. (2004). *Transformation of the welfare state: The silent surrender of public responsibility.* Oxford: Oxford University Press. Retrieved from: DOI: 10.1093/0195140745.001.0001

Healy, N. and Barry, J. (2017). Politicizing energy justice and energy system transitions: Fossil fuel divestment and a "just transition". *Energy Policy*, 108, 451–459. Retrieved from https://www.academia.edu/33675861/Politicizing_energy_justice_and_energy_system_transitions_Fossil_fuel_divestment_and_a_just_transition_?auto=citations&from=cover_page

Heyen, D. A., Menzemer, L., Wolff. F., Beznea, A. and Williams, R. (2020). Just transition in the context of EU environmental policy and the European green deal. Issue Paper under Task 3 of the 'Service contract on future EU environment policy'. Öko-institut e.V. for the European Commission, 48 pages. Retrieved from: https://ec.europa.eu/environment/enveco/growth_jobs_social/pdf/studies/just_transition_issue_paper_final_clean.pdf.

ILO (2016). ILO implementation plan 2030 Agenda for sustainable development. Retrieved from: https://www.ilo.org/wcmsp5/groups/public/---dgreports/---dcomm/---webdev/documents/publication/wcms_510122.pdf

ILO (2017). A just transition to a sustainable future – Next steps for Europe. Retrieved from: https://www.ilo.org/wcmsp5/groups/public/---europe/---ro-geneva/---ilo-brussels/documents/publication/wcms_614024.pdf

ILO (2020). Green jobs. The ILO DW for SDGs Notes Series. Retrieved from: https://www.ilo.org/global/topics/dw4sd/theme-by-sdg-targets/WCMS_561751/lang--en/index.htm

IRP (2019). Global resources outlook 2019: Natural resources for the future we want. In: B. Oberle, S. Bringezu, S. Hatfield-Dodds, S. Hellweg, H. Schandl, J. Clement, L. Cabernard, N. Che, D. Chen, H. Droz-Georget, P. Ekins, M. Fischer-Kowalski, M. Flörke, S. Frank, A. Froemelt, A. Geschke, M. Haupt, P. Havlik, R. Hüfner, M. Lenzen, M. Lieber, B. Liu, Y. Lu, S. Lutter, J. Mehr, A. Miatto, D. Newth, C. Oberschelp, M. Obersteiner, S. Pfister, E. Piccoli, R. Schaldach, J. Schüngel, T. Sonderegger, A. Sudheshwar, H. Tanikawa, E. van der Voet, C. Walker, J. West, Z. Wang & B. Zhu (eds.), *A report of the international resource panel*. Nairobi, Kenya: United Nations Environment Programme, 162 pages. Retrieved from: https://www.resourcepanel.org/reports/global-resources-outlook

Jessop, B. (2002). The changing governance of welfare: recent trends in its primary functions, scale, and models of coordination. *Social Policy & Administration*, 33(4), 348–359.

Kagan, C. & Burton, M. H. (2018). Putting the 'social' into sustainability science. In: W. L. Filho (ed.), *Handbook of sustainability science and research*. World Sustainability Series, 285–298. Switzerland: Springer International Publishing. DOI: 10.1007/978-3-319-63007-6

Koehler, G. (2016). Assessing the SDGs from the standpoint of ecosocial policy: Using the SDGs subversively. *Journal of International and Comparative Social Policy*, 2016, 1–16. DOI: 10.1080/21699763.2016.1198715

Kreinin, K. (2020). Typologies of "Just Transitions": Towards social-ecological transformation, Vienna University of Economics and Business, Institute for Ecological Economics. Working Paper Series 35/2020, 14 pages. Retrieved from: https://epub.wu.ac.at/7814/1/WP_35.pdf

Martinez-Alier, J., Temper, L., Bene, D. D. and Arnim Scheidel, A. (2016). Is there a global environmental justice movement? *The Journal of Peasant Studies*, 43(3), 731–755. DOI: 10.1080/03066150.2016.1141198

Menton, M., Larrea, C., Latorre, S., Martinez-Alier, J., Peck, M., Temper, L. and Walter M. (2019). Environmental justice and the SDGs: from synergies to gaps and contradictions. *Sustainability Science*, 15, 1621–1636. DOI: 10.1007/s11625-020-00789-8

Newell, P., Srivastava, S., Naess, L. O., Contreras, G. A. T. and Price, R. (2020). Towards Transformative climate justice: Key challenges and future directions for research. Working Paper Volume 2020, Number 540. The Institute of Development Studies, 151 pages. Retrieved from: https://opendocs.ids.ac.uk/opendocs/bitstream/handle/20.500.12413/15497/Wp540_Towards_Transformative_Climate_Justice.pdf?sequence=1&isAllowed=y

Oxfam (2022). *Inequality Kills. The unparalleled action needed to combat unprecedented inequality in the wake of COVID-19.* Oxfam International. DOI: 10.21201/2022.8465

Perry, K. P. (2021). The New 'Bond-age', climate crisis and the case for climate reparations: unpicking old/new colonialities of finance for development within the SDGs. Retrieved from: https://papers.ssrn.com/sol3/papers.cfm?abstract_id=3739103

Robra, B., and Heikkurinen, P. (2019). Degrowth and the sustainable development goals. In: L. Filho, A. Azul, L. Brandli, P. Özuyar & T. Wall (eds.), *Decent work and economic growth. Encyclopedia of the UN sustainable development goals*, 253–262. Cham: Springer. DOI: 10.1007/978-3-319-71058-7_37-1.

Schleicher, J., Schaafsma, M. and Baskar, V. (2018). Will the sustainable development goals address the links between poverty and the natural environment? *Current Opinions in Environmental Sustainability*, 34, 43–47. DOI: 10.1016/j.cosust.2018.09.004

Schlosberg, D. and Collins, L. B. (2014). From environmental to climate justice: Climate change and the discourse of environmental justice. *WIREs Climate Change*, 5(3), 359–374. DOI: 10.1002/wcc.275

Spangenberg, J. H. (2016). Hot air or comprehensive progress? A critical assessment of the SDGs. *Sustainable Development*, 25, 311–321. DOI: 10.1002/sd.1657

Supiot, A. (2020). The tasks ahead of the ILO at its centenary. *International Labour Review*, 159(1), 117–136. DOI: 10.1111/ilr.12164

Tokar, B. (2019). On the evolution and continuing development of the climate justice movement. In: T. Jafry (ed.), *Routledge Handbook of Climate Justice*, 1–13. Oxon and New York: Routledge.

UNDP (2020). The next frontier – Human development and the Anthropocene. *Human Development Report 2020*, 412 pages. Retrieved from: http://hdr.undp.org/sites/default/files/hdr2020.pdf

Velicu, I. and Barca, S. (2020). The just transition and its work of inequality. *Sustainability: Science, Practice and Policy*, 16(1), 263–273. DOI: 10.1080/15487733.2020.1814585´

Wennersten, R. and Qie, S. (2018). United Nations sustainable development goals for 2030 and resource use. In: W. L. Filho (ed.), *Handbook of sustainability science and research*. World Sustainability Series, 317–339. Switzerland: Springer International Publishing. DOI: 10.1007/978-3-319-63007-6

Winkler, I. T. and Williams, C. (2017). The sustainable development goals and human rights: A critical early review. *The International Journal of Human Rights*, 21(8), 1023–1028. DOI: 10.1080/13642987.2017.1348695

Part II

European ecological and socioecological challenges, and EU solutions

Focusing on climate change, biodiversity, resources, and Just Transition, the second part of this book turns its attention to the European Green Deal strategy and to selected areas covered by the strategy: climate change and energy; resources and circular economy; agriculture and food-systems; biodiversity and Nature's contribution to people; and Just Transition.

Part II consists of six chapters:

Chapter 5: The European Green Deal and the State of the European Environment
Chapter 6: Climate Change-Motivated Development of EU's Energy Production and Use Systems
Chapter 7: Resources and the Circular Economy
Chapter 8: The Food System and Agriculture
Chapter 9: Biodiversity and Nature's Contributions to People
Chapter 10: Just Transition in the EU

5 The European Green Deal and the state of the European environment

Anders Siig Andersen, Henrik Hauggaard-Nielsen, Thomas Budde Christensen, and Lars Hulgaard

> We should never forget that competitive sustainability has always been at the heart of our social market economy.
>
> Ursula von der Leyen, 2019

Introduction

In the second part of this book, we turn our attention to the overall European Union (EU) strategy pertaining to climate change, biodiversity, resources, and socioecological issues and to selected areas covered by the strategy: climate change and energy; resources and the circular economy; agriculture and food systems; biodiversity; and the Just Transition.

Announced by the European Commission in December 2019, the EU's new strategy—the European Green Deal—commits the EU to becoming climate-neutral by 2050 while promising to help companies to become world leaders in clean products and green technologies. The measures in the strategy are aimed at achieving significant reductions in carbon emissions. A net zero target will be given legislative force in a new Climate Law. The aim of the European Green Deal is for the EU to become the world's first "climate-neutral bloc" by 2050.

The European Green Deal covers many different areas, including: (1) the overall climate ambition of the EU; (2) sector- and system-oriented strategies regarding energy, building and construction, industry and resources, biodiversity and eco-services, food, agriculture and fisheries, mobility, and pollution; (3) levers in the sustainable transition, such as global cooperation, finance and investments, regulation and governance, innovation, and research; and (4) measures to support a just and fair transition and the participation of stakeholders and citizens.

In this chapter we present an overview of the European Green Deal and the scientific knowledge and recommendations provided by the European Environmental Agency (EEA). The first part of the chapter presents the background of the Green Deal and gives an overall characterization of the different areas covered by the strategy. The second part describes the state of the environment in Europe and the policy recommendations proposed by the

EEA. The third part analyzes the European Green Deal in the light of these recommendations.

The European Green Deal

Background

On December 11, 2019, the European Commission published a communication on "The European Green Deal" (European Commission, 2019a), accompanied by a roadmap for its implementation (European Commission, 2019b).

From the beginning of its mandate in December 2019, the new European Commission headed by President Ursula von der Leyen declared climate policy to be a top priority (von der Leyen, 2019). The emergence of the European Green Deal became possible only by the simultaneous overlapping of multiple streams that came together in 2019 (Munta, 2020: 9). First, by 2019, the perception that climate change and environmental degradation needed to be addressed had urgently penetrated deep into mainstream political thinking. In Europe, growing concern about climate change was reflected in stronger electoral support for Green parties in the 2019 European elections, especially in some larger Western Member States. Moreover, there was the emergence of grassroots movements such as "Fridays for Future" and "Youth Strike for Climate." Second, at the policy level, the momentum for a comprehensive European Green Deal had gradually been building during the last decade, and there had been a sustained evolution of the EU's legislative and non-legislative activities regarding the circular economy, clean mobility, waste policies, sustainable agriculture, resource-efficient construction, consumer rights, and other related areas. Third, the political circumstances in the European Parliament had changed in favor of the Greens, who had gained more political leverage. Von der Leyen had to balance the wishes of the EU leaders who had nominated her and the policy priorities of the Greens and the Liberals (Renew Europe), who had the power to vote her nomination down. Persuading the Socialist Frans Timmermans to manage the European Green Deal portfolio increased the credibility of the strategy. The expiry of the Europe 2020 strategy for smart, sustainable, and inclusive growth created a window of opportunity for the Commission to develop a new growth strategy that would guide the European Council's strategic agenda for 2019–2024 (Munta, 2020: 9; Siddi, 2020: 6).

Overall characterization of the European Green Deal

The EU Commission has presented the European Green Deal as a growth strategy that aims to transform the EU into a fair and prosperous society, with a modern, resource-efficient, and competitive economy. It will have no net emissions of greenhouse gases (GHGs) by 2050, and economic growth will be decoupled from resource use. Another aim is to protect, conserve, and enhance natural capital and to protect the health and well-being of citizens from environment-related risks and impacts. Moreover, the European Green Deal emphasizes that the transition must be just and inclusive. It will put people first, focusing on the regions, industries, and workers that will face the greatest challenges. The European Pillar of Social Rights will guide action to ensure that no one is left behind. According to the Green Deal, active public participation is paramount if the policies are to be accepted and successful.

The European Green Deal indicates that there is a need to rethink policies for clean energy supply that affect the economy, industry, production and consumption, large-scale infrastructure, transport, food and agriculture, construction, taxation, and social benefits. The European Green Deal stresses the importance of increasing the value assigned to protecting and restoring natural ecosystems, to ensuring the sustainable use of resources, and to improving human health. Because these areas for action are interlinked and mutually reinforcing, according to the Green Deal, attention will have to be paid to the potential trade-offs between economic, environmental, and social objectives.

The European Green Deal states that the EU should promote and invest in the necessary digital transformation. The Commission will explore measures to ensure that digital technologies can accelerate and maximize the impact of policies for tackling climate change and protecting the environment.

According to the European Green Deal, all EU actions and policies will contribute to its objectives. Policy responses will seek to maximize benefits for health, quality of life, resilience, and competitiveness. This will require coordination at all levels to exploit the available synergies across all policy areas.

The Commission will work with the Member States to step up EU efforts to ensure that current legislation and policies relevant to the European Green Deal are enforced and effectively implemented. The strategy recommends that the environmental and climate dimension should be included in the European Semester for economic policy coordination. The Semester should be refocused on the priorities of the Sustainable Development Goals (SDGs), putting sustainability and the well-being of citizens at the center of economic policy. Country reports analyzing the situation in each Member State will make it possible for the Commission and the Council of EU to issue (non-binding) country-specific recommendations. Member States will begin updating their national energy and climate plans in 2023, and these plans should reflect the new climate ambitions. The Commission will continue to ensure that all relevant legislation is rigorously enforced.

The Commission has announced that it will use the provisions in the treaties that allow the European Parliament and the Council to adopt proposals on energy taxation through the ordinary legislative procedure of qualified majority voting rather than unanimity.

As stated in the European Green Deal, public investment and increased efforts are required to direct private capital toward climate and environmental action, while avoiding a lock-in into unsustainable practices.

Furthermore, the European Green Deal notes that the global challenges of climate change and environmental degradation require a global response to promote and implement environmental, climate, and energy policies across the world. To do so, the European Commission has proposed developing "green deal diplomacy," which will focus on encouraging and supporting other countries and global stakeholders to adopt more sustainable development. By following up with diplomacy, trade policy, development support, and other external policies, the EU can act as an advocate for these initiatives.

The main areas of intervention of the European Green Deal

In the following, we will summarize some of the main areas of intervention addressed by the European Green Deal.

1. *Climate ambitions*

   The Commission will propose the first European Climate Law. This will enshrine the 2050 climate-neutrality objective in legislation. The Climate Law will ensure that all EU policies contribute to the climate-neutrality objective and that all sectors play their part. The Commission will present a comprehensive and impact-assessed plan to increase the EU's GHG emission reductions target for 2030 to at least 50 percent and toward 55 percent compared with 1990 levels. To deliver these additional GHG emission reductions, the Commission will review and propose to revise where necessary all relevant climate-related policy instruments (see also Chapter 6).

2. *Supplying clean, affordable, and secure energy*

   The European Green Deal states that further decarbonizing of the energy system is critical for reaching the climate objectives. The production and use of energy across sectors account for more than 75 percent of the EU's GHG emissions. Accordingly, the EU will prioritize energy efficiency and develop a power sector that is based largely on renewable sources, complemented by the rapid phasing out of coal and decarbonizing gas. Moreover, the EU's energy supply must be secure and affordable for consumers and businesses. The European Green Deal argues that it is important to ensure that the European energy market is fully integrated, interconnected, and digitalized.

   The Commission will propose revisions of relevant legislative measures to deliver its increased climate ambition. Furthermore, the Commission will consider extending the EU Emissions Trading System to new sectors, revising the Energy Taxation Directive, and establishing a Carbon Border Adjustment Mechanism (CBAM) for selected sectors. The Commission will also propose a new, more ambitious EU strategy on adaptations to climate change (see also Chapter 6).

3. *Mobilizing industry for a clean and circular economy*

   As stated by the European Green Deal, from 1970 to 2017, the annual global extraction of materials tripled and it continues to grow. EU industry still accounts for 20 percent of the EU's GHG emissions. The EU remains too "linear" and dependent on the throughput of new materials extracted, traded, and processed into goods and disposed of as waste or emissions. Only 12 percent of material used comes from recycling (see also Chapter 7).

The Commission will adopt an EU industrial strategy that addresses the two challenges of the green transformation and the digital transformation. Together with an industrial strategy, a new circular economy action plan will help to modernize the EU's economy, allowing the EU to benefit from the opportunities of the circular economy, domestically and globally. To simplify waste management for citizens and ensure cleaner secondary materials for businesses, the Commission will propose an EU model for separate waste collection. The Commission believes that the EU should stop exporting its waste outside of the EU and will, therefore, revisit rules on waste shipments and illegal exports. The European Green Deal states that EU industry needs "climate and resource front-runners." Priority areas include clean hydrogen; fuel cells and other alternative fuels; energy storage; and carbon capture, storage, and utilization. As an example, the Commission will support breakthrough technologies for clean steel that will lead to a zero-carbon steel-making process.

The Commission will ensure that digital technologies can accelerate and maximize the impact of policies for tackling climate change and protecting the environment. The Commission will also improve the energy efficiency and circular economy performance of the digital sector itself and assess the need for more transparency on the environmental impact of electronic communication services.

The European Green Deal states that ensuring the supply of sustainable raw materials, in particular of the critical raw materials necessary for clean technologies, digital, space, and defense applications, can be done by diversifying the supply from both primary and secondary sources.

The Green Deal argues that public authorities, including the EU institutions, should lead by example and ensure that their procurement is green (see also Chapters 6 and 7).

4 Building and renovating in an energy- and resource-efficient way

According to the European Green Deal, the construction, use, and renovation of buildings require vast amounts of energy and mineral resources (for example, sand, gravel, and cement). Buildings account for 40 percent of the energy consumed. Today, the annual renovation rate of the building stock varies from 0.4 to 1.2 percent in the Member States. This rate should double to reach the EU's energy efficiency and climate objectives. Moreover, 50 million consumers in the EU find it difficult to keep their home adequately warm.

Against this background, the Commission will encourage the EU and the Member States to conduct a "wave of renovation" of public and private buildings and will enforce the legislation on the energy performance of buildings. It will focus on the renovation of schools and hospitals and lift national regulatory barriers that inhibit energy-efficiency investments in rented and multi-ownership buildings. The Commission will also consider the possibility of including emissions from buildings in the EU Emissions Trading System.

Furthermore, the Commission will seek to ensure that the design of new and renovated buildings is aligned with the needs of the circular economy and leads to increased digitalization and climate-proofing of the building stock. The Commission has proposed working with stakeholders on a new initiative on renovation. This will include an open platform that brings together the buildings and construction sector, architects, engineers, and local authorities to address the barriers to renovation. This initiative will also include financing schemes under InvestEU (see also Chapters 6 and 7).

5 *Accelerating the shift to sustainable and smart mobility*

Transport accounts for a quarter of the EU's GHG emissions. This proportion is still growing. According to the Green Deal, to achieve climate-neutrality, a 90 percent reduction in transport emissions is necessary by 2050. Road, rail, aviation, and waterborne transport will have to contribute to the reduction.

The Commission will adopt a strategy for sustainable and smart mobility that will address these challenges and tackle emission sources. Its aims include:

- Boosting multimodal transport by increasing the capacity of railways and waterborne transport, including short-sea shipping, and making the EU transport system and infrastructure able to support new sustainable mobility services;
- Supporting the deployment of public recharging and refueling points;
- Accelerating the deployment of zero- and low-emission vehicles and vessels;
- Developing a smart system for traffic management and "mobility as a service" solutions; and
- Ramping up the production and deployment of sustainable alternative transport fuels.

Furthermore, the European Green Deal emphasizes the importance of ensuring that the price of transportation reflects its impact on the environment and on health, ending fossil-fuel subsidies, achieving effective road pricing in the EU, and ending tax exemptions such as for aviation and maritime fuels.

The European Green Deal seeks to reduce air pollution by developing more stringent air pollutant standards, including emissions standards for combustion-engine vehicles and CO_2 emission performance standards for cars and vans. Furthermore, the Green Deal states that the EU will decrease air pollution by regulating the access of the most polluting ships to EU ports, obliging docked ships to use shore-side electricity, tackling the emissions of pollutants by airplanes and airport operations, applying European emissions trading to road transport and the maritime sector, and reducing the allowances allocated for free to airlines under the EU Emissions Trading System (see also below in this chapter).

6 *Farm to fork: A fair, healthy, and environmentally friendly food system*

The European Green Deal states that European food is famous for being safe, nutritious, and high quality and that it should also become the global standard for sustainability (see also Chapter 8). Food production still results in air, water, and soil pollution, contributes to the loss of biodiversity and climate change, and consumes excessive amounts of natural resources, while a significant amount of food is wasted. At the same time, low-quality diets are contributing to obesity and diseases such as cancer.

The Commission will present a "Farm-to-Fork" strategy and launch a broad stakeholder debate covering all the stages of the food chain. The Farm-to-Fork strategy should encompass the following interventions:

- Rewarding farmers for improved environmental and climate performance;
- Motivating Member States to develop the potential of sustainable seafood as a source of low-carbon food;
- Significantly reducing the use and risk of chemical pesticides, as well as the use of fertilizers and antibiotics;
- Achieving a circular economy by minimizing the environmental impact of the food processing and retail sectors;
- Stimulating sustainable food consumption and ensuring the availability of affordable healthy food for all;
- Helping consumers to choose a healthy and sustainable diet and to reduce food waste by providing better information on where their food comes from, its nutritional value, and its environmental footprint; and
- Improving the position of farmers in the value chain.

7 *Preserving and restoring ecosystems and biodiversity*

The European Green Deal states that ecosystems provide essential services, such as food, fresh water, clean air, and shelter. They mitigate the impact of natural disasters, pests, and diseases and help regulate the climate. However, according to the Green Deal, the EU did not meet some of its most important biodiversity objectives for 2020 (see also Chapter 9).

The Commission will present a biodiversity strategy. Proposed actions will include increasing the number of protected biodiversity-rich land and sea areas by adding these to the Natura 2000 network. Member States should also reinforce their cross-border cooperation to protect and more effectively restore the areas covered by this network. The Commission will support Member States in improving and restoring damaged ecosystems to good ecological status, including carbon-rich ecosystems. The biodiversity strategy will also include proposals to green European cities and increase biodiversity in urban spaces. The Commission will consider drafting a nature restoration plan and will provide funding to help Member States to achieve this aim.

According to the European Green Deal, all EU policies should contribute to preserving and restoring Europe's natural capital, such as the Farm-to-Fork strategy (by reducing the impact of pesticides and fertilizers), fisheries policies (by reducing the impact of fishing on ecosystems and by establishing and managing marine protected areas), a new forest strategy (by increasing afforestation and preserving and restoring forests through measures that cover the whole forest cycle and respect ecological principles favorable to biodiversity and by promoting imports of sustainable products and sustainable value chains), and ocean policies (by improving the use of aquatic and marine resources, by managing the maritime space more sustainably, and by taking a zero-tolerance approach to illegal, unreported, and unregulated fishing).

8 *A zero-pollution ambition for a toxic-free environment*

According to the European Green Deal, creating a toxic-free environment requires action to prevent pollution from being generated as well as measures to clean and remedy areas affected by pollution. To protect Europe's citizens and ecosystems, the EU will monitor, report, prevent pollution in the air, water, soil, and consumer products. To address these interlinked challenges, the Commission will adopt a zero-pollution action plan for air, water, and soil.

The Commission will prioritize the following actions:

- Restoring the natural functions of ground and surface water;
- Tackling pollution from urban runoff and from new or particularly harmful sources of pollution, such as microplastics and chemicals including pharmaceuticals, and addressing the combined effects of different pollutants;
- Strengthening monitoring, modeling, and air quality plans to help local authorities achieve cleaner air;
- Revising air quality standards to align them more closely with the World Health Organization recommendations; and
- Reviewing EU measures to address pollution from large industrial installations.

To ensure a toxic-free environment, the Commission will present a sustainability strategy for chemicals. Following the European Green Deal, protecting citizens and the environment from chemicals and encouraging innovation in the development of safe and sustainable alternatives can be achieved by simplifying and strengthening the legal framework. The Commission will seek to improve the support given by EU agencies and scientific bodies in the "one substance—one assessment" process and provide greater transparency when prioritizing actions relating to chemicals. In parallel, the regulatory framework will reflect scientific evidence on the risk posed by endocrine disruptors, hazardous chemicals in products including imports, and the combined effects of different chemicals including very persistent chemicals.

9 *Finance, investments, and economic incentives in the EU*

The Commission estimates that achieving the current 2030 climate and energy targets will require €260 billion of additional annual investment, about 1.5 percent of 2018 GDP. This flow of investment will need to be sustained over time and will require the mobilization of both the public and private sectors. There are several relevant EU initiatives:

- The Commission has proposed that 25 percent of all EU programs should have climate mitigation measures. The Commission recommends the development of new revenue streams, for example, by levying a tax on non-recycled plastic-packaging waste. A second revenue stream could be to allocate 20 percent of the income from EU Emissions Trading System auctions to the EU budget.
- As part of the revision of the EU Emissions Trading System, the Commission will review the role of the Innovation and Modernization Funds, which are not financed by the EU's long-term budget.
- According to the European Green Deal, at least 30 percent of the InvestEU Fund will be assigned to fighting climate change. InvestEU also offers Member States the option to use the EU budgetary guarantee, for example, to deliver on climate-related cohesion policy objectives in their territories and regions. InvestEU will also strengthen cooperation with national promotional banks and institutions.
- The Commission will work with the European Investment Bank (EIB) Group, national promotional banks, and institutions, as well as with other international financial institutions. The EIB has set a target to double its overall lending on climate and environment sustainability from around 25 percent to 50 percent by 2025, thus becoming Europe's climate bank.

The private sector will be important in financing the green transition. Long-term signals will direct financial and capital flows to green investments and away from stranded assets. First, this will require that the European Parliament and Council adopt a taxonomy for classifying environmentally sustainable activities. The Commission will also support businesses in developing standardized accounting practices for natural capital within the EU and internationally. Second, opportunities will be provided for investors and companies by making it easier for them to identify sustainable investments that are credible. Third, climate and environmental risks will be managed and integrated into the financial system.

National budgets should also be "greened" to redirect public investment, consumption, and taxation toward "green priorities." At the national level, the European Green Deal will create the context for broad-based tax reforms and the elimination of subsidies for fossil fuels, thus shifting the tax burden from labor to pollution while taking social concerns into account. Furthermore, according to the European Green

Deal, Member States should better target value-added taxes to reflect increased environmental ambitions.

10 *Mobilizing research and fostering innovation*

New technology and disruptive innovation are important for achieving the objectives of the European Green Deal. The EU wants to increase the large-scale deployment and demonstration of new technologies across sectors and across the single market and to build new innovative value chains. Horizon Europe, in synergy with other EU programs, will play an important role in leveraging national public and private investments. Approximately 35 percent of the budget of Horizon Europe will fund new solutions for climate mitigation. Four "Green Deal Missions" will help deliver large-scale changes in areas such as adapting to climate change, oceans, cities, and soil. Partnerships with industry and Member States will support research and innovation in transportation including batteries, clean hydrogen, low-carbon steel-making, circular bio-based sectors, and the built environment. The European Innovation Council will dedicate funding, investment, and business acceleration services to start-ups and small and medium-sized enterprises. With an emphasis on experimentation and by working across sectors and disciplines, the EU's research and innovation agenda will take a systemic approach to achieving the aims of the Green Deal. The Horizon Europe program will also involve local communities.

Accessible data and interoperable systems are crucial for innovation. Combined with digital infrastructures and artificial intelligence solutions, these will facilitate evidence-based decision-making and expand the capacity of the EU to understand and tackle environmental challenges. One of the Commission's aims is that the digital transformation supports the ecological transition. An immediate priority will be to boost the EU's ability to predict and manage environmental disasters.

11 *The EU as a leader of the global sustainable transformation*

According to the European Green Deal, the EU will promote ambitious environmental, climate, and energy policies across the world by setting a credible example and following up with diplomacy, trade policy, development support, and other external policies. The EU will also continue to ensure that the Paris Agreement remains the multilateral framework for tackling climate change. In parallel, the EU will enhance bilateral engagement with partner countries.

The EU will cooperate with the G7 and G20 countries with an emphasis on supporting its immediate neighbors. Furthermore, the Commission will develop several environmental, energy, and climate partnerships with the Southern Neighborhood and within the Eastern Partnership. The EU will also engage with third countries on ending global fossil-fuel subsidies, phasing out financing by multilateral institutions of fossil-fuel infrastructure, strengthening sustainable financing, phasing out all new coal plant construction, and supporting actions to reduce methane emissions. Furthermore, the EU will work with global partners to develop international carbon markets to create economic incentives for climate action.

The European Green Deal acknowledges that the transition will reshape geopolitics, including the global economy, trade, and security. This will create challenges for many states and societies. The EU will work with partners to increase climate and environmental resilience to prevent these challenges from becoming sources of conflict, food insecurity, population displacement, or forced migration.

The EU's international cooperation will continue to help channel both public and private funds to achieve the transition. As public funds will not suffice, the EU and its Member States will coordinate their support to engage with partners to bridge the funding gap by mobilizing private finance. The Commission has proposed establishing a Neighborhood, Development and International Cooperation Instrument, which would aim to allocate 25 percent of its budget to climate-related objectives. The EU will build on the International Platform on Sustainable Finance to coordinate efforts on finance initiatives, such as taxonomies, disclosures, standards, and labels.

Possible issues with international trade arise partly because the European Green Deal states that all chemicals, materials, food, and other products that are placed on the European market must fully comply with relevant EU regulations and standards. The European Green Deal suggests different kinds of action to make this happen. For example, it lists the following planned or possible measures:

- Minimum requirements to prevent environmentally harmful products from being placed on the EU market;
- A "right to repair" and a ban on built-in obsolescence of devices, especially electronics;
- An electronic product passport with information on a product's origin, composition, repair and dismantling possibilities, and end of life handling;
- Boosting the market for secondary raw materials with mandatory recycled content;
- Revising the legislation on CO_2 emission performance standards for cars and vans;
- Not allowing imported food into EU markets that does not comply with relevant EU environmental standards;
- Regulatory and other measures to promote imported products and value chains that do not lead to deforestation or forest degradation; and
- Preventing the importation of hazardous chemicals.

Even more importantly, in relation to non-EU countries, the European Green Deal aims to decarbonize the overall energy system. However, if Europe implements a stringent climate policy while other parts of the world do not, there is a risk that emissions-intensive companies might leave the EU with its high carbon prices and relocate to places with significantly lower or no carbon prices. This is known as carbon leakage.

Thus, the European Green Deal recommends implementing a Carbon Border Adjustment Mechanism (CBAM) for selected sectors to reduce the risk of carbon leakage. The CBAM would ensure that the price of imports reflects more accurately their carbon content. The European Green Deal will ensure that this measure complies with World Trade Organization rules and other international obligations (for a critical discussion, see Chapter 11).

12 *A Just Transition leaving no one behind*

The Green Deal acknowledges that the environmental and climate proposals might deepen the existing inequalities between countries, regions, and different groups in society within Europe. Therefore, one of the main aims of the European Green Deal is to transform the EU into a fair society by putting people first with a focus on the regions, industries, and workers that will face the greatest challenges. Attention will be paid when there are potential trade-offs between economic, environmental, and social objectives. Furthermore, the Green Deal states that the European Pillar of Social Rights will guide action to ensure that no one is left behind.

The Green Deal notes that a socially Just Transition must be reflected in policies at EU and national levels. These include investment to provide affordable solutions to those affected by carbon pricing policies, for example, through public transport, as well as measures to address energy poverty and promote re-skilling. The macroeconomic coordination in the European Semester will support relevant national policies. According to the Green Deal, tax reforms can boost economic growth and resilience to climate shocks and help contribute to a more just society and to a Just Transition.

To promote a Just Transition, the main tool of the Green Deal will be the Just Transition Mechanism (see also Chapter 10). This mechanism will focus on the regions and sectors that are most affected by the transition. Support will be linked to promoting the transition toward low-carbon and climate-resilient activities. The Commission will work with the Member States and regions to help them develop their territorial transition plans. This mechanism will be in addition to the contribution from the EU's budget through all programs directly relevant to the transition, as well as existing European regional and social funds.

The Green Deal emphasizes that proactive re-skilling and upskilling are necessary to support the ecological transition. Funding from the EU will play an important role in supporting Europe's workforce to acquire the skills they need to transfer from declining sectors to growing sectors and to adapt to new processes. The European Green Deal notes that the existing Skills Agenda and the Youth Guarantee of the EU will be updated to enhance the employability in the green economy of those affected.

13 *Inclusion and citizen participation*

Since it will result in substantial change, the European Green Deal states that active public participation is necessary if the policies are to work and be accepted. People are concerned about jobs, heating their homes, and making ends meet, and EU institutions must engage with them. The European Green Deal has introduced the European Climate Pact, which aims to bring together citizens in all their diversity. Through the pact, national, regional, and local authorities, civil society, and industry will work closely with the EU's institutions and consultative bodies. The European Green Deal suggests that for companies and their workers, an active social dialog should help to anticipate and manage change.

The European Climate Pact will focus on different ways to engage with the public on climate action. First, it will encourage information-sharing and inspiration and foster public understanding of the threats and challenges of climate change and environmental degradation and on how to counter these. It will use multiple channels to do so, including events in Member States, which will be modeled on the Commission's ongoing citizens' dialogs. Second, there should be both real and virtual spaces where people can express their ideas and work together on ambitious action, both individually and collectively. Third, the Commission will work on building capacity to facilitate grassroots initiatives on climate change and environmental protection. Information, guidance, and educational modules are proposed to help the exchange of good practices (see also Chapter 10).

The Green Deal emphasizes the role of schools, training institutions, and universities in engaging with students, parents, and communities on the changes needed for a successful transition. The Commission will prepare a European competence framework to help develop and assess knowledge, skills, and attitudes on climate change and sustainable development. This framework will also facilitate the exchange of good practices in EU networks of teacher-training programs.

Furthermore, the Commission will consider revising existing regulations to improve access to administrative and judicial review at EU level for citizens and NGOs that have concerns about the legality of decisions that affect the climate or the environment. The Commission will also take action to improve access to justice in national courts in all Member States.

The state of the environment in Europe

The European Green Deal draws upon UN scientific reports on climate change and environmental challenges. In the previous chapters, we analyzed reports from the IPCC, IPBES, and IRP. In the following section, we will focus on the state of the environment in Europe based on a report published by the EEA: The European environment—state and outlook 2020: Knowledge for transition to a sustainable Europe (EEA, 2019). For 25 years, the EEA has operated as a knowledge broker at the interface between science, policy, and society in Europe in close partnership with the EU Commission. The EEA report draws on the knowledge base available to the EEA and the European Environment Information and Observation Network (Eionet), which is a partnership network between the EEA's 33 member countries. The EEA report addresses the priorities of the EU's Seventh Environment Action Program (7th EAP) and other broad frameworks, trends, outlooks, and systemic challenges. This EEA report is the sixth in a series of European environment state and outlook reports produced by the EEA since 1995, as mandated by its governing regulations.

The EEA report provides an overview of the state of and outlook for the environment and climate in Europe. It evaluates progress toward achieving established European environmental and climate policy goals, focusing primarily on 2020–2030. The report assesses ten environmental themes: (1) biodiversity and nature, (2) fresh water, (3) land and soil, (4) the marine environment, (5) climate change, (6) air pollution, (7) waste and resources, (8) chemical pollution, (9) environmental noise, and (10) industrial pollution. The report complements these by assessing environmental and climate pressures within five sectors: agriculture, marine fisheries and aquaculture, forestry, transport, and industry. Furthermore, the report assesses the systemic character of environmental and climate challenges, focusing on food, energy, and mobility systems. Finally, the report builds on these assessments to provide an integrated picture of the state of the environment in Europe, plus the trends and an outlook relevant to the priority objectives of the 7th EAP (EEA, 2019). Thus, this report provides an overall scientific foundation for discussing how Europe could respond better to environmental and climate change challenges.

Europe in the world

According to the EEA, the European economy has gone through major industrial transformations during the past two and a half centuries. Since the 1950s, the structure of the European economy has shifted from being industry-intensive toward being service-oriented. As a result, consumption patterns have also changed, with proportionally decreased spending on basic needs (for example, food) and relatively higher spending on electronic devices, recreation, and health. Overall, European consumption levels are high compared with many other world regions. For example, the average EU-28 citizen spends 3.4 times more on goods and services than the global average (EEA, 2019: 48). Imports are an important component in meeting the final European demand for goods and services, and global trade is fundamental for the European economy (EEA, 2019: 48). In 2018, Europe's exports represented more than 50 percent of its GDP (EEA, 2019: 47).

Through colonization and industrialization, Europe has played an important role in shaping global changes and challenges. Thus, the environmental consequences of European production and consumption systems can be assessed from complementary perspectives. The "territorial perspective" includes environmental pressures exerted by human activities within the European territory. The "production perspective" expands this to include pressures arising from production by European residents (companies and households), irrespective of where geographically these activities take place. The "consumption or material footprint perspective" complements these by relating environmental pressures to the final demand for goods and services. The latter includes the total environmental pressures resulting from consumption in Europe, irrespective of where geographically the production of these goods and services has resulted in environmental pressures. Therefore, the consumption perspective also includes the environmental pressures created around the world by European domestic consumption (EEA, 2019: 48).

To satisfy its consumption needs, Europe depends on resources extracted or used in other parts of the world, such as water, land, biomass, minerals, and other materials. As a result, many of the environmental impacts associated with European production and consumption occur outside Europe (EEA, 2019: 10f). The pressures associated with final European consumption are higher than the world average. Recent research suggests that the EU is a net importer of environmental impacts. Many internationally traded goods are produced in world regions with low production costs and weak environmental and labor regulations. The prices of internationally traded goods rarely incorporate the costs of environmental externalities, that is, the actual impact of the land and water used, the GHGs emitted, or the biodiversity affected. Focusing solely on the environmental impacts within Europe without considering the additional environmental impacts abroad can result in an overly positive perception of Europe's sustainability (EEA, 2019: 48f).

For example, the volume of water required to produce a commodity traded for consumption in another region is referred to as "virtual water." Estimates suggest that more than 40 percent of the water needed to produce products consumed in Europe is used outside the EU territory. With only about 7 percent of the global population, in 2009, Europe was responsible for over 28 percent of the imports of virtual water globally. Likewise, the EU countries rely heavily on "virtual land" to meet their consumption needs related to bioenergy and food production, with estimates of around 50 percent of additional land needed (arable land, pastures, and forests). The percentage of biomass products with non-EU origins that are consumed in the EU increased from about 29 percent in 1986 to 41 percent in 2007 (EEA, 2019: 49). International trade chains contribute to accelerating habitat degradation. The EU's consumption exerts considerable pressure on many biodiversity hotspots globally (EEA, 2019: 49; for further details on EU and biodiversity, see Chapter 9).

The EEA concluded that a large part of the environmental impacts associated with European consumption is exerted in other parts of the world. Between 1995 and 2011, Europe's material footprint increased across all resource and impact categories, with the largest increases being for energy use and material use (EEA, 2019: 49). Europe overshoots its share of the global "safe operating space" for several planetary boundaries, even under generous assumptions of what Europe's share of these global boundaries might be. The

European overshoots of the limits are greater than the global average for most planetary boundaries (EEA, 2019: 50ff). To an increasing degree, Europe is externalizing its pressures on key environmental issues. The EEA considers that there is still a substantial gap between the EU's 2050 sustainability vision and current overall environmental performance by the EU (EEA, 2019: 52).

However, reducing environmental pressures from the territorial perspective is the primary focus of most EU, global, and national environmental and climate policies. At present, as explained by the EEA, the territorial perspective is the only method accepted by international environmental law to account for a country's emissions and mitigation efforts. For example, commitments to limit or reduce GHG emissions under the Paris Agreement are implemented through Nationally Determined Contributions (EEA, 2019: 48). Accordingly, the EEA report focuses predominantly on the territorial perspective (for a critical discussion, see Chapter 11).

Climate and environmental progress in the EU

The summary assessment in the EEA report is structured by three overall thematic objectives to provide an overview at a European level from cross-cutting perspectives.

1 *Protecting, conserving, and enhancing natural capital*
   The EU's natural capital is not being protected, conserved, and enhanced in line with the ambitions of the 7th EAP. A low proportion of the assessed protected species (23 percent) and habitats (16 percent) were considered to have a favorable conservation status, and Europe did not meet its overall target of halting biodiversity loss by 2020. Significant progress has been made in areas such as designating protected areas. Some species have recovered, and action has been taken to address specific threats, for example, the EU initiative on pollinators. However, although successful in some areas, policy responses have been insufficient to halt biodiversity loss and the degradation of ecosystem services, even within Europe's own area. The report suggests that the prospects for 2030 are more positive, as there will be a more effective implementation of existing policies, better management of sites, and improved policy coherence, especially for sectoral policies, particularly agriculture (EEA, 2019: 322).
2 *Resource-efficient, circular, and low-carbon economy*
   Europe has been able to reduce GHG emissions and air pollution, improve resource efficiency and energy efficiency, and increase its use of renewable energy while experiencing economic growth. The EU has put the circular economy on the agenda and implemented a relevant strategy (see also Chapter 7). However, moving toward a circular economy will require traceability and a risk management approach that deals with legacy substances and long-term risks. The EEA states that a risk assessment needs to consider not only the first life of a product but also all potential

future lives and hence, different exposure scenarios from those considered in a linear economy. Efforts to clean up material flows can enhance the long-term potential for circularity (EEA, 2019: 250). According to the EEA, much remains to be done to improve the environmental sustainability of Europe's production and consumption patterns and to reach long-term policy targets and objectives. The report emphasizes that this would require consideration of the co-benefits and trade-offs between policy areas, including climate change, resource efficiency, and environmental policies, when designing new legislation. In addition, the report notes that assessment of progress does not account for the full environmental impacts of production and consumption in Europe exerted outside the region (EEA, 2019: 327).

3 *Safeguarding from environmental risks to health and well-being*

European policies have successfully reduced some risks to health and well-being, especially those from air pollution. However, human health and well-being are still affected by exposure to air pollution, noise, climate change, and hazardous chemicals. For example, the number of synthetic chemicals on the market has been estimated to be 100,000. The information available on chemical hazards is incomplete and the classification criteria do not effectively capture certain health impacts, in particular the long-term developmental toxicities associated with endocrine disruption, neurotoxicity, and immunotoxicity. Chemicals hazardous to the environment include those that are persistent, bio-accumulative, and toxic and those that are very persistent and very bio-accumulative. Furthermore, approaches are based on the hazard profile of individual substances and does not account for the effects of chemical mixtures (EEA, 2019: 238). Fully implementing and strengthening European policies is expected to reduce these impacts. According to the EEA report, developing a stronger framework that integrates environmental and health issues would be an opportunity to take a more holistic approach in which risks to health are managed by considering hazard exposure and vulnerability. This would be supported by a stronger knowledge base (EEA, 2019: 329).

The conclusions of the EEA report are clear, and the overall assessments are not promising. Policies have been more effective in reducing environmental pressures than in protecting biodiversity, ecosystems, and human health and well-being. The outlook for Europe's environment in the coming decades is described as discouraging. Even where progress has been made, such as climate change mitigation, actions need to be scaled up. Meanwhile, global megatrends, such as the continued growth in the population, economic output, and the demand for resources, and the worsening impacts of climate change are intensifying environmental problems (EEA, 2019: 418). Viewed together, the thematic and sectoral assessments in the report lead the EEA to conclude that many long-term EU environmental and climate targets will not be met with existing policy interventions if current trends continue (EEA, 2019: 338). Furthermore, the EEA concludes that, in essence, Europe, along with the rest of the world, is running out of time to avoid catastrophic impacts on the economy and society from climate change, ecosystem degradation, and overconsumption of natural resources (EEA, 2019: 418).

The EEA believes that further integrating environmental protection with policy-making, for example, for agriculture, transport, industry, and energy, and with EU spending programs is important, but the overall approach to environmental integration has not been successful (EEA, 2019: 290).

The EEA considers that this diagnosis triggers more fundamental questions. Have we truly recognized the scale of change required to achieve Europe's environmental goals? Have we fully understood the reasons for the persistence of environmental and climate problems? (EEA, 2019: 338). The EEA suggests that if environmental problems, such as biodiversity loss and climate change, have been resistant to policy interventions over several decades, that is mainly because their underlying causes have been insufficiently or ineffectively tackled (EEA, 2019: 338). The EEA argues that the scale of environmental challenges and the implications of global megatrends together imply the need for fundamental and urgent changes to our societies and economies, with significant consequences for lifestyles, jobs, and habits (EEA, 2019: 339).

This presents a fundamentally different challenge from those of the 1970s or 1980s, when specific environmental problems could be tackled with targeted instruments. According to the EEA, since the 1970s, the replication of the targeted model has led to a body of some 500 EU directives, regulations, and decisions, which today forms the most comprehensive set of environmental standards in the world. However, by the 1980s, it became increasingly clear that such targeted policies would be insufficient to address environmental problems that result from diffuse pressures from various sources, such as the unsustainable use of natural resources, environmental impacts on human health through pollution or chemical contamination, or the loss of biodiversity (EEA, 2019: 60). When the sustainable development concept began to be influential, integrating environmental concerns into other EU sectoral policies, also known as environmental integration, then became increasingly attractive (EEA, 2019: 60). Since the late 1990s, increased attention has been paid to gaining a better understanding of the systemic interlinkages between the environment, society, and the economy and understanding what policies were needed in response. This need has been reinforced with the recognition of the importance of climate change (EEA, 2019: 62).

Based on the complex and systemic character of today's sustainability challenges, the EEA assessment of the state of the environment in Europe indicates that there is a need for policy responses that differ from previous responses.

First, policy interventions must be designed to consider the environmental, social, economic, and governance dimensions of human activities, which are interconnected in many ways. Second, the roots of environmental degradation and climate change are so intrinsically linked to the structure and functioning of our societies and economies that our long-term environmental and climate goals will not be achieved without fundamental transformations in the ways we consume and produce. Third, the patterns and mechanisms of consumption and production co-evolve with each other, not only in Europe but also internationally, through trade, communication, policy, and knowledge transfer, which calls for strong coordination among the international community (EEA, 2019: 339f).

The EEA emphasizes that the 2030 agenda for sustainable development requires governments and other stakeholders to achieve the 17 SDGs and 169 associated targets, which incorporate economic, social, and environmental considerations in ways that mutually reinforce each other. The EEA notes that the UN has stressed that the agenda should be viewed as an indivisible whole in which all targets are equally important as the goals are closely interlinked (EEA, 2019: 341).

Environmental pressures from a systems perspective

The EEA argues that the EU should formulate comprehensive and integrated strategies. This implies, for example, a thorough consideration of the systemic interactions between the climate-neutral economy, the circular economy, and the bioeconomy (EEA, 2019: 344). Adopting a systemic view may help in approaching and reflecting on the complex or "wicked" problems facing Europe. It can do so by mobilizing system lenses that allow the observation of natural and social phenomena at the right scale, by zooming in and out. This can lead to the identification of the underlying structures and patterns.

Thus, the EEA report highlights how current configurations of key production and consumption systems and Europe's overall consumption patterns and levels relate to sustainability challenges. The EEA emphasizes the cross-cutting nature of those sustainability challenges, encompassing environmental, social, and economic dimensions. The report reflects on knowledge needs, societal perspectives, and policy approaches (EEA, 2019: 345). The EEA exemplifies the need for a system perspective by focusing on three systems: food, energy, and mobility. We will analyze systemic factors pertaining to energy and food systems in Chapters 6 and 8, respectively. In the next part of this chapter, we will focus on the mobility system to illustrate how the EEA applies this systemic perspective.

The mobility system

The mobility system spans resources, structures, and activities involved in moving physical objects, including people and goods. It is a complex system shaped by economic and broader societal forces, such as cultural norms and lifestyles, and has evolved over long timescales. The transport sector is just one of these components (EEA, 2019: 361). Roughly 11.5 million people, corresponding to 5.2 percent of the EU's total workforce, were employed in the transport sector in 2016, contributing €652 billion in gross value added to the economy. The manufacture of cars, trains, ships, and airplanes is an important sector in the EU. Expenditure on the building and maintenance of roads, railways, ports, and airports is huge. Moreover, increasing amounts of fuel and electricity are being used for transportation. The mobility system generates important negative impacts on ecosystems and health. Rising levels of car ownership and the growing road network have led to gains in personal mobility, but these have also caused economic, societal, and environmental problems. The spectrum is broad and ranges from direct impacts on the climate, air quality, noise pollution, biodiversity, and landscape and habitat fragmentation to more indirect impacts, such as urban sprawl and invasive alien species entering the EU in the ballast water of ships. Furthermore, transportation leads to indirect impacts in a range of sectors, including the extraction of raw materials, the production of infrastructure and vehicles, electricity generation, petroleum refining, and the recycling and disposal of materials (EEA, 2019: 362). The mobility system includes aspects that go beyond economic activity, such as personal mobility, individual behavior, infrastructure, urban and regional planning, investment, policy, and regulatory measures, and involves a multitude of actors, such as producers, users, policy makers, and civil society (EEA, 2019: 361).

According to the EEA, the mobility system has had limited success in reducing emissions and shifting toward more sustainable transport modes. While other sectors have already seen some reduction in emissions, GHG emissions from transport have increased by 26 percent since 1990 (including international aviation but excluding international shipping) (EEA, 2019: 362). The scale of change in the mobility system required to meet EU objectives is large and the timeline is short (EEA, 2019: 362).

Insights across systems

Looking across the three systems of energy, food, and mobility, it is clear to the EEA that progress is being obstructed by a variety of systemic challenges.

First, systems are characterized by lock-ins and path dependency. In part, this reflects that the system elements (technologies, regulations, infrastructures, user patterns, and so on) have co-evolved over decades to form relatively stable configurations. They are also multi-functional, implying that changes will result in a complex mix of trade-offs. Second, Europe's production and consumption systems are very often dominated by a small number of established actors. Moreover, there are marked differences in the roles and powers of actors along the value chain. Such vested interests contribute to system inertia. Third, achieving sustainability objectives is fundamentally dependent on individual and societal consumption choices, which encompass consumption levels, patterns, and lifestyles. Local initiatives are emerging, and these offer new models of consuming and producing. Yet, the choices made by individuals and governments are still largely influenced by the dominant socio-economic paradigm, which generally promotes globalization, consumerism, individualism, and short-termism. Fourth, it is also important to acknowledge the local heterogeneity of systems. Each system differs markedly across Europe and its regions, in terms of economic and infrastructural development and related consumption patterns, behaviors, and lifestyles. This implies that responses must be tailored to local realities; there are no "one-size-fits-all" solutions that apply across Europe. Fifth, systems are highly interconnected with each other, giving rise to pressures and impacts across varied ecological systems and natural resources. They are also shaped by changes in the fiscal and financial systems. This interconnectedness across systems means that system reconfiguration is likely to lead to trade-offs among sustainability outcomes. Sixth, policies can create enabling conditions to facilitate systemic change toward achieving sustainability objectives. Yet, systems differ in terms of the ambition and coverage of the main policy frameworks. Seventh, although issues such as security of supply, air pollution, and climate are recognized across energy and mobility, other environmental aspects, such as protecting natural capital, are not sufficiently covered. Governance responses are likewise oriented toward a limited set of approaches, emphasizing technologies and market-based instruments (EEA, 2019: 366f).

The EEA promotes the key idea that the many interlinkages within and between complex systems mean that there are often strong economic, social, and psychological incentives that lock society into ways of meeting its needs. Altering these systems is likely to disrupt established investments, jobs, consumption patterns and behaviors, knowledge, and values, inevitably provoking resistance from affected industries, regions, and consumers. The interactions between these diverse elements also mean that efforts to change complex societal systems can produce unintended outcomes or surprises (EEA, 2019: 367).

The EEA states that it is important to understand that the effectiveness of policy interventions can also be offset by feedback within systems. For example, technology-driven gains may be undermined by lifestyle changes and increased consumption and production, partly because improvements in efficiency tend to make a product or service cheaper and thus lead to increased production and consumption. This phenomenon is referred to as the "rebound effect" (EEA, 2019: 370; see also Chapter 4).

Furthermore, very important links between systems arise because of their shared reliance on natural systems, both as a source of resources and as a sink for wastes and emissions (EEA, 2019: 371). The concept of the "resource nexus" recognizes that food, energy, water, land, materials, and ecosystems are interconnected across space and time (see also Chapter 2). The concept supports sustainability governance by helping us to identify how best to balance socio-economic and environmental concerns (EEA, 2019: 372f).

According to the EEA, transforming production and consumption systems inevitably leads to trade-offs as well as far-reaching and uncertain impacts. Yet, established governance and knowledge systems are seldom designed to handle this kind of complexity. Policies and actions at different levels of governance—from communities to international organizations—are often developed in silos for specific sectors or issues. Similarly, research is often compartmentalized within disciplinary boundaries, while indicators and knowledge infrastructures are seldom developed and organized in ways that support a systemic understanding of challenges and responses (see also Chapter 13). Collectively, these factors make it hard to achieve adaptive governance processes that can respond rapidly to new information about the barriers, opportunities, trade-offs, and co-benefits associated with systemic change (EEA, 2019: 375).

Politics and governance

The EEA argues that to achieve sustainable system outcomes, there is a need for policies that embrace the interconnectedness of system components, interactions across systems, and links between economic, social, and environmental goals. To anticipate potential implications and unintended consequences, such interventions should be assessed against multiple criteria. These include their feasibility against ecological and biophysical constraints, their viability for the economy and society (for example, the effects on jobs, structure of the economy, and import dependency), and their ability to meet multiple sustainability goals simultaneously, both inside and outside Europe (EEA, 2019: 375).

The EEA summarizes its viewpoints regarding principles of politics and governance in six main themes:

Enable transformative change across Europe: This can be achieved by harnessing the ambition, creativity, and power of citizens, businesses, and communities to shift toward sustainable production and consumption patterns and lifestyles. Actors from diverse policy areas must work together to enable transitions. The emergence and spread of diverse and innovative ideas should be promoted by helping those working on bottom-up initiatives to learn and network. Stakeholders should be engaged in inclusive governance processes to open up a broader range of societal responses. Transitions should be socially fair, particularly for the most vulnerable in society.

Embrace the SDGs as an overarching framework for policy-making and implementation: If the goals could be more ambitious, these can be complemented with additional measures at all scales, for example, on air pollution and impacts on health. Work on meeting the SDGs in other regions should be actively supported, in particular Europe's neighborhood. Europe's diplomatic and economic influence could be used to promote the adoption of global environmental standards, including international trade rules. The outsourcing of unsustainable practices that undermine other countries' efforts to achieve the SDGs should be avoided. This "burden-shifting" can negatively affect the global achievement of the SDGs and could also feed back negatively onto Europe in areas relating to the global commons.

Realize the unfulfilled potential of existing environmental policies: This can be done via a full implementation across Europe through increased funding, capacity building, stakeholder engagement, and better coordination of local, regional, and national authorities. There is a need to increase public awareness of the co-benefits for prosperity, security, and well-being. Gaps in policy and monitoring in areas such as land, soil, and chemicals should be addressed. To produce significant and measurable outcomes, environmental goals must be integrated into sectoral policies.

Develop systemic policy frameworks with binding targets: This will mobilize and guide actions across society. Stakeholders need to be engaged in developing transformative visions and pathways that reflect the diverse realities across Europe and maximize environmental, social, and economic co-benefits. The resource nexus and ecosystem-based management approaches can avoid burden-shifting, respect environmental limits, and achieve the integrated management of natural resources.

Reorient public budgets, private investments, and financial markets toward promoting sustainability transitions: This would make full use of public resources when investing in innovative and nature-based solutions. Metrics need to be developed and adopted for measuring society's progress toward sustainability that go beyond GDP. Private spending can be mobilized and directed by shaping investment and consumption choices, including through environmental and fiscal reform and by removing harmful subsidies. The financial sector needs to be engaged in sustainable investment by implementing and building on the EU's sustainable finance action plan.

Develop knowledge and skills fit for the 21st century: This can be realized by focusing on understanding the key systems driving sustainability challenges and opportunities for change. By investing in education, lifelong learning, and R&D programs focused on sustainability, more capacity can be created for navigating a rapidly changing world. The potential of new digital technologies has to be harnessed to generate and share relevant knowledge that supports all decision makers in making choices consistent with the pathways to sustainability (EEA, 2019: 423).

Comparing policy objectives and scientific recommendations

Importantly, the European Green Deal was announced as a new growth strategy that aims to transform the EU into a fair and prosperous society, with a resource-efficient and competitive economy. Also note that the Green Deal plans to position the EU as a global leader regarding climate change and environmental degradation that can "turn an urgent challenge into a unique opportunity." It has emphasized the benefits of a green European transition as an opportunity to expand EU's export in global markets of low-emission technologies, sustainable products, and services. Furthermore, green investments will remain a marginal part of the total EU budget (around 1 percent of GDP) compared to the overall needs (Claeys et al., 2019: 8). Finally, EU research and development spending is still lower than in other major economies (Claeys et al., 2019: 13).

The EEA report (2019) emphasizes that Europe is running out of time to avoid catastrophic impacts on the economy and society from climate change, ecosystem degradation, and overconsumption of natural resources and has made several recommendations to mitigate the challenges. In many ways, the European Green Deal is aligned with these recommendations. However, the European Green Deal remains rather silent concerning the more far-reaching recommendations of the EEA. In the following, we will compare the types of solutions that are proposed in the European Green Deal with the recommendations suggested by the EEA.

1 The main policy principles for environmental and climate interventions
   First, the EEA recommends that the EU should aim to achieve *a more effective implementation of existing environmental and climate policies*. The European Green Deal is in line with this recommendation, as it stresses that the Commission will work with the Member States to step up the EU's efforts to ensure that current legislation and policies relevant to the Green Deal are enforced and effectively implemented.

   Second, the EEA recommends *strengthening the coherence of sectoral policies and integrating environmental, climate, and health consideration into other policy areas*. Under the headline "Mainstreaming sustainability in all EU policies," the European Green Deal states that all EU actions and policies will have to contribute to the European Green Deal objectives and that the policy responses must seek to maximize benefits for health, quality of life, resilience, and competitiveness. It acknowledges that it will require coordination to exploit the available synergies across all policy areas. As an example, the European Green Deal mentions that it will be necessary to rethink policies for clean energy supply that affect the economy, industry, production and consumption, large-scale infrastructure, transport, food and agriculture, construction, taxation, and social benefits.

   Third, the EEA recommends that the EU should *use resource nexus and ecosystem-based management to avoid burden shifting within the EU, respect environmental limits, and achieve integrated management of natural resources*. The European Green Deal states that all EU policies should contribute to preserving and restoring Europe's natural capital and that finding more lasting solutions to climate change require greater attention to nature-based solutions.

Fourth, the EEA recommends that the EU should *consider the environmental, social, economic, and governance dimensions of human activity from a system perspective and develop integrated interventions into the main production and consumption system of society*. The European Green Deal formulates strategic interventions into important societal systems such as industry, food, mobility, and construction and accounts for the inter-relations between environmental (climate, energy, resources, pollution, biodiversity, and ecosystem services), social, economic, and governance factors.

Fifth, the EEA recommends that the EU should *consider the trade-offs between policy areas, including climate, resources and environment and their viability for economy and society both inside and outside Europe*. The European Green Deal states that careful attention will have to be paid when there are potential trade-offs between economic, environmental, and social objectives. However, it does not mention possible trade-offs outside Europe.

Sixth, the EEA recommends that the EU should *develop and adopt metrics for measuring society's progress toward sustainability that go beyond GDP*. The European Green Deal states that the Commission will develop and adopt metrics for measuring society's progress toward sustainability that go beyond GDP.

Seventh, the EEA recommends that the EU should *increase the focus on peoples' behaviors, norms, and lifestyles*. In general, the European Green Deal focuses on how to provide the conditions for consumers to be able to plan their behavior in environmentally and climatically sound manners. As part of this, the strategy focuses on how consumer policy and product information will help to empower consumers to make informed choices and play an active role in the ecological transition. However, there are few interventions in the European Green Deal aiming at directly affecting consumer choices.

Eighth, the EEA recommends that the EU should *strengthen the regulation of pollution, chemical hazards, and the combined effects of chemical mixtures*. The European Green Deal notes that the Commission will adopt a zero-pollution action plan for air, water, and soil and develop a strategy for the sustainable use of chemicals. It emphasizes that the regulatory framework will need to rapidly reflect scientific evidence on the risks posed by endocrine disruptors, hazardous chemicals in products including imports, combination effects of different chemicals, and very persistent chemicals.

Ninth, the EEA recommends that the EU should *address gaps in monitoring in areas such as land, soil, and chemicals and ensure that integrating environmental goals into sectoral policies produces measurable outcomes*. Many of the initiatives in the European Green Deal necessitate monitoring to assess whether governments in particular but also companies are complying with the rules and meeting the standards. The European Green Deal mentions two environmental goals that need monitoring. The Commission will develop measurable objectives that address the main causes of biodiversity loss and will revise air quality standards and set up plans for monitoring air quality.

2 **Just Transition**

First, the EEA recommends that *transitions should be socially just and fair.* In the European Green Deal, the main lever for a Just Transition is the Just Transition Mechanism. As part of this, the Just Transition Fund is especially targeted at the green transformation of regions that are dependent on the production of fossil fuels. Furthermore, the European Green Deal addresses the question of energy poverty with respect to the heating of houses and the question of how to counter the regressive effects of carbon taxes. The European Green Deal also mentions that the European Pillar of Social Rights will guide action in ensuring that no one is left behind.

Second, the EEA recommends that the EU should *develop knowledge and skills fit for the 21st century* with a focus on understanding the key systems driving sustainability challenges and opportunities. The European Green Deal states that the EU will support proactive re-skilling and upskilling and support schools, training institutions, and universities in developing and assessing the knowledge, skills, and attitudes on climate change and sustainable development. In this regard, the Commission will develop the European competence framework and provide support materials and facilitate the exchange of good practices in EU networks of teacher-training programs.

3 **Levers in the sustainable transformation**

First, the EEA recommends that the EU should *reorient public budgets, private investments, and financial markets toward promoting sustainable transitions.* Financing the sustainable transition as well as investments and the role of financial markets all play a significant role in the European Green Deal. There is a focus on the importance of the sustainable transition of the EU budget, the Innovation and Modernization Fund, the InvestEU, the EIB, the taxonomy for classifying environmentally sustainable activities, and the national budgets of Member States.

Second, the EEA recommends that the EU should *harness the potential of digital technologies as enablers in the sustainable transformation.* The digital transformation and digital tools play a very important role in all aspects of the European Green Deal. The aim is to accelerate and maximize the impact of policies that tackle climate change and protect the environment. Furthermore, the Commission will consider measures to improve the energy efficiency and circular economy performance of the digital sector itself.

Third, the EEA recommends that the EU should *all actors in the sustainable transformations and support the ambitions, creativity, and power of citizens, businesses, and communities in the emergence and spread of ideas and innovations and to help bottom-up initiatives and engage stakeholders in inclusive governance processes.* According to the European Green Deal, active public participation and confidence in the transition are paramount if policies are to work and be accepted. It introduces a new climate pact for bringing citizens together in all their diversity, with national, regional, local authorities, civil society, and industry working closely with the EU's institutions and consultative bodies. For companies and workers, the European Green Deal suggests that an active social dialog will help to anticipate and successfully manage change. The Commission will work with stakeholders on a new initiative on renovating buildings. An open platform will bring together the buildings and construction sector, architects, engineers, and local authorities. Financed by the Horizon Europe program, research and innovation projects will also involve local communities in working toward a more sustainable future.

4 **Global cooperation**

The EEA recommends that the EU should *maintain strong coordination among the international community to support implementation of the SDGs, avoid the "burden shifting" inherent in the outsourcing of unsustainable practices, and develop answers on how to mitigate the environmental impact of production and consumption in Europe exerted outside Europe.* The European Green Deal contains many strategic statements and plans regarding international cooperation and EU support for other countries in managing their sustainable transformation. The CBAM should be designed to reduce carbon leakage and to prevent European Companies from outsourcing climate-harmful parts of production to countries outside the EU. The proposed regulation of the content of imported products relating to recycled materials, pollution standards, and hazardous chemicals may also prevent the outsourcing of harmful parts of European production. However, the European Green Deal remains rather silent regarding how to mitigate environmental impacts exerted outside Europe.

5 **Supporting fundamental innovations of society**

Some of the recommendations from the EEA have potentially far-reaching consequences on how the EU and the Member States are organized. In particular, there are five recommendations.

First, the EEA recommends that the EU should consider *how to better understand and deal with far-reaching and uncertain impacts.* An immediate priority in the European Green Deal is that the EU's ability to predict and manage environmental disasters needs to be boosted. To do this, the Commission will foster European scientific and industrial excellence and will develop a very highly precise digital model of the Earth. However, the Green Deal does not mention any intention to develop new ways and models to foresee different aspects of the inter-relations between, on one hand, policy interventions and, on the other, their environmental, climate, and social outcomes.

Second, the EEA recommends that the EU should *avoid the idea that techno-fixes, efficiency gains, optimization, short-termism, and market-based instruments can solve all environment and climate challenges.* The European

Green Deal does not mention techno-fixes. Its policy dependencies on technological development and the functioning of markets is, however, very apparent.

Third, the EEA recommends that the EU should *avoid lock-ins and path-dependencies and address the influence of powerful actors that work against sustainable transformations.* As the European Green Deal requires very profound changes to the European agricultural, industrial, building, transport, retail, and finance sectors, it will necessarily produce winners and losers. The European Green Deal has long-term plans for helping actors to prepare for a new future, and it supports the transition process, both politically and economically. However, the question of how to deal with path dependencies and powerful actors is not directly a part of the strategy.

Fourth, the EEA recommends that the EU should try to *avoid rebound effects that can undermine environment and climate intervention.* The European Green Deal does not mention how to deal with rebound effects. An example of a rebound effect would be if someone used the money saved on, say, energy, transportation, or food, on, say, digital products and services or holidays abroad. There is a risk that new patterns of consumption will create new environmental and climate challenges.

Fifth, the EEA recommends that the EU should consider *the need for fundamental transformations in the ways we produce and consume.* It is not quite clear what this recommendation means. In some respects, the European Green Deal aims to make fundamental changes in the way we produce and consume. However, the communication from the EU presented the European Green Deal as a growth strategy. Logically, therefore, the question of radically shifting the EU and its Member States in the direction of a non- or de-growth scenario does not apply.

Summary

In this chapter, we applied a simple structure with three parts that focused on the European Green Deal and the state of the environment in Europe. We also compared political recommendations by the EEA with the content of the European Green Deal.

The European Green Deal was announced as an overall green growth strategy that would "leave no one behind." Thus, the strategy encompasses ecological as well as socio-ecological goals. At the European level, the strategy is ambitious, as it covers a wide range of areas, such as climate; energy; industry; digitalization; the circular economy; construction and renovation; transport and mobility; agriculture and food systems; biodiversity; pollution; finance, investments, and economic incentives; research and innovation; global responsibility; Just Transition; and inclusion and citizen participation. In all areas, the European Green Deal aims to support new solutions via the European Semester, investments, market-based solutions, new sub-strategies and packages, regulations, directives, binding directions, and standards. Non-state actors and citizens are invited to participate.

The European Green Deal draws upon different scientific reports, especially the 2019 report published by the EEA. This report provides an overview of the state and outlook for the environment in Europe and for the climate, and it evaluates progress toward achieving EU policies and targets. The report covers ten environmental themes. It assesses environmental and climate change pressures within five sectors and the systemic challenges for three main sectors. It provides the scientific foundation for recommendations on how Europe could respond better to environmental and climate change. The EEA report concludes that policy responses have been insufficient to halt biodiversity loss and the degradation of ecosystem services, that much remains to be done to improve the environmental sustainability of Europe's consumption and production patterns, and that the approach to chemicals and pollution has not been effective. Much remains to be done to protect ecosystems, biodiversity, and human health and well-being. The EEA summarizes its opinions in six principles for policy and governance.

In the last part of the chapter, we compared the recommendations from the EEA with the policies and goals of the European Green Deal. Our analysis shows that there is alignment between the recommendations from the EEA and the content of the European Green Deal regarding policy principles for environmental and climate action, the Just Transition, and levers in the sustainable transformation. There are, however, important differences. The European Green Deal remains rather silent regarding how to mitigate the environmental impacts that Europe exerts outside its borders and does not mention the risks involved in so-called techno-fixes. Moreover, how to deal with powerful actors, path dependencies, and lock-ins is not directly mentioned. The risks due to rebound effects are omitted, and there may be a discrepancy between the EEA's call for fundamental transformations and the European Green Deal, which aims to achieve green growth.

In the following chapters, we will focus on five selected areas of the Green Deal, considering not only the strategy itself but also existing regulations and the follow-up sub-strategies, plans, and regulations that the EU has adopted since the announcement of the European Green Deal. Furthermore, we will draw on critical research and alternative policies for different aspects of the more specific goals and measures of the European process of sustainable transformation and discuss supplementary and alternative ways of reaching these goals.

References

Claeys, G., Tagliapietra, S. and Zachmann, G. (2019). How to make the European Green Deal work. *Policy Contribution*, issue number 14. Bruegel, 21 pages. Retrieved from: https://www.bruegel.org/wp-content/uploads/2019/11/PC-13_2019-151119.pdf

European Commission (2019a). Communication from the Commission to the European Parliament, The European Council, The Council, The European Economic and Social Committee and the Committee of the Regions. The European Green Deal, 24 pages. Retrieved from: https://eur-lex.europa.eu/resource.html?uri=cellar:-b828d165-1c22-11ea-8c1f-01aa75ed71a1.0002.02/DOC_1&format=PDF

European Commission (2019b). Annex to the communication from the commission to the European Parliament, The European Council, The Council, The European Economic and Social Committee and the Committee of the Regions. Roadmap – Key actions, 4 pages. Retrieved from: https://eur-lex.europa.eu/resource.html?uri=cellar:b828d165-1c22-11ea-8c1f-01aa75ed71a1.0002.02/DOC_2&format=PDF

EEA (2019). The European environment — state and outlook 2020. Knowledge for transition to a sustainable Europe. The European Environmental Agency, 499 pages. DOI: 10.2800/96749

Munta, M. (2020). The European Green Deal – A game changer or simply a buzzword? Friedrich Ebert Stiftung, 15 pages. Retrieved from: https://www.researchgate.net/publication/344161380_The_European_Green_Deal_A_game_changer_or_simply_a_buzzword.

Siddi, M. (2020). The European Green Deal: Assessing its current state and future implementation. FIIA Working Paper 114, 14 pages. Retrieved from: https://www.fiia.fi/wp-content/uploads/2020/05/wp114_european-green-deal.pdf

Von der Leyen, U. (2019). A Union that strives for more – My agenda for Europe. Political Guidelines for the Next European Commission 2019–2024. Publications Office of the European Union, 22 pages. Retrieved from: https://op.europa.eu/en/publication-detail/-/publication/43a17056-ebf1-11e9-9c4e-01aa75ed71a1

6 Climate change-motivated development of EU's energy production and use systems

Thomas Budde Christensen and Tobias Pape Thomsen

> This is Europe's man on the moon moment.
> Ursula von der Leyen, President of the European Commission,
> when presenting the European Green Deal, December 2019

Energy production drives the climate crisis

As part of the developed world, the countries in the EU—and the union as a whole—have a huge task in front of them, related to a transition of society toward sustainable levels of production, consumption, and pollution. Since 1990, emission levels in EU-27 have decreased by almost 25 percent, while global emissions have increased more than 50 percent (Climatewatch, 2022). In 2018, EU-27 fostered domestic GHG emissions of 3,300 megatons out of total global emissions of 48,900 megaton, corresponding to roughly 7 percent, which was half of the relative emission levels in the union in 1990 (ibid.).

Energy production still drives the climate crisis in the EU. But it is not the only factor. Overall, anthropogenic greenhouse gas emissions arise from four main sources: (1) conversion of fossil fuels, biomass, and waste for energy production and transportation; (2) agriculture, forestry, and other land use (AFOLU); (3) industrial processes with non-energy emissions like cement production; and (4) waste handling. In addition, there are abundant natural sources, which are largely outside societal control. While all sources are important and need to be addressed to mitigate climate change, the energy sector still dominates the EU emission map, as illustrated in Figure 6.1.

According to these data, emissions from transportation within the EU increased around 25 percent over the last 30 years, while emissions from industry, waste handling, and AFOLU have varied, with a net decline of 33 percent in the same period. Emissions from non-transport energy production have undergone an even more pronounced reduction in the same period, leading to a net decline in emission levels of around 37 percent in 30 years. Due to the magnitude of this sector, the reduction in non-transport energy

DOI: 10.4324/9781003319672-9

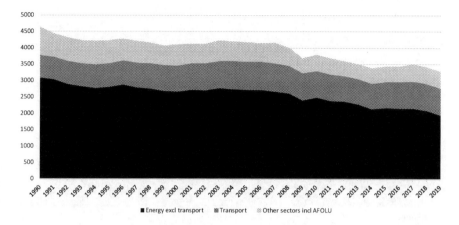

Figure 6.1 Historical domestic greenhouse gas emissions data: EU-27 (from 2020) emissions 1990–2019 (Eurostat, 2022a). AFOLU = Agriculture, Forestry and Other Land Use. CO_2e of CH_4 and N_2O calculated with a 100-year temporal scope using IPCC impact factors from Assessment Report 6 (IPCC WG1, 2022).

also governs the development in total emission levels in the same period, leading to a net reduction in total emissions of around 27 percent from 1990 to 2019 in EU27 (2020, not including Great Britain).

When investigating the total energy supply to the union, it becomes clear that the main changes are related to reductions in coal and natural gas use and increases in renewable energy sources. The historical energy supply and the related greenhouse gas emissions in EU-28 (including Great Britain) are shown in Figure 6.2.

The overall emission reductions in the EU's energy sector closely follow the decline in coal use. As a consequence, the emission reductions in EU during the last 30 years have arisen primarily from reductions in coal-based energy production. In the same period, oil-based emissions in the aggregated energy sector are almost stable (but hiding an increase in transport), while there has been a steady—and substantial—increase in emissions from natural gas use.

Energy consumption drives societal development

Use of energy both directly and indirectly fuels development of human society, and today more or less all the services and products provided to the average modern EU citizen is fueled by energy use. The energy intensity of the provided products and services vary, as does the climate impacts thereof. Correlations between energy use, on one hand, and societal development, on the other, have been established in numerous past assessments, wherein several

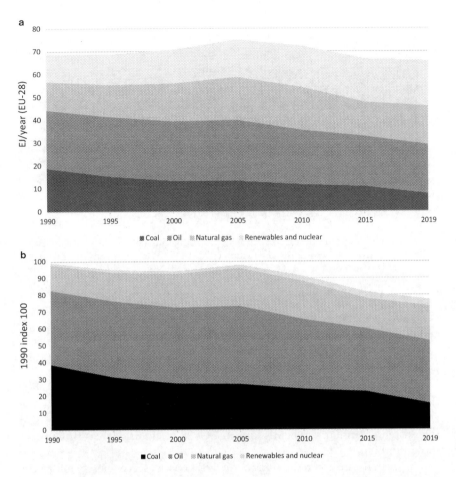

Figure 6.2 Historical energy use data (top) and greenhouse gas emissions from energy use (bottom) in EU-28 from 1990 to 2019. Energy use data from (IEA, 2022), while greenhouse gas emissions are estimated using climate impact intensity factors (100-year temporal scope) from (Silva & Raadal, 2019) & (The Netherlands Enterprise Agency (RVO), 2018).

patterns indicate that, while energy consumption is a prerequisite for economic development, especially at lower income levels, the opposite may be the case at higher income levels (Asghar, 2008; Campo & Sarmiento, 2013; Dell'ariccia et al., 2020; Esen & Bayrak, 2017; Mukhtarov et al., 2020; Nar, 2021).

However, energy is not just energy, and the specifications and characteristics of the energy produced and spent has a huge impact on its societal benefit. Low cost, high quantity, high quality, and easy implementation are some beneficial traits of energy products that increase the societal value. Low cost and high quantity are strongly related to the procurement and production processes.

The societal value of first oil was disruptive and drastically changed human society. While modern oil still provides high societal value, the costs associated with these benefits are high and retard the net gain. Two central energy system characteristics to address in this regard are Net Energy Output (NEO) and Energy Return on Energy Investment (EROI). NEO is simply "energy yield minus energy input," while EROI is "energy yield divided by energy input." While the relevance of the NEO indicator is intuitive to most, that of EROI is often less so. However, it is important to acknowledge the relative costs of energy to produce energy, and several studies have found that high complexity, modern societies require high average EROI of energy production (Lambert et al., 2014; Raugei & Leccisi, 2016). For the average production of global coal, oil, and natural gas, there has been a declining EROI for many years, and several studies have pointed out that this most likely is already having a large impact on the world economy (Hall et al., 2014; Tverberg, 2012). This may become an issue when transitioning to a low carbon energy system structure. For comparable energy carriers and services (e.g., fossil diesel and diesel from biomass), there may be a drop in EROI from around 20 to around 1–3 (2006 values); EROI for electricity produced from coal and biomass may drop from 3.6 to 1.1; and modern direct-electricity sources like off-shore wind power may reach EROI values of more than 20 in some cases (all 2013 values, UK grid) (Raugei & Leccisi, 2016; Townsend et al., 2014). In addition to the risk of increased energy consumption, it should be emphasized that renewable energy is limited—or, at least, the best sources/sites are limited—and it can be costly and often problematic to establish due to high installations costs and different types of public opposition. In addition, the planning of renewable energy production is often in competition with other land/area/resource uses and, as long as the energy system is not CO_2-neutral, any energy used in the energy system increases the climate cost of the energy services provided to society.

From a climate accounting perspective, parasitic losses and the resulting EROI and NEO metrics are typically embedded in the calculation of the climate intensity of energy production, if addressed from a suitable and adequate life cycle perspective (Raugei & Leccisi, 2016; Ulgiati et al., 2011). To illustrate some central differences among different energy production systems, the life cycle climate impact from nine different types of electricity production is compared in Figure 6.3.

Metrics like those displayed in Figure 6.3 are sensitive to method, data quality, assumption, and context of assessed system, but useful for investigating system performance and for planning development roadmaps. When using such analysis in planning a climate-oriented transition, the timing of the emissions may be crucial. While direct emissions, biogenic emissions, and methane emissions all occur annually, most emissions from infrastructure occur up front and in a very short period of time. Looking at the Solar PV case with an average emission of 66 g CO_2 per kWh, it is important to understand that this is when infrastructure cost is distributed across the entire plant lifetime and production. In reality, almost all emissions from the

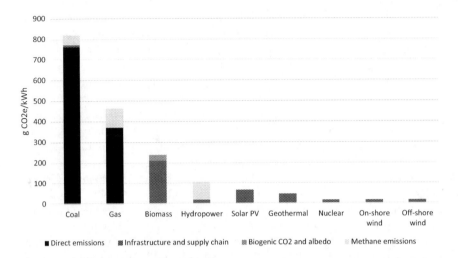

Figure 6.3 Life cycle climate impact (GWP 100 years) of electricity production. Average values from IPCC's assessment report 5, annex 3 used. Result variability not shown (Schlömer et al., 2015).

plants occur up front. This should be acknowledged in relation to already occurring climate change impact and the risk of tipping points. With some of these technologies, we need to risk a big pulse of emissions up front to have emission-free production afterwards.

So, there are costs associated with energy production and with the transition of energy production from one regime to another. These costs are economic, environmental, and even social. Some of them are known and influence the market. Some of them are hidden or unaccounted for and, therefore, do not. With imperfect cost information to enact market mechanisms and improper internalization of external costs, price and value are misaligned and a hidden burden of costs (ecological, economic, social) may be pushed/spilled to future generations and/or other parts of society (Patel, 2009).

To make good robust decisions to mitigate climate change in energy policy, an adequate level of knowledge about costs, consequences, and alternatives is required. We also need to have an open and honest discussion of how to deal, just and fairly, with the fact that different countries have different energy-prerequisites and capabilities to solve the task at hand. We are all in this together, but we are positioned very differently.

We all have different energy-prerequisites and capabilities

Access to cheap and abundant energy is a major driver in societal development, while access to clean and abundant energy is a prerequisite for a sustainable transition of the existing energy regimes. However, energy resources and procurement options are neither fairly, nor equally distributed among the world's countries or among those in the EU. Location, geography, climate, and demography all influence the situation and freedom to operate in a transition process. For example, take two extreme-end scenarios, Hungary and Sweden. Hungary currently depends on primarily fossil fuels (72 percent) and nuclear (17 percent), as well as a smaller number of renewables, biomass, and waste (11 percent), for its total energy supply (including transportation, industry, and households). On the other hand, Sweden relies mainly on renewables, waste, and bioenergy (46 percent), followed by an equal split between fossil resources (27 percent), and nuclear (27 percent) (IEA, 2022). Hungary is a relatively densely populated country with around 100 people pr m^2, landlocked with access only to lakes and with some small, distributed mountains. The population density in Sweden is just 25 people pr m^2, and the country has mountains, shorelines, and vast forest areas. According to UNDP, the main natural resources for Hungary include bauxite, coal, natural gas, fertile soils, and arable land (UNDP, 2010). For a transition of the fossil-dependent energy sector, this leaves mainly options for on-shore solar and wind power, as well as for geothermal, nuclear energy, and biobased energy. Sweden, on the other hand, has options for all major non-fossil types of energy, from biomass (forest and agriculture), wind, and solar (on- and off-shore) to wave, geothermal, hydro, and nuclear. Resource quality and quantity and climate intensity of provided energy services are not the only aspects to consider in an energy transition. The development of energy production and use systems entails a broad palette of indicators to involve in decision-making, including cost, labor qualifications, R&D strongholds, import and export balance, security of supply, energy quality of and demand for services, resources and criticality for development and maintenance, other environmental impacts, path dependency, and existing infrastructure.

The climate crisis has an inherently global nature and the uneven distribution of possibilities to develop energy sources with low climate impact thus calls for cooperation, fairness, and solidarity in the sustainable transition of energy production and consumption systems, especially in a regional context wherein more energy carriers can be distributed among countries than in a global context.

Given this background, it is the purpose of this analysis to shed light on central justice and fairness aspects of climate change related to transitions of energy production and use. This analysis focuses on the European Union as an assumed frontrunner within regional scale green transition of energy production and use. It builds on a historical, chronological presentation of the parallel development of (1) EU's Climate Change policy frameworks and (2) EU's production and use of energy from a climate perspective. The analysis also includes an assessment of trigger events, thereby forming a basis for discussing not only potentials, barriers, differences, and ambitions related to a transition of the energy sector within the EU, but also how fair and just this transition is on a local, regional, and global level.

The launch of European Union climate action policies

Today, there is a broadly established understanding and agreement that our common climate is under accelerated change, and it is driven by anthropogenic greenhouse gas emissions. Concerns on this matter have been brewing for at least 100 years, but it was not until a little more than 30 years ago that these concerns fostered global action. This has led to substantial political activity ever since. In this section, the development of EU's climate change policies is presented chronologically from initiation on global scale in 1988 to today.

Public awareness of the accelerating climate crisis ignited with the publication of the first report from the Intergovernmental Panel on Climate Change (IPCC) in 1990. The IPCC was established in 1988 and delivered its first assessment report in 1990, stating that anthropogenic emissions of GHG result in global warming. The business-as-usual scenario in the report estimates an increase in global mean temperature of about 1°C above the present value by 2025 and of about 3°C above before the end of the next century. After the release of the first IPCC assessment report in 1990, the European Council agreed on a decision to stabilize emissions of GHG by 2000 (on a 1990 level). The early discussion on European climate action also defined the three main pillars for which future climate policies in the coming 30 years would be based on: GHG reduction targets, promotion of renewable energy sources, and energy efficiency measures. These three pillars have remained the basis for European climate action policy until today (2022).

In 1991, the Commission launched the first "Community strategy to limit carbon dioxide emissions and improve energy efficiency" (European Commission, 1992), aiming to stabilize European emissions (on 1990 levels) by 2000.

In the following years, the "Specific Actions for Vigorous Energy Efficiency" (SAVE) program was initiated (1991) to promote the energy efficiency of a range of different products and services. In 1993, the first energy efficiency directive, the so-called SAVE-directive, was adopted. This was followed by the renewable energy directive adopted in 1993. Renewable energy sources were expected to provide 8 percent of energy supply by 2005, and biofuels were targeted for a market share of 5 percent of transport road fuels.

The United Nations Framework Convention on Climate Change was adopted at the Rio conference in 1992. The objective of the convention is the "stabilization of greenhouse gas concentrations in the atmosphere at a level that would prevent dangerous anthropogenic interference with the climate system." In later documents, this objective has been translated into a 2°C threshold limit to global warming and later (in the Paris Agreement) to a1.5°C threshold limit (see also Chapter 2). The convention does not in itself include legally binding emission reductions for individual countries. Rather, these are negotiated as annexes to the convention. Parties to the convention meet annually at the so-called Conferences of Parties (COP) meetings, the first of which was held in Berlin, Germany in March 1995. The first legally binding agreement to cut emission from individual countries was decided at COP3 held in the Japanese city of Kyoto in 1997. The so-called Kyoto protocol is regarded as the first global attempt to establish legally binding GHG emissions reduction. It follows the principles of the UNFCCC, including the annex structure that divides countries into three main groups (Annex I, Annex II, and Non-annex I countries). The protocol sets binding GHG reduction targets for Annex I countries covering the 37 industrialized countries and economies in transition. The European Union was included in this group of countries with one common reduction target. The overall target in the Kyoto Protocol was a reduction in GHG emission of 5 percent (relative to 1990) over a five-year reduction period 2008–2012 (labeled the first commitment period). The protocol also included three flexible market-based mechanisms: Emission Trading, Clean Development Mechanism (CDM), and Joint Implementation (JI). The European Union member states (15 at the time of the adoption) joined the Kyoto Protocol as a group, with a common GHG emission reduction target of −8 percent (relative to 1990) for the first commitment period from 2008 to 2012. The adoption of the Kyoto Protocol had a significant influence on European climate and energy policies leading to the adoption of a wide range of policies targeting reductions in GHG emissions, promotion of renewable energy sources, and energy efficiency.

European Climate Change Programme

The European Commission established the European Climate Change Programme following the adoption of the Kyoto Protocol to identify cost-efficient pathways to cut GHG emissions. The program ran over two periods and investigated a wide range of sectors, policies, and instruments to cut GHG emissions.

European emission trading system

The European emission trading system ETS was established in 2005, following the adoption of the EU ETS Directive in 2003. It was designed as a key policy instrument to deliver the needed GHG reductions to comply with the commitments under the UNFCCC Kyoto Protocol.

The ETS was established as a cap-and-trade instrument that would allow companies to trade emissions and secure the most cost-efficient reduction pathway for the European economy. The ETS Directive defines the cap in terms of CO_2 equivalents for each trading period. It covers the most carbon-intensive sectors in the economy, including power generation and heavy manufacturing industries. Companies gain access to emission allowances in two ways: (1) free allocation, whereby the companies receive emission allowances for free or (2) an auction system whereby the companies need to purchase emission allowances. During the first and second phases (2005–2012), most allowances were allocated for free. However, in the third and fourth phases (2012 onwards), most allowances were allocated through the auction system (European Commission, 2015).

The ETS was linked to the implementation of the commitments under the UNFCCC Kyoto Protocol. The first two years of the ETS (2005–2007) were designed to test and verify the infrastructure for monitoring, reporting, and verification of emissions, enabling a full operational cap-and-trade system to be in place for the first commitment under the Kyoto protocol that ran from 2008 to 2012. The ETS also allowed European companies to use emission reduction units obtained from the flexible mechanisms Clean Development Mechanism (CDM) and Joint implementation (JI) in the Kyoto Protocol to meet reduction targets under the ETS (European Commission, 2015). The ETS was expanded toward the end of the first phase in 2012, when aviation was included in the system.

2020 climate action package

In January 2007, the commission presented a collection of measures to cut GHG emissions, promote renewables, and improve energy efficiency. The package was labeled the 2020 Climate Action Package. The timing of its launch was aligned with international negotiations under the UNFCCC, where a global binding agreement was expected to be decided at COP15 in Copenhagen in 2009. The package was adopted after a legal process including the parliament and the council in December 2008. The package included three overall targets for the EU as a whole: 20 percent cut in greenhouse gas emissions (from 1990 levels); 20 percent of EU energy from renewable energy sources; and 20 percent improvement in energy efficiency. The 2020 Climate Action Package included three main policy instruments: (1) a renewed ETS Directive with an emission cap for the third allocation period (2013–2020); (2) a decision on effort sharing that covered binding annual national reduction targets for non-ETS sectors (non-ETS industries, housing, agriculture, waste, and transport with the exception of aviation) for all member states for the period 2013–2020; and (3) a revised Renewable Energy Directive (RED) with national targets for the share of renewables in electricity, heating/cooling, and transport. The RED included much-debated sustainability criteria for biofuels and was linked to a revision of the Fuel Quality Directive.

COP15 in Copenhagen

Even before the implementation of the first reduction period under the Kyoto Protocol (2008–2012), there was huge disappointment with the emission reductions achieved under the UNFCCC, primarily due to the limited scope and ambition of the Kyoto Protocol. The US did not ratify the protocol and big emitters such as China, India, Brazil, and South Africa were not even included in the first place, as the emission reduction commitments only covered the so-called Annex I countries (industrialized countries and countries in economic transition) (see also Chapter 2). Therefore, the political pressure to replace the Kyoto Protocol with a global spanning binding agreement was increasing. Hopes were raised that the COP15 in Copenhagen in 2009 could deliver such an agreement. The change in presidency in the US, where the more climate skeptical Bush administration was replaced with the Obama-Gore administration only fueled such expectations. However, the COP15 failed to deliver a global binding agreement and, instead, the much weaker Copenhagen Accord was adopted.

The Copenhagen Accord was a short 2 ½-page document drafted in the closing hours of the COP15 summit. It was a non-legally binding agreement whereby countries under the UNFCCC would submit voluntary emission reduction targets for 2020 using a range of different baselines and calculation procedures (e.g., 1990 base year, 2000, 2005, carbon intensity, business as usual). The European Union committed to reducing its GHG emissions by 20 percent (compared to 1990), in line with the already decided reduction targets in the 2020 Climate Action Package. However, the European reduction target could be increased to 30 percent, if comparable commitments were adequately made by both developed and developing countries for the period 2012–2020.

Financial crisis

Soon after the failure to agree on a global, legally binding agreement at COP15 in Copenhagen, the financial crisis struck the world economy and drew political attention away from the global climate action to economic recovery instead. Global organizations such as the UN and OECD called for green recovery plans labeled Green Economy or Green Growth strategies, but the focus on climate action had moved down the political agenda in the countries that had been leading the efforts to curb and reduce emissions. In Europe, the financial crisis influenced the economic system and caused a drop in GHG emissions of a little less than 10 percent. However, the emissions quickly returned to the original trajectory and, by 2010, GHG emissions from European member states were back on a path leading toward the 2020 emission objective, with no significant changes caused by the financial crisis to the overall slowly declining emission trend.

Paris agreement

In 2015, the Paris agreement was adopted as an annex to the UNFCCC. The agreement was based on a bottom-up approach (as opposed to the top-down approach from the failed COP15 in Copenhagen), wherein the signatories were requested to submit national climate plans prior to the COP21 meeting in Paris. Most importantly, the US and China had settled a bilateral agreement on emission reduction before the COP meeting, thereby paving the way for a global agreement. The EU's initial Nationally Determined Contribution (NDC) committed the union to reducing GHG emissions by 40 percent in 2030 (relative to 1990).

Revised directives RED2

The Renewable Energy Directive was reviewed in 2018 to increase the commitment of member states to meet an objective of 32 percent renewable energy by 2020 to support the implementation of the 20 percent emission cut objective. The revised directive also included policy instruments to support renewable energy communities and strengthened sustainability criteria for bioenergy.

European green deal

The deal was launched in December 2019 as an economic growth strategy aiming to tackle climate and environmentally related challenges while also transforming the European economy to a resource-efficient and competitive economy (see also Chapter 5). The deal included a comprehensive roadmap with several investment packages, actions, and policy instruments that cover all sectors of the European economy. Combatting climate change was naturally a central issue. Fundamental to this endeavor was the European Climate Law, designed to make climate policy objectives formulated in the Green Deal legally binding and to follow the logic of similar climate laws that had been adopted in several European member states, most notably the UK. The EU Climate Law sets overarching targets and ambitions for the European climate action policies and commits the European Union institutions and EU member states to take the necessary steps to meet these targets and objectives. The Climate Law also includes reporting and monitoring systems under which EU member states are obliged to report on policies and measures to meet the targets of the so-called National Energy and Climate Plans (NECP) (Schlacke et al., 2022). The NECPs are reviewed by the commission, which has the obligation to recommend additional measures to EU member states that are not taking appropriate measures to meet climate policy targets.

The targets of the climate law are operationalized in a series of directives and regulations that govern details on how these are met in specific sectors (Schlacke et al., 2022). These include the EU Emissions Trading Directive; the Effort Sharing Regulation; the Renewable Energy Directive; the Energy Efficiency Directive; the Regulation on Land Use, Land Use Change, and Forestry; and the Energy Taxation Directive.

The European Green Deal and the European Climate Law replaced and strengthened the existing climate ambition of 40 percent GHG reduction by 2030, as originally adopted in 2014 by the European Council prior to the COP21 meeting in Paris (European Council, 2014), with a new and more ambitious reduction target of 55 percent by 2030 and climate neutrality by 2050, defined as net zero greenhouse gas emissions by 2050. This climate policy target was included in a climate action package that was launched the following year under the headline "Fit for 55."

The Green Deal has expected broad and substantial impact, and it is in this regard acknowledged that the agreement will bring uneven burdens on various stakeholders. To address this imbalance up front, the deal includes The Just Transition Mechanism (JTM), which is a set of mechanisms and tools developed and implemented with the aim to make the transition toward climate neutrality fairer and "leave no one behind," as stated in the argumentation. The JTM involves mobilization of around €55 billion from 2021 to 2027 to not only aid and support affected stakeholders and regions, but also soften the impact of the transition enacted by the Green Deal (European Commission, 2019). In an EU context, the JTM is a milestone in the efforts to make the green transition just and fair, as discussed in detail in Chapter 10.

Fit for 55

In July 2021, the commission launched a large package of climate policy initiatives that aimed to deliver the needed reduction to achieve the targets defined in the European Green Deal and the European Climate Law. The launch of the package was also aligned with the postponed COP26, whereby signatories of the Paris Agreement to the UNFCCC were expected to deliver revised GHG emission reduction targets as a part of the ambitious mechanism. The package involved a large set of initiatives:

- A revision of the ETS: a proposal to raise the annual reduction of emission allowances from 2.2 percent to 4.2 percent; lowered emission cap; and a phase out of free allowances for aviation and the inclusion of intra-EU maritime transport emission (after a four-year phase-in period)
- An Effort Sharing Regulation that assigns emission reduction targets to individual member states for non-ETS sectors
- A regulation on carbon sinks in land use, forestry, and agriculture
- A revision of the Renewable Energy Directive aimed to increase the target for the share of renewables in gross final energy consumption from 32 percent to 40 percent by 2030 and including sustainability criteria for bioenergy. The overarching EU target for renewable energy in 2030 is additionally complemented by EU-wide and national sub-targets for certain sectors (e.g., building sector, industrial sector, and transport)
- A revision of the Energy Efficiency Directive including more ambitious annual reduction targets for energy consumption
- Stronger CO_2 emission standards for cars: raising the climate ambition related to newly registered passenger cars, increasing their CO_2 reduction target from 37 percent to 55 percent by 2030 (relative to 2021). The reduction target for light commercial vehicles is increased from 31

percent to 50 percent by 2030 (relative to 2021). in addition, an ambitious 2035 target is introduced for both passenger cars and light commercial vehicles of 100 percent, which ultimately means the phase out of fossil fueled vehicles
- Initiatives aimed at aviation and maritime fuels
- A revision of the Energy Tax Directive
- Introduction of a new so-called Carbon Border Adjustment Mechanism, aimed at pricing energy intensive products that are imported to avoid the problem of "carbon leakage"

Social effects of fit for 55

The proposed initiatives under Fit for 55, especially those related to the expansion of the ETS into the road transport and building sectors, are expected to increase energy prices across the Union, leading to potential negative economic and social impacts. The Commission therefore proposed to establish a Social Climate Fund from 2025 to 2032 to compensate vulnerable households. The allocation of funds to member states (and thereafter to the exposed households) is managed via a new policy instrument called Social Climate Plans, which are to be submitted by member states, along with the traditional National Energy and Climate Plans. The Social Climate Plans are expected to cover investments and measures to mitigate negative effects on vulnerable groups, and they include temporary income support and measures to reduce dependency on fossil fuels among vulnerable groups (Schlacke et al., 2022).

The Russian invasion of Ukraine

In March 2022, Russia invaded neighboring Ukraine, leading to radical changes in the European policies on imported natural gas and an increased focus on the rapid implementation of policy measures to reduce dependency on fossil fuels imported from Russia. Following the Russian invasion of the Ukrainian peninsular of Crimea in 2014, discussion of energy dependencies, especially those related to member states such as Germany and Italy, had already occurred for some time. The construction of the natural gas pipeline between Germany and Russia through the Baltic Sea had further sparked discussions on energy dependency and its potential implications in a conflict situation between European countries and Russia. The pipeline had also been criticized as prolonging European dependency on natural gas.

In 2021, the European Union imported 90 percent of its natural gas consumption, of which Russia was supplying 40 percent (European Commission, 2022). Additionally, oil and coal imports from Russia accounted for 27 percent and 46 percent, respectively. The natural gas was roughly used for 30 percent industry, 30 percent households, 30 percent electric power generation, and 10 percent in commercial applications. The dependency on imported natural gas differs country to country in the European Union. In

2020, Germany imported 66.1 percent of its natural gas from Russia, Poland 54.8 percent, Italy 34.3 percent, and France 36.3 percent (Eurostat, 2021). The major differences in terms of gas supply vulnerability among EU member states, combined with historic differences in political relations with Russia, initially sparked a fear that the EU would not be able to find a common ground for a natural gas policy during this crisis. Historically, eastern European countries such as Poland and Hungary had argued for less ambitious climate policies, countries like Italy and Germany had developed energy infrastructure that had created dependencies on natural gas imports, and countries like Serbia and Hungary had strong historic and political relations to the current Russian administration.

However, the Russian invasion of Ukraine, and the following thread of Russian natural gas supply disruptions, forced European member states and the European institutions to reconsider energy policies related to natural gas imports. The crisis pushed European countries closer together and caused the European Commission to present a plan, REPowerEU, aimed at reducing European natural gas dependency on Russia. The Fit for 55 already aimed to reduce the yearly natural gas consumption by 170bcm yearly by 2030 through a tripling of wind and solar capacities (and a doubling by 2025 in the meantime). The REPowerEU plan aimed at accelerating this transition toward renewable energy sources while, at the same time, increasing the import of Liquefied Natural Gas (LNG) from countries such as Qatar, the US, Algeria, and Azerbaijan. The REPowerEU was based on three pillars: (1) gas diversification focused on an increase in LNG imports from non-Russian sources as the main policy instrument in the plan and an increase in the supply of biomethane and hydrogen; (2) electrification of Europe aimed at improving European energy efficiency and increasing electricity production from wind and solar; and (3) transformation of industry aimed at increasing the electrification of industries and the uptake of renewable hydrogen.

Overview of European Union climate action policies

Looking back on the last 30 years of climate action policies in the European Union, it is evident that huge changes have occurred. The scope of policies has been expanded from narrow policies focusing on energy savings and a phase out of fossil fuels from the energy sector to a comprehensive program of policies covering almost all aspects of the European societies—one that combines sophisticated policies, market mechanisms, and regulations. For decades, energy policies in Europe were mainly a national endeavor and commitments to common climate action objectives and strategies were primarily voluntary. Over the last 30 years, a significant integration process has taken place among European Union member states, as the legal and political authority over energy policies and objectives increasingly has been transferred from the national level to EU level, followed by a sophisticated reporting and monitoring regimes covering areas such as GHG emission reductions, sharing of renewable energy sources, and implementation of biofuels and energy savings.

Major milestones in the timeline are summarized in Figure 6.4, showing when central, strategic sustainability targets were set in the EU, and dividing these targets into general reduction targets and energy technology and/or consumption targets. The figure also shows trigger events for these targets at the EU and IPCC level.

Twenty-first-century developments in EU's energy sector

The rapid developments in EU's climate policy in the 21st century have induced substantial changes in the union's energy sector and resultant impacts on global warming. In the beginning of the 2000s, the CO_2-concentration in the atmosphere reached 375 ppm, or an increase of around 2 ppm per year since the 1990 agreements (NOAA, 2022). This corresponds to an increase of 5 percent since the first IPCC report was released. In the EU, the changes in the energy system from 1990 to 2005 led to a substantial 30 percent decrease in coal consumption, while consumption of natural gas-based energy and oil increased 50 percent and 5 percent, respectively. In total, the amount of energy produced from fossil resources was almost stable from 1990 to 2005, but there was a substantial shift from coal to natural gas. All non-fossil energy production increased as well and, from a low starting point, the relative increases were drastic for some of them. Hydro increased only 8 percent and nuclear increased 25 percent. But energy produced from biomass and waste doubled, while energy produced from wind, solar, etc. almost quadrupled to 360 percent of the level in 1990. All in all, energy production in the EU increased around 10 percent, while energy-related GHG emissions decreased slightly (around 2–5 percent) from 1990 as calculated with data from (IEA, 2022; Silva & Raadal, 2019; The Netherlands Enterprise Agency (RVO), 2018). The transformation in Denmark is a good example of the approaches taken between 1990 and 2005. Some of the activities in this period included two large coal boilers were replaced with natural gas boilers and a large oil boiler was reconfigured into peak-load only (M. K. Nielsen, 2017); the country's first seven off-shore wind farms, totaling 203 wind turbines (aggregated peak production 410 MW), were deployed (Danish Energy Agency, 2022); and the first biogas plants operating on agricultural waste was built and put into operation (M. Nielsen, 2021).

In the period from 2000 to 2018, greenhouse gas emissions from non-transport energy production in EU-27 decreased 20 percent, while maintaining a net energy output to the union of 85 EJ per year. The relative emission-reductions in the 90s was substantial (more than 10 percent from 1990 to 2000), but the rate declined in the first decade of the new millennium (5–6 percent from 2000 to 2010), only to pick up pace once more in the following decade (15 percent from 2010). The decrease in greenhouse gas emissions in the last 20 years arose from a decrease in coal consumption of

Climate change-motivated development of EU's energy production 161

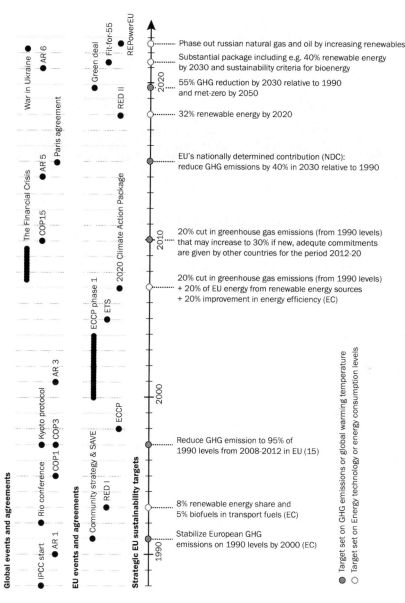

Figure 6.4 Timeline overview of major milestone agreements related to strategic sustainable development at the IPCC and EU level from 1988 to 2022.

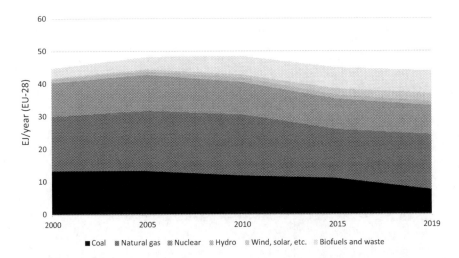

Figure 6.5 Historical energy use for non-transport purposes. Data from EU-28, years 2000 to 2019. From (IEA, 2022).

more than 40 percent, a stabilization of the natural gas consumption, and a tremendous increase in the production of non-hydro based renewable energy (850 percent in solar and wind and 250 percent in waste and bioenergy). See Figures 6.1 and 6.2 for the general development and Figure 6.5 for details of the development of specific types of energy consumption in non-transport energy production during this period. In the most recent years, this development has accelerated even further and, from 2018 to 2021, coal consumption in the EU was reduced by another 25 percent (Eurostat, 2022b).

Energy consumption for non-transport purposes in the union increased more than 10 percent for the first decade of the 2000s but decreased thereafter. As a result, the consumption level today is comparable to that of 2000. As a result of a somewhat stabilizing total energy consumption and of increasing production and consumption of renewables, non-fossil energy (including nuclear and waste) today accounts for more than 40 percent of the EU's non-transport energy.

In transport, the share of energy from renewable sources in the EU is substantially smaller, but the rate of increase is substantially higher. In 2005, the rate of renewables within EU transport was below 2 percent, which increased by a factor of five to more than 10 percent in 2020, thereby just meeting the EU's 2020 target. The contribution of different member states to meeting this target varies substantially. Half of the members underachieved on this account, and half overachieved. In Sweden, the rate of renewables in transportation is around 30 percent, while it is around only 5 percent in countries like Greece and Lithuania (European Environment Agency, 2022a). Blending of fossil fuels with biofuels (around 80 percent vegetable oil and 20 percent bioethanol (Transport & Environment, 2021) in conventional combustion engines is the major driver for this development. The inertia in the system is substantial and the process of development away from ICC-based cars is long and slow. Even in EU neighbor country Norway—where three out of four sold vehicles are electric or plug-in hybrid and all electricity is practically fully renewable—just around 3 percent of transport energy is renewable electricity (Statista Research Department, 2022). However, the development in electrification of road and rail transport is accelerating and, with the rise of requirements for non-fossil fuels in the hardly electrifiable heavy transport in aviation and the maritime sector, there is an ongoing debate about which roles electrification and biofuels should play in the coming phases of the transition in the transport sector. The palette of options includes both bio-methane from anaerobic digestion, second-generation ethanol, methanol, hydrogen, and green electricity (for more see, e.g., SLOCAT 2021; European Biogas Association, 2022; Krause et al., 2020).

The differences among member state commitments and capabilities are also still paramount in the production and use of fossil fuels, as illustrated here with the development in consumption and production of coal. While almost all countries reduced their coal use during the years 2000–2020, more than 60 percent of the total reduction occurred in the Czech Republic, France, Poland, Spain, and Greece (European Environment Agency, 2022b). Despite this massive reduction, Poland and Germany alone still accounted for more than two-thirds of the EU's total coal consumption (Eurostat, 2022b). On the production side, the differences were even more pronounced. Since 1990, coal production in the EU has decreased from 277 million tonnes per year to just around 60 million tonnes in 2021. The production in 1990 was divided among 13 member states, with Poland as the main producer and Polish hard coal production amounting to more than 140 million tonnes per year. In 2021, it was almost exclusively Poland that produced hard coal in the EU, with only a minor fraction (around 4 percent) produced in the Czech Republic. However, at the same time, Poland also accounted for the largest reduction and, in 2021, the country only produced less than 35 percent of what it produced annually in 1990 (ibid.).

Temporal scale

Transition efforts aim toward reducing the impact of the climate crisis both now and for future generations. Time to act is limited and all emissions today have long-term effects by accelerating ongoing damage events, enacting feed-back mechanisms, and irreversible developments in the socio-ecological systems (tipping points), and accumulating GHGs in the atmosphere, prolonging the perspective to reach safe levels once again. However, different GHGs have different impact patterns, and it is relevant to consider temporal scale when including impact assessments in decision-making. In the early years after 1988, there was an openness to temporal scale, including GHG

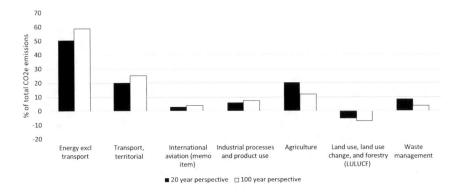

Figure 6.6 Differences in greenhouse gas emissions from various sectors as a result of the temporal scope of the accounting. Based on emission data from Eurostat (Eurostat, 2022a) and 2021 AR6 IPCC GWP characterization factors (IPCC WG1, 2022).

impact assessments, from a 20-year perspective, a 100-year perspective, and even a 500-year perspective. Today, there is an unspoken consensus about addressing climate impact on a 100-year temporal scope. This reduces the complexity of accounting schemes and decision-making processes but entails a risk of bias and blindness. The effects are mainly related to methane emissions and the related value of avoiding such emissions. Methane is a very potent GHG, though it oxidizes quickly after (on average) 11 years in the atmosphere. Calculating methane GWP in different temporal scopes is complicated, but done regularly by, for example, IPCC (IPCC WG1, 2022). Considering the option to avoid methane emissions by reducing natural gas use, optimizing biogas production or improved waste management would have a substantially higher societal value in the short-term perspective than in the long-term. The effect of limiting emissions of carbon in the form of methane into the atmosphere using the 2021 GWP accounting method would be 81–83 times higher than that of emitting the carbon into the atmosphere as CO2, when considered in a 20-year temporal scope. From a 100-year perspective, the difference would only be a factor 27–30 and the effect of methane reduction initiatives similarly smaller. Taking these aspects into consideration, accounting for EU emissions (2019 data) shows significant differences among the relative impact of the different sectors, as illustrated in Figure 6.6.

The short-term perspective may, to a larger extent, put focus on waste management and agriculture, which are major sources of methane emissions. The discussion about temporal scope in emission-accounting and decision-making becomes relevant because the effects of climate change are now here. The damage is already real. And the risk of surpassing irreversible tipping point thresholds is increasing. The value of reducing damage effects and tipping point risks should be included in decision-making, alongside long-term perspectives. Otherwise, these decisions may contribute to compromising the integrity of the socio-ecological systems required to mitigate the climate crisis in the longer term.

Impact, justice, and fairness on the path(s) ahead

Looking back on the past 30 years of European climate action policies, significant changes have been made to the scope of policies, range policy instruments, and climate ambition. Regarding the policy landscape, the scope of European climate action policies has significantly changed, leading to the inclusion of a very broad range of sectors. Whereas the first climate action policies mainly targeted the energy sector, focusing on energy savings and phase out of fossil fuels from electricity and heat production, the most recent climate action strategy Fit for 55 covers a very broad range of sectors, including energy, agriculture, industry, and buildings. It is also noteworthy that climate action policy has moved from a less significant policy area to a cornerstone of the most central EU policies—climate action is, for example, a central element in the European Green Deal. However, some elements have survived over the last 30 years, for example, the division of climate action into three main pillars: reduction of GHG emissions, promotion of renewable energy sources, and energy efficiency measures.

Regarding policy instruments, the European Union's climate policies have also undergone significant change. The European Commission has maintained a mixed policy strategy that covers initiatives taken on the EU level with initiatives taken on the member state level. The governance of the member state initiatives has also been gradually made more systematically, most recently with the adoption of the EU Climate Law and the implementation of National Energy and Climate Plans (NECP).

The first significant change to climate policy instruments came with the introduction of the ETS that was adopted in the European Union following the implementation of the UNFCCC Kyoto Protocol commitments and today (2022) remains one of the most powerful climate action policy instruments that cap overall European GHG emissions from the included sectors and facilitate trading of emission allowances to secure the most cost-efficient GHG emission reductions. Historically, the ETS has been criticized for including too many emission credits, resulting in low prices and inefficient incentives to implement climate action measures in companies covered by the system. The commission has responded by reducing the load of credits to increase prices and drive emission cuts.

The ETS has continuously been expanded to include not only power generation and heavy manufacturing industries but also aviation and maritime sectors. The most recent proposal from the European Commission, as a part of the Fit for 55 package covers a proposal to initiate an ETS-2 for the buildings and transport sectors.

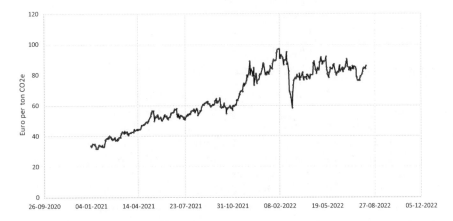

Figure 6.7 EUA (EU ETS) Futures prices, 11-8-2022 from (Ember, 2022).

A path for adequate, fair, and robust greenhouse gas emission reductions in the EU

There have been substantial changes in EU's energy systems and related reductions in greenhouse gas emissions during the last 30 years. However, since time is of the essence regarding the developing climate crisis, it is relevant to question if the rate of reduction is adequately fast and if the emission reduction goals are sufficiently ambitious. Since the EU members are generally wealthy and developed countries on a global scale, it is also relevant to question if the set targets are fair when assessed from a global justice perspective. And, if so, under which assumptions/expectations related to the efforts in the rest of the world?

The total union territorial greenhouse gas emissions from 1990 to 2019 are displayed in Figure 6.7, alongside EU's emission reduction targets for 2030 and 2050, as dictated in the climate law and agreed upon as part of the Green Deal. The chart is also fitted with a set of trend-lines extrapolating the development of historical data beyond 2050. The three trend-lines are linear regressions of the historical data (dotted) extrapolating from 2020 data either 10, 20, or 30 years back. The most positive development is found based on data going 20 years back, while data based only on the development from the last decade are further from the targets. The data indicate that substantially larger annual emission reduction effects than obtained so far are required to meet the targets. One trend-line is a polynomial extrapolation (dashed), which is closer to the targets, indicating that, to meet the targets, there needs to be either a disruptive break in the linear development trajectory or a continuously increasing rate of annual emission reductions every year from now to 2050 (Figure 6.8).

Climate change-motivated development of EU's energy production 167

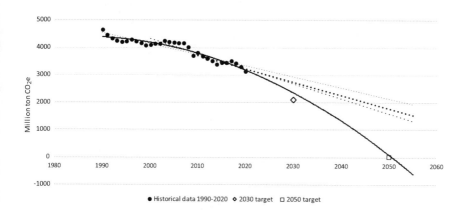

Figure 6.8 Greenhouse gas emissions (EU-27 2020 excl. Great Britain) as recorded from 1990 to 2019 (Eurostat, 2022a), calculated into CO_2e using IPCC AR6 GWP characterization factors (IPCC WG1, 2022). Included are also EU emission reduction targets in 2030 and 2050, as dictated by the Climate Law, agreed upon as part of the EU green deal (European Council, 2022). Thin trend line is based on data from 1990 to 2019. Medium trend line is based on data from 2000 to 2019. Thick trend line is based on data from 2010 to 2019.

European climate action from a global perspective

When evaluating the progress and ambition of the European Union climate action policies, a key discussion point is whether current policies adequately meet the global challenges and, for example, align European emission trajectories with the global ambition to limit global emissions on level that can secure a maximum of 1.5°C warming. The INDC commitments under the Paris Agreement seem not to deliver the needed emission reductions (see Chapter 2). Even though the European Union has played a continuous, leading role in the UN climate action negotiations under the UNFCCC, pushing for higher ambitions in the global effort to reduce emissions, one could still argue that the reductions delivered by the European Union are still not adequate and just, given the historic emissions caused by the European member states.

In addition to the discussion about development rates and Paris Agreement reduction targets, it is also relevant to discuss the fairness of addressing the current situation from present emission levels only. On top of current emission levels, there is a reasonable discussion about historical responsibility and current capability. While the EU accounts for around 7 percent of the annual emissions today, the union accounts for 16 percent of historical, anthropogenic CO_2 emissions but only 10 percent of the world population. There has been a period with centuries of over-representation in global emissions, which has played a substantial role in the region's development and current level of wealth and capabilities. The related inequity may be argued as a claim for an even larger responsibility in global greenhouse gas emission reduction than currently set. According to base-case calculations conducted with Stockholm Environmental Institute's Climate Equity Reference Calculator, using a 1990 reference and setting a 1.5°C standard pathway, the historical emission reduction responsibility of EU28 requires that the 55 percent reduction pledges, efforts, and effects are more than doubled in 2030 and that net emissions below zero must be obtained across the entire EU before 2025 (Stockholm Environment Institute, 2022). To most people, this is not even possible to imagine, let alone plan for. Thus, assessing and including the magnitude of the historical responsibility of developed nations regarding climate crisis mitigation is often left unaddressed.

European climate action from a regional perspective

The countries within the EU may be comparable on many central characteristics, but there are still substantial and relevant differences among the member states. In relation to climate change mitigation and transition of the energy sector, some of the most important differences are: (1) economic wealth, (2) natural resources valuable in energy production, (3) current energy production levels and infrastructure, (4) current emission levels, and (5) cultural and political differences. To unify the member countries in common climate change policy agreement and energy sector transition, it is essential to carefully analyze and allocate the share of burdens within the region and the related differences in capability and agency.

Fundamental differences among the European member states—for example, in terms of economic and technological capacity to implement changes and the availability of renewable resources—has made it difficult to find common ground for more ambitious climate action policies. Among the member states that are most supportive for integrated and ambitious climate action policies are countries like Austria, Denmark, France, Germany, Italy, and Sweden (Maris & Flouros, 2021). This group represents countries that, over many years, have implemented ambitious national climate action policies and strategies and, to a large extent, have also been industry leaders in developing new energy technologies. At the other end of the spectrum are countries such as Bulgaria, Croatia, Latvia, Luxembourg, Malta, and Poland with less ambitious national climate action policies and generally less support for ambitious European climate action targets and policies (Maris & Flouros, 2021). Maris and Flouros (2021) analyzed European Union member states National Energy and Climate Plans (NECPs) to identify responses, strategies, and compliance with overall European climate action policies and objectives. Based on this analysis, countries were grouped into categories according to their long-term commitment and support for European climate and energy policies (Table 6.1).

The differences in ambition, to some extent, also echo the division between "older" European Union member states in Western Europe, with

Table 6.1 EU Member States' long-term strategies in energy and climate (Maris & Flouros, 2021).

Foot-dragging	Fence-sitting	Pace-setting
Bulgaria, Croatia, Latvia, Luxembourg, Malta, and Poland	Belgium, Cyprus, Czech Republic, Estonia, Finland, Greece, Hungary, Ireland, Lithuania, The Netherlands, Portugal, Romania, Slovakia, Slovenia, and Spain	Austria, Denmark, France, Germany, Italy, and Sweden

generally stronger economies on one axis and Central and Eastern European countries that have been facing economic challenges and also have less technological capacity to implement the transition from fossil fuels to renewable energy sources on another axis. Historically, Southern European countries like Greece, Spain, and Portugal have been less supportive of ambitious climate action objectives; however, the support from these countries has been changing over the years and has often been more supportive during periods of left-wing governments. Additionally, as the scope of European Union climate action policies has been rapidly expanding, as explained above, the relation between climate action and other policy domains has also increased. This implies that climate action policies are now more likely to interfere with other policy areas that may lead member states to take national stand on some climate-related issues in order to defend policy objectives that only have little to do with climate action as such. For example, in 2021, Poland threatened to block adoption of the European Union's Climate Action Pact unless the country would get access to the European Union's pandemic recovery funds. Such political processes may distort a clear picture of the support for ambitious climate action policies.

European emissions from a local perspective

Only assessing EU policy and development on a regional or even national scale may lead to an underestimation of the complexity of the situation. In each country, there may be several local aspects that need to be considered in the larger perspective in order to understand the dynamics of development. The discussion about justice and fairness in local energy transitions relates strongly to the roles, opportunities, and obligations of various stakeholders and their inner perimeter interests. Misinterpreting, ignoring, or challenging interests at the local level may generate counter-pressure movements, manifested as NIMBY or WIIX issues and local resistance and, in more general situations, as the emergence of wide-spread public resistance like the Yellow Vest Movement in France.

Local level opposition may feed, both directly and indirectly, back to the national and supra-national level and, as such, local level dynamics may have a substantial influence on the overall development of the energy system, just as the initiatives taken on the national and supra-national level feed back into the local level. There is also a technical parallel to the discussion about governance levels, as the transition of modern energy systems involves a huge spectrum of development opportunities, from establishing new energy systems with large, centralized, and publicly owned producer units to enacting the emergence of a distributed, de-centralized system with prosumers, shareholder collectives, etc. Both governance structure and energy system structure (physical, economical) may present possibilities, as well as barriers, in the transition away from fossil-based energy.

Summary

The chapter discussed the historic and current climate of energy policies the European Union in light of the climate crisis. It opened with an analysis of how energy consumption (still) drives the major share of greenhouse gas emissions in the European Union, and some of the most prominent dynamics related to recent developments are discussed. Differences related to both quality and quantity among selected, relevant energy types were evaluated and a list of key indicators—Net Energy Output, Energy Return on Energy Investment, and Climate Intensity of various energy forms—was introduced. The following section contextualized the presented data, terms, and indicators in a discussion about how all countries have different energy prerequisites and capabilities and about how this may have a huge impact on a given country's social level of development and possibility to act in the climate crisis. Hereafter, the perspective changed to political history, with a storyline description of climate policy development on the EU and IPCC level from just before 1991, when the Commission launched the first "Community strategy to limit carbon dioxide emissions and improve energy efficiency," to today. Major political milestones and external disturbances were discussed in the context of regional development, climate impact, and energy consumption. This section ended with the EU Green Deal, Fit for 55, and the huge implications of the current war between Russia and Ukraine, before wrapping up the historical development of European Union Climate Action policies in a comprehensive timeline. The third major section of this chapter analyzed 21st-century developments in the EU's energy sector considering the findings from the first two major sections, considering both member state situations, political contexts, and major events. The chapter concluded with an open discussion about impact, justice, and fairness into the future, wherein the union's strategies and climate mitigation ambitions and obligations were evaluated on a local, regional, and global level. The chapter provided new insights into key aspects of energy production, climate impact, resource distribution, policy development, fairness, and global justice, and it questioned whether the European Union's climate impact commitments will be sufficient to deliver the needed greenhouse gas reductions and if the agreements and planned actions are fair and just from local, regional, and global perspectives?

References

Asghar, Z. (2008). Energy-GDP relationship: A causal analysis for the five countries Of South Asia. *Applied Econometrics and International Development*, 8(1).

Campo, J. and Sarmiento, V. (2013). The relationship between energy consumption and GDP: Evidence from a panel of 10 Latin American countries. *Latin American Journal of Economics*, 50(2), 233–255. DOI: 10.7764/LAJE.50.2.233

Climatewatch (2022). *Historical GHG emissions*. Database. Retrieved from: https://www.climatewatchdata.org/ghg-emissions

Danish Energy Agency (2022). *Etablerede havvindmølleparker i Danmark*. Wind Farm Portal. Retrieved from: https://ens.dk/ansvarsomraader/vindenergi/havvindmoeller-og-projekter-i-pipeline

Dell'ariccia, G., Milesi-Ferretti, G. M., Gopinath, G., Killian, L., Lee, T., Papageorgiou, C., Spilimbergo, A., Stuermer, M., and Vigfusson, R. J. (2020). Energy, efficiency gains and economic development: When will global energy demand saturate?, WP/20/253, November 2020.

Ember. (2022, August 11). *EU carbon price tracker*. Database. Retrieved from: https://ember-climate.org/data/data-tools/carbon-price-viewer/

Esen, Ö. and Bayrak, M. (2017). Does more energy consumption support economic growth in net energy-importing countries? *Journal of Economics, Finance and Administrative Science*, 22(42), 75–98. DOI: 10.1108/JEFAS-01-2017-0015

European Biogas Association (2022, July 7). *News, Brussels 7 July 2022*. News Bulletin. Retrieved from: https://www.europeanbiogas.eu/author/angela/

European Commission (1992, May 13). *A community strategy to limit carbon dioxide emissions and improve energy efficiency*. Press Statement. Retrieved from: https://ec.europa.eu/commission/presscorner/detail/en/P_92_29

European Commission (2015). *EU ETS Handbook*. Retrieved from: https://aeaep.com.ua/en/wp-content/uploads/2015/07/ets_handbook_en.pdf

European Commission (2019). *The just transition mechanism: Making sure no one is left behind*. Policy Portal. Retrieved from: https://ec.europa.eu/info/strategy/priorities-2019-2024/european-green-deal/finance-and-green-deal/just-transition-mechanism_en#introduction

European Commission (2022). *REPowerEU: Joint European Action for more affordable, secure and sustainable energy*. Retrieved from: https://eur-lex.europa.eu/resource.html?uri=cellar:71767319-9f0a-11ec-83e1-01aa75ed71a1.0001.02/DOC_1&format=PDF

European Council (2014). *Conclusions, 2030 climate and energy policy framework of 23/24 October 2014—EUCO 169/14*. Retrieved from: https://www.consilium.europa.eu/media/24561/145397.pdf

European Council (2022, June 29). *European green deal*. Policy Portal. Retrieved from: https://www.consilium.europa.eu/en/policies/green-deal/

European Environment Agency (2022a, March 10). *Use of renewable energy for transport in Europe*. Article. Retrieved from: https://www.eea.europa.eu/ims/use-of-renewable-energy-for

European Environment Agency (2022b, April 4). *Emissions and energy use in large combustion plants in Europe*. Article. Retrieved from: https://www.eea.europa.eu/ims/emissions-and-energy-use-in

Eurostat (2021). *Import of natural gas 2020–2021.* Database. Retrieved from: https://ec. europa.eu/eurostat/cache/infographs/energy_trade/entrade.html?geo=DE&year=2020&language=EN&trade=imp&siec=G3000&filter=all&fuel=gas&unit= TJ_GCV&defaultUnit=TJ_GCV&detail=1&chart=

Eurostat (2022a). *Greenhouse gas emissions by source sector (source: EEA).* Database2. Retrieved from: https://ec.europa.eu/eurostat/cache/metadata/en/env_air_gge_ esms.htm

Eurostat (2022b, March). *Coal production and consumption statistics.* Database. Retrieved from: https://ec.europa.eu/eurostat/statistics-explained/index.php?title=Coal_ production_and_consumption_statistics

Hall, C. A. S., Lambert, J. G. and Balogh, S. B. (2014). EROI of different fuels and the implications for society. *Energy Policy*, 64, 141–152. DOI: 10.1016/j.enpol. 2013.05.049

IEA (2022). *Europe.* Database. Retrieved from: https://www.iea.org/regions/europe

IPCC WG1 (2022). *Climate change 2021: The physical science basis - Working Group 1 contribution to the sixth assessment report.* In: V. Masson-Delmotte, P. Zhai, A. Pirani, S. L. Connors, C. Péan, S. Berger, N. Caud, Y. Chen, L. Goldfarb, M. I. Gomis, M. Huang, K. Leitzell, E. Lonnoy, J. B. R. Matthews, T. K. Maycock, T. Waterfield, O. Yelekçi, R. Yu & B. Zho (eds.), Cambridge University Press. DOI: 10.1017/9781009157896

Krause, J., Thiel, C., Tsokolis, D., Samaras, Z., Rota, C., Ward, A., Prenninger, P., Coosemans, T., Neugebauer, S. and Verhoeve, W. (2020). EU road vehicle energy consumption and CO2 emissions by 2050 – Expert-based scenarios. *Energy Policy*, 138. DOI: 10.1016/j.enpol.2019.111224

Lambert, J. G., Hall, C. A. S., Balogh, S., Gupta, A. and Arnold, M. (2014). Energy, EROI and quality of life. *Energy Policy*, 64, 153–167. DOI: 10.1016/j. enpol.2013.07.001

Maris, G. and Flouros, F. (2021). The green deal, national energy and climate plans in Europe: Member states' compliance and strategies. *Administrative Sciences*, 11(3). DOI: 10.3390/admsci11030075

Nielsen, M. K. (2017). *Historisk: DONG vil udfase kul* (in Danish). Berlingske. Retrieved from: https://www.berlingske.dk/virksomheder/historisk-dong-vil-udfase-kul

Nielsen, M. (2021). *Han står bag et af de første biogasanlæg i Danmark: Det har været en udfordring at udvinde grøn energi* (in Danish). JydskeVestkysten. Retrieved from: https://jv. dk/artikel/han-st%C3%A5r-bag-et-af-de-f%C3%B8rste-biogasanl%C3%A6g-i-danmark-det-har-v%C3%A6ret-en-udfordring-at-udvinde-gr%C3% B8n-energi

Mukhtarov, S., Humbatova, S., Seyfullayev, I. and Kalbiyev, Y. (2020). The effect of financial development on energy consumption in the case of Kazakhstan. *Journal of Applied Economics*, 23(1), 75–88. DOI: 10.1080/15140326.2019.1709690

Nar, M. (2021). The relationship between income inequality and energy consumption: A pareto optimal approach. *Mehmet NAR / Journal of Asian Finance*, 8(4), 613–0624. DOI: 10.13106/jafeb.2021.vol8.no4.0613

NOAA (2022). *Trends in atmospheric carbon dioxide.* Earth System Research Laboratory. Retrieved from: https://gml.noaa.gov/ccgg/trends/

Patel, R. (2009). *The value of nothing: How to reshape market society and redefine democracy (First Pica).* New York: Picador.

Raugei, M. and Leccisi, E. (2016). A comprehensive assessment of the energy performance of the full range of electricity generation technologies deployed in the United Kingdom. *Energy Policy*, 90, 46–59. DOI: 10.1016/j.enpol.2015.12.011

Schlacke, S., Wentzien, H., Thierjung, E.-M. and Köster, M. (2022). Implementing the EU climate law via the 'Fit for 55' package. *Oxford Open Energy*, 1. DOI: 10.1093/ooenergy/oiab002

Schlömer, S., Bruckner, T., Fulton, L., Hertwich, E., McKinnon, A., Perczyk, D., Roy, J., Schaeffer, R., Sims, R., Smith, P. and Wiser, R. (2015). Annex III: Technology-specific cost and performance parameters. In: O. Edenhofer, R. Pichs-Madruga, Y. Sokona, E. Farahani, S. Kadner, K. Seyboth, A. Adler, I. Baum, S. Brunner, P. Eickemeier, B. Kriemann, J. Savolainen, S. Schlömer, C. von Stechow, T. Zwickel, J. C. Minx, & T. Z. and J. C. M. Eickemeier, B. Kriemann, J. Savolainen, S. Schlömer& C. von Stechow (eds.), *Climate change 2014: Mitigation of climate change. Contribution of Working Group III to the Fifth Assessment Report of the Intergovernmental Panel on Climate Change.* Appendix 3 for assessment report 5, 1329–1356. Cambridge University Press. DOI: 10.1017/cbo9781107415416.025

Silva, M. and Raadal, H. L. (2019). Life cycle GHG emissions of renewable and non-renewable electricity generation technologies Part of the RE-Invest project. Retrieved from: https://reinvestproject.eu/wp-content/uploads/2019/11/OR_RE-INVEST_Life-cycle-GHG-emissions-of-renewable-and-non-renewable-electricity.pdf

SLOCAT (2021), *Tracking Trends in a Time of Change: The Need for Radical Action Towards Sustainable Transport. Decarbonisation, Transport and Climate Change Global, Status Report* – 2nd edition. Retrieved from: https://tcc-gsr.com/wp-content/uploads/2021/06/3.9-Renewable-Energy-in-Transport.pdf, visited 19/12-2022, pages 1-13.

Statista Research Department (2022, June 24). *Market share of electric cars (BEV and PHEV) in Norway from 2009 to 2020.* Article. Retrieved from: https://www.statista.com/statistics/1029909/market-share-of-electric-cars-in-norway/

Stockholm Environment Institute (2022, May 17). *Climate equity reference calculator data v 7.3.3 calculator v 3.0.1.* Calculation Tool. Retrieved from: https://calculator.climateequityreference.org/

The Netherlands Enterprise Agency (RVO) (2018). *BioGrace II.* Online Database and Modelling Tool. Retrieved from: https://www.biograce.net/biograce2/

Townsend, J. M., Hall, C. A. S., Volk, T. A., Murphy, D., Ofezu, G., Powers, B., Quaye, A., and Serapiglia, M. (2014). Energy return on investment (EROI), liquid fuel production, and consequences for wildlife. In J.E. Gates, D.L. Trauger, & B. Czech (eds.), *Peak Oil, Economic Growth, and Wildlife Conservation*, 29–61. New York: Springer.

Transport & Environment (2021). Biofuels - What's happening? Article. Retrieved from: https://www.transportenvironment.org/challenges/energy/biofuels/

Tverberg, G. E. (2012). Oil supply limits and the continuing financial crisis. *Energy*, 37(1), 27–34. DOI: 10.1016/j.energy.2011.05.049

Ulgiati, S., Ascione, M., Bargigli, S., Cherubini, F., Franzese, P. P., Raugei, M., Viglia, S. and Zucaro, A. (2011). Material, energy and environmental performance of technological and social systems under a life cycle assessment perspective. *Ecological Modelling*, 222(1), 176–189. DOI: 10.1016/j.ecolmodel.2010.09.005

UNDP (2010). *Climate change adaption - Hungary.* Country Profile.

7 Resources and the circular economy

Thomas Budde Christensen

> EU needs to accelerate the transition towards a regenerative growth model that gives back to the planet more than it takes, advance towards keeping its resource consumption within planetary boundaries, and therefore strive to reduce its consumption footprint and double its circular material use rate in the coming decade.
>
> European Commission, A new Circular Economy Action Plan For a cleaner and more competitive Europe (2020)

Introduction

To meet the needs of both present and future generations, there is an urgent need to develop new ways of producing and consuming that can deliver goods and services with significantly lower climate footprint, environmental impacts, and resource strain.

The modern production and consumption systems affect the natural ecosystems and deplete the resources that future generations will need to live from. Important raw materials are extracted and converted into emissions, goods, and then waste, which is later difficult to recycle for the creation of new products (Stahel, 2016).

Over the last 100 years, there has been a very close link between economic growth and resource consumption growth (Fischer-Kowalski et al., 2011). In other words, our increasing global prosperity is based on the constantly increasing consumption of energy resources, building materials, metals, and biomass, deployed to produce, for example, energy, food, infrastructure, construction, and consumer goods. When the products no longer represent a value to the consumer, they are disposed of as waste, whereby important resources are often lost. By 2050, global waste production is expected to increase by 70 percent, and most of this waste is expected to end up incinerated or dumped into landfills (EU, 2020). This process, whereby raw materials are consumed in multiple production and consumption steps and eventually returned to nature as waste, is often labeled the linear production system (Stahel, 2016).

DOI: 10.4324/9781003319672-10

A long list of policy initiatives has been implemented to reduce the environmental impacts from the European production and consumption system, including most of the waste management legislation and product regulations adopted in the European Union. The most recent policy initiative is the European Green Deal.

Following the financial crisis in 2008, European policymakers sought to find new approaches to boost economic activity, while simultaneously reducing environmental impacts. At the same time, international organizations such as OECD and United Nations Environment Program (UNEP) promoted "green growth" and "green economy" policies within the same paradigm (OECD, 2011; UNEP, 2011). This led the European Commission to publish the "Roadmap for a Resource-Efficient Europe," which aimed to increase resource productivity and decouple economic growth from resource consumption (European Commission, 2011). This roadmap was formulated as a flagship initiative under the European 2020 strategy for economic growth in the European Union. With inspiration from the Ellen MacArthur Foundation, as well as researchers from academia and in international organizations, the European Commission used the central ideas from the "Roadmap for a Resource-Efficient Europe" to launch a circular economy package in 2014. The package included a circular economy action plan and legislative proposals to revise several waste-related directives.

The European Commission presented the European Green Deal in 2019 as a policy framework to increase economic activity in Europe, while concurrently combatting climate changes, and creating a sustainable economy. A cornerstone in this policy framework was the renewed circular economy action plan (European Commission, 2020a).

The circular economy

By 2022, the circular economy concept has become widely used among academic scholars, practitioners, and policymakers. Large consultancy houses such as Accenture, Deloitte, Earnest & Young, and McKinsey and Company have published reports about the circular economy (Christensen & Hauggaard-Nielsen, 2020; Kirchherr et al., 2017) and a vast number of academic articles have been published about it (Ghisellini et al., 2016; Murray et al., 2017).

In national policies, the circular economy concept has often been used as a framework aimed at decoupling the link between resource consumption and economic growth. In China, the concept has been used for almost two decades as a broad economic model for sustainable, economic development linked to several policies associated with the "Circular Economy Promotion Law of the Republic of China" (McDowall et al., 2017; Su et al., 2013). Other countries—including Japan, the United States, Korea, and Vietnam—have also used elements of the circular economy framework to formulate sectoral policies primarily targeting the waste sector (Ghisellini et al., 2016).

Defining the concept of the circular economy

A considerable number of competing definitions for the circular economy has been suggested by policymakers, industries, and researchers. Kirchherr et al. (2017) reviewed the use of the concept in academic literature and found no more than 114 different definitions. The widespread use of the concept among a diverse group of stakeholders spanning academia, industry, and policy has gradually contributed to a significant ambiguity about the definition of the concept, its applications, its limitations, and its relations to other competing and/or overlapping frameworks that target the relation between economic development and its consequences for resources and nature. Geissdoerfer et al. (2017), for example, compared the circular economy concept to sustainable development and found several overlaps and significant differences.

The European Commission's (2014a) circular economy action plan from 2014 defined the circular economy as:

> Circular economy systems keep the added value in products for as long as possible and eliminate waste. They keep resources within the economy when a product has reached the end of its life, so that they can be productively used again and again and hence create further value.
>
> (European Commission, 2014a)

The definition remained in the revised circular action plan presented in 2015 (see description below). The 2020 action plan presents no clear definition of the circular economy, but does describe the circular economy as a regenerative growth model:

> EU needs to accelerate the transition towards a regenerative growth model that gives back to the planet more than it takes, advance towards keeping its resource consumption within planetary boundaries, and therefore strive to reduce its consumption footprint and double its circular material use rate in the coming decade.
>
> (European Commission, 2020b)

This definition refers to the concept of planetary boundaries developed by Steffen et al. (2015) as a framework to understand human impacts on ecosystems at a global scale (see also Chapter 1). In the definition, these planetary boundaries are placed as the fundamental boundaries wherein the European economy is developing. The definition furthermore is characterized as a regenerative growth model that, while continuing growth (hence a growth model), reduces its environmental impacts as measured by consumption footprint and circular material use rate. In other words, the definition targets a decoupling between economic growth and resource consumption and environmental impacts.

The circular economy as a decoupling agenda

Decoupling economic growth from resource use and environmental impacts is a key objective of many circular economy policies, and it is also formulated as an explicit aim in the 2020 European Commission Circular action plan (European Commission, 2020b).

There exist two main types of decoupling: (1) absolute decoupling, wherein resource use and pressures on the environment decline, while economic activities continue to grow and (2) relative decoupling, wherein resource use and pressures on the environment increase at a slower rate than economic activities in society.

Additionally, it is fruitful to distinguish between resource-decoupling and environmental impact-decoupling. Resource-decoupling (which can be both absolute and relative) occurs when economic activity increases faster than growth in resource consumption (e.g., use of water, energy, biomass, metals). Resource-decoupling illustrates the de-materialization of the economy and indicates that a given economy is evolving in a way in which it becomes more resource-efficient. Resource decoupling can be measured on different scales, for example, as an economic process, a sector, a national economy, or a group of national economies like the EU, as the resource use per unit of economic activity (Fischer-Kowalski et al., 2011). Decoupling can also be measured as economic activity per unit of environmental impact. Environmental impacts cover a broad range of impacts and include emissions of greenhouse gases, pollution of water resources, and waste generation. There are different methods to measure the environmental impacts, including life cycle analysis and input-output techniques (Fischer-Kowalski et al., 2011). On an aggregate level, impact decoupling may be hard to measure, as the environmental impact categories are inherently diverse. Environmental impact trends and relation to economic activities may also vary significantly from impact category to impact category, making meaningful aggregate measurements problematic (Figure 7.1).

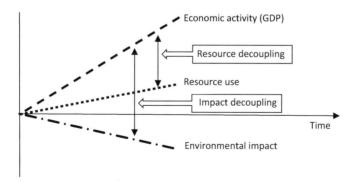

Figure 7.1 Two aspects of "decoupling" (Fischer-Kowalski et al., 2011).

A commonly used metric for measuring resource use in an economy is the so-called Domestic Material Consumption (DMC). DMC is defined by Eurostat as "the annual quantity of raw materials extracted from the domestic territory of the focal economy, plus all physical imports minus all physical exports."

The DMC indicator makes it possible to assess and distinguish between material consumption that can be ascribed to economic activities within an economy (e.g., the European economy) and material consumption generated as a consequence of demand outside the economy (exports). In a European context, this is especially important because the European economy is reliant on imports of raw materials and the import/export of goods. A problem with DMC is that it does not consider the production of upstream resource flows (and resource consumption associated with transportation) associated with the products and raw materials that are subject to export and import. These import and export flows thereby cover a hidden amount that is unaccounted for.

DMC is often, for example, by the OECD Green Growth Indicator Report or by the European Commission, used in combination with GDP as an indicator to measure the resource productivity of an economy (Hickel & Kallis, 2020). If GDP grows faster than DMC, then the economy is expanding relatively faster than the resource consumption needed for this expansion and a relative decoupling between resource consumption and economic growth is occurring.

GDP is the most common indicator for economic activity. From a circular economy perspective, a few critical remarks on its use would be in its place. GDP is a rough measure of economic activity, but it does not measure the stock or quality of the output from the economic activity. Regarding stock, GDP is a poor measure of wealth because it does not account for the stock of accumulated economic wealth in an economy. If one were to measure the wealth of a nation, then an appropriate account would consider yearly economic contribution and accumulated wealth. The GDP indicator fails to do that. Secondly, related to the question of stock, GDP does not specify *quality* of the output of the given economic activity. If, for example, economic activity in the construction sector adds to the GDP with X billion euros, the addition in the GDP is the same, regardless of whether the activities in the construction sector result in poor quality buildings that needs replacement after a short period of years or if the activity results in high quality buildings and infrastructure that generate use value for many decades.

Circular economic policies in Europe

The recycling of waste and resources has been a vital part of European policies for many decades—also before circular economy policies were developed and adopted. Historically, one of the most important pieces of European Union legislation related to the re-circulation of resources and waste is the so-called Waste Framework Directive (WFD). The WFD was first adopted in 1975 (1975/442/EC), but it has been amended several times since then, with the latest revision in 2018 (2008/98/EC). It is also integrated into the circular economy action plans and the Green Economy package (see below) as one of the most important policy instruments.

In Europe, the WFD has historically had a significant influence on how member states manage waste and resources and on the re-circulation of resources and waste back into the production of new products, services, and infrastructure. The WFD defines the basic concepts and definitions of waste and defines the roles and responsibilities among stakeholders involved with the management of waste. It also includes the influential waste hierarchy, which defines an order of preference for management of waste: (1) waste prevention, (2) preparation for reuse, (3) recycling, (4) recovery, and (5) disposal. The EU waste hierarchy can be understood as a practical way of operationalizing the 4R framework (reduce, reuse, recycle, and recover) in waste management policies. This 4R framework has been widely debated in academic literature on the circular economy. Several researchers (Kirchherr et al., 2017) have suggested expanding the 4R framework to include multiple strategies (Rs) focused on slowing, narrowing, and closing resource flows (Bocken et al., 2016).

The first circular economy action plan

In 2014, the Commission recognized the need for a broader approach to resources and waste that could link policies targeting the waste sector with new and existing initiatives focusing on product design and the manufacture of products, services, and infrastructure. This led to the development and adoption of a series of policies, strategies and regulations under the umbrella concept called Circular Economy (Table 7.1).

The first circular economy package, entitled "Towards a circular economy: A zero waste programme for Europe" was presented in 2014 (European Commission, 2014a). The circular economy package was linked to the high-level European Resource Efficiency Platform launched in 2011 (European

Table 7.1 Timeline for circular economy policy initiatives in the EU.

2011	Roadmap for a resource-efficient Europe
July 2014	Circular economy package presented
December 2015	Renewed circular economy action plan presented
January 2018	The circular economy package adopted
July 2018	Revised legislative framework on waste
June 2019	Revised fertilizers regulation
July 2019	Directive on single-use plastics
October 2019	Adoption of ten Eco-design implementing regulations
December 2019	European green deal adopted
March 2020	New circular economy action Plan adopted

Commission, 2011), which aimed to increase the resource productivity of the European economy and to decouple economic growth from resource use and its environmental impacts (European Commission, 2015).

The action plan addresses four main elements:

1 Establishment of an enabling framework to improve design and innovation procedures for a circular economy mainly through the Horizon2020 research and development program and the eco-design directive; support of investments for a circular economy, mainly through the green public procurement directive and the structural funds; and the involvement of businesses, consumers, and SMEs
2 Increase in investments in circular solutions, mainly through the public procurement directive
3 Revision of existing waste regulations and policies to support the circular economy, including, for example, revisions of the Waste Framework Directive (2008/98/EC), the Landfill Directive (1999/31/EC), and the Waste Packaging Directive (94/62/EC)
4 Definition of resource-efficiency targets for the union

However, following intense critique of the first version of the Circular Economy package as too vague and overfocused on waste management-oriented initiatives, it was retracted by the Juncker-led European Commission, whereafter the Commission announced that it would present a more ambitious action plan in late 2015 (Christensen & Hauggaard-Nielsen, 2020). This renewed circular economy action plan "Closing the loop—An EU action plan for the Circular Economy" was finally launched in December 2015 (European Commission, 2015).

The revised circular economy package was adopted in 2018, and it included an action plan for the circular economy with 54 specific actions, a strategy for plastic in the circular economy, and a report on critical raw materials for the European economy. The action plan aimed to transform the European economy to a circular economy that would boost economic competitiveness, protect manufacturing companies against resource scarcity and fluctuating prices, and create innovation and new business opportunities, thereby contributing to the European Union's overall agenda for growth and job creation (European Commission, 2015). The 54 initiatives would cover the full lifecycle of products and materials, from product design and production processes to consumption and waste management, covering instruments ranging from eco-labeling, green public procurement, and changes to the eco-design directive. However, despite the explicit focus on activities along the full lifecycle of products and materials (indicated both in the structure of the action plan and in the specific initiatives covered by the plan), waste management still played a key role in the plan to create a market for secondary raw materials to enable the flow of waste materials back into the production of new products and services (Schally, 2020).

The Circular economy monitoring framework

The monitoring of progress in the transition to a circular economy is a vital task to track and evaluate whether policies and regulations deliver the expected and needed outcomes. However, monitoring the transformation to a circular economy is inherently a complicated task. This is due to the ambiguities associated with the definition of the concept, as well as to the complexity of the challenge. The circular economy is not limited to specific products or materials, but rather covers a systemic change to the whole economy, including products and services, businesses, and business models, as well as flows and stocks of materials, products, and waste across all sectors of the European economy. The circular economy basically covers two interlinked aspects: (1) physical flows and stocks in the economy and (2) the economy of these flows (Christensen, 2021). Monitoring the circular economy thus concerns the flows and stocks of products of materials in the European economy and the economic value, costs, and revenues associated with these flows in the wider economy.

The European Union's circular economy monitoring framework was developed and adopted alongside the circular economy package adopted in 2018. The circular economy monitoring framework was inspired by the previously released Resource Efficiency Scoreboard and Raw Materials Scoreboard (European Commission, 2018a). The monitoring framework was presented on a website managed by the Eurostat that displayed regularly updated indicators. As there exists no single commonly agreed upon indicator (or set of indicators) for monitoring circularity, the monitoring framework was designed as a collection of indicators that, in sum, would enable policymakers to evaluate progress. The monitoring framework included a set of ten indicators that would measure four dimensions of the circular economy: (1) four indicators measuring production and consumption, (2) two indicators measuring waste management, (3) two indicators measuring secondary raw materials, and (4) two indicators measuring competitiveness and innovation (European Commission, 2018a). The selection of indicators was largely based on existing datasets and linked to existing policy objectives. This approach made data collection and management somewhat easier, but also meant that a more systematic approach to selection of indicators and data sets was not developed.

European Green Deal and the revised circular economy action plan

In 2019, the European Green Deal was presented by the European Commission, and the circular economy was integrated as one of the cornerstones of the deal also linking the previous circular economy policies closely to the climate policies of the Commission (European Commission, 2019). Just like in the previous circular economy package, the circular economy policy was presented as an opportunity for a transition toward sustainable development and job-intensive economy based on low-carbon technologies and sustainable products and services. With the European Green Deal, the European Commission promised to present a new circular economy action plan that included a new "sustainable product policy"; actions addressing resource-intensive industries (such as textiles, construction, electronics, and plastics); initiatives to combat so-called "green washing"; and initiatives to support the continued supply of critical raw materials for the European economy (European Commission, 2019).

The circular economy action plan "A new Circular Economy Action Plan for a cleaner and more competitive Europe" was presented in March 2020. A key element in the action plan was the revision of the product policy to push for more sustainable product designs. The main instrument here was the widening of the Eco-design directive (directive 2009/125/EC) beyond energy-related products, previously the focus of the Eco-design directive. The revision of the Eco-design directive (now launched as a regulation instead of a directive) encouraged the adoption of sustainability principles in eco-design processes. The action plan additionally addressed key product value chains associated with high resource and energy use and environmental impacts (electronics and ICT; batteries and vehicles; packaging; plastics; textiles; construction and buildings; and food, water, and nutrients). Additionally, like the previously released circular action plans, the new action plan covered a revision of waste-oriented directives and new recycling objectives with a revision of the waste framework directive (directive 2008/98/EC) as a cornerstone.

Patterns of resource consumption

There is a close link between global GHG emissions and resource extraction. According to the International Resource Panel (Oberle et al., 2019), resource extraction and processing count for around half of the total global GHG emissions. Looking at the European economy, the European Environmental Agency estimates that 18 percent of the total European GHG emissions are related to raw material extraction and processing (European Environment Agency, 2021). For the same reason, the European Commission action plan on the circular economy is closely related to the climate objective in the European Green Deal that aims at achieving climate neutrality by 2050.

By 2019, the concentration of CO_2 in the atmosphere had risen to the highest level in 2 million years (IPCC, 2021) and had created climate change at such a pace that natural ecosystems could fail, with severe consequences for humans, animals, and ecosystems (see also Chapter 1). The Paris Agreement has defined a track for the signatories of the UN Framework Convention on Climate Change (UNFCCC) toward a reduction in greenhouse gas emissions, which would ensure that the global average temperature rises by a maximum of 2°C (and preferably only by 1.5°C) to protect people, livelihoods, and ecosystems. This is regarded as a huge challenge underlined by the recent UN Environment Program's Emission Gap Report (UNEP,

2019), which shows that the countries' current climate goals are unable to deliver the needed reductions in GHG emissions and that the global emission trajectory is leading toward an increase in global average temperature above 3°C by the end of this century. In short, the reports from IPCC and UNEP highlights a "litany of broken climate promises deepening the gap between climate pledges, and reality," as formulated by IPCC president Mr. Guterres during a press conference in April 2022 for the Working Group III Mitigation of Climate Change contribution to the Sixth Assessment Report. Increased efforts are thus needed to keep global temperature below threshold limits. Resource extraction and processing make a significant contribution to global greenhouse emissions. The political GHG emission targets are unlikely to be met unless actions are taken to address emissions from resource extraction and processing.

A key driving force behind the growing resource consumption is the increase in global population. The global population has doubled from around 3.7 billion in 1970 to more than 7.7 billion in 2019 (UNDESA, 2019). The UN's global population forecasts (UNDESA, 2019) estimate that, by 2050, there will be around 9.7 billion people on the planet and, by 2100, around 10.9 billion people, despite a declining global population growth rate. Among the fastest growing populations are the 47 least developed countries, whereas wealthier countries in Europe and Northern America are projected to remain roughly about the same population size (UNDESA, 2019).

In addition, the global middle-class is expected to grow. On its own, it is a positive story that the economic development in several countries will manage to pull large parts of the global population out of poverty and provide them with access to higher living standards with better sanitation, improved diet, and greater access to consumer goods. However, if the current patterns of production and consumption are not altered to mutually accommodate the needs of present and future generations, the downside is that the growing global middle class also risks raising greenhouse gas emissions and increasing the environmental impact and the pull on critical resources and raw materials.

The combination of an expanding global economy and a growing population is driving the increased consumption of biomass, fossil fuels, metals, and minerals to provide resources, energy, food, infrastructure, construction, and consumer goods. In fact, global extraction grew from 31 billion tons in 1970 to 83 billion tons in 2019 (see also Chapter 1). Therefore, there is not only rapidly increasing global climate change according to CO_2 emissions, but also—maybe even more urgently—radically changing land-use practices that cause biodiversity loss and chemical pollution (Figure 7.2).

Looking at the geographical patterns of global extraction, Asia and the Pacific region accounts for almost two-thirds of the total global resource extraction (Oberle et al., 2019), indicating large populations in these areas. Hickel et al. (2022) show how, from 1970 to 2017, high-income countries with just 16 percent of the world's population were responsible for 74 percent of global excess resource use—driven predominantly by the United States (27

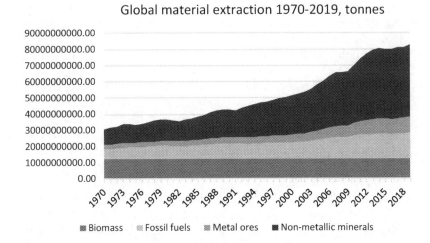

Figure 7.2 Global material extraction, from four main material categories, 1970–2019, in tons. Data from the UN International Resource Panel, https://www.resourcepanel.org/global-material-flows-database.

percent) and some major countries in the European Union (25 percent). The same study shows that the Global South is responsible for only 8 percent of resource extraction.

Resource flows and consumption in the European economy

The European economy is a huge global consumer of resources and raw materials. Large quantities of raw materials are produced domestically within Europe, but large quantities are also imported to the European economy—as resources and raw materials or as consumer products and semi-finished products.

The Sankey diagram (Figure 7.3) illustrates the total flow of materials through the European economy during 2019.

Indeed, the European economy is consuming a huge number of materials, most of which are generated domestically (77.4 percent). A large part of the materials is accumulated in the economy (as infrastructure, buildings, and products in use), amounting to 58 percent of domestically used materials. The diagram covers all materials, including fossil fuels (and other fuels such as biomass used for energy purposes). Therefore, a substantial amount of the consumed materials is released to the air as emissions (primarily CO_2) after use in the energy and transport sectors.

The diagram also illustrates what, in the literature, is considered a linear economy (Stahel, 2016), based on constant extraction of raw materials from nature, limited recycling rates, and huge emissions of "waste" to air, water,

Resources and the circular economy 185

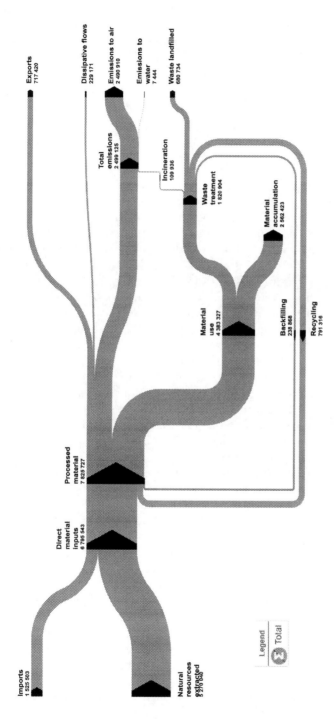

Figure 7.3 Material flows in thousands of tons per year in 2020, EU27. https://ec.europa.eu/eurostat/web/circular-economy/material-flow-diagram. The width of the band is relative to the quantity of the flow. The feedback loop in the bottom of the figure illustrates the amount of material "waste" that is recirculated back into the production of new products and services.

and landfill sites. Despite using the circular economy as a key principle for environmental and political policies, the diagram shows their weaknesses when implemented in practice. The regenerative system with resource input and waste coupling that uses design strategies with maintenance, repair, and reuse strategies meets severe challenges in bringing about perfect circles of material flows in present economic systems and business models.

Critical raw materials for the EU

Measuring resource consumption by weight, alone or in combination with economic indicators, is a straightforward approach that is useful when analyzing bulky materials such as fossil fuels, biomass, and metals. Weight-based assessments, as presented above, provide a rough overview of the total flows of materials through an economy. However, weight-based calculations might overshadow the important message that all materials are not equally important to the economy; the contribution to the economy of one ton of gravel, for example, is not the same as one ton of rare earth metals, and the resource supply risk scenarios are significantly different from material to material. Increasing political attention in the European Union is therefore given to identifying specific raw materials that are in potential future supply risk while, at the same time, important to the growth of the economy.

In Europe, a special political concern has been raised about raw material consumption and price volatility in commodity markets (European Commission, 2014b), as the European economy largely depends on imported raw materials. These concerns were raised in the period leading up to the launch of the first circular economy action plan, presented in 2014 by the European Commission. Additionally, rapid industrialization and urbanization in growth economies in countries like China, India and Brazil were seen as a present and future driving force for further competition for critical raw materials (European Commission, 2014b). Based upon this concern, the EU Critical Raw Materials Program was established to identify the most critical raw materials to the European economy and to develop policy responses that could mitigate negative consequences to the European economy.

The EU Critical Raw Materials Program has defined a list of raw materials that are both particularly important for the European economy and associated with high supply risk (European Commission, 2020d). The list was first published in 2011, and it is updated every three years. The first list included 14 materials but has grown for every time it has been published. The most recent list (published in 2020) now covers 30 materials, that are used in, for example, electronics, wind turbines, and fertilizers for agriculture (European Commission, 2020c). The rapid growth in the number of materials on the list (14 materials on the first, 20 on the second, 27 on the third, and 30 on the fourth) is an indicator of a rising concern over future supply risks of critical raw materials.

The CRM lists illustrates first, that vital economic sectors in the European economy are vulnerable to resource shortage and price fluctuations and, second, that this vulnerability is increasing over time, as the number of materials placed on the list of critical materials increases every time a new list is published.

To convert the knowledge generated in the program about critical raw materials into policy responses, a set of policy reports has been published from the program. In 2018, a policy report was published on CRM and the circular economy describing potential EU policies and actions to recirculate CRMs within the European economy (European Commission, 2018b). In 2019, the EU Joint Research Center published a report on the potential for the extraction of raw materials from mining waste and landfills (Blengini et al., 2019) and, in 2020, the EU Commission published a report on the relation between critical raw materials and strategic technologies (batteries, fuel cells, wind turbines, traction motors, photovoltaics, robotics, drones, 3D printers, and ICT materials) and sectors (renewable energy, electric mobility, and defense and space) in the European economy (Bobba et al., 2020). The latter was structured as a foresight study that investigated demand and potential supply risks for 2030 and 2050.

Overall, the policy suggestions and recommendations on critical raw materials coming from the EU Commission focus on pathways for recycling CRMs that are already in the European production and consumption system placed either within products and infrastructure or in the waste flows ending in incineration plants or in landfill sites. The concept of circular economy is used by the European Commission as a vehicle to loop critical raw materials back into the economic sectors once the products become waste, thereby reducing supply dependency on countries outside the EU.

Less attention is given to critically debating the long-term sustainability of the current European production and consumption system, although the data presented clearly indicate that the European economy is heading toward critical supply risks associated with strategic sectors and technologies.

Evaluating the circular economy policies as a decoupling strategy

Given the rapid increase in resource consumption and potential future resource scarcity scenarios, combined with an increasing number of raw materials placed on the EU CRM list, the key question is whether the proposed policies and strategies for the circular economy are appropriate and sufficient to ensure the development of a sustainable production and consumption system in the European Union.

Looking at the European economy, it appears that a relative decoupling has taken place over the last 20 years, as the gross domestic product (GDP) has increased, while domestic material consumption (DMC) decreased between 2006 and 2012 and has remained more or less stable since 2012. An "absolute

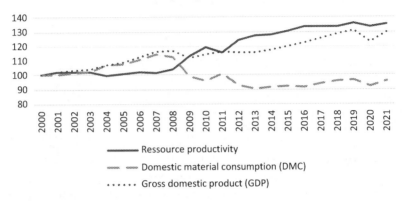

Figure 7.4 Development of resource productivity in comparison between GDP and DMC (European Union 2000–2020): https://ec.europa.eu/eurostat/statistics-explained/index.php?title=Material_flow_accounts_and_resource_productivity.

decoupling" took place in the years following the financial crisis, when DMC declined. However, the European economy "recovered" (in the sense that the economy returned to growth rates similar to before the crisis) and, from 2012 onwards, the DMC has been relatively stable, and GDP has increased. The Covid-19 pandemic caused a small decline in economic activity and DMC in 2020, but the economy and material consumption appear to have regained 2019 levels by 2021 (Figure 7.4).

As indicated earlier, an important problem about measuring resource productivity as the relation between GDP and DMC is that the DMC indicator does not provide the full picture of material consumption in the economy. For example, DMC excludes upstream material consumption associated with the production and transportation of imported goods (Hickel & Kallis, 2020). Significant parts of manufacturing processes, especially those that are associated with large upstream material consumption such as material extraction, take place outside the EU and remain unaccounted for in the DMC indicator. For the EU, this may result in misleading assumptions about the resource productivity of the economy, thereby overestimating the resource-productivity of the European economy.

The circular economy, economic growth, and sustainable development in the EU

The European Green Deal was launched in 2019 as a strategy aimed at boosting the economy and tackling climate and environmental-related challenges.

According to the European Commission, the Green Deal is an economic growth strategy "that aims to transform the EU into a fair and prosperous society, with a modern, resource-efficient and competitive economy where there are no net emissions of greenhouse gases in 2050 and where economic growth is decoupled from resource use" (European Commission, 2019, p. 1). The revised circular economy action plan was launched as a cornerstone of the Green Deal package, aiming to facilitate the transition toward a regenerative growth model for the European economy that would keep resource consumption within planetary boundaries and reduce the resource consumption footprint (European Commission, 2020b).

The European Green Deal and the European Commission's action plan on circular economy both rely upon the assumption that policy interventions can incrementally adjust the European economy, increase resource-productivity, and reduce environmental pressures. This philosophy is presented as a so-called regenerative growth model, wherein a combination of product policies, involving eco-design methods and regulations; interventions in the consumption stage, involving product labeling and green public procurement strategies; and ambitious waste targets, focusing on recycling and reuse of products and materials close material loops and decouple material consumption from economic growth.

The European economy is based on an enormous input of natural resources, amounting to more than 6.5 billion tons per year (although the input is stabilizing and not increasing), most of which is emitted to sinks (primarily as air emissions and solid waste placed in landfills). A smaller amount is accumulated in the economy (primarily as products, buildings, and infrastructure), and only a limited amount is actually circulated back into the construction of new products, services, and infrastructure. This flow of materials through the European production and consumption system is best described as a linear flow and not a circular economy. The European economy is therefore far from a circular economy, understood as an economic system that

> Keep[s] the added value in products for as long as possible and eliminate waste. [It keeps] resources within the economy when a product has reached the end of its life, so that they can be productively used again and again and hence create further value.
> (European Commission, 2014a)

Looking critically on key indicators to measure the relation between resource consumption and economic growth, however, the picture seems to suggest that only a relative decoupling has taken place over the last ten years—one in which domestic material consumption has stabilized, whereas economic growth (measured as gross domestic product) has continued along an increasing trend line. Consequently, the resource productivity of the European Union's economy is increasing. What has been achieved so far based on the last three circular economy action plans is thus best described as a stabilization of the resource flows through the European economy in a situation wherein economic activity has increased.

Additionally, looking at potential future supply risk scenarios for the European economy, the critical raw materials for the EU program indicate that supply risks associated with economically important raw materials are increasing every time the list is updated, indicating that the European economy is at risk of supply shortages associated with raw materials that are critical for key technologies (including batteries, fuel cells, wind turbines, traction motors, photovoltaics, robotics, drones, 3D printers, and ICT materials) and sectors (renewable energy, electric mobility, and defense and space) in the European economy.

Summary

This chapter explores the relation between resource consumption and economic growth. The chapter discusses and evaluates whether circular economy policies proposed and implemented by the European Union have managed to decouple economic growth from resource consumption. The chapter begins with a theoretical discussion about the concept of the circular economy and an analysis of how the circular economy is conceptualized in European Union policies. The analysis identifies the concept of decoupling as a central element in the circular economy action plans adopted by the European Union, especially linked to the "regenerative growth model" in the most recent circular economy action plan from 2020. This analysis is followed by a presentation of different theoretical approaches to understanding the concept of decoupling economic growth from resource consumption and environmental impacts on an economy. The chapter then analyzes circular economy policies as they have been adopted in the European Union over the last decade. The analysis presents the key elements of the two circular economy action plans that have been adopted (in 2015 and 2019), the latter as a cornerstone of the European Green Deal launched in 2019 by the European Commission as a strategy aimed at boosting the economy and tackling climate and environmental-related challenges. The analysis of circular economy policies in the European Union is followed by an analysis of the historic patterns of resource consumption in the European economy. The analysis points toward the need for looking simultaneously at gross material flows (typically measured statistically in tons) and at raw materials that are economically critical to the economy but may appear in smaller amounts and less evident in overall material flow charts. Finally, the article combines the analysis of resource consumption and economic growth to evaluate whether the adopted circular economy policies have managed to create a decoupling of resource consumption from economic growth in the European economy. The analysis concludes that the European economy consumes large quantities of resources, generates large amounts of wastes, and only manages to circulate a smaller percentage of the resources back into production of new products and services. On the positive side, the analysis indicates that a relative decoupling (but not absolute decoupling) between economic growth and resource consumption has taken place over the last ten years and that the resource productivity of the European economy therefore has increased. Finally, the analysis concludes that the list of critical raw materials for the European economy is increasing and that the European economy is at risk of supply shortage associated with raw materials critical to strategic technologies in the economy.

References

Blengini, G.A., Mathieux, F., Mancini, L., Nyberg, M.;Viegas, H.M. (Editors), Salminen, J., Garbarino, E., Orveillon, G., Saveyn, H., Mateos Aquilino, V., Llorens González, T., García Polonio, F., Horckmans, L., D'Hugues, P., Balomenos, E., Dino, G., de la Feld, M., Mádai, F., Földessy, J., Mucsi, G., Gombkötő, I., Calleja,I. (2019). *Recovery of critical and other raw materials from mining waste and landfills: State of play on existing practices*, EUR 29744EN, Luxembourg: Publications Office of the European Union, ISBN 978-92-76-08568-3, doi: 10.2760/600775, JRC116131.

Bobba, S., Carrara, S., Huisman, J., Mathieux, F., and Pavel, C. (2020). *Critical raw materials for strategic technologies and sectors in the EU: A foresight study.* Luxembourg: Publications Office of the European Union.

Bocken, Nancy M.P., Ingrid de Pauw, Conny Bakker, and Bram van der Grinten. (2016). Product Design and Business Model Strategies for a Circular Economy. *Journal of Industrial and Production Engineering* 33(5): 308–20. https://doi.org/10.1080/21681015.2016.1172124.

Christensen, T. B. (2021). Towards a circular economy in cities: Exploring local modes of governance in the transition towards a circular economy in construction and textile recycling. *Journal of Cleaner Production*, 305, 127058. DOI: 10.1016/jjclepro.2021.127058

Christensen, T. B. and Hauggaard-Nielsen, H. (2020). Circular economy: Practices, Knowledge bases and novelty. *The Journal of Transdisciplinary Environmental Studies*, 18(1), 2–16.

European Commission (2011). *Communication from the Commission to the European Parliament, the Council, the European Economic and Social Committee and the Committee of the Regions, Roadmap to a Resource Efficient Europe.* Brussels: European Commission.

European Commission (2014a). *Communication from the Commission to the European Parliament, the Council, The European Economic and Social Committee and the Committee of the Regions. Towards a circular economy: A zero waste programme for Europe.* Brussels: European Commission. DOI: 10.1017/CBO9781107415324.004

European Commission (2014b). Report on critical raw materials for the EU, Report of the Ad hoc Working Group on defining critical raw materials. Retrieved from https://ec.europa.eu/docsroom/documents/10010/attachments/1/translations/en/renditions/pdf

European Commission (2015). *Communication from the Commission to the European Parliament, the Council, the European Economic and Social Committee and the Committee of the Regions, Closing the loop - An EU action plan for the Circular Economy.* Brussels: European Commission.

European Commission (2018a). *Communication from the Commission to the European Parliament, the Council, the European Economic and Social Committee and the Committee* of the Regions, on a monitoring framework for the circular economy. Brussels: European Commission. Retrieved from: https://ec.europa.eu/info/strategy/international-strategies/global-topics/sustainable-development-goals/eu-

European Commission (2018b). *Report on critical raw materials and the circular economy* Luxembourg: Publications Office of the European Union.

European Commission (2019). *Communication from the Commission to the European Parliament, the Council, the European Economic and Social Committee and the Committee of the Regions, The European Green Deal*. Brussels: European Commission.

European Commission (2020a). *Circular economy action plan - For a cleaner and more competitive Europe*. Brussels: European Commission. Retrieved from: https://eur-lex.europa.eu/resource.html?uri=cellar:9903b325-6388-11ea-b735-01aa75ed71a1.0017.02/DOC_1&format=PDF

European Commission (2020b). *Communication from the Commission to the European Parliament, the Council, the European Economic and Social Committee and the Committee of the Regions, A new Circular Economy Action Plan For a cleaner and more competitive Europe*. Brussels: European Commission.

European Commission (2020c). *Communication from the commission to the European Parliament, the Council, the European economic and social committee and the committee of the regions. Critical Raw Materials Resilience: Charting a Path towards greater Security and Sustainability*. Brussels: European Commission. Retrieved from: DOI:10.1007/978-3-030-40268-6_9

European Commission (2020d). *Study on the EU's list of critical raw materials.* Luxembourg: Publications Office of the European Union, 2020. DOI: 10.2873/11619

European Environment Agency (2021). Improving the climate impact of raw material sourcing. Luxembourg: Publications Office of the European Union. DOI: 10.2800/722698

Fischer-Kowalski, M., Swilling, M., von Weizsäcker, E. U., Ren, Y., Moriguchi, Y., Crane, W., Krausmann, F., Eisenmenger, N., Giljum, S., Hennicke, P., Romero Lankao, P., Siriban Manalang, A., and Sewerin, S. (2011). *Decoupling natural resource use and environmental impacts from economic growth, A report of the working group on decoupling to the international resource panel*. Nairobi: United Nations Environment Programme. Retrieved from: https://www.resourcepanel.org/file/400/download?token=E0TEjf3z

Geissdoerfer, M., Savaget, P., Bocken, N. M. P. and Hultink, E. J. (2017). The circular economy – A new sustainability paradigm? *Journal of Cleaner Production*, 143, 757–768. DOI: 10.1016/j.jclepro.2016.12.048

Ghisellini, P., Cialani, C. and Ulgiati, S. (2016). A review on circular economy: The expected transition to a balanced interplay of environmental and economic systems. *Journal of Cleaner Production*, 114, 11–32. DOI: 10.1016/j.jclepro.2015.09.007

Hickel, J. and Kallis, G. (2020). Is green growth possible? *New Political Economy*, 25 (4), 469–486. DOI: 10.1080/13563467.2019.1598964

Hickel, J., O'Neill, D. W., Fanning, A. L. and Zoomkawala, H. (2022). National responsibility for ecological breakdown: A fair-shares assessment of resource use, 1970–2017. *The Lancet Planetary Health*, 6(4), e342–e349. DOI: 10.1016/S2542-5196(22)00044-4

IPCC (2021). Summary for Policymakers. Climate Change 2021: The Physical Science Basis. Contribution of Working Group I to the Sixth Assessment Report of the Intergovernmental Panel on Climate Change. DOI: 10.1017/9781009157896.001

Kirchherr, J., Reike, D. and Hekkert, M. (2017). Conceptualizing the circular economy: An analysis of 114 definitions. *Resources, Conservation and Recycling*, 127(September), 221–232. DOI: 10.1016/j.resconrec.2017.09.005

McDowall, W., Geng, Y., Huang, B., Barteková, E., Bleischwitz, R., Türkeli, S., Kemp, R. and Doménech, T. (2017). Circular economy policies in China and Europe. *Journal of Industrial Ecology*, 21(3), 651–661. DOI: 10.1111/jiec.12597

Murray, A., Skene, K. and Haynes, K. (2017). The circular economy: An interdisciplinary exploration of the concept and application in a Global context. *Journal of Business Ethics*, 140(3), 369–380. DOI: 10.1007/s10551-015-2693-2

Oberle, B., Bringezu, S., Hatfield-dodds, S., Hellweg, S., Schandl, H., Clement, J., Authors, C., Cabernard, L., Che, N., Chen, D., Droz-, H., Ekins, P., Fischerkowalski, M., Flörke, M., Frank, S., Froemelt, A., Geschke, A., Haupt, M., Havlik, P., and Kaviti, J. (2019). *Global resources outlook 2019: Natural resources for the future we want. In Summary for policy makers.* A Report of the International Resource Panel United Nations Environment Programme. Nairobi, Kenya. Retrieved from: https://www.resourcepanel.org/file/1172/download?token=muaePxOQ

OECD (2011). *Towards green growth* (OECD Green Growth Studies). Paris: OECD Publishing. DOI: 10.1787/9789264111318-en

Schally, H.-M. (2020). Introduction. In: S. Eisenriegler (ed.), *The circular economy in the European Union, an interim review* (pp. 1–7). Springer.

Stahel, W. R. (2016). The circular economy. *Nature*, 531(7595), 435–438. DOI: 10.1038/531435a

Steffen, W., Richardson, K., Rockström, J., Cornell, S. E., Fetzer, I., Bennett, E. M., Biggs, R., Carpenter, S. R., de Vries, W., de Wit, C. A., Folke, C., Gerten, D., Heinke, J., Mace, G. M., Persson, L. M., Ramanathan, V., Reyers, B. and Sörlin, S. (2015). Planetary boundaries: Guiding human development on a changing planet. *Science*, 347(6223). DOI: 10.1126/science.1259855

Su, B., Heshmati, A., Geng, Y. and Yu, X. (2013). A review of the circular economy in China: Moving from rhetoric to implementation. *Journal of Cleaner Production*, 42, 215–227. DOI: 10.1016/j.jclepro.2012.11.020

UNDESA (2019). *World population prospects 2019.* Department of Economic and Social Affairs. United Nations, Department of Economic and Social Affairs, Population Division. DOI: 10.18356/3e9d869f-en

UNEP (2011). *Pathways to sustainable development and poverty eradication a synthesis for policy makers.* Nairobi: United Nations Environment Programme. www.unep.org/greeneconomy

UNEP (2019). *Emissions gap report 2019.* Nairobi: United Nations Environment Programme.

8 The food system and agriculture

Henrik Hauggaard-Nielsen and Niels Heine Kristensen

If we tried to produce all the food needed in 2050 using today's production systems, the world would have to convert most of its remaining forest, and agriculture alone would produce almost twice the emissions allowable from all human activities.

Tim Searchinger, World Resources Institute

Introduction

The European Environment Agency (2019a) defines a food system as all the elements (for example, environment, people, inputs, processes, infrastructures, and institutions) and activities that relate to the production, processing, distribution, preparation, and consumption of food and to the outputs of those activities, including socio-economic and environmental outcomes; food system actors include those directly involved in food chain activities, as well as governments and private actors. This chapter focuses on terrestrial ecosystems, agriculture, and deliverables to European food tables, while acknowledging the relevance of commercial fisheries and aquaculture in the EU (see Chapter 5).

The main share of land in Europe is used by agriculture, with a relatively high impact on the environment. This also means that the aquatic and terrestrial ecosystems cannot be dealt with separately because of their interconnectedness through water systems. By the mid-1970s, water protection had already been prioritized by the EU, with legislation on fish waters, shellfish waters, bathing waters, and groundwaters—especially addressing pollution from urban wastewater and from agriculture. From that perspective, EEA (2019a) highlights that 45 percent of assessed fish and shellfish stocks in Europe's seas are not in good shape. Indeed, there is a need for greater ambition in terms of reducing the impacts of agricultural activities on biodiversity, fresh water, marine pollution, green-house gas (GHG) emissions, ammonia emissions, and soils. Special attention is paid to the strategies developed and applied by the European Common Agricultural Policy (CAP) not only to meet the EU Green Deal's objectives, but also to ensure a transition to a more sustainable agri-food system that engages

DOI: 10.4324/9781003319672-11

the actors in the global supply chains—short or complex—following the Farm-to-Fork strategy (see Chapter 5).

In these regards, it is important to remember that European agri-food systems are diverse, with considerable regional variability. Local conditions, national markets, and national regulations have shaped the pathway of these contextualized systems. The role of the agri-food system in different regions ranges from very little to very strong. Nevertheless, from an economic perspective, agriculture and food are by far the world's largest business, acting as stewards of enormous land areas linked to environmental, nutritional, and social factors. The same also goes for the EU in terms of employment, turnover, and value added (EEA, 2019a), as some 13 million enterprises and 29 million workers produce, process, distribute, prepare, and sell food and beverages (Eurostat, 2022). Global food production is bigger than ever. Paradoxically, around 815 million people still suffer from hunger, while 1.9 billion are diagnosed as overweight or obese (IAASTD, 2009). Although the transition to more sustainable agri-food systems is on major political agendas, it remains a big challenge to govern agri-food systems within a safe and just operating planetary space. To understand our modern food system's structure and function, a 50–100year historical perspective can be helpful.

New political realities and urgent economic, social, and food production challenges from the ruins of WWII formed the beginnings of the modern European food system. Replacing the common land and labor productive factors by increased use of new technologies was the main factor behind a rapid increase in production (Martín-Retortillo & Pinilla, 2015). The implementation of substantial agricultural machinery—together with chemical fertilizers, pesticides, the development of intensive livestock breeding, improved breeds of animals, genetic selection of seeds, and the expansion of irrigated farming—ushered in an industrial agricultural transformation that focused on maximizing farm efficiency and thereby replacing more traditional diverse and locally adapted agricultural systems that had been managed with ingenious practices for both community food security and agrobiodiversity conservation (Altieri, 2004). Today, European farming systems are dominated by a mainstream farming regime with very simplified rotations and intensified animal husbandry, degrading ecosystem services like terrestrial soil carbon sequestration, water quality regulation, and pest control that influence greenhouse gas emissions and resilience toward extreme weather conditions (for example, Magrini et al., 2016; Wezel et al., 2014). Overall, progress toward sustainable outcomes is still limited, including unhealthy diets (EEA, 2019a).

It is estimated that global crop production will need to double by 2050 to meet projected food demands, and concerns are increasing about whether humanity will be able to continue to feed itself within the planetary boundaries (see also Chapter 1). Beltran-Peña et al. (2020) conclude that, without major food system innovations, food self-sufficiency is likely to decline despite increased food production through sustainable agricultural intensification, since projected food demand will exceed potential production. The same authors underline the fact that most countries in Africa and the Middle East will continue to be heavily reliant upon imports throughout the 21st century, despite following a very optimistic sustainable production scenario. Historical agri-food ambitions about independence, food self-sufficiency, and security are moving up the political ladder, as very much highlighted by the Russian invasion and adjacent Ukraine crisis (IPES-FOOD, 2022). A shift from feed toward food crops for more direct human consumption is put forward in EU, with examples that show diverting just 8 percent of EU feed crops to be enough to offset the loss of grain imports from Ukraine (IPES-FOOD, 2022). At the same time, it is important to understand that, every year in the EU, around 88 million tonnes of food are lost along the supply chain or simply wasted at the household level, with corresponding estimates as high as EUR 143 billion (EEA, 2019a). Production concentrations, specialization, and standardization are shaping the entire food system, discouraging the more traditional local and regional food production and connected businesses (Fitzgerald, 2005). Moreover, geographical concentration embeds unequal actor relationships and possible inequalities in market access. The CAP, launched in 1962, was justified by agri-business uncertainties and the environmental impact of farming, with a cost-effective ambition not only to keep the rural economy alive by promoting jobs in farming, agri-food industries, and associated sectors, but also to maintain soils and biodiversity. Nevertheless, according to, for example, Pe'er et al. (2019), these trends are still favored by the CAP, as are dominating approaches, to reach economic profitability in agri-food systems; these include continued structural development of increasing farm size (economy of scale), technological development such as automatization and communication technology, and the elimination of labor costs to approach lowest-cost production methods. Understanding major lock-ins at the structural and practical level is important when devising the development and implementation of new pathways, including the global concentration of power and alternative routes for more decentralized agri-food systems. Only 4 percent of the CAP budget goes to financing dedicated agri-environment-climate measures (Négre, 2021), with payments concentrated on bigger farms in the richest regions with the fewest farm jobs. A similar concentration exists on the retail and distribution of food, as strong price competitions for consumer goods have caused downstream price pressure on primary producers. Embedded in the dominating retail chains strategy is a "private label" concept (Dhar & Hoch, 1997). Private label offers the consumer a recognizable category of products, often with built-in criteria on the environment and animal welfare, but often without a traceability to the origin of the product, except that regulated in relation to food safety and nutrition. This situation is reaching a level whereat farmers have trouble telling the public the final destination of their specific products. This is a critical situation when investigating the global food system from production (farm) to plate (fork)—or vice versa—to provide sufficient broader perspectives into policymaking decisions. An exception to this is organic certification and labeling, which has been regulated at the EU level since 1991 in all member countries, following continuous updates, with the most recent applied on January 1, 2022 (EU, 2018).

In large part due to the CAP, the EU today is the world's largest exporter of agricultural products, taking around one-quarter of global agricultural exports (Rayner et al., 2008). This also includes imported, or virtual, land used to produce the traded products (see Chapter 5). Nevertheless, such a system motivated either by profit or by state interests has failed to sustain farmer livelihoods and to address food quality and health. Today, we are faced with several negative impacts of industrial food production and consumption on the environment and climate change. Furthermore, when targeting global markets, farmers are part of a global intellectual property regime (Clancy & Moschini, 2017) giving up rights such as saving seed for next growing season or repairing their own equipment. Thus, it can be argued that the distribution of wealth gains attributable to the agricultural production is, to an increasing degree, claimed by input suppliers. EEA (2019a) argues that, if current practices with fewer, larger, and more capital-intensive farming systems continue without additional policy interventions, it is likely that the food system will be shaped by increased competitiveness and export orientation, rather than by the meeting of health, environmental, and economic goals.

In other words, today's agri-food sector is extensively embedded in the institutions of modern societies, which implies that changes in agri-food sociotechnical structures necessarily involves changes in knowledge structures, governance models, and networks far beyond the sector itself. In this respect, both national and EU research programs play an important role.

Judging by the EU research funding priorities (for example, Horizon programs), adaptation of multi-actor and cross-sectoral approaches seems to be almost a prerequisite. This means engaging practitioners (primary producers, processors, retailers, food service providers, consumers), public and private institutions (governmental institutions, NGOs, industry), and citizens to co-create, test, and demonstrate solutions from production to consumption. The Horizon requirement demonstrates understanding and increased implementation speed on a European scale, as well as increased emphasis toward regional and sectoral needs within an environmental, socioeconomic, geographical, and cultural context. The requirements indicate a change of paradigm that integrates social sciences and humanities with technical and natural science expertise to maximize the returns to society from research investments and to foster collaboration, bridge building, and the breaking down of silos among actors in the food chain (see also Chapter 13). Nevertheless, the open question is whether these programs can create a momentum for increased European food sovereignty by shortening the food value chains with more genetically and spatial diverse cropping systems that can deliver high quality and varied foods? Critics argue that the current innovation paradigm in EU policies locks the food system into a vicious cycle of "techno-fixes" and short-termism that reinforces trends toward intensive, large-scale monoculture-based production, despite their demonstrable harm and trade-offs across environmental and socio-economic issues (EEA, 2019a). Creating alternatives, however, and potential implications on jobs remains unclear.

The Farm-to-Fork strategy, which is at the heart of the European Green Deal (see Chapter 5), aims to address these challenges and accelerate the transition to sustainable agri-food systems. However, before being able to scale up, such innovations require supply side factors to be considered, including regional infrastructures and capacities, as well as demand side factors like knowledge level, finance, and trust. Nevertheless, scaling up organic farming practices in the EU is exemplary with the 1990s breakthrough based upon public interests, increasing consumer demand followed up by political support—possibly with a momentum of economic challenges in the dominating conventional agricultural sector. While direct CAP support for farmers in pillar I (direct payments to farmers) has been the dominating instrument, pillar II (rural development policy) has been the minor for decades. From 2014 to 2020, pillar II has been added to objectives on climate. For the 2023–2027 period, the EU communication "places an emphasis on sustainable development, the preservation of natural resources, and the need to ensure generational renewal" (see also Chapter 9).

Impact on the very basis of the food we grow

Agri-food systems are a major driver of climate change (Vermeulen et al., 2012) due to their massive land use change and biodiversity losses (Foley et al., 2005) contributing to the crossing of several of the proposed "planetary boundaries" (see Chapter 1) that attempt to define a safe operating space for humanity in a stable Earth system (Rockström et al., 2009; Steffen et al., 2015). According to the Farm-to-Fork strategy (see Chapter 5), consumption of whole-grain cereals, fruits, vegetables, legumes, and nuts is insufficient, while consumption of red meats, sugars, salt, and fats exceeds recommendations. Plant-based foods have a key role to play in protein, climate, and health traditions but nonetheless have a very low degree of use in Europe. At the same time, the world's population is expected to grow to almost 10 billion by 2050, enhancing agricultural demand with a dietary transition toward higher consumption of meat and thereby adding further pressure on natural resources. If no mitigation measures are taken, these demand-side trends may increase environmental impacts by 50–90 percent by 2050, pushing the food system beyond environmental limits (Springmann et al., 2018).

Agriculture affects the functioning of Earth's systems through various impact channels (Foley et al., 2005), contributing 214 ± 67 petagrams of carbon to the atmosphere from land-use change since the beginning of the Industrial Revolution, or almost equivalent to the estimated 270 ± 30 petagrams of carbon from fossil fuel combustion (Zomer et al., 2017). This development has transgressed the planetary boundaries for biosphere integrity and biogeochemical flows, increasing the risk of their exceedance for land-system change and freshwater use (Rockström et al., 2009; Steffen et al., 2015).

Over the past 50 years, land use, livestock production, and soil and nutrient management have nearly doubled greenhouse gas emissions, and projections suggest a further increase by 2050 (IPCC, 2019). The EU's agricultural sector accounted for 10 percent of the EU's total greenhouse gas emissions (EEA, 2019b), including carbon losses from land use practices, methane (CH_4) arising from livestock enteric fermentation, stored animal manure, and nitrous oxide (N_2O) derived from organic and mineral nitrogen (N) fertilizers soil applications. In fact, CH_4 and N_2O are responsible for more than 80 percent of this total. The majority of CH_4 is produced in the rumen, and it is thus affected by the quantity and quality of the supplied animal feed. When manure is applied as crop fertilizer, nitrifying and denitrifying soil bacteria produce the most N_2O when N is abundant relative to crop demand (Carter et al., 2012). N_2O emissions can vary widely depending on land use, crop type, soil temperature, and soil aeration controlled by soil organic matter content and original soil texture. The highest N_2O emission rates have been shown to occur with artificial N fertilization for intensive agriculture under wetter soil conditions, with up to >80–85 percent water filled soil pore space (de Carvalho et al., 2022). Thus, mitigation requires increasing efficiency of N use in crop production in time and space, including improved manure management in animal-production systems.

Another perspective on efficiency centers on cropping systems and strategy modifications. Jensen et al. (2020) suggest that, by intercropping grain legumes with cereals, the species complementarity of N_2 fixation (legume) and soil-N derived from mineralization (cereal) could reduce global fertilizer N production and use by about 26 percent and significantly reduce CO_2 and N_2O emissions from agriculture. Following the plant-based food trends, increasing grain legume market pulls could likewise provide crop diversification opportunities to combat several self-reinforcement mechanisms that lock-in the current system (Magrini et al., 2016). In this way, practice transformations may reduce the combined area required for food production, while providing additional ecosystem functions and services that lead to more sustainable land use (Della Rossa et al., 2022).

European food consumption contributes to about 17 percent of EU household greenhouse gas emissions (Ivanova et al., 2017), with 20 percent of the food produced in the EU being wasted (Stenmarck et al., 2016). Such waste represents lost surfaces of arable land, and it is possibly intensifying the farming systems through, for example, specialization by fertilizer and pesticide use and mechanization, which can lead to the disintegration of farmland features, landscape homogenization, and soil degradation. This means a lack of productivity, which is very critical in a future with more and more unforeseen weather patterns requiring the opposite. This calls for a strategy aimed at a more adaptive and resilient system. Motivating actors for such transitions might be challenged by common reduced awareness of production and consumption interactions, with consumers having limited knowledge about ecosystem functions and service utilized to produce the sourced crop. In addition, for food security reasons, the EU needs to combat global shocks and disruptions in supply chains by reshaping EU agri-food systems to mitigate socio-economic impacts. However, the concentration of power in large, globally networked, and vertically integrated companies is massive—from primary producers to actors downstream in the supply chains. For example, the ten biggest retail companies in the EU have a combined market share of over 50 percent, exerting a large influence over producers and consumers (EEA, 2019a).

Covering the whole food system from the soil to the social and political movements shaping the organization of human societies (Egmose et al., 2021), agroecology appears to be a cornerstone for the sustainable transformation of European agriculture (Wezel et al., 2009). Agroecology values and principles support the Farm-to-Fork Strategy (see also Chapter 5), with the ambition to accelerate transition to a sustainable food system and the Biodiversity Strategy for 2030 setting specific goals for EU's long-term nature conservation policy (see also Chapter 9) and thereby influencing the strategy on adaptation to climate change.

According to IPCC predictions, if effective countermeasures are not taken, climate change will lead to a 5–30 percent reduction in global food production capacity by 2050 (IPCC, 2019). As one of the hallmark signs of climate change, this is partly caused by the impact on the relationship between biodiversity and ecosystem functions and reinforced by more frequent extreme weather events like heavier rain and surface winds. In some places, drought will be the main challenge and, in others, it will be storms. It is expected that the growing of major crops like maize, rice, soybean, and wheat may have yield fluctuations caused by inter-annual climate variability ranging between 18 and 43 percent (Vogel et al., 2019), causing a serious threat to global food security. At the same time, a series of problems such as soil erosion, degradation, chemical pollution, and loss of biodiversity caused by current practices (Rockström et al., 2017) have further weakened the resistance of agriculture to global climate change (Lobell et al., 2011).

In general, inputs and technology development have created a uniformity, regularity, and symmetry of crop individuals dominating current global agriculture and reducing crop diversity (Jensen et al., 2020) that influences ecosystem functions and services, weakening the resistance of agriculture to global climate change (Altieri et al., 2015). Such a lack of responsiveness ability poses a serious threat to global food security.

World Soil Day is a United Nation (UN) initiative held annually on December 5 to focus attention on the importance of healthy soils to meet future challenges. That is about food quality and human health, but also about the sequestering of more carbon, increased water infiltration, and improvement of wildlife and pollinator habitats to support productivity and profits. Unfortunately, focusing on short-term productivity has neglected a significant deterioration of these important functions and services. Most evidently, soil organic matter has been mineralized, resulting in reduced soil fertility, reduced water holding capacity and infiltration rate, deterioration of soil structure leading to increased erosion damage, greenhouse gas emissions, and reduced biodiversity (Lal, 2004). This, in turn, has incurred compensating costs for additional fertilizer, watering systems, fuel for tilling compacted soils, and additional weed treatments. Moreover, landscape simplification in the use of crops, clearing of hedges, and field drainage to achieve a more homogenous landscape that is easier to manage rationally with larger machinery has caused a continued loss of agroecosystem functions and services above- and belowground (IPES-Food, 2016).

The European Commission has proposed several initiatives to accelerate the transition toward agroecology throughout Europe (Wezel et al., 2018). Agroecology combines principles like diversity, knowledge co-creation and sharing, synergies, efficiency, recycling, resilience, human and social values, culture and food tradition, responsible governance, and circular-solidarity economy (EU, 2021; FAO, 2018). Thus, agroecology is highlighted as a sustainable practice to promote and scale-up in the European Green Deal and in the Farm-to-Fork and Biodiversity strategies possibly supported by future common agricultural policy eco-schemes. From this perspective, policy development is important to develop more sustainable agri-food systems supported by the many actors already engaged, including policies for attracting and involving actors not engaged today as a part of designing the agri-food institutions to meet near-future political goals and agreements. EEA (2019a) proposes that influencing the food environment could be an important lever for changing dietary composition (see Willett et al., 2019), reducing food waste, and supporting more sustainable production. The ideal would be to engage suppliers, retailers, and service providers to shape the "food environment" framed by the physical, social, and economic surroundings that influence what people eat. However, there is no overarching policy addressing the food system in Europe; rather, there are multiple policies across many different domains.

Lack of environmental impact of the Common Agricultural Policy

The dominating development paths of European food chain actors underline the fact that policy interventions have facilitated the engineering of supply chain efficiencies and consolidated existing chains supported by legislative changes, tax incentives, and changes in labor practices. This is obviously also linked to the developments of the global agri-food systems, wherein farmers buy inputs such as seed, mechanization (production, distribution and utilization of a variety of equipment for field operations and and primary processing), fertilizer, and pesticides from the same few global entities, while selling to just a few food processors and traders. Corporations have entered the agri-food systems, acquiring numerous smaller companies and merging with large competitors at a speed never seen before—including retailers where most of us get our food. One example is the purchase of Monsanto, the world's top producer of genetically engineered seeds and associated agro-chemicals, by the pharmaceutical and agro-chemical giant Bayer in May 2016 in a US$66 billion deal (Clapp, 2018). The seed industry mega-mergers are seen as a fundamental indicator of a shift from a competitive sector composed primarily of small, family-owned firms to an industry dominated by a small number of transnational pharmaceutical/chemical corporations (Howard, 2018). Compared to 50 years ago, the crop varieties consumed by humans is decreasing, and crop diversity has significantly declined (FAO and WHO, 2019). Just four crops—wheat, maize, rice, and potato—account for approximately 60 percent of global food sources (Altieri et al., 2015; see also Chapter 1).

In the IPES-Food & ETC Group (2021) report, deep worries about trends in the development and governance of agri-food systems and especially about the power and roles of the bio-digital giants are raised. For example, the fertilizer company Yara (yara.com) invested significantly in digital farming devices for precision farming practices by teaming up with IBM (ibm.com/products/agriculture), whose products are integrated with John Deere equipment (deere.com/en/technology-products/precision-ag-technology). Such strategies are denoted "precision agriculture," which is now poised to leverage big data to optimize input use at extremely refined levels and to expand the use of robotics in revolutionary applications (Clancy & Moschini, 2017). IPES-Food & ETC Group (2021) argue that these bio-digital conglomerates are primed to unleash big data and digital DNA into the world's pharmacies, food markets, and financial systems.

Developing a systemic policy framework for food—connected across the Sustainable Development Goals and EU policies—could potentially mobilize and guide contributions from many policy areas and provide a basis for a broad range of actors to explore pathways for the system's transition (EEA, 2019a). Such redesigning of the governance of farming activities through multi-sectoral governance models that extend the farming units into wider agri-food systems have been taken up by civil society groups through innovative networks and association like Community Supported Agriculture (CSA), Alternative Food Networks (AFN), box schemes, cooperative farming, and share farming. Fundamental enablers of system changes may promote larger transitions to sustainability supported by political initiatives to realign sectoral policies across production, processing, distribution, and consumption. In addition, municipal and regional institutions and authorities could establish sustainable procurement policies for food, food policy councils, meal policies, roadmaps, and other incentives for converting conventional farming systems into organic and/or other alternative farming models—including public food services in school canteen, elderly homes, and kindergartens. One unique example is the city of Copenhagen, where almost 90 percent of food served in schools and other institutions is now certified organic food and where a climate policy is being implemented on food procurement and practices with the aim of reducing climate impact from the municipal food system by 25 percent by 2025 (Anonymous, 2019).

The general objective for the future CAP is that it should play a crucial role in managing the transition toward a sustainable food system and in supporting European farmers. Aligned with Green Deal objectives, a political agreement on a new CAP (ec.europa.eu) was announced in a press release dated June 25, 2021 to target Farm-to-Fork and Biodiversity strategies that integrate environmental and climate legislation. On the table is €270 billion earmarked for the CAP for the period of 2023–2027. However, NGOs like Greenpeace, the European Environmental Bureau (EEB), BirdLife, Friends of the Earth Europe, and the World Wide Fund for Nature (WWF) criticized the provisional agreement's lack of solutions to fight the urgent climate and biodiversity crises.

According to Brown et al. (2021), the failure of EU agricultural subsidies to achieve their environmental objectives is not due to a lack of knowledge about agricultural expansion and intensification as key drivers of biodiversity and ecosystem services loss. These processes are not only driven by socio-economic and technological forces, but also supported by public policies. Furthermore, in recent years, the scientific literature offers several suggestions of needed systemic changes and specific management practices necessary to better maintain soil health and biodiversity functions and services. EEA (2019a) basically concludes that CAP interventions have failed to meet the urgency of the problems that we face as a society in the near future. The agency asks for a necessary fundamental sustainability transition in the European food system.

Some concepts are included in the CAP, including fallow land, some degree of agroforestry, and preservation of field margins. However, there must be greater adoption of environmentally beneficial management practices by Europe's farm-to-fork actors for the CAP to be effective. It is recommended to take more actor-driven objectives as a starting point and to involve non-academic actors, as well as scientists, in a process of cross-inspiration, knowledge sharing, and collective learning in order to overcome the implementation gap between research and practice (see also Chapter 13).

Farmers and additional food chain actors are very different regarding their acreage, background, age, and experiences (Aare et al., 2021a). A classical subsidy compensation for lost income and additional cost philosophy might be too simple. Instead, a more open co-innovation space around common resources requires learning processes involving knowledge concepts, perceptions, routines, rules, and regulations at the level of the social and economic contexts in which the actual actors operate. Innovations must be negotiated and locally adjusted by relevant actors not only to be effective but also to overcome apparent resistance to political environmental objectives (Hansen et al., 2020)

The successor of Horizon 2020 is Horizon Europe, which continues approaches that support the market uptake of innovation, including the scale-up of breakthrough innovators, while integrating sustainable development goals. A shift from activity-driven approaches toward impact-driven strategies is emphasized. See Table 8.1 with exemplary research projects listed from recent EU research programs with this chapter authors as partners. From this active participation doing cross-disciplinary research it is concluded that changing priorities in such ways challenges the current systems, causing potential conflicts within review offices, disciplinary academic societies, and institutions. Despite, for instance, the emergence of additional research issues not necessarily foreseen in the original and approved research project, only minor opportunities for adjusting projects are possible according to funding bodies' rules and traditions for status reporting. Likewise, strong traditions, cultures, and norms embedded in the food system can challenge potential transitions to other possibly more sustainable and diversified agri-food systems of the future.

The strategy of promoting knowledge sharing to discuss principles rather than tailor-made solutions is gathering increasing attention. This strategy should also be addressed with the new CAP to be implemented beginning in January 2023, which is supposed to be "fairer, greener, more flexible," with higher environmental and climate ambitions aligned with Green Deal objectives (www.ec.europe.eu). Some CAP components of direct payments are still mandatory (conditionality) based upon good agricultural and environmental conditions, including appropriately preventing soil erosion, maintaining soil structure, sustaining permanent grasslands, protecting biodiversity, and managing water. More interestingly, 25 percent of the direct payments will be allocated to eco-schemes, providing stronger incentives for climate and environment-friendly farming practices such as organic farming, agroecological practices, precision farming, agroforestry, and carbon farming, as well as animal welfare improvements. It should be noted, however, that a two-year learning period (2023–2024) is allowed in the case that an EU country spends less than 25 percent because of a lower take-up by farmers than planned.

Based on simpler rules, each member state will prepare a strategic plan to implement the policy, allowing them to take local conditions into account. This might require forcing local/regional/national food system actors to "unlearn" current knowledge and break with current value chain actor networks to increase adaptive capacity or transition and innovation. This is not an easy task. And what about the Farm-to-Fork strategy ambitions to reduce pesticide, set a threshold on food waste, and rely on renewable energy to create a sustainable food system? There exist major conflicts between those who want to continue expanding an industrial farming model and others who prefer a distributed and local economy scale to obtain a more ecologically friendly form of agriculture. The latter encounter arguments about decreasing Europe's agricultural production, rising prices, and greater dependence of the EU on imports. On the other hand, why not realize that environmentally friendly farming will come with a cost that is typically not included in

Table 8.1 Exemplary research projects from recent EU research and innovation program Horizon 2020 (almost €80 billion) conducted by this chapter authors to address EU policy priorities to tackle critical food system and agriculture challenges.

Project	Outcome
Remix (www.remix-intercrops.eu/) was funded to re-co-design current cropping systems based on 11 case-study platforms across Europe. This multi-actor approach aimed at understanding the reason that such ancient crop diversification practices—shown to have the potential to contribute to productive, resilient, and environmentally friendly cropping systems less dependent on external inputs than current dominating cropping traditions—are almost never utilized in the European cropping landscape.	In the work program under the project, issues of equity became apparent that perceived benefits primarily are of relevance to farmers or, adversely, that farmers could be left alone with the risks of failure, unless contractual arrangements are changed.
Legvalue (www.legvalue.eu) was funded to work under a "multi-actor approach" to ensure adequate involvement of the farming sector in developing sustainable legume-based farming systems and agri-feed and food chains. Across 15 pilots (case studies), benefits of legume production were exemplified. In addition, the project demonstrated that a more valuable and diverse market could create financial benefits for all in the value chains, when it aimed at delivering social and environmental benefits.	Knowledge deficits on crop production and transformation were identified, highlighting the need for new organizational arrangements to generate interactions and shared rules across value-chain actors. Combinations of organizational, network, and system levels seemed to be key to pilot case successes.
The Food Trails Project (www.foodtrails.milanurbanfoodpolicypact.org) bridges 11 cities with universities to map these cities' food policy programs and strategies and to co-create roadmaps and living labs for developing and implementing food policies that cover green transition goals.	The participating cities represent a diversity of developing food policies, including implementing a transition, using 90 percent organic food, establishing food councils, supporting school food programs, supporting SMEs and local farmers, and establishing school gardens.
Nextfood (www.nextfood-project.eu) gathers 19 partners to map, train, and develop the competences of observation, dialog, reflection, participation, visionary thinking, and facilitation through 12 case-based action learnings for transitions toward more sustainable agri-food and forestry systems.	Its specific aim is that systemic cross-disciplinary and -sectoral approaches produce responses to the need for education that enable the young generation to deal with complex agroecological food sustainability challenges.

present industrial farming, despite the strong evidence-based arguments for alarming longer-term climate and biodiversity costs?

With the EU ambition to reach 25 percent of organic land by 2030, it is important to remember that this development started as an alternative to the dominating globalized food system. Now, more than 30 years after the organic agri-food system was introduced, this is still only a fragment of the total market characterized by a growing organic conventionalization (Guthmann, 2004) as it tries to meet the very same global low-cost food regime retailer logics in contrast to the direct argument for change when the whole organic movement was initiated. Institutional lock-ins for the development of an alternative agri-food system indeed exists, which is also reflected in challenging access to relevant knowledge, advisors, regulation, financing, and research. Developing the next new agri-food systems—based on more plant-based foods—will most probably face similar lock-ins and challenges.

Traditional product-specific policies could be replaced by a more producer- or even value chain-based policies. To support such development, more attention needs to be dedicated to perspectives that include multilevel participation, opening the science-policy in EU more toward citizen involvement and participation. Such attention may open for a more robust innovative food policy domain of locally based companies, communities, associations, and institutions that lowers single-actor risks. However, major differences within and among the Member States may reduce the overall impact.

Another difficulty is certainty for payment support to food systems that provide public goods in the form of rural, cultural, environmental, and climate-friendly agriculture benefits that are not sufficiently rewarded on the market (Scown et al., 2020). From the learning of the decade-long CAP regulatory history, with the aim of increasing agricultural productivity while ensuring a fair standard of living for the agricultural community through, for example, ensuring market stability, we must conclude that it still fails to adequately address citizens' concerns regarding the sustainability of farming, the environment, and climate change.

Necessary interventions to transform the food system

Since the Neolithic Period, agriculture has been fundamental for the social, cultural, and economic condition of humankind. Farmers are not only food and fiber providers, but also shepherds of ecological services such as pollination and biodiversity conservation while preserving soil productivity for future generations. However, self-reinforced decline in soil organic matter through the interplay of human and natural processes (Rockström et al., 2017) reduces natural capital at a speed never seen before, lowering productivity capacity even as the world population is fast-growing (Steffen et al., 2015). These social challenges and future environmental tipping points are critically put forward by the IPES-Food & ETC Group (2021), highlighting food system corporate consolidations across all sectors that influence power relations and possibly affect key information flows between, for example, governmental bodies, scientists, and wider civil society organizations.

No doubt, mechanisms of the global market have put the modern farmers under considerable pressure—economically as well as socially—challenging their ability to introduce new management practices. In Europe, farm sizes have increased by about 30 percent since 2005, with fertilizer use and the use of other types of agrichemical inputs showing similar trends that negatively influence biodiversity indicators like the Farmland Bird Index (ec.europa.eu/eurostat). Without a more radical transformation, this development is expected to continue driving agricultural intensification even further in Europe, independent of the greening of the new CAP, leading to a continuing decline of farmland biodiversity and quality.

Involving sectoral experts from the public and private sectors with a modeling exercise, Rega et al. (2019) show that, if appropriate land use and land management choices are put in place, Europe could maintain its current agricultural production levels in 2040, while halting harm to environment and biodiversity. It sounds almost too good to be true. However, food security and environmental sustainability create trade-offs in land use practices. The intensification agenda harms future land productivity and, in turn, agricultural trade and market prices. Basically, the EU faces a situation with a detrimental risk in the long-term to lose the functioning of fundamental ecological processes. In saying that, strong traditions, cultures, and norms are embedded in the farming profession, to support potential transitions to other more diversified agricultural practices.

Following IPES-Food & ETC Group (2021), scenarios for the transformation of agribusiness versus civil society options can be used to illustrate radically different pathways to follow, with a critical eye toward existing economic and power structures.

Scenario 1 is about agribusiness as usual. This means a situation with increased climate change challenges, situated environmental challenges, and severe political actions trying to preserve and widen existing power structures and capitalist modes of production. This implies the risk that the keys to the food system are handed over to the bio-digital mega-corporations, data platforms, and private equity firms. Ecosystems are engineered through data gathered in the sky in centralized computer systems with robotics and drones taking over field operations. An internet of farming things is thus born. This also goes downstream into the consumer part of the system, with data harvested from online activities combined with metadata generated from the use of digital wallets and automated food services. In this way, demand can be tracked with nudging opportunities and other tools for the reshaping of food culture.

Scenario 2 is about civil society as unusual. This means a situation with civil society defining initiatives while developing deeper, wider, and more effective collaborations. A food movement is strengthened and able to challenge corporate concentrations, causing a fundamental governance reconfiguration that weakens dominating agribusiness controls. Much more inclusive transformation processes are realized to promote diversified agroecological systems and accelerate alternative markets and dietary shifts. Local/regional/national Food Policy Councils collaborate based on deliberative dialogs to strengthen the participation of social movements, ancient practices, and the redirection of financial flows by NGOs. Despite oppositions and diverging priorities, civil society can operate more collaboratively through a diversity of forms and scales of action, making it a powerful and very dynamic change-maker (see also Chapter 11).

From what we know today, scenario 1 will be almost incapable of bringing the planet and its agri-food systems back within a safe operating space (Rockström et al., 2009; Steffen et al., 2015) with a risk to continue to generate inequalities, food insecurity, and harmful environmental impacts. Already today, we face a situation in which mainstream European farming systems have led to a rapid degradation of biodiversity, soil carbon sequestration, and water quality and to increased greenhouse gas emissions. Greater mechanization and use of inputs are symbols of nature control, rather than of the design of farming systems that mimic nature to support ecosystem services.

In scenario 2, engaging different forms of knowledge of academic and non-academic actors—whether implicit, explicit, experiential, informal or formal—is a possibility to obtain knowledge that is both scientifically credible and socially valuable and that supports a more democratic and sustainable management of common land (Aare et al., 2021a, 2021b). Urgently needed new food system development pathways can be addressed in dissimilar ways and from different perspectives, including confrontations with and integration of multiple perspectives, insights, experiences, and ideas.

Such an impact-driven framework in research and policy programs may mark a paradigm change toward much more participatory processes, providing close-to-real-time information to handle complex problems while ensuring implementation and continuous communication. However, a paradigm shift is not realized overnight. Hauggaard-Nielsen et al. (2021) conclude that the open interactions within a multi-actor approach facilitate increased trust and reliability across traditional disciplinary boundaries, creating fertile working linkages and constructive cross-collaborations. However, the same authors underline that it is simultaneously important to remember that, when project partners are back home again in their normal professional working environments, rules for accrediting research, procedures for promotions, and other criteria for academic life, such as advancements, may threaten to undermine this attempt to rethink research and practices (see also Chapter 13).

Fundamental theoretical and political questions concerning the development of the food system in Europe and the interrelations between the EU and the world

The need for a sustainable transition of the agri-food systems is well-documented by research-based studies. From an overall theoretical perspective, three dominating methods to tackle this need have been suggested: (1) incremental innovations and optimizations of existing production regimes currently focusing on further development of effective technologies that can reduce greenhouse gas emissions; (2) radical innovations involving the potential redesign of the wider agri-food system; and (3) concepts that combine these approaches.

Major questions related to the development of sustainable and resilient food systems have been formulated based on a wide range of identified lock-ins that hinder market integration and the provision of added-value to farmers and connected value chain actors. The lock-ins are embedded in many levels:

- Structural and institutional lock-ins (investment, policies, path dependencies, funding mechanisms of research)
- Economic lock-ins (export orientation, expectation of change)
- Intellectual lock-ins (compartmentalized, sectorial short-term thinking, certain discourses about feeding the world)
- Societal lock-ins (concentration of power in the food chain, cultural lock-ins, no societal consensus on how and at what cost we can produce food)
- Technological lock-ins (agriculture and food research, complexity of technology, cost of technology)

Existing research-based knowledge has been disseminated to decision-makers in the EU and in national democratic boards. However, there is a lack of possible new directions creating flourishing market avenues and niches providing economic profitability and added-value to farmers and actors in the agri-food value chain (Hauggaard-Nielsen et al., 2021). Thus, despite carbon-neutral targets by 2050 that involve a number of defined efforts policy success will depend heavily on further research and innovation for speeding up knowledge transfer strategies for authorities, producers, and end-users, including the transnational development of knowledge and standards. The SCAR (2020) foresight report by a team of European experts outlines the steps ahead and declares that humanity is neither in a "safe" nor "just" operating space. Drawing upon the COVID-19 pandemic experience that showed a lack of resilience to stressors and shocks, a drastic transformation of the way that we produce and consume food and exploit natural resources is put forward as necessary, underlining the fact that incremental improvements are no longer sufficient. Indeed, accelerating changes are required toward severe environmental threats, as well as interrelated social and economic stressors, including the depopulation of rural areas, low levels of entry into farming as an occupation, and poor rates of return for the majority of farm gate produce.

One simple way to illustrate the complexity is to note the fact that the price of food does not include the negative environmental, economic, and social externalities that are directly and indirectly associated. This is critical for a novel development of future systems. The socio-economic outcome of sustainable systems should be based on true cost accounting with premiums for climate change mitigation, soil fertility, and biodiversity building strategies.

Current practices exhaust productive capacity and more environmentally responsible and climate-smart solutions need maturity to be able to reverse deteriorations. The true cost of food is devalued with market power generation within the global food supply chains, educating consumers to spend a comparatively low share of total consumption on food as one of the most fundamental materials for the survival of living beings. Egmose et al. (2020) explain that the interconnectedness of crises that cannot be separated from the results of historical and structural notions of mastery and extraction toward renewed attentiveness and human engagement (see also Chapter 12). Thus, as almost all main policies are interconnected, increased emphasis toward improving the involvement of sectorial and horizontal policies is recommended based upon a multi-actor approach that includes practitioners.

It is easier than it sounds, however. It requires that we look at the constraints to change—the path dependencies and lock-ins. New policies meet a tradition in a socio-technical food landscape deeply embedded in cultural and normative values, as well as global and national trends, such as economic growth and the broader political situation that influences, positively or negatively, the route toward system innovation. Another policy level and target are the regimes providing orientation and direction to the activities of the social groups operating within the dominant systems and their shared routines, rules, and norms that provide stability and, by their very nature, resist radical change. A major obstacle to unlocking the lock-ins emerges from the evolution of the farming model toward intensification and the individual identity and capabilities of farmers. To challenge innovation stagnation by regime actors, support to subsystems can be suggested in which new technologies; new rules and legislation; and new institutions, concepts, and ideas can be developed and experimented with (Geels, 2020).

The EAT-Lancet Commission Report provides a quantitative assessment of several primary sector-relevant planetary boundaries to meet a future with a more plant-based global diet (Willett et al., 2019). It could be regarded as a recognition of the coupled links between healthy people, healthy societies and a healthy planet to consider for boosting innovation policies that address the whole system, in which desired transitions should occur. That being said, it is important to remember that the EU Farm-to-Fork Strategy supports this by setting out guiding principles for a robust and resilient food system with a need to strengthen interrelations between ecosystems, supply chains, consumption patterns, and planetary boundaries. However, moving from intensification and specialization (simplification), driven by both policy objectives and advancing technology and leading to major changes in farm management, is not trivial. Indeed, policy-makers need to reconnect agri-food systems to societal aims (needs) to succeed in the goal to deliver safe and nutritious foods, while respecting planetary boundaries, rewarding novel organizations and connected value-chain actors, and showcasing business models for the future.

Summary

The dominant food systems have transformed radically through centuries. Conveying plentiful and affordable food to the people was an overall aim for the initial EU CAP policies in the 70s, with a vision of making remote areas of EU feed the centers of the EU and thereby securing a higher self-sufficiency with food. Since then, the EU CAP policy has been deregulated to better match the global agri-food systems bulk markets, with a major contemporary mega-trend being the development of the scientific-industrial agri-food regime dominated by centralized and (often) global economic private actors who interact with public policymakers in both national and transnational public regulatory and economic institutions.

Despite being very cost-effective, agri-food systems face challenges of unequal power, safety, and inequality at the system level and offer an example of the possible pitfalls associated with socio-ecological transformation. This has resulted in a structural development that has negatively impacted the environment and the socio-economic life of rural, peri-urban, and urban communities. For many people in contemporary Western societies—and those of the EU especially—access to food seems trivial. But it is not. Historically, agri-food systems have experienced a series of transformations caused by socio-economic, environmental, and many other events and crisis. Now again, the agri-food system is realizing transformative changes to meet societal goals related to negative environmental impacts on water systems, biodiversity, and climate, including negative health impacts caused by population dietary preferences. The recent crisis in Ukraine has intensified the need for adding food security to this agenda. Although their economic power is minor, the development of counter trends has been documented. This includes not only NGOs and other ideal actor groups, but also public policymakers in both national and transnational public regulatory and economic institutions.

Food movements have been developing a variety of cooperative practices in recent decades, giving access to shorter distances to farmers and, at the same time, opening markets for more sustainable production systems, typically of organic or regenerative origin. As more of these decentralized movements have practiced either international cooperation or the inspiration of ideas instead of commodities, they have supported democratic policy processes to balance the influence of the concentrated powers of the agri-food system. Through such initiatives, we now see that both civil society food movements and cities reach out to farmers and farmer groups to work on integrating common goods into their farming practices.

Since the 1980s, pioneering farmers and farmer movements like organic farmers have been working on developing new alliances with food movements and cities. These days, the plant-based food movement can be identified as a possible carrier of a similar radical game changer for the agri-food system. Food system change agents may be stimulated by a growing recognition of: (1) commodity price competition that tends to exclude the development of new pathways and more radical sustainable production systems and (2) "eating is an agricultural act," meaning the development of regulatory and structural frameworks that give the eater better access to food and information for more sustainable food production practices.

To reach EU food system goals, society calls for farmers and other actors to take a more prominent role in developing the agri-food system to protect the environment, mitigate climate change, and ensure the quality of the food we eat. Farmers cannot do all this at their own risk. They need support for systematic collection and dissemination of experiences; verification of effects on soil, plants, and climate; and easy access to novel/adapted means of production. Agents with the power of transformative decision-making can particularly support the development of conditions for farming that integrate societal, environmental, and ethical needs with market conditions for agri-food chain actors.

In Chapter 11 of this book, more regulatory scopes and possible interventions will be addressed, including how science, NGOs, practitioner organizations, communities, and other active society actors can influence decision-makers to provide recognition for real-life efforts to combat the burning platforms that we face. In the next chapter, we will focus on biodiversity in the EU and biodiversity governance. As we shall see, agriculture and food systems play an important role regarding biodiversity loss. Therefore, the transformation of agriculture and food systems may also play an important role in solving biodiversity challenges.

References

Aare, A. K., Lund, S. and Hauggaard-Nielsen, H. (2021a). Exploring transitions towards sustainable farming practices through participatory research: The case of Danish farmers' use of species mixtures. *Agricultural Systems*, 189, 103053. DOI: 10.1016/j.agsy.2021.103053

Aare, A. K., Egmose, J., Lund, S. and Hauggaard-Nielsen, H. (2021b). Opportunities and barriers in diversified farming and the use of agroecological principles in the Global North: The experiences of Danish biodynamic farmers. *Agroecology and Sustainable Food Systems*, 45(3), 390–416. DOI: 10.1080/21683565.2020.1822980

Altieri, M. A. (2004). Linking ecologists and traditional farmers in the search for sustainable agriculture. *Frontiers in Ecology and the Environment*, 2, 35–42. DOI: 10.1890/1540-9295(2004)002

Altieri, M. A., Nicholls, C. I., Henao, A. and Lana, M. A. (2015). Agroecology and the design of climate change-resilient farming systems. *Agronomy for Sustainable Development*, 35, 869–890. DOI: 10.1007/s13593-015-0285-2

Anonymous (2019). Københavns kommunes Mad- og Måltidsstrategi. Retrieved from: https://www.maaltider.kk.dk/for-borgere/mad-og-maaltidsstrategi. Accessed 3.8.2022

Beltran-Peña, A. A., Rosa, L. and D'Odorico, P. (2020). Global food self-sufficiency in the 21st century under sustainable intensification of agriculture. *Environmental Research Letters*, 15, 095004. DOI: 10.1088/1748-9326/ab9388

Brown, C., Kovacs, E., Herzon, I., Villamayor_Tomas, S., Albizua, A., Galanki, A., Grammatikopoulou, I., McCracken, D. I., Olsson, J. and Zinngrebe, Y. (2021). Simplistic understandings of farmer motivations could undermine the environmental potential of the common agricultural policy. *Land Use Policy*, 101, 105136. DOI: 10.1016/j.landusepol.2020.105136

Carter, M. S., Hauggaard-Nielsen, H., Heiske, S., Jensen, M., Thomsen, S. T., Schmidt, J. E., Johansen, A. and Ambus, P. (2012). Consequences of field N2O emissions for the environmental sustainability of plant-based biofuels produced within an organic farming system. *GCB Bioenergy*, 4(4), 435–452. DOI: 10.1111/j.1757-1707.2011.01132.x

Clancy, M. S. and Moschini, G. (2017). Intellectual property rights and the ascent of proprietary innovation in agriculture. *Annual Review of Resource Economics*, 9, 53–74. DOI: 10.1146/annurev-resource-100516-053524.1

Clapp, J. (2018). Mega-mergers on the menu: Corporate concentration and the politics of sustainability in the global food system. *Global Environmental Politics*, 18, 2. DOI: 10.1162/glep_a_00454

de Carvalho, A. M., dos Santos, D. C. R., Ramos, M. L. G., Marchão, R. L., Vilela, L., de Sousa, T. R., Malaquias, J. V., de Araujo Gonçalves, A. D. M., Coser, T. R., de Oliveira, A. D. (2022) Nitrous oxide emissions from a long-term integrated crop–livestock system with two levels of P and K fertilization. *Land*, 11, 1535. DOI: 10.3390/land11091535

Della Rossa, P., Mottes, C., Cattan, P. and Le Bail, M. (2022). A new method to co-design agricultural systems at the territorial scale - Application to reduce herbicide pollution in Martinique. *Agricultural Systems*, 196, 103337. DOI: 10.1016/j.agsy.2021.103337

Dhar, S. K. and Hoch, S. J. (1997). Why store brand penetration varies by retailer. *Marketing Science*, 16, 208–227. https://doi-org.ep.fjernadgang.kb.dk/10.1287/mksc.16.3.208

EEA (2019a). The European environment — state and outlook 2020. Knowledge for transition to a sustainable Europe. DOI: 10.2800/96749

EEA (2019b). Annual European Union greenhouse gas inventory 1990–2017 and Inventory report 2019. EEA Report No 6/2019. Submission under the United Nations Framework Convention on Climate Change and the Kyoto Protocol. Retrieved from: https://www.eea.europa.eu/publications/european-union-greenhouse-gas-inventory-2019

Egmose, J., Jacobsen, S. G., Hauggaard-Nielsen, H. and Hulgård, L. (2021). The regenerative turn: On the re-emergence of reciprocity embedded in living ecologies. *Globalizations*, 18(7), 1271–1276. DOI: 10.1080/14747731.2021.1911508

EU (2018). Regulation (EU) 2018/848 of the European Parliament and of the Council of 30 May 2018 on organic production and labelling of organic products and repealing Council Regulation (EC) No 834/2007. Retrieved from: http://data.europa.eu/eli/reg/2018/848/oj

EU (2021). Resilience and transformation. Report of the 5th SCAR Foresight Exercise Expert Group - Natural resources and food systems: Transitions towards a 'safe and just' operating space. European Commission Directorate-General for Research and Innovation. DOI: 10.2777/025150

Eurostat (2022). Manufacturing statistics - NACE Rev. 2. Retrieved from: https://ec.europa.eu/eurostat/statistics-explained/index.php?title=Manufacturing_statistics_-_NACE_Rev._2

FAO (2018). The 10 elements of agroecology: Guiding the transition to sustainable food and agricultural systems. Retrieved from: http://www.fao.org/3/i9037en/i9037en.pdf

FAO and WHO (2019). Sustainable healthy diets – Guiding principles. Rome. Retrieved from: https://www.who.int/publications/i/item/9789241516648

Fitzgerald, D. (2005). Eating and remembering. *Agricultural History*, 79, 393–408. http://www.jstor.org/stable/3745162

Foley, J. A., DeFries, R., Asner, G. P., Barford, C., Bonan, G., Carpenter, S. R., Chapin, F. S., Coe, M. T., Daily, G. C., Gibbs, H. K., Helkowski, J. H., Holloway, T., Howard, E. A., Kucharik, C. J., Monfreda, C., Patz, J. A., Prentice, I. C., Ramankutty, N. and Snyder, P. K. (2005). Global consequences of land use. *Science*, 309, 570–574. DOI: 10.1126/science.1111772

Geels, F. (2020). *Transformative innovation and socio-technical transitions to address grand challenges*. Directorate-General for Research and Innovation, European Commission, Publications Office, Brussels. https://data.europa.eu/doi/10.2777/967325

Guthmann, J. (2004). The trouble with 'Organic Lite' in California: A rejoinder to the 'Conventionalisation' debate. *Sociologia Ruralis*, 44, 301–316. DOI: 10.1111/j.1467-9523.2004.00277.x

Hansen, E. M. Ø., Egmose, J., Lund, S. and Hauggaard-Nielsen, H. (2020). The role of experience exchange groups in farmers' practice transitions: The case of reduced tillage in Danish conventional farming. *Agroecology and Sustainable Food Systems*, 44(8), 1012–1032. DOI: 10.1080/21683565.2020.1726550

Hauggaard-Nielsen, H., Lund, S., Aare, A. K., Watson, C. A., Bedoussac, L., Aubertot, J-N., Chongtham, I. R., Bellostas, N., Topp, C. F. E., Hohmann, P., Jensen, E. S., Stadel, M., Pinel, B. and Justes, E. (2021). Translating the multiactor approach to research into practice using a workshop approach focusing on species mixtures. *Frontiers of Agricultural Science and Engineering*, 8(3), 460–473. DOI: 10.15302/J-FASE-2021416

Howard, P. (2018). Global seed industry changes since 2013, 31 December 2018. Accessed 8 April 2022. https://philhoward.net/2018/12/31/global-seed-industry-changes-since-2013/

IAASTD (2009). International Assessment of Agricultural Knowledge Science and Technology for Development (IAASTD) (2009). Agriculture at a crossroads: Synthesis report. Retrieved from: https://wedocs.unep.org/20.500.11822/7862.

IPCC (2019). *Climate change and land: An IPCC special report on climate change, desertification, land degradation, sustainable land management, food security, and greenhouse gas fluxes in terrestrial ecosystems*. P.R. Shukla, J. Skea, E. Calvo Buendia, V. Masson-Delmotte, H.-O. Pörtner, D. C. Roberts, P. Zhai, R. Slade, S. Connors, R. van Diemen, M. Ferrat, E. Haughey, S. Luz, S. Neogi, M. Pathak, J. Petzold, J. Portugal Pereira, P. Vyas, E. Huntley, K. Kissick, M. Belkacemi & J. Malley (eds.). Retrieved from: https://www.ipcc.ch/srccl/

IPES-Food (2016). From uniformity to diversity: A paradigm shift from industrial agriculture to diversified agroecological systems. International Panel of Experts on Sustainable Food systems. Retrieved from: https://ipes-food.org/_img/upload/files/UniformityToDiversity_FULL.pdf

IPES-FOOD (2022). Another perfect storm? How the failure to reform food systems has allowed the war in Ukraine to spark a third global food price crisis in 15 years, and what can be done to prevent the next one. Retrieved from: https://ipes-food.org/_img/upload/files/AnotherPerfectStorm.pdf

IPES-Food & ETC Group (2021). A long food movement: Transforming food systems by 2045. Retrieved from: https://www.ipes-food.org/_img/upload/files/LongFoodMovementEN.pdf

Ivanova, D., Vita, G., Steen-Olsen, K., Stadler, K., Melo, P. C., Wood, R. and Hertwich, E. G. (2017). Mapping the carbon footprint of EU regions. *Environmental Research Letters*, 12, 054013.

Jensen, E. S., Carlsson, G. and Hauggaard-Nielsen, H. (2020). Intercropping of grain legumes and cereals improves the use of soil N resources and reduces the requirement for synthetic fertilizer N: A global-scale analysis. *Agronomy Sustainable Development*, 40, 5. DOI: 10.1007/s13593-020-0607-xensen 2020

Lal, R. (2004). Soil carbon sequestration impacts on global climate change and food security. *Science*, 304, 1623. DOI: 10.1126/science.1097396

Lobell, D. B., Schlenker, W. and Costa-Roberts, J. (2011). Climate trends and global crop production since 1980. *Science*, 333, 616–620. DOI: 10.1126/science.1204531

Magrini, M-B. Anton, M., Cholez, C., Corre-Hellou, G., Duc, G., Jeuffroy, M-H., Meynard, J. M., Pelzer, E., Voisin, A-S. and Walrand, S. (2016). Why are grain-legumes rarely present in cropping systems despite their environmental and nutritional benefits? Analyzing lock-in in the French agrifood system. *Ecological Economics*, 126, 152–162. DOI: 10.1016/j.ecolecon.2016.03.024

Martín-Retortillo, M. and Pinilla, V. (2015). Patterns and causes of the growth of European agricultural production, 1950 to 2005. *The Agricultural History Review*, 63(1), 132–159. http://www.jstor.org/stable/43698008

Négre, F. (2021). Second pillar of the CAP: Rural development policy. Fact Sheets on the European Union – 2021. Retrieved from: https://www.europarl.europa.eu/factsheets/en/sheet/110/second-pillar-of-the-cap-rural-development-policy

Pe'er, G., Zinngrebe, Y., Moreira, F., Sirami, C., Schindler, S., Müller, R., Bontzorlos, V. A., Clough, D., Bezák, P., Bonn, A., Hansjürgens, B., Lomba, Â., Möckel, S., Passoni, G., Schleyer, C., Schmidt, J. and Lakner, S. (2019). A greener path for the EU Common agricultural policy. *Science*, 365, 449–451. DOI: 10.1126/science.aax3146

Rayner, G., Barling, B. and Lang, T. (2008). Sustainable food systems in Europe: Policies, realities and futures. *Journal of Hunger and Environmental Nutrition*, 3, 145–168. DOI: 10.1080/19320240802243209

Rega, C., Helming, J. and Paracchini, M. L. (2019). Environmentalism and localism in agricultural and land-use policies can maintain food production while supporting biodiversity. Findings from simulations of contrasting scenarios in the EU. *Land Use Policy*, 87, 103986. DOI: 10.1016/j.landusepol.2019.05.005

Rockström, J., Gaffney, O., Rogelj, J., Meinshausen, M., Nakicenovic, N. and Schellnhuber, H. J. (2017). A roadmap for rapid decarbonization. *Science*, 355, 1269–1271. DOI: 10.1126/science.aah3443

Rockström, J., Steffen, W., Noone, K., Persson, Å., Chapin, III, F. S., Lambin, E., Lenton, T. M., Scheffer, M., Folke, C., Schellnhuber, H. J., Nykvist, B., De Wit, C. A., Hughes, T., van der Leeuw, S., Rodhe, H., Sörlin, S., Snyder, P. K., Costanza, R., Svedin, U., Falkenmark, M., Karlberg, L., Corell, R.W., Fabry,

V. J., Hansen, J., Walker, B. H., Liverman, D., Richardson, K., Crutzen, C. and Foley. J. (2009). A safe operating space for humanity. *Nature*, 461, 472–475. DOI: 10.1038/461472a

SCAR (2020). Resilience and transformation: Report of the 5th SCAR Foresight exercise expert group - natural resources and food systems, transitions towards a 'safe and just' operating space. European Commission, Directorate-General for Research and Innovation, Publications Office. Retrieved from: https://data.europa.eu/doi/10.2777/025150

Scown, M. W., Brady, M. V. and Nicholas, K. A. (2020). Billions in misspent EU agricultural subsidies could support the sustainable development goals. *One Earth*, 3(2), 237–250. DOI: 10.1016/j.oneear.2020.07.011

Springmann, M., Clark, M., Mason-D'Croz, D., Wiebe, K., Bodirsky, B. L., Lassaletta, L., de Vries, W., Vermeulen, S. J., Herrero, M., Carlson, K. M., Jonell, M., Troell, M., DeClerck, F., Gordon, L. J., Zurayk, R., Scarborough, P., Rayner, M., Loken, B., Fanzo, J. and Willett, W. (2018). Options for keeping the food system within environmental limits. *Nature*, 562(7728), 519–525. DOI: 10.1038/s41586-018-0594-0

Steffen, W., Richardson, K. Rockström, J, Cornell, S. E., Fetzer, I., Bennett, E. M., Biggs, R., Carpenter, S. R., De Vries, W., De Wit, C. A., Folke, C., Gerten, D., Heinke, J., Mace, G. M., Persson, L. M., Ramanathan, V., Reyers, B. and Sörlin, S. (2015). Planetary boundaries: Guiding human development on a changing planet. *Science*, 347, 736, 1259855. DOI: 10.1126/science.1259855

Stenmarck, Å., Jensen, C., Quested, T. and Moates, G. (2016). Estimates of European food waste levels. European Commission (FP7), Coordination and Support Action – CSA. DOI: 10.13140/RG.2.1.4658.4721

Vermeulen, S. J., Campbell, B. M. and Ingram, J. S. I. (2012). Climate change and food systems. *Annual Review of Environment and Resources*, 37, 195–222. https://doi-org.ep.fjernadgang.kb.dk/10.1146/annurev-environ-020411-130608

Vogel, E., Donat, M. G. and Alexander, L. A., Meinshausen, M., Ray, D. K., Karoly, D., Meinshausen, N. and Frieler, K. (2019). The effects of climate extremes on global agricultural yields. *Environmental Research Letters*, 14, 054010. https://iopscience.iop.org/article/10.1088/1748-9326/ab154b

Wezel, A., Bellon, S., Doré, T., Francis, C., Vallod, D. and David, C. (2009). Agroecology as a science, a movement and a practice. A review. *Agronomy for Sustainable Development*, 29, 503–515. DOI: 10.1051/agro/2009004

Wezel, A., Casagrande, M., Celette, F., Vian, J.-F. F., Ferrer, A. and Peigné, J. (2014). Agroecological practices for sustainable agriculture. A review. *Agronomy for Sustainable Development*, 34, 1–20. DOI: 10.1007/s13593-013-0180-7

Wezel, A., Goette, J., Lagneaux, E., Passuello, G., Reisman, E., Rodier, C. and Turpin, G. (2018). Agroecology in Europe: Research, education, collective action networks, and alternative food systems. *Sustainability*, 10, 1214. DOI: 10.3390/su10041214

Willett, W., Rockström, J., Loken, B., Springmann, M., Lang, T., Vermeulen, S., Garnett, T., Tilman, D., DeClerck, F., Wood, A., Jonell, M., Clark, M., Gordon, L. J., Fanzo, J., Hawkes, C., Zurayk, R., Rivera, J. A., De Vries, W., Majele Sibanda, L., Afshin, A., Chaudhary, A., Herrero, M., Agustina, R., Branca, F., Lartey, A., Fan, S., Crona, B., Fox, E., Bignet, V., Troell, M., Lindahl, T., Singh, S., Cornell, S. E., Srinath R. K., Narain, S., Nishtar, S. and Murray, C. (2019).

Food in the Anthropocene: The EAT-Lancet Commission on healthy diets from sustainable food systems. *Lancet* (London, England), 393(10170), 447–492. DOI: 10.1016/S0140-6736(18)31788-4

Zomer, R. J., Bossio, D. A., Sommer, R. and Verchot, L. V. (2017). Global sequestration potential of increased organic carbon in cropland soils. *Scientific Reports*, 7(1), 15554. DOI: 10.1038/s41598-017-15794-8

9 Biodiversity and nature's contributions to people

Thorkil Casse and Henrik Hauggaard-Nielsen

> ...We need to change the way we produce, consume, and trade. Preserving and restoring our ecosystem needs to guide all our work.
>
> The President of the European Commission, Ursula von der Leyen, in her vision for a greener Europe (EC, 2019a)

Introduction

According to the Intergovernmental Science-Policy Platform on Biodiversity and Ecosystem Services (IPBES, 2019) degradation of the Earth's land surface through human activities is negatively impacting the well-being of at least 3.3 billion people, pushing the planet toward a sixth mass species extinction and costing more than 10 percent of the annual global gross product in loss of biodiversity and ecosystem services. The European Green Deal (see Chapter 5) and the Biodiversity Strategy for 2030 (EC, 2020a) indicate an ambitious biodiversity recovery plan (Hermoso et al., 2022). This means, for instance, to protect at least 30 percent of the EU's land area, strictly protect one-third of the EU's protected areas, plant 3 billion trees, and reverse the decline of pollinators. However, analogous aims were agreed upon in various previous policies (Paleari, 2022), without ever being met (EC, 2020). A European standard bird index shows a decline of 34 percent from 1990 to 2017 in open lands and a constant trend in forest areas (European Court of Editors, 2020). The same report argues that the number of birds and butterflies has decreased by 30 percent over just three decades. A study from Germany on insect decline has drawn the attention of several news media due to a drop of 82 percent over 27 years (Hallman et al., 2017). Later, it was questioned whether the conclusion was correct, since insect total biomass was measured instead of the number of total insects or species.

Current trends of biodiversity loss and reduced ecosystem health pose a serious threat to food security, very much linked to global warming, droughts, and frequent extreme weather events. Radical transformative solutions are needed to halt and reverse them. This chapter focuses on terrestrial ecosystems with an awareness of the multiple pressures across Europe that affect

DOI: 10.4324/9781003319672-12

species and habitats, leading to cumulative impacts on inland aquatic or marine biodiversity and reducing the overall resilience.

In accordance with the European Commission's State of Nature Report (EC, 2020b), the European Environment Agency (EEA, 2021) calls for urgent actions to combat Europe's continued alarming biodiversity decline. A utilitarian approach to nature exploitation has pushed uncontrolled consumption and expansion of infrastructure and trade at the expense of biodiversity (IPBES, 2019). The most frequently reported pressures for both habitats and species stem from agriculture (see also Chapter 8), which reflects the relative scale of agricultural and the intensified land-use practices almost abandoning more extensive practices (EC, 2020). Today, European farming systems are dominated by intensified crop monocultures and animal systems that indicate simplification rather than ecological connectedness and resilience-building, leading to severe pressures toward ecosystem functioning and services. Thus, society and consumer demands for ample and inexpensive foods result in unsustainable land-use practices that require increased political attention toward ecosystem preservation and restoring strategies—with, for example, the enlargement of existing Natura 2000 areas to protect, maintain, and restore Europe's biodiversity. In a seemingly self-contradictory way competitiveness in the agricultural sector is fundamentally dependent on the long-term resilience of ecosystems regulating services (climate, flood, disease, and water regulation); provisioning services (freshwater); supporting services (nutrient cycling, soil formation, primary production); and biodiversity-related interactions (see also Chapter 1).

Today, extension of the agricultural area under high-diversity landscape (see Chapter 8) is improved and can potentially be used to a higher degree. The European Commission (EC, 2020a) has declared that it will propose legally binding EU nature restoration targets, possibly underlining the political priorities compared to the traditional voluntary approaches in this policy area (IPBES, 2018). The European Green Deal (See Chapter 5) could indicate a paradigm change with continental priorities toward a better integration of biodiversity conservation across sectoral policies (Hermoso et al., 2022). Thus, biodiversity conservation (development) is a significant part of the socioeconomic challenges addressed by the European Green Deal to fight the impacts of climate change on society (see also Chapter 6) influencing our consumption forms shaping relations with other humans and the broader ecology (Egmose et al., 2021). In this perspective it is important to remind us of that EU policies are not limited to continental priorities due to subscriptions to international agreements and conventions with more global efforts to combat severe biodiversity losses.

Direct drivers enumerate agriculture and harvesting as mentioned, as well as mining, infrastructure building, and tourism (with mixed effects). All these active human interactions influence living organisms like animals, plants, insects, bacteria, and nonliving components like rocks, soil, water, and sunlight. The total demand for living and nonliving has increased six times from 1970 (IPBES, 2019), indicating the pressure on the survival of the living organisms in an ecosystem depending upon the capacity to adapt to sometimes very unforeseen climate change elements within its community challenging a resilient functioning. IPBES (2019) considers governance an overarching factor. Net exporters of biodiversity products come from Africa and Asia, opposite net importers from the EU and the US (IPBES, 2019), which also means that trade impacts global biodiversity through the "virtual" water, land, and deforestation contained in EU imports (see also Chapter 5). According to EEA (2020), more than half of Europeans land and water consumption footprints occur outside Europe, including those due to goods imported into the EU and consumed by Europeans. Importing virtual land (and other resources) is representing a real financial risk, as resource prices are expected to increase in the future. This also means that both public and private actors must start to address their total land use and work to reduce it. Full-life products are addressed in the European Green Deal (see Chapter 5) with the aim to develop more environment-friendly (and longer-lasting) products. Specific land uses and global value chains influence biodiversity quality.

In search of an assessment of the weight of different drivers behind the decline in biodiversity, we find no clear answer. The main difficulty becomes clear in assessing how much a change in land use translates into modifying the availability of biodiversity. Biodiversity is challenging to measure across countries, and it is difficult to link species changes to agricultural practices. The concrete connections are hard to establish, whether the focus remains concentrated on life cycle assessments or on global value chains. The best choice is to refer to a baseline stage of biodiversity or potential natural vegetation. Most studies are limited in geographical scope, and there is considerable variability in biodiversity among different kinds of natural vegetation (see, e.g., Gabel et al., 2016). Even a regional assessment is not easy to conduct, and indicators tend to be limited to water consumption and raw materials in global value chain analysis of ecological exchanges (Rivera-Basques et al., 2021). Developing comprehensive research methods in the global value chains-biodiversity nexus is at a very early stage.

Compared to the climate crisis and global models of changes in the mean surface temperature, ecological processes tend to be more local, chaotic, and less predictable (Borie et al., 2021). The European Union is participating in the setup and implementation of the IPBES work program to develop ideas and models to address the correlation between biodiversity conservation and economic development (EC, 2021a). This includes conflicts about United Nations (UN) functions between the interests of the Global North and the Global South. For example, India and Indonesia have demanded financial subsidy schemes by IPBES, whereas the US and EU were strongly against any design suggestions on funding mechanism (Vadrot, 2014). Western countries have defended looking at "ecosystem services," whereas several Latin American countries have deemed this approach overly neoliberal. IPBES continues to struggle to define a common notion engaging several institutions to play a pivotal role. In this sense, the IPBES approach is ambitious and holistic, but less concrete.

A possible solution to unite different viewpoints is by introducing the concept of Nature's Contribution to People (see also Chapter 1). This notion is broader than the notion of ecosystem services and highlights the ability of ecosystems to adapt to, for example, climate change as an important intrinsic value. Egmose et al. (2021) argue that the biodiversity crises, embedded in connected problems, can be regarded as destroying human and ecological livelihoods. What we encounter is essentially a crisis in the relations among humans and broader environmental and social concerns, and it begs the questions of how we should organize ourselves and our societies. The value of keeping an ecosystem in shape can easily be underestimated. The challenge, however, is to get from a more comprehensive concept to policy recommendations (Pascual et al., 2017), including the recognition of the full impacts of trade both within and outside the EU (see also Chapters 7 and 11). This more open approach integrates values in biophysical, socio-cultural, economic, health, and other terms.

In this chapter, we will discuss different approaches to the valuation of biodiversity losses, drivers of biodiversity losses, and thoughts about protection and the engagement of stakeholders in the pursuit of a sustainable future.

Biodiversity valuation

Biodiversity might be the most fundamental feature of our planet with every living thing, including man, involved in complex networks and dynamic interactions. Different branches of science build their estimates of biodiversity and losses on different traditions and premises and thus the actual measurements used—biologists and economists being one example of non-identical definitions of biodiversity. Many biologists note that biodiversity is not to be confounded with ecosystem services and that economic valuations often neglect regulation services (Farnsworth et al., 2015). The same authors find that public surveys to evaluate biodiversity focus on naturalness and overestimate recreational values and their accessibility compared to the value of remote forests. Other examples could be mentioned. Economists may argue the ability to direct environmental policy by correctly pricing nature to optimize resource management (Spash & Hache, 2022). This might go for reduced crop yields due to erosion, fish stock, and similar, whereas more complex ecosystem matters like soil health—including the ability to recycle nutrients, purify water, and absorb atmospheric carbon—are more unfamiliar topics for economists.

In an analysis of the leading 18 contributions, IPBES (2019) suggests a compromise among biologists, economists, and politicians. In these 18 contributions, main areas cover anything from habitat creation and pollination to air quality regulation and water and energy production. The link to biodiversity is more evident in some cases than in others. For instance, with the eye of an economist collaborating with engineering water purification provided by filtration in ecosystems can be substituted by cleaning human-made facilities. However, is it that simple to estimate the biodiversity loss and its cost by contemplating the establishment costs of artificial water cleaning facilities? The authors think not. Reduced natural water purification may indicate drought risks having an impact on water resources and agriculture production, influencing soil erosion, and reducing carbon sequestration. IPBES (2019) mentions examples wherein the connection is lacking completely or challenging to establish, such as more social science-oriented consequences with loss of identity for people for whom a species or a forest represents important functional and cultural meaning if a habitat is significantly changed, or even destroyed. There is a need to identify exemplary cases for relevant benefit estimation. One important observation from the IPBES Plenary meeting in 2022 in Bonn was the absence of comparative studies of different valuation methods. At one extreme, a pure utilitarian approach to a species, habitat, or ecosystem benefit and, at the other, a value to local people in non-monetary terms (personal observation, T. Casse). The absence of benefit estimations may be due to internal scientific and/or political disagreement illustrated by, for example, the IPBES 2019 report noting declines in habitat conservation, pollination diversity, increase in pollution, and water runoff, but staying silent on the impact on Nature's Contributions to People.

Data collection from 238 valuation papers in Europe and Central Asia revealed a ponderance of non-material values in more than 50 percent of the studies. Habitat creation and physical and psychological experiences are the specific areas of biodiversity that people appreciate as top priorities (Christie et al., 2019). Other studies have approached the valuation theme by assuming that land value expresses a proxy of ecosystem values. Estimating global loss of production due to poor land management in drylands formed the base of the worldwide conclusion that the quantification of net primary production could help to understand the productive function of ecosystems and biodiversity (Zika & Erb, 2009). Nevertheless, the same authors did not claim that this work could replace biodiversity loss estimations. Another example is Tilman et al. (1997), underlining that loss of soil fertility (and thereby food productivity) in isolation can be misleading when showing positive relations with increasing biodiversity (Tilman et al., 1997). Interestingly, the work of Carrasco et al. (2014) to value biodiversity-rich areas in the tropics showed a link between economic activity, accessibility, and land values, but no connection between ecosystem values regarding land monetary estimation and the location of biodiversity hotspots.

Using the EU 2030 Biodiversity Strategy that sets protection targets, the agenda to protect an area of high biodiversity value can be exemplified. This EU initiative is based upon the arguments that present protected areas are not sufficiently large to safeguard biodiversity at the EU level and that they require improved governance. However, this is challenging for scholars and planners to convince at the policy level in economic terms with short-term estimations most often indicating marginal economic values, despite the principal economic natural resource values provided by biodiversity initiatives such as fiber and food production, carbon storage, water infiltration, recreation, and improved extreme weather events resilience. Alternatives could disregard economic value and instead focus on the cost/effectiveness relation regarding the protection of specific species or ecosystem services. This was done in a Danish case, with the objective to protect about 900 terrestrial species and to identify the areas to realize this protection. The conclusion was that 13 percent of Danish forests require protection, with the costs of discontinued production-oriented forest management representing the main economic obstacles (Petersen et al., 2016). In another national report from a Danish region, carbon sequestration benefits originating from forest protection efforts played an essential role in the economic calculus (Termansen et al., 2017). However, none of the two reports seek to estimate biodiversity per se in economic terms.

Drivers of biodiversity loss

One challenge reaching a global goal of biodiversity protection is the bias toward studies of climate impact on biodiversity. Classifying many scientific papers published from 2006 to 2016, Mazor et al. (2018) found that 40 percent of all efforts discussing drivers of biodiversity losses focused on climate changes. Only 5 percent contemplated pollution, and another 5 percent overexploitation.

One possible way to identify where species are most threatened or thrive clean of significant human impacts is to combine the distribution of threats to biodiversity—including buildings, croplands, pasture lands, railways, and roads—with the International Union for Conservation (IUCN) Red List of threatened species' spatial distribution. In one example, Allan et al. (2019) shows that mammals are primarily under threat (52 percent), and one-quarter of the endangered species experience threats in 90 percent of their distributed land due to electric infrastructure, buildings, and agriculture. Europe and North America are gradually becoming more impacted or affected by such threats, with several Southeastern countries experiencing the highest probability of losing biodiversity based on such mapping studies (Allan et al., 2019).

From a historical perspective, the European Common Agricultural Policy (CAP) has supported large intensive farming systems. Land ownership has become concentrated in fewer large holdings in EU countries, managed by a limited number of corporate firms. In 2012, farms of more than 100 ha, 3 percent of all farms, controlled 50 percent of the agricultural areas (van der Ploeg et al., 2015). This has only increased over the last decade. Thus, while the proportion of cultivated land in the EU is relatively stable over time, the number of farms is in steep decline. It should be noted then that nearly 40 percent of the EU budget finances the Common Agricultural Policy (CAP), of which 40 percent consists of direct payments to this decreasing number of individual farmers (Pe'er et al., 2020; see also Chapter 8). The same authors favor a shift from direct payments to payments for public goods to support a multi-functional farming system and moves beyond a narrow focus on support to higher productivity systems. In a reflection paper, the EU Commission acknowledges that more efforts to sustain biodiversity are needed (EU, 2020a), with only 23 percent of species and 16 percent of habitats in good shape (EU, 2019b). A new biodiversity strategy was adopted in 2020 and defines a target to have a least 30 percent of non-protected species showing a positive trend by 2030. The link to the CAP is not spelled out in the biodiversity strategy, though land-use changes have highly impacted the quality of biodiversity in the EU.

The establishment of eco-schemes in the new CAP (due to begin January 2023) may be a promising tool to support biodiversity objectives, as it provides a more contextualized result-based approach to bridging ecosystem functions and services with actual land-use practices, as well as a more socio-political influence on food production. However, current evidence of former experiences of eco-schemes is inconclusive. Arnott et al. (2019) report positive outcomes with small mammals in the UK, but with no improvement in plant biodiversity in the Netherlands. The method of comparing two different sites over time and collected from various countries can be disputed. However, this may still be the best alternative without a comprehensive study of all EU countries. The eco-schemes are intended to increase incitements to manage farm areas to create wildlife-friendly habitats using such subsidy schemes. Examples of biodiversity strategies could be flower blocks using specific partridge-friendly seed mixtures providing habitat, for example, for birds that can eat the insects while providing nesting and winter cover from predators. Beetle banks at arable margins and hedgerows are other examples of high-quality habitats that could potentially be reintroduced.

The Farm-to-Fork strategy (see Chapters 5 and 8) has the ambition to push forward a global transition to sustainable food systems, in close cooperation with its international partners. When evaluating food systems, direct and indirect biodiversity impacts from the global trading of agricultural products can be hidden. The current "as cheap as possible" dominating food markets require production at the lowest possible cost, often obtained through more intensification and possible further land clearance. With Denmark as an example as one of the most cultivated countries in the world, fragmentation of natural terrestrial habitats is causing an urgent situation wherein 11 out of 17 terrestrial habitat types is considered unfavorable by the EU Habitats Directive (Fredshavn et al., 2019). On a European and even global scale, expansion of agricultural land is the main driver for deforestation. Chaudhary and Kastner (2016) matched maps of crop yields with extinct species, globally and regionally, and then combined it with trading patterns to show that a total of 83 percent of regional confined species were lost due to domestic consumption by populous countries like India, Indonesia, and China. The same authors highlight that about 17 percent were lost due to exports—with imports into

China and the US having the highest species losses compared to species lost to local consumption. Another study transposed projections of future agricultural cover with habitats of all known amphibians, birds, and mammals and estimated that nearly 90 percent of the 17,400 species would lose part of their typical habitats, and 10 percent of those species would lose more than 25 percent of their habitat extent to agricultural expansion (Williams et al., 2020). IPBES (2019) estimate that 32 million global hectares of primary or forest land were lost between 2010 and 2015, linked to the production of imported commodities like soybean, beef, wood, and coffee, partly to European citizens. This is to underline the complex and multiple connections between Europe as the world's largest exporter of agri-food products in economic terms, while massive imports occupy global land resources and increase climate change, biodiversity loss, and critical social injustices in some places.

In response to this business-as-usual scenario, Williams et al. (2020) suggests changing global production patterns to meet sustainable food production limitations and promoting regional opportunities and healthier diet—most often with a higher plant-based diet proportion. According to more nutritious diets, the EU Farm-to-Fork strategy describes the current food consumption patterns as unsustainable from both environmental and health points of view, exceeding as they do recommendations for the average intakes of energy, etc. People need to eat much more plant-based seasonal foods like whole grains, nuts, a variety of vegetables and grain legumes like beans, lentils, peas, and chickpeas. If such diet demands should lead to a real market pull, it would imply a shift from cereal-dominated rotations for fodder production to a much more diverse crop rotation (in time and space). Such potential enhancement of diversity of crop species promotes biodiversity conservation through new hosts for a more extensive range of species, from plants to insects, birds to mammals, above- and belowground (Brussaard et al., 2007; Perfecto et al., 2003).

Deforestation is also linked to the distribution of biodiversity through wildfires, and selective logging removing one or more trees and leaving the rest intact—a more sustainable alternative to the dominating clear-cutting strategies of removing a larger forest area completely (Barlow et al., 2016). Using satellite photos and a global forest model, Curtis et al. (2018) listed four drivers of equal importance: permanent land-use changes, forestry, shifting or slash-and-burn agriculture, and wildfires. Urbanization has only a marginal influence on global deforestation. Finally, Brodie et al. (2021) claim that the functional diversity of mammals in southeast Asia and South America declines mostly due to habitat loss and harvest. In areas of exceptionally high threat, such as Indonesia and Argentina-Venezuela, habitat destruction is a more vital type of threat than harvesting. Aiming at improving the quantity and quality of EU forests to strengthen their protection, restoration, and resilience, the new EU Forest Strategy for 2030 (EU, 2021b) sets a vision and concrete actions to meet new environmental conditions according to highly uncertain weather extremes and other impacts of future climate change. This also includes an expected increase of socio-economic functions and services.

Protection of biodiversity

The European Natura 2000 network is an ambitious protection framework to designate terrestrial and marine biodiversity areas (EC, 2020a). The EU combined two directives related to habitats (92/43/EEC) and birds (79/409/EEC). In 2016, management of protection extended to 18 percent of the total land in the EU where endangered mammals had their total range area covered, except for six species, with likewise 84 percent of birds covered in just 16 percent of the Natura 2000 network (van der Sluis et al., 2016). However, over the years, scholars and politicians have had lengthy debates about the effectiveness of protected areas and whether to leave full or partial protection of species/ecosystems to local people. This is indeed not only the case for indigenous communities in the Global South, for example, but a stated part of the EU Forest Strategy to ensure vibrant rural areas with thriving populations (EU, 2021b).

Participatory processes can legitimize state decisions and increase trust between public servants and the population. The question is whether the achievement in biodiversity protection in Europe is the result of actor involvement or the outcome of a top-down planning exercise (see also Chapter 11).

A debate is ongoing in Europe about how to involve all stakeholders in the designation process of new protected areas. Among negative impacts are overcrowding in protected areas and the uneven distribution of benefits for the community. In a review of studies analyzing social impacts of protected areas in Europe, half of them mentioned benefits and the other half negative issues (Jones et al., 2020). Benefits could include control of illegal fishing and the recognition of territorial rights, whereas the negative effects could include increasing bureaucratic procedures and new conflicts among different users. The authors did not attempt to weight benefits vs. costs, but 70 percent of studies referred to positive impacts, though this figure can be biased because the studies ended up with pure qualitative conclusions. While social impact studies are available, we know little about the designation of Nature 2000 areas in Europe or about local reactions.

Zafra-Calvo and Geldmann (2020) have looked at the possible trade-off between well-functioning protected areas and local support and satisfaction, and they showed a negative correlation between the two variables. However, increasing human pressure did not affect this negative correlation. One notorious problem inherited in the establishment of protected areas is underfunding. In a survey from Slovakia, 75 percent answered that Natura 2000 represented an obstacle to economic activities (Brescancin et al., 2018). Accordingly, including more than 2,000 protected areas and their management reports, Coad et al. (2019) find that only 25 percent of the all-natural regions dispose of adequate financial resources to hire staff and execute needed actions within their budget limits—only 20 percent reported sufficient financial resources. In the face of low funding, habitat loss and degradation follow. Geldmann et al. (2018) discussed various management methods, including design, planning, and monitoring. They concluded that only capacity and resources (budget and staff education) were significantly correlated to the increase in animal population in 73 protected areas around the globe.

Although not numerous, examples exist of effective participatory approaches in management of protected areas or co-management, for example, in England and Spain (Hermoso et al., 2022). Likewise, in a Natura 2000 implementation study in six EU member states, Blondet et al. (2017) concluded that stakeholder involvement was relatively high, but with involvement happening rather late in the process, toward the implementation phase. Another reflection from the work of Blondet et al. (2017) was that participation never included ordinary, average citizens, leaving out the most worrisome public actors in the future management practice changes process and leaving all the space for people and organizations with invested interests marked their opinions. Though Natura 2000 sites offer opportunities to private landowners (in the form of compensation) and a promotional tool to potentially profit through tourism activities, a substantial challenge to the EU system is to shift roles from pure top-down decision-making to orchestration, mediation, and coordination (see also Chapter 11).

Data-based considerations for biodiversity protection

Biodiversity protection tends to favor isolated areas such as sites on high slopes and within a certain distance of towns or villages (Joppa & Pfaff, 2009). In this way, it is easier to obtain governmental approval when, for instance, pressures from major agriculture actors are minor. Venter et al. (2018) discuss whether agricultural costs of land or the threat to biodiversity was the main objective of creating new protected areas by looking at the 2004–2009 and 2010–2014 time periods and then confirming that planners continue to declare new protected areas in isolated regions. This might be a result of governments supporting agricultural production by rewarding output or lowering input prices, not necessarily in the favor of local support and regional development. With increasing world populations and a rise in global food demand, this pressure to biodiversity might remain or even increase. However, isolated areas will not be enough to meet biodiversity targets (EU, 2020a) and a more reflective understanding is required to link biological richness and cultural diversity on both geopolitical and biogeographic terms. Agriculture's external impacts are counterproductive, and it is a fundamental challenge to provide access to many of the same resources as agricultural producers have currently (Foley et al., 2011). Brazil could be an example of such challenges, with Sampaio et al. (2007) calculating that, if the Amazon rainforest's area decreases by 40 percent of its expanse in the 1970s, it could not grow back to deliver past ecosystem functions and services. Nobre (2019) follow up on these findings by concluding Brazil managed to reduce its annual deforestation by 75% from 2005 to 2014- even as the value of agricultural production increased by 75 percent from 2005 to 2014—even as the value of agricultural production increased by about 200 percent over the same timeframe through support by "progress" in science and technology. Much of the former virgin Amazon soil is today transformed into drier, hotter savanna with detrimental consequences for the sustainability of the region's remaining natural vegetation and people. A parallel is the rise of large-scale land deals, or "land grabbing," taking place in the EU and influencing food security, food sovereignty, rural employment, and vitality (EP, 2016).

Unless comprehensive dietary changes take place (see Chapter 8), including eco-functional intensification strategies (Jensen et al., 2015), the situation may even worsen as food prices experience shocks from climate disturbances and geopolitical stressors. Until recently, the scientific community could not measure patterns and trends in land use and management. However, newer data is available. For instance, satellite-based forest cover estimates can be used to substitute laborious data production on biodiversity indicators. The question is the quality of such forest cover proxy for biodiversity protection. Ghoddousi et al. (2022) see a methodological problem, as they claim that 40 percent of global terrestrial protected areas are not in forested nature places. Along the same lines, data beyond the case-study level are very scarce compared to the Nature's Contribution to People's approach. Likewise, economic growth per se is not recognized as the main factor behind biodiversity degradation, only as one out of several indirect drivers. Other direct and indirect drivers include transitions from biomass to other energy sources, property rights, community governance, and trade. Furthermore, a disconnect appears between consumers and ecosystems that produce commodities, resulting in a lack of awareness of the impact of consumer choices. Moreover, out of a list of 150 peer-reviewed papers on protected area effectiveness, Ghoddousi et al. (2022) found only nine containing more than one dimension. A major inherent problem is the urge to scale up smaller or single case studies, which requires an agreement on indicators that are easy to collect. Today, this is not even close to being in place globally.

Furthermore, counterfactual methods in comparing protected areas to non-protected areas to estimate what would have happened without an intervention sound convincing from a statistical viewpoint. Still, they come with pitfalls mostly related to limited knowledge and understanding of causal relationships. Using more sophisticated methods should not replace socio-economic comprehension of the context in which protected areas are founded (dos Santos Ribas et al., 2020). Rich species and ecosystem diversity is the fundamental basis, and we need to improve our understanding of these comprehensive and complex interactions. It is true that new methodologies and technologies come not only with a range of opportunities, but also with associated risks, and thus they can be used for good or for bad.

In most studies related to biodiversity protection, the assumption rests on an alleged trade-off between conservation and development (agricultural expansion). While most observers believe this is true, others discuss the trade-off or hard choices in analyzing specific cases. Results of calculating the net economic benefits of nature conservation versus development of 62 sites worldwide, collected from peer-reviewed articles, showed that, in 24 cases, total conservation benefits outweighed the private costs of development. Data are comprehensive but too complex to assess the quality of the study without digging into the details. Most benefits include water provision or high-water quality (Bradbury et al., 2021).

An alternative approach is to depart from the traditional land-based study of conservation benefits versus opportunity costs (foregone earnings when land is protected). In a study from Madagascar, villagers living close to protected areas are better off in income and welfare than those living far from biodiversity-rich sites (Casse et al., 2022). One circumstance was that public services came from tourist facilities, replacing the state functions. Other studies employing a similar with/without approach in other countries may reveal if the Malagasy observation is unique. Studies from China, for example, find identical positive effects of tourism and poverty reduction and increased local inequality if communities engage in creating tourism facilities (Ma et al., 2019). If a tourist company depends directly on the health of the surrounding ecosystem, investments in biodiversity management is straightforward. However, and for Europe with about 50 percent land in rural landscapes used for agriculture, there is a need to develop opportunities to contribute to biodiversity protection/restoration while, at the same time, utilizing it as a sustainable resource for increasing economic viability (see Chapter 8).

Whether the protection of nature has positive impacts on local people beyond income generation is a long debate, and a few studies of possible win-win scenarios will not silence the skepticism. In China, nature reserves hosting the giant pandas have reduced pressure from cattle grazing and increased local participation in conservation projects. However, the socio-economic impact for households living inside the nature reserves is marginal, and China does pay ecological compensation to households to decrease household dependency on fuelwood collection (Ma et al., 2020). Not all developing countries can offer compensation, and even lower-income households in developed countries face a trade-off between conservation and development. From a governance perspective, this is covered by the so-called "second pillar" of the CAP, prioritized to restore, preserve, and enhance biodiversity in farms and forests across the EU, including Natura 2000 payments. With the new CAP (2023–2027), one out of nine specific objectives are "to preserve landscapes and biodiversity." In principle, each member state can spend at least 25 percent of their direct payments budget on eco-schemes; however, a member state may spend less than 25 percent in case of a lower-than-planned take-up by farmers. The question about biodiversity development using crop diversification strategies in time and space on agricultural land is less predominant (see Chapter 8).

A transformation need will enable an accelerated response to biodiversity decline by adopting new practices. This would also mean that the conservation planning techniques need to a higher degree to deal with possible mismatches between costs to leave current practices and benefits to improve the changes for appropriate longer-term conservations. This may require policy mixes to succeed in cases such as land-use zoning and other land management practices. Sometimes, the problem can be that specific landowners finds it unclear whether potential promotion of biodiversity can change the business model by penalizing crop yields due to lack of internal biological functions and services to reduce or avoid the use of external (and costly) fertilizers and pesticides. Such risk may require value chain actor involvement to support a systemic change toward self-sufficiency and food supply security increasing overall resilience through biodiversity-building strategies. Is it possible that the benefits of nature conservation can outweigh the private costs of development? McPhee et al. (2021) underline several conditions to achieve such a comprehensive challenge: (1) the connection with Nature and the living system, which is at the heart of the sector and acts as a common context and opportunity for change; (2) the need for "real-life" experimentation because agroecological innovation is rooted in space, territory, or place; (3) consideration that the high social value is therefore of serious political concern; and (4) consideration of the integrated constellation of institutions, actors, and knowledge in the agri-food sector because changes affect the entire system, as well as sectorial and national specificities.

Such development can be regarded as a radical opposition strategy to the dominating technological-driven changes that have been the primary driving force for increasing agricultural productivity and promoting agricultural development in Europe (see Chapter 8). Today, many farmers realize that this strategy leaves them with a vulnerable cropping system with a low level of resilience to accumulate unforeseen climate change hazards, while production costs are rising (employee wages, land prices, fertilizer costs, building construction, new machine technologies, fuels), increasing investment needs and potential depths. Crop diversity strategies are a radical alternative, leaving more space to biological interactions and endorsing self-regulation in the arable cropping strategies and less direct farmer operations. The trust in this type of strategy is challenging for self-understanding, culture, values, and norms in the local networks, where most farmers live their lives (Mass et al., 2020).

Local stewardship practices multiply in many areas with a huge number of environmental issues. Studies analyze factors that support or undermine stewardship initiatives, but do not offer definition or framework. Bennett et al. (2018) suggests a focus on actors, motivations, and capacity. Often overlooked, the authors mention as crucial capacity, local communities, and general governance. Internally, stewardship success is determined by the speed of action and, externally, by its political feasibility. In accordance with Bennett et al. (2018), other authors identify three leverage points to increase the impact of stewardship from minor, local interventions to broad, societal transformations (Chapin III, 2022). They call upon changing visions, shifting social norms, and engaging influential scholars. Adding rights to nature equips courts to pressure states for specific ecosystem components like rivers.

Reconciliation of stakeholders' different views has failed to halt biodiversity loss, with threefold increases of agricultural production since 1970 and an industrial timber increase that is up to 50 percent relative to 1970 (IPBES, 2019). While land degradation has reduced 25 percent over the same period, 25 percent of all animal and plant species are threatened by extinction, several within decades. Until today, stewardship arrangements or stakeholder agreement have not allowed for any substantial changes in the human exploitation of natural resources.

Complicating the picture is stakeholders opposing a priori central decisions to expand protected areas. Voluntary arrangements may coordinate with systematic central conservation efforts to reach a more viable and balanced result (Paloniemi et al., 2018). Another approach could be to enhance back and forth political moves and not define a fixed outcome (Brites et al., 2021). In an exercise of zonation in Finland, three analyses were promoted, showing that ecological optimization overlapped with ecological optimization by excluding solutions of adverse farmer reactions. Paloniemi et al. (2018) attributed the highly positive result to using a spatial approach. In a Brazilian case, continuous meeting rounds among stakeholders to agree on implementing a forest conservation code led to softening of initial conflicts (Brites et al., 2021). A study on German and Austrian farmers' perception of agri-environment schemes confirmed solutions should move away from static proposals and look upon them more as a process with continuous interactions among stakeholders (Maas et al., 2021). Both farmers and scientists maintain a positive attitude toward the value of biodiversity. All three studies point to a relatively low perceived importance of scientific evidence held by farmers or practical stakeholders.

In a final comment on the challenges of engaging multiple stakeholders to preserve biodiversity, Reed et al. (2019) list essential factors to enhance a biodiversity agenda: (1) stay away from rigid solutions and accept "the need to navigate complex challenges"; (2) recognize all stakeholder views; (3) include governance aspects in negotiating a deal; and (4) acknowledge that incentives play a pivotal role in influencing ideas and perceptions.

Summary

From a terrestrial system perspective, this chapter reveals the importance of healthy ecosystems to support biodiversity development, while highlighting the socio-economic value in the context of potential climate change tipping points that lead to accelerating declines—the sixth mass species extinction, with severe regional, national, and continental economic consequences. There is an urgent need for actions to combat Europe's continued biodiversity decline very much influenced by the increasing scale of agricultural and intensified land-use practices. Biodiversity governance needs to be addressed as part of the way we produce, consume, and trade. Both the European Green Deal and the Biodiversity Strategy for 2030 indicate a biodiversity recovery plan. The establishment of eco-schemes in the new CAP (2023–2027) supports climate and biodiversity objectives, indicating a more socio-political influence on agricultural practices and landscape planning, although evidence of the former experiences of eco-schemes is evaluated as inconclusive.

The definition of biodiversity is challenging, covering anything from habitat creation and pollination to air quality regulation, water, energy production, and more. Different definitions influence biodiversity benefit estimations, in some cases due to monodisciplinary approaches, including internal academic discussions with a clear lack of understanding, when addressing issues across mutual interspecific interactions, including the impact on Nature's Contributions to People.

EU supports IPBES as an international independent body working to strengthen the science-policy interface for biodiversity and ecosystem services qualifying EU policies beyond continental priorities. The Farm-to-Fork strategy (see Chapters 5 and 8) has the ambition to push forward a global transition to sustainable food systems, in close cooperation with its international partners. Without a doubt, trade impacts biodiversity decline, with more than half of European land and water consumption footprints occurring outside of Europe. However, it is concluded that developing comprehensive research methods in the global value chains-biodiversity nexus is at a very early stage (see Chapters 2 and 8). It is a critical obstacle for further development, also when it comes to the socio-economy dilemma between conservation and development (agricultural expansion). Examples exist from case-studies, but they have never been compared to each other. Without clear agreement on biodiversity functions and services, estimation of economic values for potential compensation is demanding. Currently, biodiversity impacts only represent marginal financial benefits and thereby limited optimization interests by stakeholders. There is a need to address the correlation between biodiversity conservation/building and longer-term economic sustainable development.

Biodiversity is about preserving and redeveloping, but also about a wide range of other important benefits to society and the economy via the flow of ecosystem services. It is not only a matter of reducing agricultural environmental impacts, but also of supporting additional business models within tourism and recreation. In the next chapter of this book, we will take a closer look at the broader social aspects of ecological challenges and solutions, with a special focus on Just Transition in the EU.

References

Arnott, D., Chadwick, D., Harris, I., Koj, A., and Jones, D. L. (2019). What can management option uptake tell us about ecosystem services delivery through agri-environment schemes? *Land Use Policy*, 81, 194–208. DOI: 10.1016/j.landusepol. 2018.10.039

Allan, J. R., Watson, J. E. M., Di Marco, M., O'Bryan, C. J., Possingham, H. P. and Atkinson, S. C. (2019). Hotspot of human impact on threatened terrestrial vertebrates. *PLOS Biology*, 17(3). DOI: 10.1371/journal.pbio.3000158

Barlow, J., Lennox, G. D., Ferreira, J., Berenguer, E., Lees, A. C., Mac Nally, R., Thomson, J. R., Ferraz, S. F., Louzada, J., Oliveira, V. H., Parry, L., Solar, R. R., Vieira, I. C., Aragão, L. E., Begotti, R. A., Braga, R. F., Cardoso, T. M., de Oliveira, R. C., Jr, Souza, C. M., Jr, Moura, N. G. and Gardner, T. A. (2016). Anthropogenic disturbance in tropical forests can double biodiversity loss from deforestation. *Nature*, 535(7610), 144–147. DOI: 10.1038/nature18326

Bennett, N. J., Whitty, T. S., Finkbeiner, E., Pittman, J., Basett, H., Gelcich, S. and Allison, E. H. (2018). Environmental stewardship: A conceptual review and analytical framework. *Environmental Management*, 61, 597–614. DOI: 10.1007/s00267-017-0993-2

Blondet, M., de Koning, J., Borras, L, Ferranti, F., Geitzenauer, M., Weiss, G., Turnhout, E. and Winkel, G. (2017). Participation in the implementation of Natura 2000: A comparative study of six EU member states. *Land Use Policy*, 66, 346–355. DOI: 10.1016/j.landusepol.2017.04.004

Borie, M., Mahony, M., Obermeister, N. and Hulme, M. (2021). Knowing like a global expert organization: Comparative insights from the IPCC and IPBES. *Global Environmental Change*, 68, 102261. DOI: 10.1016/j.gloenvcha.2021.102261

Bradbury, R. B., Butchart, S. H. M., Fisher, B., Hughes, F. M. R., Engwall-King, L., MacDonald, M. A. and Merriman, J. C. (2021). The economic consequences of conserving or restoring sites for Nature. *Nature Sustainability*, 4, 602–608. DOI: 10.1038/s41893-021-00692-9

Brescancin, F., Dobsinska, Z., de Meo, I., Salka, J. and Paletto, A. (2018). Analysis of stakeholders' involvement in the implementation of the Natura 2000 network in Slovakia. *Forest Policy and Economics*, 89, 22–30. DOI: 10.1016/j.forpol.2017.03.013

Brites, A. D., de Mello, K., Tavares, P. A., Metzger, J. P., Rodrigues, R. R., Moin, P. G., Pinot, L. F. G., Joly, C. A. and Fernandes, J. F. A. (2021). Science-based stakeholder dialogue for environmental policy implementation. *Conservation, and Society*, 19(4), 225–235

Brodie, J. F., Williams, S. and Garner, B. (2021). The decline of mammal functionality and evolutionary diversity worldwide. *PNAS*, 118(3), e1921849118. DOI: 10.1073/pnas.1921849118

Brussaard, L., de Ruiter, P. C. G. and Brown G. (2007). Soil biodiversity for agricultural sustainability. *Agriculture Ecosystems & Environment*, 121, 233–244. DOI: 10.1016/j.agee.2006.12.013

Carrasco, L. R., Nghiem, T. P. L., Sunderland, T. and Koh, L. P. (2014). The economic valuation of ecosystem services fails to capture the biodiversity value of tropical forest. *Biological Conservation*, 178, 163–170. DOI: 10.1016/j.biocon.2014.08.007

Casse, T., Razafintsalama, M. H. and Milhøj, A. (2022). A trade-off between conservation, development, and tourism in the vicinity of the Andasibe-Mantadia National Park, Madagascar. *SN Social Sciences*, 2, 12. DOI: 10.1007/s43545-021-00309-0

Chaudhary, A. and Kastner, T. (2016). Land use biodiversity impacts embodied in international food trade. *Global Environmental Change*, 38, 195–204. DOI: 10.1016/j.gloenvcha.2016.03.013

Curtis, P. G., Slay, C. M., Harris, N. L., Tyukavina, A. and Hansen, M. C. (2018). Classifying drivers of global forest loss. *Science*, 361(6407), 1108–1111. DOI: 10.1126/science.aau3445

Chapin III, F. S., Weber, E. U., Benett, E. M., Biggs, R., van den Bergh, J., Adger, W. N., Crépin, A. S., Polasky, S., Folke, C., Scheffer, M., Segerson, K., Anderies, J. M., Barrett, S., Cardenas, J. M., Carpenter, S. R., Fischer, J., Kautsky, N., Levin, S. A., Shogren, J. F., Walker, B., Wilen, J. and de Zeeuw, A. (2022). Each stewardship: Shaping a sustainable future through interacting policy and norm shift. *Ambio*, 51, 1907–1920. DOI: 10.1007/s13280-022-01721-3

Christie, M., Martin-Lopéz, B., Church, A., Siwika, E. and Szymonczyk, P. (2019). Understanding the diversity of values of 'Nature's contributions to people': Insights from the IPBES Assessment of Europe and Central Asia. *Sustainable Science*, 14(5), 1267–1282. DOI: 10.1007/s11625-019-00716-6

Coad, L., Watsom, J. E. M., Geldmann, J., Burgess, N. D., Leverington, F., Hockings, M., Knights, K. & Marco, M. D. (2019). Widespread shortfalls in protected area resourcing undermine efforts to conserve biodiversity. *Frontiers in Ecology and the Environment*, 17, 259–264. DOI: 10.1002/fee.2042

Dos Santos Ribas, L. G., Pressey, R. L., Loyola, R. and Bini, L. M. (2020). A global comparative analysis of impact evaluation methods in estimating the effectiveness of protected areas. *Biological Conservation*, 246, 108595. DOI: 10.1016/j.biocon.2020.108595

EEA (2020). The European environment — state and outlook 2020. Knowledge for transition to a sustainable Europe. Chapter 1 Assessing the global-European context and trends. Retrieved from: https://www.eea.europa.eu/publications/soer-2020

EEA (2021). State of nature in Europe: A health check. European Environment Agency. Retrieved from: https://www.eea.europa.eu/themes/biodiversity/state-of-nature-in-the-eu/state-of-nature-2020-subtopic

Egmose, J., Jacobsen, S. G., Hauggaard-Nielsen, H. and Hulgård, L. (2021). The regenerative turn: On the re-emergence of reciprocity embedded in living ecologies. *Globalizations*, 18(7), 1271–1276. DOI: 10.1080/14747731.2021.1911508

EC (2019a). European Commission, Directorate-General for Communication, Leyen, U. 2019 A Union that strives for more: My agenda for Europe: political guidelines for the next European Commission 2019–2024, Publications Office. Retrieved from: https://data.europa.eu/doi/10.2775/753401

EC (2019b). Towards a sustainable Europe by 2030, Reflection Paper. Retrieved from: https://www.eesc.europa.eu/en/our-work/opinions-information-reports/opinions/reflection-paper-towards-sustainable-europe-2030

EC (2020a). EU biodiversity strategy actions tracker. Retrieved from: https://dopa.jrc.ec.europa.eu/kcbd/actions-tracker/public/groups/completed

EC (2020b). Report from the Commission to The European Parliament, The Council and The European Economic and Social Committee. The state of nature in the European Union Report on the status and trends in 2013–2018 of species and habitat types protected by the Birds and Habitats Directives. COM/2020/635 final. Retrieved from: https://eur-lex.europa.eu/legal-content/EN/TXT/PDF/?uri=CELEX:52020DC0635&from=EN

EC (2021a). Proposal for a directive of the European Parliament and of the Council amending Directive 2003/87/EC as regards aviation's contribution to the Union's economy-wide emission reduction target and appropriately implementing a global market-based measure. COM (2021)552 final. Retrieved from: https://eur-lex.europa.eu/legal-content/EN/TXT/PDF/?uri=CELEX:52021PC0552&from=EN

EP (2016). Extent of farmland grabbing in the EU. In: J. Franco, S. Kay & J. Peuch (eds.), *European parliament, directorate-general for internal policies of the Union*. https://data.europa.eu/doi/10.2861/686177

EU (2021b). New EU Forest Strategy for 2030 – communication from the commission to the European parliament, the Council, the European Economic and Social committee and the Committee of the regions. COM (2021)575 final. Retrieved from: https://ec.europa.eu/environment/pdf/forests/new_EU_forest_strategy_2030.pdf

European Court of Editors (2020). Biodiversity on farmland: CAP contribution has not halted the decline. *Special Report,* 13. Retrieved from: https://www.business-biodiversity.eu/36681/Newsdetailseite/ebbc_index01.aspx?newsid=112165&newsrefid=36615&row=0&newsrefaddcoid=&nafrom=&nato=?utm_source=newsletter&utm_medium=email&utm_campaign=2_2020&utm_content=text

Farnsworth, K. D., Adenuga, A. H. and de Groot, R. S. (2015). The complexity of biodiversity: A biological perspective on economic valuation. *Ecological Economics,* 120, 350–354. DOI: 10.1016/j.ecolecon.2015.10.003

Foley, J., Ramankutty, N., Brauman, K., Cassidy, E., Gerber, J. S., Johnston, M., Mueller, N. D., O'Connell, C., Ray, D. K., West, P. C., Balzer, C., Bennett, E. M., Carpenter, S. R., Hill, J., Monfreda, C., Polasky, S., Rockström, J., Sheehan, J., Siebert, S., Tilman, D. and Zaks, D. P. M. (2011). Solutions for a cultivated planet. *Nature,* 478, 337–342. DOI: 10.1038/nature10452

Fredshavn, J., Nygaard, B., Ejrnæs, R., Damgaard, C., Therkildsen, O. R., Elmeros, M., Wind, P., Johansson, L. S., Alnøe, A. B., Dahl, K., Nielsen, E. H., Pedersen, H. B., Sveegaard, S., Galatius A. and Teilmann, J. (2019). Bevaringsstatus for naturtyper og arter – 2019 Conservation status of habitat types and species -2019. Habitatdirektivets Artikel 17-rapportering. Aarhus Universitet, DCE – Nationalt Center for Miljø og Energi, 52 s. Videnskabelig rapport nr. 340. Retrieved from: http://dce2.au.dk/pub/SR340.pdf

Gabel, V. M., Meier, M. S., Köpke, U. and Stolze, M. (2016). The challenges of including impacts on biodiversity in agricultural life cycle assessments. *Journal of Environmental Management,* 181, 249–260. DOI: 10.1016/j.jenvman.2016.06.030

Geldmann, J., Coad, L. Barnes, M. D., Craigie, I. D., Woodley, S. and Balmford, A. (2018). A global analysis of management capacity and ecological outcomes in terrestrial protected areas. *Conservation Letters,* 11, e12434. DOI: 10.1111/conl.12434

Ghoddousi, A., Loos, J. and Kuemmerle, T. (2022). An outcome-oriented, social-ecological framework for assessing protected area effectiveness. *BioScience,* 72, 201–212. DOI: 10.1093/biosci/biab114

Hallmann, C. A., Sorg, M., Jongejans, E., Siepel, H., Hofland, N., Schwanm, H., Stenmans, W., Müller, A., Sumser, H., Hörren, T., Goulson, D. and de Kroon, D. (2017). More than 75 percent decline over 27 years in total flying insect biomass in protected areas. *PLoS ONE,* 12(10), e0185809. DOI: 10.1371/journal.pone.0185809

Hermoso, V., Carvalho, S. B., Giakoumi, S., Goldsborough, D., Katsanevakis, S., Lenontiou, S., Markantonatou, V., Rumes, B., Vogiatzakis, I. N. and Yates, K. L. (2022). The EU biodiversity strategy for 2030: Opportunities and challenges on the path towards biodiversity recovery. *Environmental Science and Policy,* 127, 263–271. DOI: 10.1016/j.envsci.2021.10.028

IPBES (2018). The IPBES assessment report on land degradation and restoration. In: L. Montanarella, R. Scholes & A. Brainich (eds.), *Secretariat of the intergovernmental science-policy platform on biodiversity and ecosystem services.* Bonn, Germany, 744 pages. DOI: 10.5281/zenodo.3237392.

IPBES (2019). *Global assessment report on biodiversity and ecosystem services of the intergovernmental science-policy platform on biodiversity and ecosystem services.* E. S. Brondizio, J. Settele, S. Díaz & H. T. Ngo (eds.), Bonn, Germany: IPBES secretariat. 1148 pages. DOI: 10.5281/zenodo.3831673.

Jones, N., Graziano, M. and Dimitrakopoulos, P. G. (2020). Social impacts of European protected areas and policy recommendations. *Environmental Science and Policy*, 122, 134–140. DOI: 10.1016/j.envsci.2020.06.004

Joppa, L. N. and Pfaff, A. (2009). High and far: Biases in the location of protected areas. *PLoS ONE*, 4(12), e8273. DOI: 10.1371/journal.pone.0008273

Ma, B., Cai, Z., Zheng, J. and Wen, Y. (2019). Conservation, ecotourism, poverty, and income inequality: A case study of nature reserves in Quinling. *China, World Development*, 115, 236–244. DOI: 10.1016/j.worlddev.2018.11.017

Ma, B., Zhang, Y., Huang, Y. and Wen, Y. (2020). Socio-economic and ecological direct and spillover effects of China's giant panda nature reserves. *Forest Policy and Economics*, 121, 102313. DOI: 10.1016/j.forpol.2020.102313

Mass, B., Fabian, Y., Kross, S. M. and Richter, A. (2021). Divergent farmer and scientist perceptions of agricultural biodiversity, ecosystem services, and decision-making. *Biological Conservation*, 256, 109065. DOI: 10.1016/j.biocon.2021.109065

Mazor, T., Doropoulos, C., Schwarzmueller, F., Gladish, D., Kumaran, N., Merkel, K., Di Marco, M. and Gagic, V. (2018). Global mismatch of policy and research on drivers of biodiversity loss. *Nature Ecology & Evolution*, 2, 1071–1074. DOI: 10.1038/s41559-018-0563-x

McPhee, C., Bancerz, M., Mambrini-Doudet, M., Chrétien, F., Huyghe, C. and Gracia-Garza, J. (2021). The defining characteristics of agroecosystem living labs. *Sustainability*, 13(4), 1718. DOI: 10.3390/su13041718

Nobre, C. A. (2019). To save Brazil's rainforest, boost its science. *Nature*, 574, 455. DOI: 10.1038/d41586-019-03169-0

Paleari, S. (2022). The impact of the European Green Deal on EU environmental policy. *The Journal of Environment & Development*, 31(2), 196–220. DOI: 10.1177/10704965221082222

Paloniemi, R., Hujala, T., Rantala, S., Harlio, A., Salomaa, A., Primmer, E., Pynnöen, S. and Arponen, A. (2018). Integrating social and ecological knowledge for targeting voluntary biodiversity conservation. *Conservation Letters*, 11(1–10), e12340. DOI: 10.1111/conl.12340

Pascual, U., Balvanera, P., Díaz, S., Pataki, G., Roth, E., Stenseke, M., Watson, R., Dessane, E. B., Islar, M., Kelemen, E., Maris, V., Quaas, M., Subramanian, S., Wittmer, H., Adlan, A., Ahn, S., Al-Hafedh, Y., Amankwah, E., Asah, S. T., Berry, P., Bilgin, A., Breslow, S., Bullock, C., Caceres, D. M., Daly-Hassen, H., Figueroa, E., Golden, C., Gomez-Baggethun, E., González-Jiménez, D., Houdet, J., Keune, H., Kumar, R., Ma, K., May, P. H., Mead, A., O'Farrell, P., Pandit, R., Pengue, W., Pichis-Madruga, R., Popa, F., Preston, S., Pacheco-Balanza, D., Saarikoski, H., Strassburg, B., van den Belt, M., Verma, M., Wickson, F. and Yagi, N. (2017). Valuing nature's contributions to people: The IPBES approach. *Current Opinion in Environmental Sustainability*, 26–27, 7–16. DOI: 10.1016/j.cosust.2016.12.006

Pe'er, G., Bonn, A., Bruelheide, H., Dieker, P., Eisenhauer, N., Feindt, P. H., Hagedorn, G., Hansjürgens, B., Herzon, I., Lomba, Â., Marquard, E., Moreira, F., Nitsch, H., Oppermann, R., Perino, A., Röder, N., Schleyer, C., Schindler, S., Wolf, C., Zinngrebe, Y. and Lakner, S. (2020). Action needed for the EU Common

Agricultural Policy to address sustainability challenges. *People and Nature*, 2(2), 305–316. DOI: 10.1002/pan3.10080

Perfecto, I., Mas, A., Dietsch, T. and Vandermeer, J. (2003). Conservation of biodiversity in coffee agroecosystems: A tri-taxa comparison in southern Mexico. *Biodiversity and Conservation*, 12, 1239–1252. DOI: 10.1023/A:1023039921916

Petersen, A. H., Strange, N., Anthon, S., Bjørner, T. B. and Rahbek, C. (2016). Conserving what, where, and how? Cost-efficient measure to conserve biodiversity in Denmark. *Journal for Nature Conservation*, 29, 33–44. DOI: 10.1016/j.jnc.2015.10.004

Reed, J., Barlow, J., Carmenta, R., Vianen, J. and Sunderland, T. (2019). Engaging multiple stakeholders to reconcile climate, conservation, and development objectives in tropical landscapes. *Biological Conservation*, 238, 108229. DOI: 10.1016/j.biocon.2019.108229

Rivera-Basques, L., Duarte, R. and Sánches-Choloiz, J. (2021). Unequal ecological exchange in the era of global value chains: The case of Latin America. *Ecological Economics*, 180, 106881. DOI: 10.1016/j.ecolecon.2020.106881

Sampaio, G., Nobre, C. Costa, M. H., Satyamurty, P., Soares-Filho, B. S. and Cardoso, M. (2007). Regional climate change over eastern Amazonia caused by pasture and soybean cropland expansion. *Geophysical Research Letters*, 34, L17709. DOI: 10.1029/2007GL030612

Spash, C. L. and Hache, F. (2022). The Dasgupta review deconstructed: An exposé of biodiversity economics. *Globalizations*, 19(5), 653–676. DOI: 10.1080/14747731.2021.1929007

Termansen, M., Konrad, M., Levin, G., Hasler, B., Thorsen, B. J., Aslam, U., Andersen, H. E., Bojesen, M., Lundhede, T. H., Panduro, T. E., and Strange, N. (2017). Udvikling og afprøvning af metode til modellering af økosystemtjenester og biodiversitetsindikatorer - med henblik på kortlægning af synergier og konflikter ved arealtiltag [Development and testing of a method for modeling ecosystems and biodiversity indicators - with a view to mapping synergies and conflicts in area measures]. Aarhus Universitet, DCE – Nationalt Center for Miljø og Energi, 81 s. - Videnskabelig rapport fra DCE - Nationalt Center for Miljø og Energi nr. 226. http://dce2.au.dk/pub/SR226.pdf

Tilman, D., Knops, J., Wedin, D., Reich, P., Ritchie, M. and Siemann, E. (1997). The influence of functional diversity and composition on ecosystem processes. *Science*, 277(5330), 1300–1302. DOI: 10.1126/science.277.5330.130

Vadrot, A. B. M. (2014). The epistemic and strategic dimension of the establishment of the IPBES: 'epistemic selectivities' at work. *The European Journal of Social Science Research*, 27, 361–378. DOI: 10.1080/13511610.2014.962014van der Sluis, T., Foppen, R., Gillings, S., Groen, T., Henkens, R., Hennekens, S., Huskens, K., Noble, D., Ottburg, F., Santini, L., Sierdsema, H., van Kleunen, A., Schaminee, J., van Swaay, C., Toxopeus, B., de Vries, M. W., and Jones-Walters, L. (2016). *How much biodiversity is in Natura 2000?; The "Umbrella Effect" of the European Natura 2000 protected area network*. Wageningen: Alterra Wageningen UR, University & Research centre, Alterra report 2730B. https://data.europa.eu/doi/10.2779/950442

van der Ploeg, J. D., Franco, J. F. and Borras Jr, S. M. (2015). Land concentration and land grabbing in Europe: a preliminary analysis. *Canadian Journal of Development Studies / Revue canadienne d'études du développement*, 36(2), 147–162. DOI: 10.1080/02255189.2015.1027673

Venter, O., Magrach, A., Outram, N., Klein, C. J., Possingham, H. P., Di Marco, M. and Watson, J. E. (2018). Bias in protected-area location and its effects on long-term aspirations of biodiversity conventions. *Conservation Biology*, 32, 127–134. DOI: 10.1111/cobi.12970

Williams, D. R., Clark, M., Buchanan, G. M., Ficelota, G.F., Rondinini, C. & Tilman, D. (2020). Proactive conservation to prevent habitat losses to agricultural expansion. *Nature Sustainability*, 4, 314–321. DOI: 10.1038/s41893-020-00656-5

Zafra-Calvo, N. and Geldmann, J. (2020). Protected areas to deliver biodiversity need management effectiveness and equity. *Global Ecology and Conservation*, 22, e01026. DOI: 10.1016/j.gecco.2020.e01026

Zika, M. and Erb, K. H. (2009). The global loss of net primary production resulting from human-induced soil degradation in drylands. *Ecological Economics*, 69(2), 310–318. DOI: 10.1016/j.ecolecon.2009.06.014

10 Just Transition and the EU

Lars Hulgaard and Anders Siig Andersen

> A socially just transition is essential to winning the support and confidence of working people for the major changes to the economy that are needed to save the planet from climate change (...). It's clear trade unions need a much greater role in designing and delivering a just transition if the European Commission wants to move to a green economy in a genuinely fair way that doesn't risk a rise in climate scepticism and a populist backlash.
>
> European Trade Union Confederation,
> Confederal Secretary Ludovic Voet, 2020

Introduction

Research into environmental and climate justice is framed by concepts such as equality, human rights, collective rights, and historical responsibilities for environment and climate. As noted in the third chapter of this book, many UN knowledge providers draw on the deeply interwoven notions of distributional, procedural, recognition, and intergenerational aspects of equality and justice, and they place the emphasis on who bears the costs of environment problems and climate change, as well as the actions taken to address it and those involved in shaping the responses. In this chapter, we primarily address Just Transition from the European perspective, but also introduce critical perspectives from the Global South on how the European "club" of some of the richest countries in the world have included a global justice perspective only to a very limited degree.

First, we describe inequalities in Europe, emphasizing socioecological inequalities. Second, we highlight how the distributive and procedural aspects of environmental and climate justice are dealt with in the European Green Deal and its follow-up interventions and how the different elements regarding these interventions have been criticized. Third, we present alternative ideas for a Just Transition proposed by the Green New Deal for Europe Coalition in the Blueprint for Europe's Just Transition (2019). Fourth, we introduce a Global South perspective, viewing EU policies regarding Just Transition as Eurocentric and taking too limited responsibility for global socioecological justice.

Inequalities in Europe

Providing the backdrop for dealing with the issue of Just Transition in the context of the European Green Deal, we start by outlining some of the existing inequalities in the EU. Mainly, we base our account on a series of publications issued by the European Foundation for the Improvement of Living and Working Conditions (Eurofound). The Eurofound is a tripartite European Union Agency established in 1975. Its role is to provide knowledge of social, employment, and work-related policies. According to the Eurofound, inequalities have risen in Europe in recent decades, due to factors such as globalization, technological change, taxation policy, and the aftermath of the 2008 global financial crises. The Eurofound further states that these inequalities are hampering economic growth and can lead to social conflict, reduced participation in society, and increased social exclusion. In line with other contemporary longitudinal research into patterns of inequality (Piketty, 2020), the Eurofound divides inequalities into two general categories "income inequality" and "wealth inequality." Furthermore, the Eurofound focuses on the social impact of COVID-19 (Eurofound, 2019; 2021a; 2021b)

Income and wealth inequalities in Europe

Following the financial crises in 2008, income inequality increased between countries and within countries in the EU. In-work poverty and the working poor account for a substantial group among workers. In addition, there are various forms of fraudulent work and self-employment in the EU, with severe implications for working conditions and for social protection. Unemployment and its associated decline in income is the main reason for income inequality. Wolf et al. (2021) however, note that unemployment figures for individual countries differ widely. When COVID-19 hit, many European countries had hardly recovered from the post-2008 financial crises. Pre-COVID-19 unemployment levels ranged from 2 percent in the Czech Republic, 3.1 percent in Germany and 3.3 percent in Poland to 10 percent in Italy, 14.1 percent in Spain, and 17.3 percent in Greece. Youth unemployment rates were 29.2 percent in Italy, 32.5 percent in Spain, and 35.2 percent in Greece before the COVID-19 crisis (Wolf et al., 2021: 101). Quality of life for people in the lowest income quartile improved less between 2011 and 2016 than for others (Eurofound, 2021a). Large differences remain between Member States and between socioeconomic groups in ratings of quality of welfare services, especially health services. Women in the lower income quartile are particularly at higher risk of mental health problems, and women continue to carry out most of the unpaid household and care work. Some groups, particularly the (long-term) unemployed, are much more likely to experience feelings of social exclusion. In addition, the share of European workers living in poverty is on the rise. In 2016, 118 million Europeans—nearly one out of four—were at risk of poverty or social exclusion, with rates of homelessness increasing across the continent. Almost 25 million children under the age of 18 are at risk of poverty or exclusion (von der Leyen, 2019). Furthermore, in 2018, nearly 50 million people in the EU were affected by energy poverty understood as a condition in which individuals or households are not able to adequately heat or provide other required energy services in their homes at an affordable cost. According to the Eurofound, for the first time in decades, younger generations from low-income groups and the middle classes will have fewer opportunities for upward social mobility than their parents' generation (Eurofound, 2021a). To many communities and entire European regions, this has been the situation at least since the beginning of the financial crisis. However, in 2005, even before the crisis, a young Spanish intellectual coined the concept "Mileurista" as a metaphor for her own economic situation and conditions for future livelihood. Thus, mileurista literally means a person who owns maximum €1,000 a month and has no prospect of breaking the glass ceiling for a better life. In the European context, this amount of money is rarely enough for getting by and not enough to build a family. Thus, the mileurista generation is bound to their family homes while working on short contracts.

In the EU, however, wealth inequality is even greater than income inequality. The EU is characterized by an enormous gap in wealth: the gross assets of those in the top wealth quintile in the 21 EU Member States examined by the Eurofound are 60 times larger than those in the bottom wealth quintile. The Eurofound states that investigating the distribution of wealth is a major challenge because there is very limited access to data on hidden wealth. Around 8 percent of the global financial wealth of households is held in tax havens, three-quarters of which goes unrecorded. Accordingly, hidden wealth, which is almost entirely held by the rich, seriously complicates any analysis of wealth inequality (Eurofound, 2021b).

The Eurofound has also investigated the consequences of COVID-19 for increased inequality. It concludes that existing inequalities are widening because of the disproportionate impact of the pandemic on vulnerable groups. These findings show that difficulties in making ends meet have increased significantly among those already in a precarious situation. At the same time, trust in national governments has decreased (Eurofound, 2021c).

Inequalities pertaining to climate change and environmental solutions

In general, the European Green Deal acknowledges that measures to combat environment and climate challenges might by themselves deepen existing inequalities between Member States, regions, and different groups in society. Having studied the possible negative social impact of the European Green Deal, Heyen et al. (2020) broadly distinguish between potential impacts on: (1) jobs, workers, and regions; and (2) households and consumers. The first perspective deals with workers and their communities, emphasizing the need for better and decent jobs, social protection, more training opportunities, and greater job security for all workers affected by global warming and climate change policies (Heyen et al., 2020: 11). The second perspective focuses on promoting a transition wherein the costs are distributed progressively and wherein everyone's essential needs for housing, transport, and energy use are met (Heyen et al., 2020: 11).

Regarding the possible negative impacts from each of the two perspectives, Heyen et al. (2020) reach the following conclusions:

Jobs, workers, and regions

- Jobs may not emerge equally among different sociodemographic /socioeconomic groups, skill levels, and regions;
- New "green" sectors may have inferior labor conditions such as pay, job security, worker protection, and worker rights;
- Destabilization, shrinkage, or preventing further innovation of "brown" industries may lead to job losses; and
- Regions currently dependent on "brown" sectors could struggle with rising unemployment, shrinking tax revenues, and public spending, possibly lowering infrastructure endowments and quality of life in the regions, increasing territorial and social inequities.

Households and consumers

- Some saving opportunities, for example, regarding the use of energy might not be (easily) available for everybody because of high upfront investment costs or because the investment depends on others;
- Opportunities for (return on) investment in new "green" technologies might not be (easily) available for low-income households;
- New "green" plants may involve impairments of neighbors; and
- Green taxes and increasing prices for CO^2-intensive products and services can disproportionately affect their affordability for low-income households or other vulnerable groups.

(Heyen et al., 2020: 13)

Regarding the overall distributive effects of the climate change and environmental aspects of the European Green Deal, Heyen et al. assess that these can be serious and manifold. Given that these impacts will affect a situation that is already marked by distributive inequalities, it seems important to focus on how issues of inequality are addressed in the implementation of the European Green Deal. In the following part of the chapter, we will highlight how the Green Deal seeks to provide answers to these challenges, as well as present some critical voices that address the main actions of the strategy.

Just Transition and the European Green Deal

The European Green Deal was approved at a time when Europe was recovering from economic and sovereign debt, migration crises, and Brexit negotiations. This was also a time marked by increasing inequalities in the EU and among the Member States (EEA, 2019: 47). Simultaneously, new work patterns and lifestyles were emerging. With rapid and pervasive technological change, more jobs are likely to be automated and the demand for highly skilled qualifications is expected to rise. Although this creates new opportunities, it also poses challenges for individuals, such as needs for increasing mobility and new skills, and for governments to prevent mass unemployment and job insecurity. The EEA mentions that the development in inequalities may lead to growing social discontent, which is one of the highest obstacles to environmental and climate sustainability (EEA, 2019: 47).

Acknowledging the risks of increased inequalities, one of the main aims stated by the European Green Deal has been to transform the EU into a fair society by putting people first and paying attention to the regions, industries, and workers who will face the greatest challenges. As further mentioned in Chapter 5 of this book, the European Green Deal states that the European Pillar of Social Rights will guide action in ensuring that no one is left behind. In the following, we will describe some of the major initiatives pertaining to Just Transition that have been approved by the EU on the heels of the European Green Deal: the Just Transition Mechanism, the European Pillar of Social Rights, and measures to prevent future socially disfavoring consequences of carbon price regulation.

The Just Transition mechanism

To promote a Just Transition, the main tool of the European Green Deal is the Just Transition Mechanism. The Just Transition Mechanism focuses primarily on the regions and sectors that are most affected by the socioecological transition because they depend on fossil fuels or carbon-intensive processes. This mechanism is an addition to the contribution of the EU's budget through programs directly relevant to the transition, as well as existing European regional and social funds.

The Just Transition Mechanism is based on three pillars: the Just Transition Fund (primarily grants), InvestEU (guarantees), and the Public Sector Loan Facility. In May 2020, following the recent developments related to the COVID-19 crisis, the EU approved the idea that its long-term budget should be coupled with the NextGenerationEU (a temporary instrument to support recovery from COVID-19). Some of the money from this recovery plan should act supplemental to finance the Just Transition Mechanism.

In the following, we present the three pillars of the Just Transition Mechanism.

1 The first pillar is the Just Transition Fund. Proposed in January 2020, it is intended to alleviate the impact of the transition by financing the diversification and modernization of local economies and by mitigating the negative repercussions for employment. The fund is meant to provide

support to territories facing serious socioeconomic challenges deriving from the transition process toward the climate-neutral economy of the Union by 2050 (Sabato & Fronteddu, 2020: 29). The Commission expected a total of €30–€50 billion in investments. The initial Commission proposal would have provided the Just Transition Fund with €7.5 billion of its own budget from 2021 to 2027. An amendment proposed in May 2020 would have raised the funds' resources to €10 billion and a top-up of €30 billion from the European recovery instrument, the Next Generation EU. The EU leaders, however, decided to cut the budget of the Just Transition Fund to €7.5 billion from the Multiannual Financial Framework (MMF) and €10 billion from the Next Generation EU, which is less than half of the amount proposed by the Commission (see also Chapter 11). Most of the funding will be allocated to regions with the biggest transition challenges. Member States will have freedom to determine their Just Transition territories as long as they meet the criteria. The focus will remain on the most negatively affected regions based on the economic and social impacts from the transition, in particular in regard to expected adaption of workers or job losses in fossil fuel production and the transformational needs of industrial facilities with the highest greenhouse gas intensity. To unlock funding from the Just Transition Fund, EU countries will have to prepare Territorial Just Transition Plans that identify the eligible territories, and they will have to ensure that the plans are consistent with their National Energy and Climate Plans (see also Chapter 6).

2   The second pillar of the Just Transition Mechanism is a Just Transition Scheme that has been established under InvestEU. It aims to crowd in private investments in support of the Just Transition. The InvestEU Fund consists of an EU budget guarantee for the financial products provided by the implementing partners. The Just Transition Scheme is expected to attract €45 billion of private investment (including €1.8 billion of public guarantees) (Sikora, 2021: 694f). In the EU's long-term budget, an additional €6.1 billion from Next Generation EU has been added to the budget guarantee. Investments can be guaranteed by the Just Transition Scheme, if they help to find new sources of growth that could include projects for decarbonization, economic diversification of the regions, energy, transport, and social infrastructure (Fleming & Mauger, 2021: 172).

3   The third pillar of the Just Transition mechanism is a public loans facility channeling funds from the European Investment Bank (EIB), partly guaranteed by the EU budget. The Public Loans Facility will be supported by €1.5 billion from the EU budget and €10 billion in lending by the European Investment Bank to mobilize between €25 and €30 billion of public investment. The logic of the public sector loan facility is to lend money to local authorities to finance projects that do not generate revenue and would otherwise not get financed. According to Fleming and Mauger, typically, infrastructures would fit within this range, with

examples such as energy and transport infrastructure, district heating networks, and renovation or insulation of buildings (Fleming & Mauger, 2021: 173).

The EU Commission warns that if a Member State does not seriously aim to reach climate neutrality by 2050, its plan will not be validated and, therefore, no project will be financed by any of the three pillars of the Just Transition Mechanism (Fleming & Mauger, 2021: 173f). On June 29, 2020, a Just Transition Platform was launched. It aims to assist EU countries and regions to unlock the support available through the Just Transition Mechanism via a single access point for support and knowledge related to the Just Transition (Fleming & Mauger, 2021: 180).

Despite the development of an EU legal framework for regional justice, some critiques have been voiced. One point of criticism concerns the narrow interpretation of the concept of Just Transition that the European Commission is promoting. In the political discourse, the vocabulary tends to be very inclusive and notions of solidarity, fairness, and justice feature regularly with an overall focus on people and citizens. However, Fleming and Mauger state that, when analyzing the proposed legislation, its main focus is on particular groups like workers and jobless citizens, rather than on people in a particular region as a whole. In addition, the solidarity under the Just Transition Mechanism will only apply within the identified regions, though there are plenty of justice issues in the energy transition to climate neutrality in all regions of the EU. The fact that, for example, the territorial Just Transition plans are being redacted by Member States and the local authorities without the obligatory involvement of local inhabitants underlines this restricted vision of a Just Transition (Fleming & Mauger, 2021: 180).

Furthermore, regarding trade-offs, Sabato and Fronteddu (2020) argue that the European Green Deal sets no clear priorities among environmental, economic, and social objectives. Accordingly, the authors address the need for comprehensive analysis of synergies and trade-offs among the objectives, initiatives, and recommendations proposed by the EU, including the social objectives. They argue that this would require a high degree of policy integration and coordination among the various institutional actors responsible for economic, social, and environmental policies and an improvement of their analytical capacities.

An important role is to be played by the European Semester's Country Reports. These documents have the potential to provide a more comprehensive analysis of the situation in Member States and of possible (positive or negative) interactions among initiatives in different policy domains (Sabato & Fronteddu, 2020: 36). As part of the COVID-19 temporary recovery plan, the European Parliament and the Council of the European Union have issued new EU Regulation 2021/242, "Establishing the Recovery and Resilience Facility" (the European Parliament and the Council of the European Union, 2021). This regulation describes revisions to the European Semester for economic policy coordination that should strengthen the implementation of the European Green Deal, the European Pillar of Social Rights, and the UN Sustainable Development Goals. According to the regulation, Member States should adopt National Recovery and Resilience Programs, Strategies, and Investments Plans. In addition to measures that strengthen the competitiveness, growth potential, and sustainable public finances, reforms based on solidarity, integration, social justice, and a fair distribution of wealth should also be introduced. The aim of this regulation is to create quality employment and sustainable growth, ensuring equality of, and access to opportunities and social protection, protecting vulnerable groups, and improving the living standards of all Union citizens. The Member States concerned shall report twice a year in the context of the European Semester on the progress made in the achievement of its recovery and resilience plan, including the operational arrangements.

Carbon pricing and Just Transition

The European Green Deal proposes carbon pricing as an important measure to prevent climate change (see also Chapters 6 and 11). Looking at economic incentives from a justice and equality perspective, carbon pricing can be anything from moderately regressive (China, the United States) and distribution-neutral (Canada) to moderately progressive (India). Sweden delivers an example of using carbon taxes while reconciling decreases in climate impact and taking care of potential caused inequalities. Sweden introduced climate taxes in the 1990s, with support schemes for households followed by a tax reduction for low-income households in 2004. This made Sweden one of the few industrialized countries to have reduced its carbon dioxide emissions between 1990 and the early 2010s, while sustaining and keeping inequalities under control (UNDP, 2020: 168).

The European Green Deal notices that coherence of climate and environment policies and holistic approaches are often a precondition for ensuring that they are perceived as fair (see also Chapter 5). Accordingly, the Green Deal states that the need for a socially Just Transition must be reflected in policies at the EU and national level. This includes investment to provide affordable solutions to those affected by carbon pricing policies—for example, through public transport—as well as measures to address energy poverty and promote re-skilling. According to the European Green Deal, well-designed tax reforms in the Member States can boost economic growth and resilience to climate shocks and help contribute to a fairer society and to a Just Transition. The EU, however, leaves it to the individual Member States to ensure that the regressive elements of carbon pricing and rising energy prices are offset by progressive elements of other parts of the tax and subsidy system.

In accordance with the EU, Claeys et al. (2019) argue that it will be important to use the revenues from a more comprehensive carbon pricing system to compensate the citizens most affected by the rise in carbon prices. To do this, they suggest that money raised from taxing emissions be returned to citizens in the form of a so-called dividend. This could take the form of lump sum transfers like in Switzerland, where two-thirds of the revenues from carbon levies go back to the population through this means. Alternatively, the money could be more directly targeted at the lower deciles of the income distribution (Clayes et al., 2019: 16).

Transparency is important if a government or an institution wants to determine individual emissions based on what each person consumes and how each invests in stocks. Governments would need information on individual asset ownership. In a handful of countries, such information on the ultimate beneficiaries of asset ownership is available (e.g., Norway). However, in most countries, it remains extremely opaque after decades of financial deregulation and disinterest in financial transparency matters. This highlights the importance of data transparency in the fight against tax evasion (see Piketty, 2020).

Procedural justice and the European Green Deal

Procedural justice is about the access of citizens, workers, and communities to influence the green transition through various forms of participatory governance. It is well known that big companies and organizations have rich opportunities to promote their views vis-a-vis the EU Commission and that they invest large sums in lobbyism. Furthermore, as Newell and Simms point out, it may be a danger to public participation that the emphasis on urgency and crisis management could frame responses in terms of top-down interventions from elite actors and the coercive powers of the state. This could diminish scope for more pluralistic, bottom-up, inclusive, and deliberative pathways to sustainable transformation (Newell & Simms, 2020: 5).

The need for procedural justice is both argued by referring to the resistance of different groups and by referring to participation as a fundamental lever of the green and Just Transition.

From a resistance point of view, Heyen et al. (2020) argue that transformational processes do not happen without trade-offs, conflicts, and resistance, since they disrupt and challenge established investments, jobs, behaviors, knowledge, and values. In the case of climate change and other sustainability transitions, the decline of incumbent firms (e.g., in the oil and coal business) can have negative (regional) economic and employment effects. Regions that lack diversification and have a limited capacity for innovation will face the greatest challenge, as will workers with skills that are in less demand or an inability to acquire new skills. Moreover, if energy or other commodity prices rise because of environmental transitions, this may disproportionately affect low-income households. Both effects are likely to provoke resistance against transitions, even more so when they are politically initiated or pushed forward. Recent examples are protests by the French Yellow Vests against rising fuel taxes and the protests of German coal miners against a coal phase-out (Heyen et al., 2020: 8).

From a lever of transition point of view, the EEA argues that, to enable transformative change across Europe, the EU should harness the ambition, creativity, and power of citizens and communities to shift toward sustainable consumption patterns and lifestyles; promote the emergence and spread of diverse ideas and innovations by helping bottom-up initiatives to learn and network; engage stakeholders in inclusive governance processes to open up a broader range of societal responses; and ensure that transitions are socially fair, particularly for the most vulnerable in society (see also Chapter 5).

The EU Commission acknowledges that the most effective public participation takes place at the national, regional, and local level. Nonetheless, according to the Commission, public participation should also be encouraged or coordinated by the EU. In a Policy Brief from the EU, Colli (2021) examines specific options for public participation in policymaking and discusses the extent to which each option is already included in the European Green Deal.

To Colli, movements such as Fridays for Future and mass climate marches across Europe have demonstrated the public pressure for stringent climate policies, and public and stakeholder inclusion has been shown to be an essential aspect to ensure social buy-in and coherence between local and EU policy priorities (Colli, 2021: 1). Colli focuses mainly on the question of democratic legitimacy of policies by ensuring that multiple points of view are considered and stresses that the EU suffers from a democratic deficit (Colli, 2021: 1). Participation is important not only because the policy output is more likely to take public concerns into account, but also because those consulted can gain a sense of ownership through participation (Colli, 2021: 2).

Pertaining to the plans of the EU to support participation, Colli differs among three measures that she both acknowledges for their intentions and criticizes for their limited efficiency in reaching their stated goals:

Public consultations: Consultations are the main choice of participatory mechanism for the European Commission, as they are inexpensive to organize (particularly online) and can easily allow for answers from a range of groups. However, research shows that stakeholder consultations do not always allow for true public participation. Many public consultations do not reach a large enough public to elicit individual submissions or ask questions that are too technical for ordinary citizens to answer. Stakeholder consultations, therefore, have the potential to signal different positions to the EU institutions, but are limited in the extent to which they can facilitate public participation (Colli, 2021: 2).

Citizens' assemblies: These fora allow regular citizens to learn about, debate, and discuss particular issues, as well as subsequently draft recommendations to be voted on in parliament. Citizens' assemblies are supposed to facilitate public participation beyond the sub-section of the population that usually engages with and participates in politics, while also establishing a formal procedure that ensures that the recommendations provided are usable. This, however, relies on the willingness of the formal political institutions to pay attention to and abide by the results. When this is not the case, it can degrade trust in the process. The representativeness of many citizens' assemblies is also questionable, as they usually require a significant time contribution, which may limit the participation of certain sub-groups (Colli, 2021: 2f).

Local projects: The final means for public participation is through participatory projects. These usually take place at the local level, as direct public participation is the backbone of these projects. Local projects require citizens to participate fully, for example, in the process of transitioning away from fossil fuels, setting their own priorities, and considering local features. The downside of such projects can be their limited geographic impact, as they require scaling up or incorporation into broader policies to have large-scale impact (Colli, 2021: 3).

Colli explains that the Just Transition Platform provides an example of a hybrid, ongoing form of public consultation. The platform consists of three main work-streams: a website to help actors ask technical and administrative questions to the Commission; project and expert databases to help with information sharing; and a forum for dialog on Just Transition involving local and national stakeholders, social partners, public authorities, and EU institutions. To Colli, however, it is important to note that the platform is dependent on pre-existing projects on the national and local level, as it aims to bring these projects together. Moreover, it links to the relatively narrow regional scope of the Just Transition Mechanism, which may limit its potential for more expansive participation (Colli, 2021: 3f).

The EU Climate Pact, launched on December 16, 2020, aims to create a network of projects and initiatives throughout the EU. It differs from the Just Transition Platform as it is not only specifically about Just Transition, but also about climate initiatives more generally. Its goal is to move beyond policies and laws and encourage citizen actions, providing a platform to share ideas and best practices among "people across all walks of life." It aims to raise awareness and support specific actions. There have been three initiatives announced as part of the Climate Pact. The first is "Climate Pact Ambassadors." The second involves a partnership with the global climate campaign "Count Us In," where citizens can pledge to take different steps toward reducing their own carbon footprint. Third, other individuals and organizations are encouraged to organize "satellite events" for the Climate Pact, which can be public debates, conferences, and workshops (Colli 2021: 4).

Colli also mentions the Conference on the Future of Europe. This conference is not a specific measure announced under the European Green Deal, but in its communication, the Commission has promised to ensure that the green transition features prominently in the debate on the future of Europe. A first key difficulty—as with EU action more generally—will be to reach citizens with lower levels of mobility, less knowledge of English, and less awareness of the EU. These citizens are often members of communities, who will be most affected by climate change and transition, and it is therefore vital that they are able to provide their own input. Second, lessons learned from other participatory mechanisms such as the European Citizens' Initiative show the importance of ensuring that there is a guarantee that the recommendations collected during the conference will lead to actual policy change (Colli, 2021: 4). However, Colli notes, it seems unlikely that the design of the conference will ensure true public participation. First, it has a very short timeframe: about 12 months from start to finish, not long enough to organize a citizens' assembly or interactive and creative forms of participation, even using digital platforms. Second, the complex structure of the conference makes it unlikely to be easily understood by citizens not familiar with EU processes. Finally, the results of the Conference on the Future of Europe will be communicated in a non-binding report to the three EU institutions, each of which will examine how to follow up on the report (Colli, 2021: 5).

According to Colli, three questions arise that will need to be answered to promote coherent, effective public participation as part of the European Green Deal (Colli, 2021: 5).

1   Who are we trying to reach, and how can we get there?
     The first question reflects a continuous problem for the EU: reaching and exchanging with people beyond already-committed EU supporters or people interested in political affairs. This will be a key challenge for participatory mechanisms, and it will require specific design choices to ensure not only that networks contribute to expanding local projects' reach, but also that a range of citizens are able to participate in the Conference on the Future of Europe (Colli, 2021: 5).
2   How can we structure the exchange and participation?
     The EU's focus on creating decentralized networks of local and regional projects, especially through the Climate Pact, increases the likelihood of including a range of actors and reduces the risk of failed forced "-top-down" participation. A key issue, however, will be to ensure that the multitude of projects do not compete for attention and that there is added value in the EU coordinating these networks. This means that the initiatives should be designed to ensure that resources are efficiently used and that lessons learned from these local projects do feed into broader EU policies (Colli, 2021: 5f).
3   How do we make the exchange count?
     The planned efforts of the EU regarding citizen participation insufficiently allow for expressing the needs of the citizens through real involvement. It is, however, important to make sure that the involvement of citizens leads to concrete policy change and input. Otherwise, these participatory mechanisms risk becoming "window-dressing," giving the impression of democratic legitimacy without really contributing to the policy process (Colli, 2021: 6).

The Horizon 2020 program and procedural Just Transition

As noted, the EU acknowledges that all areas of the Green Deal, from climate action to zero pollution, require citizens' active support at all stages of the transitions. The EU also acknowledges that workable solutions, accepted and taken-up at scale, can only be found through the active participation of all people concerned. Nevertheless, the EU considers it a difficult challenge for the EU, as well as for the Member States, to support the participation of citizens and workers, especially in vulnerable positions. Therefore, as part of the Horizon 2020 framework program, the EU has put forward a call for research and innovation projects investigating "European capacities for citizen deliberation and participation in the Green Deal." The call received 1,550 applications (Colli, 2021: 1).

The topic of the call covers citizen deliberation and participation. Projects retained will establish transnational networks of experts, researchers, practitioners, and relevant civil society organizations specialized in deliberative democracy and civic participation across Europe. Experts on gender equality and climate justice should also be included. They will be expected to share good practice, tools, and resources and implement participatory and deliberation processes on priority issues to deliver on the Green Deal, both at the level of local communities and at a wider scale. Vulnerable and marginalized categories of the population, minorities, and various age groups, including both youth and the elderly generation, as well as both urban and rural areas, will be considered and included. Gender balance will be ensured, and gendered issues will receive specific consideration .

Successful projects are expected to contribute to specific impacts, including:

- Feeling of ownership and engagement through citizen deliberation and participation across Europe;
- Participatory identification of solutions contributing to the European Green Deal;
- Enhanced involvement of citizens in the implementation of the European Green Deal and of the future Horizon Europe missions;
- Stronger trust in policy and science institutions among citizens on European Green Deal issues;
- Commitment and buy-in from a broad spectrum of social groups across Europe to support the European Green Deal targets and to engage in the co-creation and co-implementation of transition pathways, including activation of citizens through social innovation; and
- In the longer term, contribution to one or several of the Sustainable Development Goals.

On the one hand, the aim of projects financed by the call will be to increase citizens support and active contribution to implementing the European Green Deal. On the other hand, the aim of the projects will be to increase citizens' trust in the political system and in science.

Blueprint for Europe's Just Transition

Until now, in this chapter, we have highlighted elements in the implementation of the European Green Deal pertaining to different aspects of the Just Transition and listed some critical considerations. In this part of the chapter, we will follow up on the critical reflections by providing insight into an alternative proposal to the European Green Deal.

Issued by the Green New Deal for Europe Coalition just before the approval of the European Green Deal, the Blueprint for Europe's Just Transition (Blueprint, 2019) presents an alternative approach to the socioecological transformation of Europe. In the Blueprint, the coalition formulates a comprehensive policy package to deliver environmental and climate change justice in Europe and around the world. The Blueprint intends to develop answers to what is conceived as three interconnected main crises of Europe. The first is the economic crisis, with rising levels of poverty, insecurity, and homelessness across the continent. The second is the climate and environmental crisis, with severe consequences for Europe's front-line communities. The third is the crisis of democracy. Across the continent, people are disconnected from the loci of political decision-making not only in Brussels, but also in the communities where they reside (Blueprint, 2019: 9).

The Green New Deal for Europe includes three distinct institutions:

1   The Green Public Works is a historic investment program to kickstart Europe's Just Transition.
2   The Environmental Union is a package of legislation to align EU policy with the scientific consensus, enshrining the principles of sustainability and solidarity in European law.
3   The Environmental Justice Commission is an independent body to research, monitor, and advise EU policymakers on how to advance the course of environmental justice.

(Blueprint, 2019: 9)

Furthermore, the Green New Deal for Europe focuses on how civil movements may affect EU policy development and implementation as pertains to sustainable socioecological transformation through the formation of a transnational movement and people's assemblies.

In many aspects, the Blueprint differs from the European Green Deal, most fundamentally by applying a bottom-up, instead of a top-down, perspective. Overall, the political suggestions in the Blueprint emphasize public spending, active democratic participation, solutions to European inequality based on solidarity, shifting powers from centralized institutions to the people of Europe, a specific focus on environment and climate legal justice, and a direct mobilization of the people of Europe to secure a socioecological Just Transition.

In the following, we will highlight each of the three institutions in the Blueprint focusing on Just Transition, i.e., distributional, recognitional, procedural, and intergenerational justice (see also Chapters 3, 4, and 11). In the European Green Deal, Just Transition is an important aspect of suggested interventions. The notion, however, is primarily attached to specific measures like the Just Transition Mechanism and the European Pillar of Social Rights. In contrast, as the different aspects of Just Transition lie at the heart of the Green New Deal for Europe, considerations concerning Just Transition are integral parts of most proposed solutions.

The green public works (GPW)

The Green Public Works (GPW) is suggested as an investment program to deliver Europe's transformation. It links economic aims with a vision of environmental and climate justice: decarbonizing Europe's economy, reversing biodiversity loss, and guaranteeing decent jobs across the continent. According to the Blueprint, the private sector is, at best, agnostic to the core principle underpinning every aspect of the Green New Deal for Europe—economic justice. Therefore, the green transformation calls on investments not just in projects that can generate profits for investors, but also in initiatives that produce social returns, thereby enhancing community resilience and wellbeing (Blueprint, 2019: 30).

The Blueprint states that the GPW should be financed entirely through green bonds issued by the European Investment Bank (EIB), which will direct idle funds to parts of the continent suffering from unemployment, poverty, and climate and environmental breakdown (Blueprint, 2019: 9). The governance of the GPW would aim to empower communities and facilitate links between them. Investment decisions should be devolved to sub-European authorities, where members of the community actively participate in deciding their direction. GPW should earmark funding for all national governments, regional governments, and municipal governments that agree to a shared set of fundamental principles, including democracy, transparency, and sustainability. Democracy is a guiding principle of the Green New Deal for Europe. It aims to shift power back to the people—both over their lives and over the future of Europe. The GPW carries forward that principle, empowering communities to make meaningful decisions over how money is spent and to collaborate across their borders (Blueprint, 2019: 37).

The GPW will also make use of public procurement strategies to ensure that funds invested into local communities remain in local hands. Public procurement must be subject to strict requirements on the use of sustainable materials and energy, as well as framed to prioritize worker-led organizations, cooperatives, and community projects. The GPW will distribute funds directly to these authorities, allowing them to decide democratically on their destination, on the condition that they collect detailed data about the progress of project implementation (Blueprint, 2019: 37). According to the Blueprint, putting the public in the driving seat of community development will deepen the culture of sustainability and the consensus around the benefits of a green transition. The GPW thus aims to address the crisis of democratic legitimation in the EU, providing political means through which Europeans can participate in the economic transformation (Blueprint, 2019: 37f). To enhance horizontal information-sharing and political decision-making across the continent, the Blueprint suggests establishing a Green Solidarity Network to unite twinning and cooperation arrangements between municipalities, regions, farmers, and communities (Blueprint, 2019: 38f).

The investments of the GPW aim to reorient the European economy away from private wealth accumulation and toward socioecological sustainable development, focusing on areas such as housing and energy poverty, mobility, rural communities, workers' rights, cooperatives, and reproductive and care work. In the following, we will focus on how the GPW aims to achieve its goals.

Housing and energy poverty: The program will restore, maintain, and retrofit existing housing stock for sustainability and commit a massive investment to bring Europe's homes to a standard of energy efficiency that minimizes the need for active energy systems for heating and cooling, increases health and comfort, and dramatically reduces their ecological footprint. The GPW will equip every European community with solar panels, heat pumps, energy, and heat storage facilities, as well as other tools essential to reducing emissions. These programs will be subject to suitability and affordability criteria, prioritizing neighborhoods in the greatest need and households least able to afford refurbishing their homes. Where practical, the GPW will purchase and refurbish unoccupied private housing for public use. Europe's 38 million vacant homes will be mobilized to eliminate homelessness and housing insecurity. The redevelopment of housing at this scale will be based on a holistic approach, allowing for integrated approaches to housing, mobility, and services for communities (Blueprint, 2019: 41).

Energy infrastructure. The program will be based on an integrated approach to energy across generation, transmission, distribution, and management. The GPW will mobilize public resources for public investments to support the public ownership of energy utilities, ensuring fairer pricing and control of supply for Europe's residents. Any new investment in energy grids and other utilities by the GPW will bring these essential services into public hands. Once power distribution and transmission are in public hands, the GPW will invest in the decentralization of power generation to regions, municipalities, neighborhoods, and even individual homes, where solar panels and energy storage solutions can create significant cost savings for households.

Mobility: A pan-European Mobility Cohesion Fund will ensure that every European community has access to agile, clean, and inexpensive transport options (Blueprint, 2019: 9f). Within Europe's towns and cities, trams, electric buses, trains, and other modes of transport will form part of a connected public transport infrastructure, ensuring that every community is well-connected. These services will be made free or low-cost to all users to maximize use and accommodate people with any disability, including by making assistance available without pre-booking. Bicycle routes will be insulated from automobile traffic (Blueprint, 2019: 47).

Rural communities: The GPW will redirect EU's agricultural policy that is allocating most resources to multinational agribusiness to support regenerative practices across farming, fishing, and forestry, ensuring that Europe's rural communities become an engine of the environmental recovery (Blueprint, 2019: 10). In particular, the GPW will emphasize the need for creating new green jobs in rural communities: green and cottage industries, nature preservation, rewilding, organic farming, forestry and forest products, and other regenerative activities (Blueprint, 2019: 36). The investments in rural communities will be grounded in participatory approaches that engage with farmers, fishermen, and rural communities to understand their needs and concerns.

Workers' rights: The GPW will ensure that workers and communities in Europe will benefit in terms of health and the stability of their environment, as well as in job opportunities and income. And it will ensure that the jobs created in Europe will not be supported through environmental devastation elsewhere (Blueprint, 2019: 35). The Green New Deal for Europe is committed to extending democracy to new frontiers. In addition to democratizing public investment decisions, it will also be a catalyst for the democratization of private workplaces—establishing a new pact between owners and workers. To bring about this transformation, funding under the GPW will be tied to a radical transformation in labor practices, including (1) a reduction in working time; (2) better commuting policies; (3) worker participation; (4) the promotion of diversified worker ownership funds; and (5) retraining of workers to adapt to decreases in material production (Blueprint, 2019: 51). Furthermore, it will implement an income guarantee for workers in carbon-intensive industries that will be phased out by law.

Cooperatives and community projects: According to the Blueprint, cooperatives and community projects show the way forward. By radically allocating finance to local communities, the GPW will inject the necessary funding to develop durable, long-term cooperative structures that empower local communities and support the democratization of the economic sphere. By tying funding to standards of worker participation and empowerment, it will support private businesses in reforming their working standards (Blueprint, 2019: 49).

Reproductive and care work: Finally, the GPW will recognize that reproductive and care work represents a significant amount of time allocated for personal, household, and community wellbeing and the protection of and struggle for human rights. The GPW, therefore, includes provision for a Care Income. This can be made available to people who are not formally employed but are engaged on a full- or part-time basis in care—for example, parents caring for their children, children caring for their elderly parents, and community members caring for each other and the environment (Blueprint, 2019: 35).

The Environmental Union (EnU)

According to the Blueprint, on its own, an investment plan like the Green Public Works (GPW) is insufficient to address the climate and environmental crises. A much broader legislative package is necessary to rein in environmentally destructive practices and realign policymaking with scientific consensus (Blueprint, 2019: 56). This package is called the Environmental Union. The Environmental Union will replace the principle of competition with that of solidarity, putting the interests of workers, communities, and the environment first. It will also enshrine respect for the natural world in law, introducing penalties for polluters, and formally recognizing "ecocide" as a punishable offence (Blueprint, 2019: 10). However, as the suggested proposals pertaining to the Environmental Union are more focused on environment and climate issues than on the Just Transition in the EU, we will turn our focus to the third pillar of the New Green Deal for Europe.

The environmental justice commission (EJC)

According to the Blueprint (2019), confronting environment and climate challenges cannot be separated from the question of social justice. Whether it is a carbon tax or a plastic ban, climate policies have massive ramifications for who gets what and how. This is the reason that the Green New Deal for Europe will establish an Environmental Justice Commission, an independent body with the mandate to monitor the progress of the green transition, investigate questionable practices, and advise EU authorities on how to redress Europe's role in environmental injustice around the world (Blueprint, 2019: 77).

The Environmental Justice Commission will be tasked with evaluating intersectional justice in the context of a changing climate, creating a new space for frontline communities to voice their concerns and demands, and advising EU authorities on how best to respond (Blueprint, 2019: 82). The work on intersectional justice will apply across different areas, including health, employment, education, and mobility. In each of these areas, the commission will aim to identify barriers to equal distribution, recognition, and participation, as well as to advise EU authorities on how best to eliminate them, ensuring that all those who live in Europe are included in the green transition. The commission will also examine how Europe can deal with intergenerational justice. In particular, the commission will evaluate Europe's economic and environmental policies and their potential impacts on future generations. It will consider an explicit legal protection for future generations, which entitles them to make claims on existing environmental policy (Blueprint, 2019: 11).

A transnational movement and people's assemblies

The Blueprint argues that a social movement for a Green New Deal for Europe cannot afford to ignore the EU as a set of powerful coordinating institutions and the locus of continental political mobilization capable of responding at scale to the immediacy of the challenge ahead. According to the proposal, the EU Commission's European Green Deal provides a clear target for activists to mobilize around (Blueprint, 2019: 17). The Green New Deal for Europe, however, acknowledges that it is not possible to expect the leaders of the EU to lead its implementation. That is the reason that the Blueprint includes two pathways to the Green New Deal for Europe.

Regarding the first pathway, the Blueprint suggests building a transnational movement around the concerns of front-line communities across the continent (Blueprint, 2019: 19). The idea is that local action that is coordinated transnationally can target every level of the EU's legislative process. Similarly, national-level lawsuits on areas ranging from environmental justice to social rights can build up a body of European case law, thereby setting precedents and building momentum for further action (Blueprint, 2019: 21).

In the second pathway, the Blueprint sets out a plan to organize People's Assemblies at the municipal, regional, national, and European levels to deliberate and deliver policies (Blueprint, 2019: 19). Self-organized municipal assemblies are the smallest core unit feeding into regional assemblies and upward. Each level is responsible for developing its own set of priorities and policy recommendations (Blueprint, 2019: 23). According to the Blueprint, the European Peoples' Assembly would not only give structure, motivation, and purpose to the social movement behind a Green New Deal for Europe, but it would also help to fill the democratic deficit at the heart of the EU (Blueprint, 2019: 25).

Europe's Just Transition in the light of a Global South perspective

The European Green Deal is focusing on Green Growth and a Just Transition within the EU. Viewed from a Global South perspective, this focus omits both historical and present responsibility of the "rich club of European countries" to take on its global socioecological responsibility. From a Global South perspective, the contradiction between economic growth and global socioecological sustainability constitutes a major conceptual and practical problem. The challenge is double. The first challenge concerns the commitment to global sustainability and inclusion. The second challenge concerns a deeper revision of the dominant epistemologies and a search for epistemologies that can lead a way out that would be attractive for the majority of people inhabiting the Earth.

In his book *Ideas to Postpone the End of the World*, Ailton Krenak, the Brazilian leader of the Alliance of Forest Peoples, reflects on the concept of sustainability (Krenak, 2020). Krenak is one of the few remaining of the Krenak People in the state of Minas Gerais in Brazil. A few years back, he was invited to give a lecture on sustainability at the University of Brasilia. In his book, he reflects on the event:

> Being in the company of those people made me reflect on the myth of sustainability, invented by corporations to justify their theft of our idea of nature. No company on this earth is sustainable, no matter what they say. But these companies and even whole sectors opportunistically appropriate the concept of sustainability for its marketing value.
>
> (Krenak, 2020)

Krenak is so-called indigenous and shows how we are connected through a history of colonization between the Global South and the Global North. Furthermore, in the Global North, inequality and the absence of sustainability are, among other things, a consequence of the dominant economic model, as pointed out by researchers such as Thomas Piketty (2020) and Joseph Stiglitz (Nobel laureate, economics).

According to these Global South perspectives, the first task is to make visible the paradox between "growth" and "sustainability" as a basis for a just, green transition. This means better understanding the scope for various economic models and programs such as circular economy, doughnut economy, solidarity economy, and feminist economy. Secondly, it means to ask the non-essentialist question about possible other epistemologies that may lead to a socioecological sustainable world that is not a mere reflection of economic acquisition (see also Chapter 12). Global South perspectives question how heterodox economic models and non-essentialist epistemologies could possibly contribute to a profound Just Transition for the benefit not only for the richest, but also for all peoples and life on Planet Earth?

Following this, from a Global South perspective, we also need to ask how policies on Just Transition and climate change mitigation originating in Europe must be evaluated when looked upon from post-colonial perspectives and epistemologies of the South. According to Siddiqi (2022), policy makers, also in Europe, should begin by asking if "the agents of colonial modernity—states, markets, and financial institutions—adapt to climate change and reduce hazard risk without erasing and "muting" the subaltern?" (Siddiqi, 2022). The erasion and muting of subaltern peoples is a matter of what the Portuguese scholar Boaventura de Sousa Santos coined "epistemicide" (Santos, 2008). Neither colonialism nor post-colonialism can happen without the erasion of the knowledge underpinning the societies and subjects of coloniality of power. In a research paper on carbon colonialism, Eberle et al. (2019) claim that the mitigation of climate change and hazard risks are promoted by agents of colonial modernity, who continue the "colonial thought patterns and structures that continue to exist and work in favor of former colonial powers" (Eberle et al., 2019). The hope for a more relational and regenerative being in the world lies in the ongoing unraveling of the "One-World doctrine" given the "growing visibility of struggles to defend mountains, landscapes, forests and so forth by appealing to a relational and pluri-ontological understanding of life" (Escobar, 2015: 21). From a Global South perspective, the criticism of the Just Transition aspects of the European Green Deal are not only about the strictly European focus and the neglect of global responsibility but, also about the epistemic construction and legitimization of at post-colonial order (see also Chapter 12).

Summary

The notion of Just Transition is an important pillar of the European Green Deal. In the EU, in the aftermath of the financial crises and only exacerbated by the COVID-19 crises, income and wealth inequality, social mobility, poverty, and precarious work conditions have followed a downward trajectory. At the same time, measures to deal with environment and climate change challenges could put even more Europeans at risk. This is evident when focusing on regions dependent on fossil fuels extraction. Vulnerabilities, however, may also arise because of increasing energy prices and the general transition from "brown" to "green" jobs. Without targeted actions, there will be winners and losers, and many types of inequality in Europe may rise to new levels.

Primarily, the European Green Deal focuses on financing the transition of fossil fuel dependent regions. As part of the Just Transition Mechanism, the Just Transition Fund aims at financing the diversification and modernization of transitionary regions. The Just Transition Scheme shall crowd in investments in support of a Just Transition, and the aim of the public-loans facility is to channel money to green projects that would otherwise not get financed. Originally, the commission proposed to allocate €30 billion from the Next Generation EU (COVID-19 recovery). This amount, however, was reduced to €10 billion by EU leaders. Secondary, as part of the European Semester, the commission has asked the EU countries to implement green reforms based on solidarity, integration, social justice, and a fair distribution of wealth, and it calls on the countries to invest in affordable housing, transportation, and energy. The individual countries, however, can decide whether they will decide to follow these calls or not. Some further criticisms of the Just Transition aspect of the European Green Deal can be summarized in the following points:

- The narrow and regionalized concept of a Just Transition;
- The weak EU regulation regarding the priorities of different aims;
- The missing incentives pertaining to policy integration and coordination;
- The neglect of possible trade-offs among environmental, social, and economic goals; and
- The lacking demand of returning carbon and other tax revenues to vulnerable citizens and communities.

The European Green Deal emphasizes the need for citizen participation in developing and realizing the stated aims, on the one hand, to draw on the power, competences, creativity, and fantasy of ordinary people and communities, and, on the other, to prevent the deal from getting obstructed. The EU measures are public consultations, citizens' assemblies, local projects, the Climate Pact, the Conference of the Future for Europe, and Horizon 2020 projects. As highlighted in the chapter, these initiatives could be questioned from several reasons

- As a centralized institution, it is difficult for EU to reach people, who are not already committed EU-supporters;
- It is difficult for the EU to secure that local projects add value to the overall project of the European Green Deal; and
- It is difficult for the EU to translate citizens proposals into EU policies.

This implies that there is a risk that the EU is not involving the people who are most necessary to involve, if it wants to prevent the obstruction of the European Green Deal; that EU money are spent with too little overall outcome; and that the involved people experience their participation as "window-dressing" that does not really influence policies.

To contrast the European Green Deal with some further reaching suggestions for a Just Transition, we have highlighted an alternative strategic proposal published by the Green New Deal for Europe Coalition. This strategy aims not only to prevent climate change and environmental challenges from undermining social equality and justice in Europe, but also to secure the participation and crucial influence of citizens, communities, and workers. The strategy focuses on finance, regulation, and justice. In all areas—ranging from housing, energy poverty, and mobility to rural communities, workers, and care work—it seeks to strengthen democracy, to decentralize power, and to increase ownership to decisions. At the same time, the strategy seeks to strengthen the regulative power of the EU based on expanded forms of participative and deliberative democracy and grass root pressure. Contrasting the European Green Deal and the Green New Deal for Europe highlights many different considerations and suggestions on how to promote socioecological sustainable development in Europe. It also indicates that the formulation of the European Green Deal has been deeply dependent on the different views and power interests of the European countries.

In the last part of the chapter, we looked upon the European Just Transition from a Global South perspective. From this perspective, the European Green Deal is viewed as euro-centric, omitting the historical and present responsibility of the "rich club of European countries" to take on global socioecological responsibility and insisting too much on continuing growth in the Global North. This critique also contains epistemic aspects, pointing at the need to recognize different epistemologies.

In the third part of the book, we will elevate our perspective to more general and cross-cutting understandings, including of government and governance, policies and political paradigms, ontological and epistemological issues, and knowledge creation. In the next chapter, we apply an overall perspective on government and governance issues and solution paradigms pertaining to the UN and to the EU, as well as to ecological and socioecological issues.

References

Blueprint (2019). The green new deal for Europe, 94 pages. Retrieved from: https://report.gndforeurope.com/cms/wp-content/uploads/2020/01/Blueprint-for-Europes-Just-Transition-2nd-Ed.pdf

Claeys, G., Tagliapietra, S. and Zachmann, G. (2019). How to make the European Green Deal work. *Bruegel Policy Contribution,* 13, 1–21. Retrieved from: https://www.econstor.eu/bitstream/10419/237632/1/168713524X.pdf

Colli, F. (2021). A transition for the citizens? Ensuring public participation in the European Green Deal. European Policy Brief, nr. 68 2021. *Egmont Royal Institute for International Relations,* 7 pages. Retrieved from: https://www.egmontinstitute.be/content/uploads/2021/04/EPB68.pdf?type=pdf

Eberle, C., Münstermann, E., and Siebeneck (2019). Carbon colonialism. A postcolonial assessment of carbon offsetting. Research Paper. University of Bonn / United Nations University, 1–34. Retrieved from: https://www.researchgate.net/publication/337622634_Carbon_Colonialism_A_postcolonial_assessment_of_carbon_offsetting

EEA (2019). *The European environment — state and outlook 2020. Knowledge for transition to a sustainable Europe.* The European Environmental Agency, 499 pages. DOI: 10.2800/96749

Escobar, A. (2015). Thinking-feeling with the Earth: Territorial struggles and the ontological dimension of the epistemologies of the South. *Revista de Antropoloía Iberoamericana,* 11(1), 11–32.

Eurofound (2019). *A more equal Europe? Convergence and the European Pillar of social rights.* Luxembourg: Publications Office of the European Union, 22 pages. Retrieved from: https://www.eurofound.europa.eu/sites/default/files/ef_publication/field_ef_document/ef19050en.pdf

Eurofound (2021a). *Wealth distribution and social mobility.* Luxembourg: Publications Office of the European Union, 102 pages. Retrieved from: https://www.eurofound.europa.eu/sites/default/files/ef_publication/field_ef_document/ef20034en.pdf

Eurofound (2021b). *Living, working and COVID-19 (Update April 2021): Mental health and trust decline across EU as pandemic enters another year.* Luxembourg: Publications Office of the European Union, 21 pages. Retrieved from: https://www.eurofound.europa.eu/sites/default/files/ef_publication/field_ef_document/ef21064en.pdf

Fleming, R. C. and Mauger, R. (2021). Green and just? An update on the 'European Green Deal'. *Journal for European Environmental & Planning Law,* 18, 164–180. Retrieved from: https://brill.com/view/journals/jeep/18/1-2/article-p164_164.xml.

Heyen, D. A., Menzemer, L., Wolff. F., Beznea, A., and Williams, R. (2020). Just Transition in the context of EU Environmental Policy and the European Green Deal. Issue Paper under Task 3 of the 'Service contract on future EU environment policy'. Öko-institut e.V. for the European Commission, 48 pages. Retrieved from: https://ec.europa.eu/environment/enveco/growth_jobs_social/pdf/studies/just_transition_issue_paper_final_clean.pdf.

Krenak, A. (2020). *Ideas to postpone the end of the world.* Canada: Anansi Press.
Newell, P., and Simms, A. (2020). How did we do that? Histories and political economies of rapid and just transitions. *New Political Economy.* DOI: 10.1080/13563467. 2020.1810216
Piketty (2020). *Capital and ideology.* Cambridge, MA: Harvard University Press, 1104 pages.
Sabato, S., and Fronteddu, B. (2020). A socially just transition through the European Green Deal? Working Paper 2020.08, European Trade Union Institute, 40 pages. Retrieved from: https://www.etui.org/sites/default/files/2020-09/A%20socially %20just%20transition%20through%20the%20European%20Green%20Deal-2020-web.pdf.
Santos, B. d. S. (2008). *Another knowledge is possible.* Beyond Northern epistemologies. London: Verso.
Siddiqi, A. (2022). The missing subject: Enabling a postcolonial future for climate conflict research. *Geography Compass,* 16(5), 1–13.
Sikora, A. (2021). European Green Deal – legal and financial challenges of the climate change. *ERA Forum,* 21, 681–697. Retrieved from: https://doi.org/ 10.1007/s12027-020-00637-3
The European Parliament and the Council of the European Union (2021). Regulation (EU) 2021/241 Of the European Parliament and of the Council of 12 February 2021 establishing the Recovery and Resilience Facility 75 pages. Official Journal of the European Union. Retrieved from: https://eur-lex.europa.eu/ legal-content/EN/TXT/PDF/?uri=CELEX:32021R0241&from=EN
UNDP (2020). The next frontier - Human development and the Anthropocene, 412 pages. Retrieved from: http://hdr.undp.org/sites/default/files/hdr2020.pdf
Von der Leyen, U. (2019). A Union that strives for more – My agenda for Europe. Political Guidelines for the Next European Commission 2019–2024. Publications Office of the European Union, 22 pages. Retrieved from: https://op.europa.eu/ en/publication-detail/-/publication/43a17056-ebf1-11e9-9c4e-01aa75ed71a1
Wolf, S. Teitge, J., Mielke, J., Schütze, F., Teitge, J. and Jaeger, C. (2021). The European Green Deal – More than climate neutrality. *Intereconomics,* 56(2), 99–107. Retrieved from: https://link.springer.com/content/pdf/10.1007/s10272-21-0963-z.pdf

Part III
Cross-cutting issues
Governance, the "Anthropocene", and interdisciplinary research

The third part of this book focuses on three main themes: ecological and socioecological government and governance in the UN and the EU as well as theoretical and political paradigms underlying or confronting dominant political responses; different conceptualizations of the "Anthropocene" and its drivers; and different types of interdisciplinary research and knowledge creation.

Part III consists of three chapters:

Chapter 11: Ecological and Socioecological Governance in the UN and the EU
Chapter 12: Decentering Humanity: the Anthropocene and the Perils of Anthropocentricity
Chapter 13: Interdisciplinary Research and Knowledge Creation

11 Ecological and socioecological governance in the UN and the EU

Anders Siig Andersen, Thomas Budde Christensen, and Lars Hulgaard

That Gross National Product counts air pollution and cigarette advertising, and ambulances to clear our highways of carnage. It counts special locks for our doors and the jails for the people who break them. It counts the destruction of the redwood and the loss of our natural wonder in chaotic sprawl (…) the gross national product does not allow for the health of our children, the quality of their education or the joy of their play. It does not include the beauty of our poetry or the strength of our marriages, the intelligence of our public debate or the integrity of our public officials.

Robert Kennedy, 1968

Introduction

In the first two parts of this book, we have highlighted ecological and socioecological challenges and solutions at the UN and the EU levels. In this third part of the book, we focus on three main themes: ecological and socioecological government and governance in the UN and the EU (Chapter 11); conceptualizations of the "Anthropocene" (Chapter 12); and interdisciplinary research and knowledge creation (Chapter 13).

In the present chapter, we critically compare and reflect on the structural and procedural aspects of governance in the UN and the EU and, furthermore, on differing paradigms regarding solutions pertaining to climate change, environment, and socioecological issues. To achieve the common goal of securing the Earth as a just and safe place for humans to live, as well as of preserving nature for future generations to come, action is crucial, and governance is a precondition for coordinated action. First, we present different ideal types of structural and procedural government and governance, before analyzing UN and EU government/governance by applying this typology as a theoretical lens. Second, we highlight the compositions of different paradigms for strategies and solutions that underpin policies, responses, and governance in the UN and the EU: market-based technological and socioecological modernization. Third, we present paradigms that are situated at the margin of and conflicting with hegemonic paradigms: technological escapist and quick fix, nationalist, and socioecological transformative.

DOI: 10.4324/9781003319672-15

Concepts of government and governance

The notion of government covers the activities of public authorities at the global, regional, national, and subnational levels, whereas the notion of governance focuses particularly on the interplay between state and non-state actors. Generally, in this book, we have applied the term "governance" as the overall notion covering government and governance. In the following, we will differ between the two notions. According to government and governance theory, government and governance structures may be categorized as monocentric, multilevel, polycentric, or hybrid. Processes of government and governance may be interventionist, regulatory, or catalytic. As theoretical concepts, structures, and processes should be regarded as ideal types that are partly overlapping. In the following, we shall briefly explain differences and similarities between the concepts to provide a theoretical context for assessing the different types of UN and EU government/governance.

Government and governance structures

Monocentric (or centralist) government often implies (quantifiable) goals, legally binding instruments, and the possibility of reinforcing decisions if countries or citizens do not follow the rules. In nation states, centralist government that combines monocentric legislative, judicial, and executive power is founded in many constitutions.

Multilevel government denotes structures wherein decision-making, implementation, assessment, and follow-up is divided between the centralized and decentralized levels of a system—i.e., when different levels of government share or transfer responsibility among each other (Jänicke & Rüdiger, 2019: 10). In contrast to centralized government, in multilevel government, partners at different levels have negotiated and agreed upon their dispersed influence on decision-making.

Polycentric systems of governance do not have a central authority that exerts significant hierarchical authority (Jordan et al., 2018: 361). In polycentric governance structures, there are several centers of decision making that are formally independent, and non-governmental actors play a crucial role.

Hybrid forms of government and governance imply that two or three of the mentioned types of government/governance structures function simultaneously.

Procedures of government and governance

Interventionist government procedures are a main characteristic of the positive state. The concept of the positive state shares many of its properties with the concept of the bureaucratic state (Weber). The positive state defends or promotes public interests by using direct forms of intervention (Prontera & Quitsow, 2022: 520).

The regulative state represents an indirect approach to governance. The main goal of the regulative state is to promote efficient and competitive markets and to avoid market failures via regulation and market-orientated policies in order to increase technological advantages. The notion of the regulative state shares some properties with the notions of new public management and the competition state, which are rooted in a neoliberal economic tradition and promote deregulation, privatization, the transformation of public institutions to function in quasi-markets as semi-private entities, and the ability of all citizens to increase their competitiveness vis-a-vis each other and the citizens of other nations (Prontera & Quitsow, 2022: 520).

The catalytic state aims at leveraging the resources of non-state actors in pursuit of its policy goals. In the catalytic state, governments try to augment their resources through complex, ad hoc consortiums composed of other states, multinational institutions, banks, corporations, and other non-state actors. The most important type of state institution in the catalytic state is a partnership of government with non-state entities. The catalytic state works by "orchestration" through intermediaries, rather than directly, applying soft instruments—e.g., persuasion, convening of relevant actors, material, ideational support (finance, guidance, technical assistance), and reputational incentives (recognition of endorsement, naming, and shaming) (Abott, 2018: 194). The concept of the catalytic state has some resemblance with the concept of the entrepreneurial state. Recognizing that politicians cannot solve complex and wicked problems on their own, according to this concept, they should limit themselves to formulating visions, introducing incremental reforms (experiments), and entering into partnerships with outside actors such as organizations, companies, citizens, and universities (Nielsen, 2021).

There are obvious connections among government/governance structures and procedures. Usually, direct intervention is attributed to centralist government and orchestration by the catalytic state is associated with polycentric governance structures. In practice, however, neither government/governance structures nor procedures function completely separate from each other. Although there are clear differences between the UN and the EU in the composition of structures and procedures, as we shall see in the following, hybrid structures and procedures are dominant.

Characterization of government and governance structures and procedures in the UN and the EU

Structures and procedures in the UN

In Chapter 2 of this book, we presented the UN Convention on Climate Change (UNFCCC) and characterized the Paris Agreement (2015) as based on goals and National Determined Contributions (NDCs). The main goal of the Paris Agreement is to limit global warming to well below 2°C, preferably 1.5°C, and to achieve a climate neutral world by mid-century. All ratifying partners are under commitments, but these vary. Monitoring, reporting, and reviewing are based on the Enhanced Transparency Framework (ETF). The "ambition" or "rachet" mechanism implies the expectation that countries will formulate progressively stronger targets. The Paris Agreement provides a framework for financial, technical, and capacity building support to countries who need it. In the Paris Agreement, non-governmental actors are assigned a (voluntary) role to participate in reaching the goals of the agreement. In many ways, the Convention on Biological Diversity (CBD) and the follow-up Strategic Plan for Biodiversity and the Aichi Target (2010) share many government/governance features with the Paris Agreement, as it works through National Biodiversity Strategies and Plans (NBSAPs). The goals, however, are less specific than the main goals of the Paris Agreement (see also Chapter 2). The resource area is governed by a 10-year Framework of Programs of Sustainable Consumption and Production (10YFP) (UN, 2012). The One Planet Network is the main implementation agency of the 10YFP. Within the resource area, there are no UN conventions, no clear targets, and no national determined contributions. Moreover, the One Planet Network has only a coordinating, collaborating, and advisory role. Regarded from an overall perspective, government/governance of the climate area is somewhat stronger than government/governance of the biodiversity area, while the resource area has very weak government/governance structure and procedures. The 2030 Agenda of Sustainable Development and the Sustainable Development Goals (SDGs) (UN, 2015) reiterate many of the ecological goals and targets from the Paris Agreement, the Strategic Plan for Biodiversity, and the Aichi Targets. Pertaining to the resources area, however, the goals and targets are expressed more precisely than in the 10YFP (see also Chapter 2).

Across these areas, global assessments commissioned by the UN predominantly show that stated climate change, biodiversity, and resource goals and targets have not been reached and that development has continued to progress in ecologically unsustainable directions.

The Paris Agreement, the Strategic Plan for Biodiversity/the Aichi Targets, and the ten Year Framework of Programs on Sustainable Consumption and Production Patterns (10YFP) all contain aims and goals directed at socioecological sustainable development, understood as the differentiated social effects of ecological challenges and interventions within a context of freedom and safety, as well as distributional, recognitional, procedural, and intergenerational equality. The 2030 Agenda of Sustainable Development, however, is the primary UN Treaty targeting socioecological sustainability, integrating as it does ecological, economic, and social aims, goals, targets, and indicators. The governance model of the 2030 Agenda and the Sustainable Development Goals (SDGs) resembles the overall model pertaining to climate change and biodiversity. The SDGs contains many goals, targets, and indicators directed at the global level. However, each government (or group of countries such as the European Union) sets its own targets through National Determined Contributions, and each government decides how targets should be implemented into planning processes, policies, and strategies. Governments are expected to deliver Annual Progress Reports based on the indicator framework of the SDGs and quadrennially Global Sustainable Development Reports, followed up and reviewed, however, only by the states themselves (see also Chapter 2).

The first Global Stocktaking of the 2030 Agenda and the SDGs delivered by the first Global Sustainability Report concluded that the world is not on track to achieve the SDGs by 2030.

In general, the UN government/governance model can be characterized as multilevel and catalytic. It operates through goalsetting and national determined contributions. Primarily, the role of the UN is to orchestrate the activities of member states, who are obliged to document transparency and accountability through common and uniformed systems of monitoring and reporting. The "ambition mechanism" in the Paris Agreement put a moral obligation on member states to increase their promises regarding GHG emissions. The other agreements do not contain this type of mechanism. This implies that the main government/governance procedures within UN system are primarily soft—i.e., goalsetting, transparency frameworks, and "naming and shaming," without the possibility of enforcing decisions. This means that progress is fully dependent on the actions of member states. Measured against outcomes, this does not seem to be sufficiently effective.

All the UN agreements pertaining to climate change and the environment also represent elements of polycentric governance, as non-governmental actors are encouraged to make their own voluntary contributions. In the Paris Agreement, non-governmental actors are supported through procedures of counseling, reporting, knowledge dissemination, and sharing. Coen et al. (2020) highlight three types of non-governmental actors that are part of the UN governance structure: (1) informal intergovernmental organizations, e.g., G7, G20, Major Economic Forum (MEF); (2) regional intergovernmental organizations, e.g., the European Union (EU), the African Union (AU), the Association of Southeast Asian Nations (ASEAN); and (3) non-state and sub-state actors, e.g., cities and other sub-state authorities, non-governmental organizations (NGOs), private business actors, and public-private initiatives (Coen et al., 2020: 35ff). It is, however, difficult to hold non-state actors responsible for actions, progress, and outcomes.

This means that all the agreements are based on the good will of the participating countries, who have agreed on the main outcomes of scientific analysis and, furthermore, the use of common and uniform systems for setting targets, monitoring, reviewing, and reporting on targets. Because there are no enforcement mechanisms for individual countries and because countries decide their goals themselves, free riding is a risk to be considered. The transparency measures of the system, however, offer opportunities for national, regional, and global state and non-state actors to hold the system, as well as each other, accountable for any lack of progress in reaching the stated goals.

Structures and procedures in the EU

The EU combines the principles of supra-nationality and intergovernmentalism, which are displayed in its multilateral government structures and its procedures. The European Commission, the European Parliament, the European Court of Justice, and the European Central Bank are supranational institutions representing European interests. National governments are represented in the European Council of the European Union as intergovernmental EU institutions. The EU commission is the central executive body, representing the supranational idea of the EU (Treude, 2022: 20f).

The EU single market was introduced with the European Single Act (1987) and complemented in the Treaty of Maastricht (1993), introducing an economic and currency union and a supranational monetary and currency policy. In the European Council, the EU Member States are responsible for the national fiscal and economic policies and for setting policy orientations. Instead of assigning the task to EU institutions, Member States orient their respective national policies to common objectives (Treude, 2022: 22f). With the European Semester (2010), the EU has established an alignment process of national budgetary and economic policies aimed at macroeconomic balance. The semester is an annual cycle of economic and fiscal policy coordination. The commission drafts country specific recommendations that are revised and adopted by the council, and member states take recommendations into account when preparing their next year's national budget (Treude, 2022: 26).

In contrast to the UN, in the EU, there are several types of binding legal acts, which are applied in different ways, including through regulations that bind all Member States directly, directives that bind the Member States to achieve a particular objective but leaving it to the Members States to decide how it should be transposed into national law, and binding decisions that can be addressed to Member States, groups of people, or even individuals. The Court of Justice of the European Union ensures that EU legislation is interpreted and applied in the same way in each Member State. The court has the power to settle legal disputes between Member States, EU institutions, businesses, and individuals.

By adopting the European Green Deal as a new holistic strategy, the EU aims to develop a sustainable and inclusive market economy that reconciles competing objectives of growth, environmental protection, and social well-being. The European Green Deal has been integrated in the European Semester as the new control instrument of European economic policy. Furthermore, measures for economic recovery that have been adopted to recover from the Covid-19 pandemic have partly been orientated toward the social sustainability goals of the European Green Deal (Treude, 2022: 37; see also Chapter 10).

Whereas multilateralism is at the center of EU economic policy, the area of the environment has been addressed with targeted and binding instruments, including 500 EU regulations, directives, and decisions that can be characterized as monocentric and interventionist (see also Chapter 5). As we have highlighted in Chapters 6 to 10, the European Green Deal is generally implemented into already highly regulated fields pertaining to climate change, biodiversity, resources, and social policies such as the sectors of energy, industry, digital, building, transportation, waste handling, and agriculture, as well as into labor market and social issues. New sector specific strategies such as the "Farm to Fork Strategy," new laws such as the "European Climate Law," new packages such as the "Fit for 55 package," and new mechanisms such as the "Just Transition Mechanism" have been followed up by adopting new or by changing existing regulations, directives, decisions, standards, and mechanisms. Non-state actors are supported in their delivery of voluntary contributions.

The overall balance between the application of hard and soft regulation differs among areas. The regulation of all areas, however, can generally be characterized as hybrid, combining monocentric, multilevel, and polycentric government/governance structures, as well as interventionist, regulative, and catalytic procedures. Compared to the UN, the EU has a much stronger organizational structure and applies a much more complex and diverse set of measures through a mixture of common goals and legally binding interventions.

Political and theoretical paradigms underlying UN and EU solutions

In this part of the Chapter, we will highlight different paradigms for strategies and solutions regarding ecological and socioecological challenges that underlie the policies and governance of the UN and the EU: (1) market-based and (2) socioecological modernization. First, we will present and critically discuss the work of the economist William Nordhaus. His arguments for market-based solutions are attached to a neoliberal economic paradigm. In the case of Nordhaus, however, they are also attached to the notion of technological development and what he defines as "clubs of the able and willing." In this part of the Chapter, we will also critically highlight the application of market-based solutions by the UN and the EU. Second, we will explain the socioecological modernization paradigm that covers a much broader and more complex suite of solutions. The core notion of this paradigm is green growth. Performed by a variety of government and governance structures and procedures at the UN and the EU levels, the paradigm is directed at reshaping many societal structures and processes, while simultaneously preserving the basic economic rationale for development, which is growth through technological development. The socioecological modernization paradigm, however, also emphasizes the promotion of social justice and the counteracting of prevailing inequalities. The paradigm draws inspiration from a comprehensive toolbox ranging from market-based, financial, and technological solutions to direct interventions (EU) and tools directed at cultural change, learning, and skills development.

The market-based approach to climate change: the work of William Nordhaus

The foundations of the market-based approach to analyzing and formulating solutions to environmental and climate challenges are clearly expressed by the neoclassical economist William Nordhaus, who received the Nobel Prize in Economics in 2018. Nordhaus is best known for his contribution to modeling the link between climate change and GDP development, counteracting market failures using carbon taxes or cap and trade pointing to a specific carbon tax level to achieve the optimal cost-benefit between taxes and reducing CO_2 emissions. He is further renowned for his proposal of climate clubs as supranational organizational solutions to the challenges of implementation. Nordhaus reflects on what he regards as the fundamental problem posed by climate change in stating that climate is a public good. He defines "public good" as activities whose costs or benefits spill outside the market and are not captured in market prices. According to Nordhaus, the two key attributes of a public good are, first, that the cost of extending the output to an additional person is zero ("nonrivalry") and, second, that it is impossible to exclude individuals from enjoying it ("non-excludability"). Viewed from a market perspective, global public goods are economic externalities that resist the control of both markets and national governments (Nordhaus, 2019: 2). To correct "market failures," Nordhaus proposes raising the market price of CO_2 and other GHG emissions either by putting a regulatory limit on the amount of allowable emissions and allowing trading ("cap-and-trade") or by levying a tax on carbon emissions (Nordhaus, 2019: 13).

Nordhaus has initiated the development of the so-called Dynamic Integrated Model of Climate Change and Economy (DICE) to measure the optimal cost benefit equilibrium between carbon taxes and global temperature. The model combines a neoclassical growth model with a model that describes the effect of greenhouse gas emissions on global temperatures. Nordhaus' premises are that: (1) laissez-faire capitalism generates a suboptimal outcome by emitting too much CO_2; and (2) we should only reduce carbon emissions to the extent that doing so maximizes the present value of future utility from consumption. Nordhaus further argues that, in the view of most economists, the balancing of costs and benefits is the most satisfactory way to develop climate policy (Nordhaus, 2019: 11).

In the 2016 version of the DICE model, Nordhaus estimated that the economic consequences of damages regarding global GDP to be 2 percent of output at a 3°C global warming and 8 percent of output with a 6°C warming (Nordhaus, 2019: 9). Nordhaus states that, however attractive a temperature target may be as an aspirational goal, the target approach is questionable because it ignores the costs of attaining the goal. In economic terms, his conclusion was that 4°C of global warming would be too costly because of the damages from climate change and that using carbon taxes to attain a goal of less than 3°C of global warming would be too costly to reach, especially for poorer nations. Thus, Nordhaus concluded that a cost-benefit optimum with standard damages would raise temperatures to over 3°C in 2100 (Nordhaus, 2019: 12). He acknowledged that this was quite far from the goals of the Paris Agreement and the scientific recommendation from the IPCC.

In a paper published in 2021, now recognizing the international climate objectives (2°C) formulated in the Paris Agreement, Nordhaus changes his recommendations by stating that the introduction of carbon taxes without rapid technological decarbonization will be too costly to produce deep abatement, and, similarly, that rapid technological decarbonization by itself will not induce deep abatement. Therefore, he proposes to use these two solutions in combination (Nordhaus, 2021: 1). In his paper, he also elaborates further on the proposal on climate clubs already mentioned in his 2019 paper, combining his interrelated economic and technological solution with the voluntary formation of international treaties.

Nordhaus criticizes the global agreements on climate change under the UNFCCC (the Kyoto Protocol and the Paris Agreement) because, in his opinion, very little coordinated abatement has taken place. He states that "free riding" is a major obstacle to the solution of global externalities and that, without an appropriate incentive structure, no individual country has an incentive to cut its emissions sharply. He claims that, if there is an international agreement, nations have a strong incentive not to participate, letting other nations carry the burden. According to Nordhaus, the outcome is a noncooperative free-riding equilibrium in which few countries undertake strong climate change policies. As an alternative, Nordhaus argues for his model of climate clubs (Nordhaus, 2021: 1).

In his proposal, a climate club is a coalition of countries based on a target of carbon price and organized to encourage high levels of participation and abatement. The central feature of the club model is that the structure includes both obligations in terms of strong abatement and penalties for either nonparticipation or failure to meet the club obligations. For example, he suggests that countries might agree that each country should implement policies that produce a minimum domestic carbon price of $50 per metric ton of CO_2. The target price might apply to 2025 and rise over time at 3 percent per year in real terms and carbon prices might be determined by a cap-and-trade system or by carbon taxes (Nordhaus, 2021: 1).

His main analytical concept is a "supportable policy." This type of policy designates the upper bound on a tax contribution to the public good—one that is compatible with the incentives contained in the agreement. In his analysis, two important parameters are the rate of decarbonization and the rate of technological change in the backstop technology. The backstop technology is the set of technologies that can produce zero net carbon emissions at minimum cost (Nordhaus, 2021: 5). Nordhaus states that technological improvements provide powerful boosts to the club incentive because they lower the cost of participation.

Nordhaus further argues that trade sanctions without rapid technological decarbonization will be too costly to induce deep abatement and that rapid technological decarbonization by itself will not induce deep abatement because of free riding by some countries. However, according to his study, providing incentives to participate—e.g., by introducing carbon taxes that will increase the competitiveness and innovation of non-carbon using technologies or by politicians deciding to allocate carbon tax revenue to technological innovation—the clubs can achieve the international objectives (Nordhaus, 2021: 2).

Modeling the efficiency of climate clubs, he examines club incentives, along with a rapid rate of decarbonization (2 percent per year faster than historical rates) and a rapid decline in the cost of the backstop technology (at 4 percent per year, instead of 1 percent in his base assumption). Based on these assumptions in his model, global emissions will be slightly negative in 2050, and global temperatures will stay within the 2°C limit (Nordhaus, 2021: 2). According to Nordhaus, the major conditions for a successful club include the following: (1) a public good–type resource that can be shared; (2) cooperative arrangement, including the cost, that is beneficial for each of the members; (3) exclusion of nonmembers at a relatively low cost to members; and (4) stable membership in the sense that no member wants to leave (Nordhaus, 2021:2). He indicates that the European Union (EU) is the most relevant contemporary example of a multinational club with the benefits of a single market (Nordhaus, 2021: 3).

In addition, Nordhaus indicates that the main risks for a climate club will be the potential for trade retaliation. He states that this problem is particularly severe for small clubs. If a single small region creates a climate club, then other countries can offset any penalties through actual or potential retaliation. On the other hand, Nordhaus argues, with large clubs, countries that are outside the club will have little leverage to offset penalty tariffs, especially if they are small and act individually. Based on his model, Nordhaus estimates that a core club of the EU and United States would induce other countries to join until all regions have joined the club (Nordhaus, 2021: 5).

Criticism of market-based solutions

The British-Australian economist Steve Keen, recognized for his criticism of neoclassical economics as inconsistent, unscientific, and empirically unsupported, highlights the fact that forecasts by economists of the economic damage from climate change have been much more modest than predictions by scientists about possible damages to the biosphere (Keen, 2020: 1). He regards William Nordhaus as one of the main figures within the neoclassical group of economists. Keen focuses on the fact that Nordhaus and likeminded economists omit 86–90 percent of GDP from their models, as they use the relationship between temperature and GDP (in different areas of the United States) today as a proxy for the impact of global warming over time. He also criticizes the mismatch between the estimates of economists and natural scientists regarding projections of climate change impact and damages. He points out that the work of neoclassical economists has been used to calibrate the "Integrated Assessment Models" (IAMs) that have largely guided the political responses to climate change. Furthermore, he indicates that neoclassical economists have been involved in writing the formal reports of the IPCC and that their conclusions carry very much weight with politicians (Keen, 2020: 2).

According to Keen, Nordhaus argues that only few sectors in society will be directly affected by climate change. Nordhaus especially mentions agriculture and forestry. He estimates that approximately 3 percent of US national output is produced in highly sensitive sectors, another 10 percent in moderately sensitive sectors, and about 87 percent in sectors that are negligibly affected by climate change. He has justified his assumption on the basis that, for the bulk of the economy, manufacturing, mining, utilities, finance, trade, and most service industries, it is difficult to find major direct impacts of the projected climate changes over the next 50–75 years (Keen, 2020: 13). Keen criticizes the fact that Nordhaus equates climate to the weather and thereby underestimates political, demographic, and economic forces. The implication is that only if an activity is exposed to the weather is it vulnerable to climate change (Keen, 2020: 5). In this context, Nordhaus has calculated optimum temperatures for each of the sectors that he expects to be affected by climate change, excluding the list of sectors that he assumes will be unaffected (Keen, 2020: 6). Only to a very limited degree are the fixed numbers and the rather linear progression applied by Nordhaus in accordance with more holistic analyses of the system impacts of climate change.

According to Keen, in predicting the impact on GDP on increasing global temperatures, Nordhaus has assumed that the same coefficients that he found for the relationships between temperature and Gross State Output (GSP) per capita between different parts of the United States can be used for an estimate of the future impact of warming all over the world. Keen argues that this method is very questionable and highlights the fact that it has resulted in subsequent studies by other economists, which have concluded that increasing global temperatures caused by global warming would be beneficial to the economy (Keen, 2020: 7).

Keen concludes his analysis by stating that, if activities that occur indoors actually will be subject to climate change and if the temperature to GDP relationships across space cannot be used as proxies for the impact of global warming on GDP, then the conclusions of Nordhaus and other neoclassical economists will turn out to be false. Arguing solely by rejecting Nordhaus' assumption that almost 90 percent of the economy will be unaffected by climate change, Keen states that it will be at least one order of magnitude more damaging to the economy than the numbers that Nordhaus implies. Furthermore, he claims that it could be far worse if, in fact, climate change does lead to the transgression of tipping points and the catastrophic outcomes that some natural scientists predict (Keen, 2020: 22; see also Chapter 1).

In a paper in "The Ecologist," Dale (2018) criticizes the fact that Nordhaus has based his model on a high discount rate at 6 percent, which implies a rapid and continuous economic growth. Dale argues that this scale of predicted growth will exacerbate the climate crisis and impose the costs of the problems generated by the present to future generations. More generally, and in line with Keen, Dale criticizes Nordhaus for translating ethical questions into a utilitarian cost-benefit analysis and for neglecting the risk of non-linear paths of climate change (Dale, 2019: 3).

Market-based solutions in the UN and the EU

Market-based solutions to climate change are promoted by the UN and the EU. In 2017, 21 individual emission trading systems existed at the global, regional, national, and subnational levels (Biedenkopf & Wettestad, 2018: 243). Negotiated as part of the United Nations Framework Convention on Climate Change (UNFCCC), the Kyoto Protocol encouraged the formation of carbon markets. Furthermore, the concept of Voluntary Carbon Offset (VCO) has allowed for the participation of companies and other entities to earn carbon credits by investing in emission reduction activities in developing countries (Okereke, 2018: 328). As mentioned, during negotiations of the Paris Agreement, it was proposed to adopt a new framework to replace and strengthen the market-based mechanisms from the Kyoto Protocol. However, these provisions have not yet been applied (see also Chapter 2).

At the European level, the revision of the EU Emission Trading System (ETC) directive for phase 4 (2021–30) is part of the Fit for 55 package (see also Chapter 6). The European Commission has adopted a set of proposals that include abandoning the international credit system in favor of the European ETC system, improving the ETS system to promote effectiveness and price stability, and expanding it to new sectors (Treude, 2022: 37).

The EU commission also plans to introduce a Carbon Border Adjustment Mechanism (CBAM) to correct international competitive distortions at the EU border and to prevent EU companies from "flagging out" (see also Chapter 6). The CBAM system will work as follows: EU importers will buy carbon certificates, corresponding to the carbon price that would have been paid had the goods been produced under the EU's carbon pricing rules. Conversely, once a non-EU producer can show that they have already paid a price for the carbon used in the production of the imported goods in a third country, the corresponding cost can be fully deducted for the EU importer. Initially the CBAM will apply to imports of cement, iron, steel, aluminum, fertilizers, and electricity. The ETC and the CBAM are connected, as an effective ETS exerts cost-based pressure toward the introduction of a CBAM (Bongardt & Torres, 2022: 178).

Criticism of market-based solutions in the UN and the EU

Market-based solutions have been criticized by many environmental and climate movements and NGOs, critical scholars, the International Panel of Climate Change (IPCC), and the Intergovernmental Platform on Biodiversity and Ecosystem Services (IPBES) (see also Chapters 2 and 4). As highlighted in this Chapter, part of the criticism is directed at the theoretical and empirical foundation of Integrated Assessments Models such as the DICE. Much critique, however, has been directed at the ecological and socioecological implications of applying market-based solution aimed at the reduction of GHG emission—including the formation of clubs and border adjustment mechanisms.

IPCC and IPBES express considerable worries that allowing businesses to fund nature-based solutions such as reforestation, afforestation, or the planting of bioenergy crops over vast areas presents significant risks to biodiversity (see also Chapters 2 and 4). From a socioecological point of view, these types of ecological risks often translate into risks of local communities in the Global South losing their livelihoods because of land grabbing. As highlighted in Chapter 3, comparable challenges may rise when investing in low-emission technology, "climate-smart" agriculture, and the building of flood defenses. This means that market-based solutions pose a double challenge. First, they enable countries and businesses in the Global North to continue their emissions of GHG. Second, they create risks for biodiversity and local populations in the Global South. Compared to free market systems, both types of risk are reduced, but not eliminated, in cap-and-trade systems that put a limit to emissions under a public jurisdiction. Carbon taxes and cap-and-trade systems may support socioecological sustainability if revenue is redirected to reach social aims. There are, however, only few examples of this actually happening. The market for Voluntary Carbon Offset (VCO) has been criticized for being a mechanism for greenwashing, as well as an emotional Band-Aid for the rich, as consumption and use of services lead to continuing GHG emissions, e.g., by flying, and it has been further criticized as a method for green washing because private green investment projects are not monitored nearly as strictly as public systems (Okereke, 2018: 329). Furthermore, the risk of double counting is inherent in complex differentiated systems with many actors that function independently of each other (see also Chapter 3).

The EU is a market-based union that takes advantage of the size of its market and its common financial policy. This has strengthened the EU's competitiveness vis-à-vis external competitors and strengthened internal integration regarding the conditions for internal movement of products, services, money, people, knowledge, and ideas. The European Carbon Transfer (ECT) system and the plan for a Carbon Border Adjustment Mechanism (CBAM) are integrated parts of this market logic. Over time, the EU has partially changed its strategy to green growth, meaning that the union now strives to become a world leader in the production and sale of green technologies and the knowledge and services accompanying these technologies.

To prevent the risk of carbon leakage and to counteract the risk of unequal competition, the EU has planned to introduce the CBAM. The double construction intended by the EU of a cap-and-trade system and a border adjustment mechanism is very much in line with the recommendations proposed by Nordhaus. In implementing this combined model, the EU takes the risk of market retaliations, while counting on the fact that the market power of the union will prevent this from happening. In the view of Nordhaus, the EU can be considered as a "club" of some the richest countries in the world. Introducing the CBAM will create a space to secure and increase its market power and its future economic competitiveness. The EU Parliament has adopted the commission's CBAM proposal. However, the World Trade Organization, competing countries, and the EU Council of Ministers may challenge final the adoption.

As we have already outlined different criticism of carbon markets and cap-and-trade systems (see Chapters 4 and 6), here we will concentrate on criticism directed at the EU proposal of a Border Adjustment Mechanism. First, border adjustment mechanisms as the CBAM aim to correct "market-failures" that leverage the burdens of carbon taxes by taking money from outside competitors, when they are trading across the borders of a given jurisdiction. Countries within the borders get the opportunity to further their competitive advantages through technological innovation. Countries outside the borders are placed in a less competitive position. First, this means, that countries characterized by lower levels of technological development will find it more difficult to sell their raw materials and products. Second, it implies that countries with a higher level of technological development will find it easier to adapt to the new market conditions. Basically, in the global context, poorer and less technologically developed countries may be pressured to reduce their costs by intensifying work, reducing labor costs, and reducing companies' costs for environmental and occupational health-oriented purposes. In addition, this may reduce tax revenues and weaken the provision of public welfare goods, as well as public initiatives directed toward climate change mitigation and adaption and the prevention of biodiversity loss. As Nordhaus describes it, club constructions for rich nations can correct for market failures, as well as promote technological innovation. However, poorer and technologically less developed countries, especially in the Global South, are at risk of paying a high price ecologically, socially, and economically. Instead of promoting the SDGs, this might prevent the goals from being realized. Furthermore, leapfrogging seems unlikely to happen if rich "country clubs" indirectly counteract technological developments in the Global South via market-based solutions. To correct the failures of this type of market-based solution, countries in the Global North could strengthen their financial and technical support to the countries in the Global South and reconstruct trade relations on a more equal basis (see also Chapter 4).

Socioecological modernization

Ecological modernization is a paradigm for environmental and climate change policy that emphasizes the role of eco-innovation and positive trade-offs between ecology and economy (Jänicke, 2008; Mol & Jänicke, 2009). The ecological modernization narrative incorporates ideas from the market-based paradigm, however, with a further emphasis on the role of the state, a stronger focus on the social implications of climate and environmental policy, and an increased focus on the importance of technological change, industrial action, and innovation, in addition to market mechanisms (Kreinin, 2020: 5).

The term ecological modernization was coined in the 1980s and especially gained momentum in Germany with impact on both academia and policy, primarily in social-democratic circles and the green party, but also in broader European political thinking (Jänicke, 2008). Central to the ecological modernization paradigm is the redefinition of the state-market relation (Mol & Jänicke, 2009). Traditional environmental policies focused on environmental protection through laws and regulation aimed at industrial market-actors. Ecological modernization theory and policies focused on how the same market mechanisms and actors could be involved in developing technological innovations that would reduce environmental impacts. The role of the environmental policies was to stimulate investments (both private and public) in green technologies, combined with market-based regulations focusing on the internalization of externalities. The ecological modernization theories did not suggest revolutionary new approaches to environmental policies and industrial organization, but rather suggested a reformist strategy to environmental policy (and academic theory) that used market-mechanisms and technological development incentives to develop and implement greening processes within the European economy (Mol & Jänicke, 2009).

The "green growth" and "green economy" strategies that were suggested by the UNEP (UNEP, 2011) and OECD (OECD, 2011) following the financial crisis shared the same idea of decoupling economic growth from environmental impacts through policies that would drive investments and innovation in low-carbon and resource-efficient technologies and systems. In the same period, following the financial crisis, the European Union adopted the "Europe 2020" strategy (European Commission, 2010) focused on smart, sustainable, and inclusive growth, to a large extent based on the same fundamental idea of creating continued economic growth, while simultaneously reducing environmental impacts through eco-innovation, increased resource productivity, and public and private investments in environmentally friendly products, and technologies (Jänicke, 2012). As analyzed in Chapter 5, the European Green Deal follows the same modernist approach; however, compared to the Europe 2020, it has more ambitious climate targets and an altogether broader coverage, even as it maintains a focus on resource productivity. Compared to the Europe 2020 strategy, the European Green Deal expands the scope of the paradigm from ecological to socioecological modernization by tying the climate and environmental targets to multiple policy areas that emphasize the need for a fair and just transition to a green economy. Fundamentally, the socioecological modernization paradigm is based on the idea that supranational institutions, governments, and non-government actors can assist with the transition to socioecological sustainable development by designing policies aimed at green economic growth and by taking social considerations into account without changing, however, the fundamental structures, power relations, and driving forces of society.

Although in different versions, pertaining to policies as well as scientific assessment and recommendations, the socioecological modernization paradigm has become hegemonic at the UN and EU levels. The UN, however, primarily governs through goals, targets, and indicators and by orchestrating the policies of national states and, to a lesser extent, the actions of non-state actors. Although the adopted UN agreements are based on the socioecological modernization paradigm, this implies that the UN leaves it to the member states to decide which types of solutions they want to apply. Contrary to the UN, the EU has adopted a range of solutions that corresponds to the solutions inherent in the socioecological modernization paradigm.

In the following, first, we will characterize the specific version of the socioecological modernization paradigm that has been implemented by the EU. Within this paradigm, however, there are marked differences between what has been adopted and which possible policies, strategies, and actions could be adopted, still respecting the basic preconditions of the paradigm of green growth through technological innovation and simultaneously promoting social equality and justice. Therefore, secondly, we will highlight differences between adopted EU and UN responses to the socioecological challenges and the greater variety of solutions that have been recommended by UN and EU anchored scientific reports.

Socioecological modernization in the EU

As mentioned, the EU has applied market-based solutions in the form of a cap-and-trade system, and it plans to apply a carbon border adjustments mechanism. This corresponds with the ideas fostered by neoclassical economists on carbon taxes/cap and trade, border adjustments, and clubs. However, the dominant feature of the European Green Deal is its attempt to mainstream all policy areas to fit the green growth agenda while "leaving no one behind." Against this backdrop, a series of new initiatives already have been initiated and more are planned. These initiatives cover the vast areas of climate change, energy, industry, transport, building and renovation, agriculture and food, biodiversity, pollution, Just Transition, research and innovation, citizen and stakeholder participation, and finance. To a certain degree, as accounted for in Chapters 5 to 10, the EU has adapted its responses to the Covid-19 crisis to support the goal of a green and fair transition and, motivated by the Ukrainian

War, has tried to advance the green agenda by referring to the need for European energy security.

As outlined in Chapter 5, the European Green Deal version of green modernization aims to secure a more efficient implementation of environmental and climate policies, to improve the coherence and efficiency of sectoral policies, to promote nature-based solution, to consider trade-offs, to increase the focus on behaviors and lifestyles, and to strengthen the regulation of pollution. Regarding Just Transition, the EU has implemented the Just Transition Mechanism and acknowledged the challenges caused by energy poverty and the need to mitigate the regressive effects of carbon taxes. Furthermore, the EU aims to develop knowledge and skills relevant to the green transition. Not all plans suggested by the commission have been adopted as intended. The EU is a multilateral organization of countries in different situations and with different national interests. Within most areas, decisions can only be adopted if there is an agreement between the countries. However, the EU version of the socioecological modernization paradigm is much stronger than the UN version of the same paradigm. Nonetheless, in respect to the green growth imperative, there are many possibilities of improvement regarding policies and implementation at the EU and UN levels.

Criticism from within: The UN version of the socioecological modernization paradigm

The dominant goal-based governance system in the UN is criticized by UN-sanctioned knowledge providers such as the IPBES and the IPCC. For example, an IPBES-IPCC workshop report on the biodiversity-climate change nexus criticizes the fact that biodiversity and climate change have been addressed separately by the UN and suggests more integrated approaches (Pörtner et al., 2021). Furthermore, it suggests that the principle of goal-based governance should be extended with complementary rule-based governance, including requirements and prohibitions, and that goals should be strengthened pertaining to climate change mitigation and adaption, as well as to biodiversity and the biodiversity-climate change nexus (see also Chapter 2).

In the area of climate change, the Production Gap Report (SEI et al., 2021) criticizes UN governance as not influential enough. Taking stock of progress pertaining to climate change, the report suggests strengthening measures to reduce the demand for fossil fuels and recommends actions to secure a decline in fossil fuel production. For example, the report suggests a rapid, just, and equitable winddown of global fossil fuel production, restrictions on fossil fuel exploration and extraction, and a phasing out of government support for fossil fuel production (see also Chapter 2).

Assessing the SDG outcomes (Independent Group of Scientists 2019), the first Global Sustainability Report criticizes the fact that the goal-based model applied by the UN increases the risk of negative trade-offs between goals globally, among countries, and especially between the Global North and the Global South (see also Chapter 3). As an alternative to the implementation of single goals and targets, the report suggests targeting intertwined ecological, economic, and social systems, pointing out six entry points and four levers. However, in formulating what should be done by whom, the report does not specifically mention the role of the UN. Instead, it addresses international actors, governments, local city authorities, organizations, the private sector, and civil society. The report, however, also points at several critical issues that should be addressed at the global level, thereby indirectly pointing at the UN:

- *Structures:* The deprivation of people is due not only to the lack of technical and financial resources, but also to deeply rooted structures of social and political inequality, discriminatory law, and social norms. Aspects of current organization and production can have socially detrimental and catastrophic environmental consequences.
- *GDP:* The universal use of GDP as a measure of guiding economic policy and human development constrains and undermines the 2030 Agenda.
- *Technological solutions*: Technological solutions alone cannot deliver the necessary transition.
- *Fossil fuels:* Direct and indirect government support of fossil fuels, low global subsidies for renewables and the fossil fuel industry's activities directed against scientifically documented CO_2 emissions are undermining the realization of climate goals.
- *The global commons:* The management of the global commons must explicitly address environmental injustice, avoiding unequal use of resources and repairing the damage already caused.
- *Movements and activists*: Movements supporting the global commons such as divestment, agroecology, and environmental justice should be supported in their activities, and the killings of civil rights activists, journalists, and trade union leaders should be prevented.
- *Bottom-up innovation:* Transformative change means harnessing bottom-up innovation, including indigenous knowledge at the grassroots level and in the informal sector.

(See also Chapter 3).

The criticism and suggestions in the scientific reports do not explicitly question the underlying green growth message of the socioecological modernization paradigm. Rather, criticism is directed at the goal-based model of governance, fundamental structural and organizational issues, discrepancies between stated goals and actions, and top-down types of interventions. For example, criticism is directed at economical and ideological power relations between "brown" vs. "green" nation states and industries, the Global North vs. the Global South, privatization vs. public ownership, nation states vs. vulnerable groups, authoritarian regimes vs. civil groups fighting for their "rights," and government control vs. bottom-up innovation. Underneath the suggestions from the UN knowledge providers, the general message is that the UN, as an organization dependent on agreements between member states, has neither been strong enough to address some of the more fundamental forces driving socioecological risks and challenges, nor been able to address important barriers for realizing the stated aims and goals. Furthermore, the message is that this could be different.

Criticism from within: The EU version of the socioecological modernization paradigm

According to the EEA, the roots of environmental degradation and climate change are intrinsically linked to the structure and functioning of societies and economies (see Chapter 5). Therefore, the EEA recommends that the EU considers the need of fundamental transformations in the ways that we produce and consume, as well as a shift away from the dominant socioeconomic paradigm, which generally promotes globalization, consumerism, individualism, and short-termism. The EEA promotes the key idea that the many interlinkages within and between complex systems implies that there are often strong economic, social, and psychological incentives that lock society into ways of meeting its needs. Structural and institutional lock-ins can be embedded at many levels and can include economic lock-ins, technological lock-ins, intellectual lock-ins, societal lock-ins, and cultural lock-ins (see also Chapter 8). Radically altering systems is likely to disrupt established investments, jobs, consumption patterns and behaviors, knowledge, and values, inevitably provoking resistance from affected industries, regions, and consumers. The interactions among these diverse elements also mean that efforts to change complex societal systems can often produce unintended outcomes or surprises. Given this context, the EEA recommends that the EU should counteract lock-ins and path-dependencies and address the influence of powerful actors that work against sustainable transformations.

To the EEA, it is important to understand that the effectiveness of policy interventions such as decoupling and the circular economy can be offset by lifestyle changes and increased consumption and production, partly because improvements in efficiency tend to make a product or service cheaper and thus lead to increased production and consumption. This phenomenon is referred to as the "rebound effect" (see also Chapters 4, 5, and 7). The EEA recommend that the EU should try to avoid rebound effects that can undermine environment and climate intervention.

Trade-offs among different systems arise because of their shared reliance on natural systems, both as a source of resources and as a sink for wastes and emissions (see Chapter 5). The concept of "resource nexus" recognizes that food, energy, water, land, materials, and ecosystems are interconnected across space and time. It supports sustainability governance by helping to identify how best to balance socioeconomic and environmental concerns. The EEA recommends that the EU should base its interventions on careful considerations of this nexus.

A socially Just Transition includes investments to support innovative solutions in regions affected by abandoning fossil fuels and compensatory interventions such as tax dividends directed at those most negatively affected by carbon pricing policies, the risk of energy poverty, rising transportation costs, and de-skilling vis-à-vis new demands caused by the green transition. As accounted for in Chapter 10, to support a Just Transition, the EU provides funding mechanisms such as the Just Transition Mechanism and implementing the proposal of a Social Climate Fund. The EU, however, could also examine other means of influencing countries' redistribution of the burdens of the green transition, such as through taxation and investment policies.

Procedural justice is about the participation of citizens, workers, and communities in the green transition. Big companies and organizations have rich opportunity to promote their views. Furthermore, it may be a danger to public participation that the emphasis on urgency and crisis management could frame responses in terms of top-down interventions from elite actors and the coercive powers of the state. This could diminish scope for more plural, bottom-up, inclusive, and deliberative pathways to sustainable transformation. The process of sustainable transition needs civil society-defining initiatives to develop deeper, wider, and more effective solutions. To involve citizens, one suggestion has been to establish local/regional/national councils (agriculture) that collaborate based on deliberative dialogs to also strengthen the participation of social movements and NGOs (see also Chapter 8).

Interventions into complex and intertwined ecological, economic, and social systems carry the risks of trade-offs and unintended consequences. Therefore, such interventions should be assessed against multiple criteria. These include feasibility against ecological and biophysical constraints, their viability for economy and society (e.g., effects on jobs, structure of the economy, import dependency), and their ability to meet multiple sustainability goals simultaneously, both inside and outside Europe (see also Chapter 5).

From a global perspective, Europe depends heavily on resources extracted or used in other parts of the world. Focusing solely on the environmental and social impacts within Europe, without considering the additional impacts abroad, results in an overly positive perception of Europe's sustainability. Europe overshoots its share of the global "safe operating space" for several planetary boundaries (see also Chapter 5). This suggests that there is still a substantial gap between the EU's sustainability vision and current overall EU environmental performance. At present, the territorial perspective is the only method accepted by international environmental law to account for a country's emissions and mitigation efforts. Nonetheless, the EEA recommends that the EU should avoid outsourcing unsustainable practices that undermine other countries' efforts to achieve the SDGs, while this "burden shifting" could negatively affect the global achievement of the SDGs and could also feed-back negatively on Europe in areas relating to the global commons (see also Chapter 5).

The different proposals to strengthen EU regulation and other responses to the interrelated ecological, economic, and social challenges cover many areas such as better addressing structural drivers, lock-ins, and rebound effects; considering the resource nexus; improving measures to support a Just Transition, strengthening procedural justice; and taking on responsibility for the global socioecological challenges that are co-produced by the EU. Fundamentally, these proposals are not (necessarily) problematizing the socioecological modernization paradigm. However, given the construction of the EU as an organization that heavily relies on Member States and their very different national circumstances and interests, some of the proposals will be very difficult to adopt and implement. Climate and environment diplomacy is a central part of the European Green Deal, but the EU has displayed no willingness to be held directly accountable for the socioecological consequences of its system of production and consumption that are played out elsewhere, including in the Global South.

Political and theoretical paradigms underlying alternative solutions

In this section of the Chapter, we will highlight paradigms underlying solutions of ecological and socioecological challenges that, to a varying degree and in different ways, are conflicting with the hegemonic paradigms. We have chosen to focus on three very different paradigms: technological escapist and quick fix, nationalist, and socioecological transformative.

Technology-based and quick fix strategies

The technology-based escape and quick fix strategies, such as geoengineering, have very different aims but share an optimistic believe in human's Promethean ability to solve problems by means of technology. They also share a neglect of socioecological considerations.

In general, escape strategies build on the acknowledgement that climate is bound to change, that natural biodiversity will be lost, and that many of the planet's resources will be depleted. For example, escape strategies aim to escape from the planet, to escape into a digital world, or to escape from the dependency on eco-system services. Technologists and billionaires talk of the need to abandon a degraded Earth altogether and are taking the first steps to develop Mars-bound spaceships. This is a very elitist strategy that accepts the forecasted inhabitability of Planet Earth, aiming at providing solutions for the minor few. The long-term vision of the 3D Google Metaverse and similar technological projects is a departure from the physical world, which implies that humans do not have to directly encounter nature or other people any longer. All activities and encounters with people and nature—including production and work, buying, and selling—may, in principle, happen by connecting to a computer and acting through an avatar. By living in the fully developed Metaverse, people only need little space, digitally ordered food, physical health services, 3D devises, different types of sensors, and a computer. What matters socially and economically is what people do and what they own within the virtual space. More far-reaching solutions are proposed by some variants of transhumanism, which argue that humans should cease their physical existence and evolve into uploaded digital beings. These strategies may be characterized as technology-based adaption strategies to a future situation with a totally degraded biosphere, containing no socioecological considerations. Biological science contributes with suggestions on how humans could detach from the natural biosphere. To compensate for the loss of biodiversity and explore possibilities of future human survival on a devastated planet, scientists have begun to experiment with ways to synthesize ecosystem-services, such as pollination or other natural processes, to grow crops underground, to use bioreactors, and to modify genes to increase biological resilience. Again, these types of techno-biological strategies build on the inevitable erosion of the biosphere and miss socioecological reflections.

Geoengineering is the predominant quick fix strategy to reduce atmospheric CO_2 by negative emission technologies, targeting the manipulation of the planetary environment to counteract anthropogenic climate change. Geoengineering techniques can be divided into two strategies: Carbon Dioxide Removal (CDR) and Solar Radiation Management (SRM). Carbon dioxide can be removed by carbon capture and storage, enhancing ocean uptake of CO_2 through ocean fertilization, increasing seawater alkalinity, and accelerating mineral weathering to transform carbon dioxide into stable mineral forms. These types of solutions are in the phase of development to be fully functional at greater scales, their exact efficiency, however, is unknown, and some of the techniques pose unknown risks to the biosphere (see also Chapter 2). Solar radiation management techniques are designed to reduce the solar radiation that reaches the Earth's surface, e.g., by injecting particles into the stratosphere to simulate the effects of volcanic eruptions (Adelman, 2018: 1). Scientists warn that climate manipulation may contain irreversible consequences because they cannot be certain of how the biosphere will respond to forced interventions. This includes the possibility that it could lead to feedback processes that increase so-called acid rain and exacerbate ocean acidification. Climate manipulation may also slow down or reverse the recovery of the ozone layer and reduce global rainfall, while, at the same time, increasing flooding and intensifying extreme weather events (Adelman, 2018: 3). From a socioecological point of view, the effects of an attempt by one or more countries to manipulate their climate may increase conflicts because these effects will not be limited to a single country. Adelman concludes that substantial parts of the world may experience greater risk when geoengineering is applied than when the effects of GHG are unabated (Adelman, 2018: 8). Thus, such quick fixes need careful consideration regarding possible consequences like reduced governance pressure for immediate CO_2 emission reductions.

Nationalist strategies

In general, the term "nationalism" refers to the pursuit of national interests at the expense of supranational or intergovernmental interests. In politics, however, there are many examples of the pursuit of national interests taking place within specific arenas, while the pursuit of other interests takes place in a coordinated and supranational manner. In the EU, on the one hand, it has been impossible to formulate and adopt a common immigration and refugee policy because of the political articulation of strong national diverging interests. On the other hand, in the field of climate change, it has been possible for national governments to formulate common objectives and guidelines for political action. Yet, in the field of climate change national governments still continue to balance national and supranational interests. The articulation of national interests is linked to political power relations, which are, in turn, dependent on several other factors such as business structures, path-dependencies and lock-ins pertaining to energy supply, and voter affiliations to political parties. As accounted for in Chapter 6, based on national circumstances and dependencies, some EU countries act more skeptically than other countries regarding the change from fossil fuels to renewable energy. Furthermore, as highlighted in Chapter 10, some countries, such as the Frugal Four (Austria, Denmark, the Netherlands, and Sweden), advocate against a large distributive European budget and collective EU debt. Accordingly, they took an oppositional stand to the original proposition from the commission regarding the level of subsidies for the promotion of a just and green transition in the wake of Covid-19. Although most EU countries continue to balance national special interest and common EU interests, they do not want to be perceived as nationalists. Other parties, however, perceive the term "nationalist" as a proof of their loyalty to the citizens of the nations that they represent.

In the European context, most of these nationalist parties are critical of meeting global challenges through global responses. Their nationalist views may build on climate denial assumptions or state interests in continuing fossil fuel production, but not necessarily. Schaller and Alexander (2019) have studied the European situation and provided empirical evidence on the nexus between right-wing populism and climate change. Their investigation for Adelphi, an independent think-and-do tank in Europe for climate, environment, and development focuses on what they define as the strongest 21 European right-wing populist parties. Their point of departure is a perceived threat that the increasing share of climate-skeptics in European countries could undermine ambitious climate policy proposals and obstruct national governments in passing laws and filling both the EU and UN mechanisms (Schaller & Alexander, 2019: 44).

Within the right-wing populist spectrum, Schaller and Alexander map out significant variations in terms of climate change frames and arguments. They differ between three types of policies: the denialist/skeptic, the disengaged/cautious, and the affirmative. They reach the following conclusions: (1) seven denialist/skeptic parties cast doubt on the scientific evidence on human-induced climate change or explicitly reject this evidence. Furthermore, some of these parties argue that CO_2 is not a pollutant but an indispensable component for all life on Earth, that governments are suppressing this fact, or that political actors strategically use scientifically disputed climate change arguments to draw financial resources (taxes) from the population; (2) eleven disengaged/cautious parties have no position on climate change or attribute little importance to the problem. According to Schaller and Alexander, parties of this variety often emphasize the uncertainty around the impacts of emissions in the atmosphere and the effects of climate policy. On the one hand, some of these parties argue that Earth's climate changes naturally over time, and that we know too little about what affects these changes. On the other hand, some of these parties simultaneously promote visions of national environmental actions and renewable energy deployment; and (3) three affirmative parties focus on nationalist strategies to oppose immigration, while simultaneously recognizing the danger that climate change poses to the world and their own countries. They tend to acknowledge the global character of climate change, support research into climate change and technological solutions, highlight climate related extreme events, and even propagate global solutions (Schaller & Alexander, 2019: 12).

Most right-wing populist parties in the sample generally oppose EU action and rules that impact national sovereignty, regarding sustainable energy and climate policies (Schaller & Alexander, 2019: 23). Internationally agreed climate targets—from the UN to the EU—are mostly considered over-ambitious, ideological, and harmful to consumers and national economies (Schaller & Alexander, 2019: 24). According to Schaller and Alexander, the most common arguments put forward by many parties in the sample are that: (1) climate policies (renewable support schemes, efficiency laws, emissions trading, or carbon taxes) harm the economy and the competitiveness of national industries; (2) climate policy has unjust effects such as higher energy prices and it will cost people their jobs and undermine social justice; and (3) increasing wind and solar power, among other renewable energy sources, would impact the natural value of national and local environment and landscapes (Schaller & Alexander, 2019: 14ff). The authors state that several right-wing populist parties exhibit a kind of "green patriotism" that strongly supports environmental conservation to preserve biodiversity, but not climate action. They argue that this kind of "eco-nationalism" is based on ethnic conservative interpretations of nature conservation (Schaller & Alexander, 2019: 38).

Furthermore, Schaller and Alexander highlight that most of the narratives used to counter climate and energy policies are fundamentally rooted in economic or social justice grievances and climate action is perceived as an elitist issue. They state that anger has its roots in long-standing social grievances about the unequal merits of market liberalization, perceived threats to prosperity, and one's culture, security, and stability (Schaller & Alexander, 2019: 3). They criticize the fact that most established parties have pursued a type of fact-based, but highly technocratic, climate discourse that often neglects citizens' expectations. They further argue that this elite steering of the transformation has itself contributed to the proliferation of mistrust in science, democratic institutions, and multilateralism, and that it is hence part of the problem (Schaller & Alexander, 2019: 47).

Therefore, the authors argue for new ways of conceiving climate policy. On the one hand, policies must be comprehensive, multi-sectoral, and more creative to alleviate social inequality. On the other hand, the story of climate change needs a new positive framing and a progressive narrative to inspire the imagination and to empower citizens (Schaller & Alexander, 2019: Introduction). Schaller and Alexander state that the success of climate policies depends upon constructive deliberation, honest assessment of synergies and trade-offs, and the creation of popular support for transformative change. Rather than viewing climate action as a technical problem and framing it as such, they recommend that a credible and positive narrative is needed wherein climate policy measures are embedded and framed as societal policy. In this context, they also argue that it can be valuable to acknowledge that the multilateral project of globalization, climate policies, and fundamental societal changes have unjust effects if they remain unmanaged and that taking concerns seriously and acknowledging the truth contained within populist narratives—from corruption to the repercussions of neoliberalism—would be an important step to regain trust (Schaller & Alexander, 2019: 47).

Socioecological transformation strategies

The socioecological transformation paradigm refers to a radical transformation of the current socio-metabolic regime—i.e., the set of flows of materials and energy a society needs to reproduce itself. This is different from the concept of socioecological modernization, as described in the text above, which refers to green innovation-centered incremental transitions within the current economic system. Proponents of the socioecological transformation paradigm suggest not only that the market should not be governing resource allocation, but instead be embedded within society, but also that production should be socialized, democratized, and re-located to serve the purpose of the emancipation of humans and nature and of freedom from repression and exploitation (Kreinin, 2020: 5f).

According to this paradigm, unequal global relations are the result of historic exploitation and colonialism. International trade and financialization of the commons are viewed as a continuation of colonial relations, as well as a source of environmental injustice and damage. It is fundamental to the paradigm that environmental, social, and economic crises are inherent to an expansionist economic system. The socioecological transformation paradigm includes insights from Marxism and solidarity economy, new visions of society and "the good life" past current consumption and material-based expressions of living well, ideas of socializing the commons, ecofeminist perspectives, a critique of productivism, a concern for North-South relations, and an explicit politicization of the private and social-[re]production work and care work, as well as a critique of the primacy of paid labor as the basis of societal organization (Kreinin, 2020: 6).

In the following, we shall return to the proposal of a Green Deal for Europe that we have already touched upon in Chapter 10. Then we shall elaborate on some of the main themes and solutions that are highlighted within the socioecological transformation paradigm regarding degrowth, the role of capital accumulation in increasing ecological and socioecological risk, the financialization of the commons, and suggestions from a Global South perspective of a radical bottom-up approach to organizing the interplay between local, national, regional, and global socioecological actions and solutions.

Green deal for Europe

As outlined in Chapter 10, in 2019, the Green New Deal for Europe Coalition published the Blueprint for Europe's Just Transition, which contained the proposal of a Green Deal for Europe (see Chapter 10). This proposal contains some elements that correspond to a proposal from US Congresswoman Alexandria Ocasio-Cortez, who presented a proposal for a House Resolution to create a Green New Deal in 2019. The range of proposals in the Blueprint, however, are more radical in their scope than the Green New Deal (Samper et al., 2021: 10f).

The blueprint addresses three global, as well as European, crises regarding the economy, environment, and democracy, and it presents a set of proposals for ecological and socioecological transformation attributed to the ideas of non-/degrowth, based on a widened concept of democracy. To realize its aims, the Blueprint suggests the establishment of three new institutions: an investment program, a package of legislation aimed at ecological and socioecological issues, and an Environmental Justice Commission. Some of the solutions proposed in the blueprint resemble proposals in the European Green Deal, such as the commitment to a rapid and massive deployment of renewables, the decarbonization of transport and agriculture, new or refurbished zero-carbon affordable housing, and reforestation and ecological restoration. Still other proposals in the Blueprint point to the need for more radical transformations:

- *Finance:* Adopt a multi-stakeholder governance model for the European Central Bank; make it prioritize employment, social progress,

and environmental protection; abandon the dominant model of public-private financing; and invest in the transition directly.
- *Global trade:* Renegotiate the World Trade Organization rules to include human rights, including the right to the benefits of science, a clean environment, and labor standards.
- *Companies:* Introduce punitive capital requirements for investments in fossil fuel and environmentally destructive projects and codify a duty on directors to invest in renewable and sustainable energy, transport, buildings, and other practices.
- *Taxation:* Replace the EU emissions trading scheme with a fee-and-dividend system, introduce legislation to shut down tax havens, and introduce additional fiscal measures, such as an environmental damage tax and a financial transaction tax, to generate funds to support communities on the frontline of the climate and environmental crises.
- *Public ownership:* Support the public buy-out of utilities companies across EU member states.
- *Decent and democratic jobs:* Spend funding on guaranteeing decent local public jobs to all European residents based on a three-day weekend or four-day work week with lower overall working hours, support the emergence of workplace democracy across the continent, focus investment on worker cooperatives and community-led projects based on municipal or local ownership, and fund a Care Income to compensate activities like care for people, the urban environment, and the natural world.

Underneath the different proposal is a commitment to respecting the Planetary Boundaries and to promoting radical democratization, Just Transition, decent work, reduced work time, work security, and income guaranty for informal work. Furthermore, the Blueprint aims at controlling the dynamics of capitalism, decreasing the power of company owners and shareholders, and promoting non-growth or degrowth. Although, from a technical and organizational point of view, many of the suggestions in the Blueprint appear "realistic," they also represent fundamental criticisms of many aspects of the power structures and economic dynamics that the European Green Deal relies upon. The core object of this criticism is directed at the green growth imperative. In the following, we shall highlight further aspects of the degrowth paradigm.

Degrowth

In a report issued in 2021, the UNDP states that initiatives aiming at socioecological sustainable transformation will be subject to filtering and that we need to re-examine the values and priorities driving that filtering. If it is just the invisible hand of deregulated markets doing the filtering, based on short-term financial gains that concentrate power with the few, outcomes that promote sustainability, equity, or collective flourishing are highly unlikely: "After all, that filter got us in the mess in the first place" (UNDP, 2020: 104). Furthermore, the UNDP argues that many of the processes and systems of today need to change, including consumerism, business models of unlimited economic growth, and the displacement of impacts and dependencies across geographies and generations. The UNDP acknowledges that diverging from an unsustainable present implies losses for those who disproportionately benefit or aim to benefit from business as usual (UNDP, 2020: 37) and that redressing inequalities in human development is paramount to avoid the capture of political processes by narrow interests that want to preserve status quo (UNDP, 2020: 41). This view of the UNDP contrasts with the idea that the neoliberal economic model, economic liberalization, and global competitiveness are the universal remedy that promises a socioecological sustainable future for the Earth and all its inhabitants. However, the varying proposals in UN reports from UNDP, IPCC, IPBES, and IR, as well as policies implemented by the UN, have been criticized for directing problem-solving at the level of the immediate appearance of problems, rather than at the level of their root causes. This duality reflects a deeper controversy between proponents of a green growth concept and proponents of a degrowth concept (see also Chapter 4).

However, the concept of degrowth is not only expressed by radical movements and scholars. In 2021, in a short text, "Growth and narratives for change," the European Environmental Agency (EEA) formulates the questions: "Are there alternatives to the present EU growth scenario?" and "Could the European Green Deal, for example, become a catalyst for EU citizens to create a society that consumes less and grows in other than material dimensions?." The EEA highlights the fact that a global decoupling of economic growth and resource consumption is not happening and that recent studies find no evidence of absolute decoupling between growth and environmental degradation having taken place on a global scale (see also Chapter 6). The EEA explains the low potential for decoupling via circularity by outlining that a very large share of primary material throughput is composed of: (1) energy carriers, which are degraded through use, as explained by the laws of thermodynamics, and cannot be recycled; and (2) construction materials, which are added to the building stock, which is recycled over very long periods. EEA interprets this in the light of Tainter's (1988) study of the collapse of complex societies: as complexity increases, there are diminishing marginal returns on improvements in problem-solving; hence, improvements at the local scale have a very small impact on the overall system (EEA, 2021).

To the EEA, an absolute reduction of environmental pressures and impacts would require fundamental transformations to a different type of economy and society, instead of incremental efficiency gains within established production and consumption systems. Historically, however, the EEA highlights that modern states have embraced economic thought that focused on economic growth and conceptualized social and environmental problems as externalities. As a result, growth is culturally, politically, and institutionally ingrained. Worldwide, the legitimacy of governments cannot be separated from their ability to deliver economic growth and provide employment.

Thanks to economic growth, the portion of the world's population living in extreme poverty has fallen. The EEA states, however, that economic growth has not contributed to decreasing inequality, either among or within countries (see also Chapter 3).

The EEA argues that, while the planet is finite in its biophysical sense, infinite growth in human existential values, such as beauty, love, and kindness, as well as in ethics, may be possible. Society is currently experiencing limits to growth because it is locked into defining growth in terms of economic activities and material consumption. In this context, the EEA asks the question: what could be achieved in terms of human progress if the European Green Deal is implemented with the specific purpose of inspiring European citizens, communities, and enterprises to create innovative social practices that have little or no environmental impacts yet still aim for societal and personal growth? According to the EEA, the fundamental values of the EU are human dignity, freedom, democracy, equality, and the rule of law, and they cannot be reduced to or substituted by an increase in GDP (EEA, 2021).

The EEA then asks the open question: how can society develop and grow in quality (e.g., meaning, solidarity, empathy), rather than in quantity (e.g., material standards of living), and how can this be done in a more equitable way? Furthermore, it asks: what are we willing to renounce to meet our sustainability ambitions? Instead of insisting on green growth, the EEA suggests that we think about possibilities of achieving sustainability by innovating lifestyles, communities, and societies that consume less and yet are attractive to everybody (EEA, 2021).

It is, of course, remarkable that an EU knowledge institution questions the Green Growth Paradigm that underlies the European Green Deal. By doing so, the EEA highlights the serious challenges and the little progress that is facing the EU and the world. As accounted for in Chapter 4, critical scholars regard degrowth as the negation of both "brown" and "green" capitalism, as well as of the corresponding established power structures. The degrowth discourse questions the growth model and perceives it as ecologically irresponsible. Proponents of degrowth fight for ecologically responsible economies, protection and restoration of ecological commons, and anti-consumerist lifestyles (Ossewaarde & Ossewaarde-Lowtoo, 2020: 2). Robra and Heikkurinen point out that, for some scholars and activists, the critique of growth has led to a stark critique of capitalism within the degrowth movement due to the argument that capitalism is the main driver of today's society and, furthermore, that capitalism requires growth to function (Robra & Heikkurinen, 2019: 3). In the next section, we will highlight some of the characteristics of such anti-capitalist approaches (see also Chapter 12).

Anti-capitalism approaches

In his book "After Capital" (2018), Venn argues that, if one wants to critically analyze the current crisis and contribute to the formulation of alternatives, it will be necessary to understand the underlying economic and political forces that are driving development (Venn, 2018: 58). From his eco-Marxist and anti-capitalist point of view, Venn regards development as anchored in the material, institutional, discursive, technological, and historical constituents of a world economy driven by ceaseless growth, accumulation at a global scale, and destructive technologies (Venn, 2018: 60). Venn explains that, historically, the capitalist system was set up in the period of European colonialism and imperialism (Venn, 2018: 75). Although, colonies formally have been set free, according to Venn, the colonial "heritage" still plays a very important role. To maximize profits, post-colonies have become the sites for outsourced production by companies and financial institutions from the Global North, as well as by companies and institutions placed in the Global South. Venn states that geopolitical organizations such as the IMF, the World Bank, and forums such as G7 and G20 have helped to promote this new post-colonial world order (Venn, 2018: 82f; see also Chapter 4).

Focusing on ecological and socioecological challenges, Venn argues that the problems of climate change, biodiversity loss, resource depletion, and increasing global, regional, and national inequalities are driven by geo-economic forces tied to global capitalism and its inherent compulsion for unlimited growth to sustain accumulation (Venn, 2018: 63). In the Global North, the post-war period has been founded on a social contract among capital, state, and citizens—one built on the negotiated sharing of economic wealth between profits and wages, a redistribution of wealth through taxation, and the provision of social and health security. The basis for this contract has been an agreement on the need for continuous economic growth. The iterations of growth across many parameters—GDP, output and sales by firms, levels of consumption, incomes, the size of profit and thus shareholder value, private wealth accumulation, etc.—is so prevalent that one forgets that it is as man-made as the historic development of a capitalist economy (Venn, 2018: 61). Venn emphasizes that competition functions as a regulative idea determining calculation across all sectors of the global economy and all aspects of society and individual behavior (Venn, 2018: 82). He highlights a broad variety of examples that confirm his view that the competition for resources and growth undermines effective actions directed at ecological and socioecological challenges (Venn, 2018: 59).

Especially focusing on difficulties in preventing disastrous climate change, Venn argues that the most important barrier is the massive wealth already locked up in assets tied to fossil reserves, as fossil fuel companies are dependent on the value of the reserves that they already own to attract investments. Indeed, proposals of divestment are regarded as catastrophic by the petro-industrial complex. Accordingly, it applies a great variety of measures to prevent such proposals from gaining ground (Venn, 2018: 57).

Venn is not very explicit about possible practical dimensions of post-capitalist transformations. He states that a post-capitalist world should be based in a worldview in which solidarity, empathy, being-with, and being-for-the-other are prioritized and that it should be based on property regimes that prioritize common ownership. Moreover, he asserts that it should avoid the centralization and bureaucratization of decision-making processes and instead embrace decentralized network arrangements that try to find a balance between the efficiency of systems and autonomy at the regional or localized level of decision-making. He also states that international institutions and binding agreements would be necessary for tackling big issues like climate change and resource management at the global level. Finally, he mentions that it would be important for all citizens to learn how to participate in democratic institutions and to live in collectivities, while developing values and activities that "feed the spirit" (Venn, 2018: 141ff).

Likewise grounded in the eco-Marxist approach, while focusing on the financialization of the commons, Foster argues that proponents of market capitalism view the financialization of ecosystem services not previously incorporated within the economy—building on global carbon markets and conservation finance—as an answer to the global ecological crisis that is constituting a new financialized ecological regime. According to Foster, this monetization of the environment allows for an enormous expansion of the circuit of exchange value (Foster, 2022). The first published estimates of the global value of natural capital/ecosystem services led to a new asset class and a market consisting of trillions of dollars. Spatial mapping of natural capital indicates that there is a high concentration of terrestrial ecosystem assets in the equatorial regions, particularly in the Brazilian Amazon and the Congo Basin. Marine ecosystem assets are highest in Southeast Asia and along coastlines. Indigenous territories cover some 24 percent of the earth's land surface and contain 80 percent of the Earth's remaining healthy ecosystems and global biodiversity priority areas, making these primary targets for expropriation and conversion into marketable natural capital. Sub-Saharan Africa is a target since it is estimated that around 90 percent of land is untitled, with the result that many Indigenous communities that have lived in these areas for untold years lack official land titles and that their land is, therefore, open to land grabbing (Foster, 2022).

Foster indicates that the financialization of nature is promoting a Great Expropriation of the global commons, thereby replacing the laws of nature with the laws of commodity value (Foster, 2022). The financialization of biodiversity involves mechanisms of packaging multiple ecosystem goods and services, including biodiversity, for sale. In this process, the global commons are cut up and monopolized by a few private interests, who turn them into revenue streams to be bundled together as financial assets. From an eco-Marxist point of view, Forster argues that to monetize the environment is ultimately to draw it into the market and to subject it to the dynamic of accumulation, which make a sustainable relation to the environment impossible. He further argues that the concept of natural capital is an attempt to monetize ecosystem services to generate a social and historical relation in which the entire Earth is for sale. He criticizes the fact that the system of original expropriation, which was the basis of the creation of the industrial proletariat, will metamorphose into a more universal dispossession and the creation of a global environmental reserve army of the dispossessed (Foster, 2022).

To Foster, the response to such a destructive system should be a universal struggle for nature and humanity, demanding a peoples' sovereignty of the Earth and of production. He argues that the global resistance of Indigenous communities, together with peasant subsistence producers, to increasing land grabs is one of the most important developments of our time. He suggests that the goal of this resistance should ultimately be one of sustainable human development, necessarily coupled with struggles of the dispossessed to resist capitalism, racism, colonialism, imperialism, and ecological devastation (Foster, 2022).

Bottom-up alternatives

Within the socioecological transformation paradigm, some bottom-up practices are not only grounded locally in their catering to local needs of participants and members, but also aimed at building trans-local networks of coordination. Katherine Gibson articulates this as a global endeavor of people taking back their economy to encounter the hegemonic framework of market fundamentalism. She has done this in pioneering the fields of diverse economies and community economies (Gibson-Graham & Dombroski, 2020). Here, the authors are linking to the critical trend in socioecological transformation by outlining "ethical ways of living on our dangerously degraded planet." There is a global surge in such practices that represent a reorientation vis a vis institutionalized politics, in the sense that they are "more oriented towards building constructive and thoroughly organized alternatives rather than appealing to formal institutions by putting pressure on them to change their political decisions" (Forno & Graziano, 2014: 2). Thus, agents of socioecological transformation are realizing a type of political action that is both designed to cater to the livelihoods of members and participants and to function as a "tool to bring different collectives together, helping them to develop common strategies" (Forno & Graziano, 2019: 3) Following Forno and Graziano (2014 and 2019), such post-capitalist practices, which they label "Sustainable Community Movement Organizations" (SCMOs), are aimed at rebuilding social bonds through alternative and sustainable networks of production, exchange, and consumption. In their mapping of SCMOs in Italy in the area of solidarity purchasing and factory recovering groups (Forno & Graziano, 2019), the authors have identified new forms of integrated political and economic bottom-up actions that have increased in number and covered areas in the wake of the multiple crises. Other institutionalized forms of trans-local practices can be found in the ecovillage movement, permaculture, community supported agriculture, various forms of regenerative practices in agriculture, and social enterprises—particularly within the framework of solidarity economy. Furthermore, in general, these practices form a connection to the post-colonial view characterizing the framework of epistemologies of the South (Escobar, 2016; Santos, 2014; see also Chapter 12).

Summary

In this Chapter, we highlighted different notions of government and governance procedures and structures to characterize UN and EU government and governance pertaining to climate change, resources, biodiversity, and socioecological issues. We have argued not only that UN governance structures and procedures are primarily based on goals, national determined contributions, transparency, and accountability, but also that they are rather weak when compared to the EU. Relating the different areas, however, UN government and governance is characterized by different levels of precision, scope, and strength. The government and governance procedures of the EU are much more complex in combining monocentric, multilevel, and polycentric structures, as well as interventionist, regulative, and catalytic procedures. In the EU, market-based and technological solutions are combined with investments, research and innovation, binding regulations, highly developed mechanisms of coordination, participation of non-state actors and citizens, and the dissemination of information.

In the following section of the Chapter, we discussed two paradigms regarding ecological and socioecological conceptualizations and the solutions underlying UN and EU strategies and policies: (1) neoliberal market-based; and (2) socioecological modernization. We have chosen to present the ideas of William Nordhaus as a prominent representative of the neoliberal market-based paradigm. His main proposal combines carbon taxes, technological de-carbonization, and climate clubs. The theoretical modeling and empirical foundation of the work of Nordhaus, however, have been criticized by other economists as being inconsistent, unscientific, and unsupported by evidence. Market-based solutions are promoted by the UN and the EU. Carbon taxes were part of the Kyoto Agreement that also introduced the concept of Voluntary Carbon Offset (VCO). The EU has implemented the EU Emission Trading system and proposed a Carbon Border Adjustment Mechanism (CBAM). Market-based solutions have been criticized by scholars, as well environment and climate movements and NGOs, who argue that: (1) enterprises in the Global North are provided an opportunity to continue their carbon emissions; (2) the funding of nature-based solutions represents a risk to biodiversity; (3) these types of risk translate into socioecological risks for communities in the Global South; (4) VCOs may be used as a mechanism for green-washing; and (5) carbon border adjustment mechanisms may create pressures in the Global South that undermine ecological and socioecological conditions.

The socioecological modernization paradigm incorporates market-based solutions, and, furthermore, applies government and governance measures pertaining to a very broad range of economic, technological, and organizational solutions that focus on ecological and socioecological issues. Acknowledging the basic principles of the socioecological modernization paradigm, UN knowledge providers suggest that stronger actions could be taken: (1) goal-based governance should be supplemented with forms of government that include requirements and prohibitions; (2) siloed models of tackling environmental and climate change challenges should be abandoned in favor of more systemic approaches; (3) climate change and biodiversity depletion should be addressed in an integrated matter; (4) much more efficient measures should be implemented to reduce fossil fuel demand and production; (5) deeply rooted structures generating different types of inequality should be addressed; (6) technological solutions should not stand alone; (7) management of the global commons should address inequality and injustice more directly; and (8) environment, climate, and social movements, alongside grass root initiatives and indigenous knowledge, should be supported. Pertaining to the implementation of the socioecological modernization paradigm by the EU, the EEA suggests a variety of measures to strengthen responses by addressing structural drivers, lock-ins, and rebound effects, considering the resource-nexus, improving measures to support a Just Transition, and taking much stronger responsibility for the global ecological and socioecological challenges that are co-produced by the EU.

In the last section of the Chapter, we presented three different paradigms, which contrast the paradigms of market-based solutions and socioecological modernization: (1) technology-based escape and quick fix; (2) nationalist; (3) and socioecological transformative paradigms. The first category includes different forms of geoengineering, ideas of how to physically escape from the planet or into digitalized 3D universes, and biological strategies of how to survive if faced with a degraded biosphere. Many scientists have assessed geoengineering solutions as dangerous due to their unpredictable effects, whereas escape strategies do not aim to propose viable solutions to the ecological and socioecological challenges. Generally, nationalist strategies are opposed to supranational solutions based on different types of arguments, including, e.g., that they harm national economies and have unjust effects. Nationalist strategies are often based on climate change denial, but not necessarily. As argued in the Chapter, their acceptance by citizens may be grounded in economic and social grievances and anti-elitists notions. Socioecological transformation strategies refer to proposals of radical societal transformations. We presented radical democratic and equality-oriented solutions proposed by the Green New Deal for Europe Coalition, degrowth ideas as formulated by the European Environment Agency, anti-capitalist approaches, and ideas of bottom-up alternatives. What these types of solutions hold in common are, for instance, ideas about less market and corporate power, more participatory democracy connected to state power, and confrontation of the fundamental drivers that are creating ecological and socioecological challenges and the divide between the Global North/Global South.

In the next Chapter, we will elaborate further on some of these paradigms from the general perspective of the "Anthropocene," which is argued to represents an epochal shift in the (different) ways that we construct and understand the relationship between humans and nature.

References

Abott, K. W. (2018). Orchestration. Strategic ordering in polycentric governance. In: A. Jordan, D. Huitema, Assens H. van & J. Forster (eds.), *Governing climate change*. Cambridge University Press. Retrieved from: https://www.cambridge.org/core/product/033486F6DA7F2CD1F8F3D6011B17909B

Biedenkopf, K., and Wettestad, J. (2018). Harnessing the market. Trading carbon allowances. In: A. Jordan, D. Huitema, Assens H. van & Forster, J. (eds.), *Governing climate change*. Cambridge University Press. Retrieved from: https://www.cambridge.org/core/product/033486F6DA7F2CD1F8F3D6011B17909B

Coen, D., Kreienkamp, J., and Pegram, T. (2020). *Global climate governance*. Cambridge Elements, Cambridge University Press. DOI: 10.1017/9781108973250

Bongardt, A. and Torres, F. (2022). The European Green Deal: More than an exit strategy to the pandemic crisis, a building block of a sustainable European economic model. *JCMS*, 60(1), 170–185. DOI: 10.1111/jcms.13264

Dale, G. (2018). The Nobel Prize in climate chaos: Romer, Nordhaus and the IPCC. *Ecologist*, 12th October. Retrieved from: https://theecologist.org/2018/oct/12/nobel-prize-climate-chaos-romer-nordhaus-and-ipcc

EEA (2021). Growth without economic growth. In '*Narrative for change' series*, European Environment Agency Publications, Briefing no. 28/2020 (13 pages). Retrieved from: https://www.eea.europa.eu/publications/growth-without-economic-growth. doi: 10.2800/492717

European Commission (2010). Europe 2020. Retrieved from: https://ec.europa.eu/eu2020/pdf/COMPLET percent20EN percent20BARROSO percent20 percent20 percent20007 percent20- percent20Europe percent202020 percent20-percent20EN percent20version.pdf

Escobar, A. (2016). Thinking-feeling with the Earth: Territorial struggles and the ontological dimension of the epistemologies of the South. *Revista de Antropologia Iberoamericana*, 11(1), 11–32.

Forno, F. and Graziano, P. (2014). Sustainable community movement organisations. *Journal of Consumer Culture*, 14(2), 139–157.

Forno, F. and Graziano, P. (2019). From global to local. Political consumerism in times og multiple crises. *European Societies*, 5, 1–23. Retrieved from: DOI: 10.1080/14616696.2019.1616793

Foster, J. B. (2022). The defense of nature: Resisting the financializaton of the Earth. *Monthly Review - An Independent Socialist Magazine*, 73(11). Retrieved from: https://monthlyreview.org/2022/04/01/the-defense-of-nature-resisting-the-financializaton-of-the-earth/

Gibson-Graham, J. K., and Dombroski, K. (2020). *The handbook of diverse economies*. London: Edward Elgar.

Independent Group of Scientists (2019). Independent Group of Scientists appointed by the Secretary-General, Global Sustainable Development Report 2019: *The Future is Now – Science for Achieving Sustainable Development*. New York: United Nations.

Jänicke, M. (2012). "Green growth": From a growing eco-industry to economic sustainability. *Energy Policy*, 48, 13–21. DOI: 10.1016/j.enpol.2012.04.045

Jänicke, M. and Rüdiger K.W. (2019). Leadership and lesson-drawing in the European Union's multilevel climate governance system. *Environmental Politics*, 28(1), 22–42. DOI: 10.1080/09644016.2019.1522019

Jordan, A., Huitema, D., Assens H. van and Forster, J. (2018). Governing climate change polycentrically: Setting the scene. In: A. Jordan, D. Huitema, Assens H. van & J. Forster (eds.), *Governing climate change*. Cambridge University Press, 29–46. Retrieved from: https://www.cambridge.org/core/product/033486F6DA7F2CD1F8F3D6011B17909B

Keen, S. (2021). The appallingly bad neoclassical economics of climate change, *Globalizations*, 18(7), 1149–1177 (1–29), DOI: 10.1080/14747731.2020.1807856Kreinin, H. (2020). Typologies of "Just Transitions": Towards social-ecological transformation, Institute for Ecological Economics (Wienna University), Working Paper Series 35.

Mol, A. P. J., and Jänicke, M. (2009). The origin and foundations of ecological modernisation theory. In: A. P. J. Mol, D. A. Sonnenfeld & G. Spaargaren (eds.), *The ecological modernisation reader, environmental reform in theory and practice*, 17–27. New York: Routledge.

Nielsen, S. W. (2021). Entreprenørstaten: Hvorfor vælgernes ønsker forsvinder op i den blå luft – og hvordan vi fikser det, eng.: The Entrepreneurial State: Why voters' wishes disappear into the blue air – and how do we fix it?, Gads Forlag.

Nordhaus, W. (2019). Climate change: The ultimate challenge for economics. *American Economic Review*, 109(6), 1991–2014. DOI: 10.1257/aer.109.6.1991

Nordhaus, W. (2021). Dynamic climate clubs: On the effectiveness of incentives in global climate agreements. *PNAS*, 118(45), 2–6. DOI: 10.1073/pnas.2109988118

OECD (2011). Towards green growth (OECD Green Growth Studies). OECD. DOI: 10.1787/9789264111318-en

Okereke, C. (2018). Equity and justice in polycentric climate governance. In: A. Jordan, D. Huitema, Assens H. van & J. Forster (eds.), *Governing climate change*, 320–337. Cambridge University Press. Retrieved from: https://www.cambridge.org/core/product/033486F6DA7F2CD1F8F3D6011B17909B.

Ossewaarde, M. and Ossewaarde-Lowtoo, R. (2020). The EU's Green Deal: A third alternative to green growth and degrowth? *Sustainability*, 12, 2–15. DOI: 10.3390/su12239825

Pörtner, H. O., Scholes, R. J., Agard, J., Archer, E., Arneth, A., Bai, X., Barnes, D., Burrows, M., Chan, L., Cheung, W. L., Diamond, S., Donatti, C., Duarte, C., Eisenhauer, N., Foden, W., Gasalla, M. A., Handa, C., Hickler, T., Hoegh-Guldberg, O., Ichii, K., Jacob, U., Insarov, G., Kiessling, W., Leadley, P., Leemans, R., Levin, L., Lim, M., Maharaj, S., Managi, S., Marquet, P. A., McElwee, P., Midgley, G., Oberdorff, T., Obura, D., Osman, E., Pandit, R., Pascual, U., Pires, A. P. F., Popp, A., Reyes-García, V., Sankaran, M., Settele, J., Shin, Y. J., Sintayehu, D. W., Smith, P., Steiner, N., Strassburg, B., Sukumar, R., Trisos, C., Val, A. L., Wu, J., Aldrian, E., Parmesan, C., Pichs-Madruga, R., Roberts, D. C., Rogers, A. D., Díaz, S., Fischer, M., Hashimoto, S., Lavorel, S., Wu, N., and Ngo, H. T. (2021). IPBES-IPCC co-sponsored workshop report on biodiversity and climate change, IPBES and IPCC. DOI: 10.5281/zenodo.4782538

Prontera, A. and Quitzow, R. (2022). The EU as catalytic state? Rethinking European climate and energy governance. *New Political Economy*, 27(3), 517–531. DOI: 10.1080/13563467.2021.1994539

Robra, B., and Heikkurinen, P. (2019). Degrowth and the sustainable development goals. In W. L. Filho et al. (eds.), *Decent work and economic growth*. Springer Nature Switzerland. DOI: 10.1007/978-3-319-71058-7_37-1

Samper, J. A., Schockling, A. and Islar, M. (2021). Exposing the political frontiers of the European green deal. *Politics and Governance*, 9(2), 8–16. DOI: 10.17645/page.v9i2.3853

Santos, B. D. S. (2014). *Epistemologies of the South. Justice against Epistemicide*. London: Routledge.

Schaller, S., and Alexander C. (2019). *Convenient truths: Mapping climate agendas of right-wing populist parties in Europe*. Berlin: Adelphi. Retrieved from: https://www.adelphi.de/en/system/files/mediathek/bilder/Convenient percent20Truths percent20- percent20Mapping percent20climate percent20agendas percent20of percent20right-wing percent20populist percent20parties percent20in percent20Europe percent20- percent20adelphi.pdf

SEI, IISD, ODI, E3G, and UNEP (2021). *The production gap report 2021*. Retrieved from: http://productiongap.org/2021report

Treude, S. (2022). European economic policy and the European Green Deal: An institutionalist analysis- Research Report. Wissenschaftliche Schriften des Fachbereichs Wirtschaftswissenschaften, No. 35, Hochschule Koblenz - University of Applied Sciences, Fachbereich Wirtschaftswissenschaften, Koblenz. http://hdl.handle.net/10419/248441

UN (2012). A 10-year framework of programs on sustainable consumption and production patterns. Annex to the letter dated 18 June 2012 from the Permanent Representative of Brazil to the United Nations addressed to the Secretary-General of the United Nations Conference on Sustainable Development. Retrieved from: https://sdgs.un.org/documents/aconf2165-10-year-framework-programmes-o-19090

UN (2015). General Assembly, Transforming our world: The 2030 Agenda for Sustainable Development, 21 October, A/RES/70/1. Retrieved from: https://www.refworld.org/docid/57b6e3e44.html

UNDP (2020). The next frontier - Human development and the Anthropocene, 412 pages. Retrieved from: http://hdr.undp.org/sites/default/files/hdr2020.pdf

UNEP (2011). Pathways to sustainable development and poverty eradication - A synthesis for policy makers. In: *Towards a GREEN economy*. Retrieved from: www.unep.org/greeneconomy

Venn, C. (2018). *After capital. Sage series: Theory, culture & society*. Sage Publications, 172 pages.

12 Decentering humanity

The Anthropocene and the perils of Anthropocentricity

Anders Siig Andersen and Lars Hulgaard

> We are at a unique stage in our history. Never before have we had such an awareness of what we are doing to the planet, and never before have we had the power to do something about that. Surely, we all have a responsibility to care for our Blue Planet. The future of humanity and, indeed, all life on earth now depends on us.
>
> Sir David Attenborough

Introduction

In Chapter 11 of this book, we focused on governance structures and procedures and different political paradigms underlying solutions to socioecological challenges. In this chapter we shift our attention to different philosophical and social science paradigms aiming to understand the fundamental character of the contemporary human and planetary condition. We take our point of departure in the notion of the "Anthropocene." Loosely but quite radically, the term defines a new conceptualization of the relationship between people and nature. It suggests that we have entered a new geological epoch in which the human species is now the dominant Earth-shaping force. Hereby, it unsettles the philosophical, epistemological, and ontological ground on which the natural sciences as well as the social sciences/humanities have traditionally stood. The notion of the Anthropocene, however, is differently defined within varying scientific paradigms and, furthermore, questioned and criticized by several scholars as well as activists. Yet, the Anthropocene has quickly become much more than a geochronological term.

Natural scientists regard the Anthropocene as a period in which people and nature are dynamically intertwined and embedded in the biosphere, placing shocks and extreme events as part of this dynamic: "Humanity has become the major force in shaping the future of the Earth system as a whole" (Folke et al., 2021: 834; see also Chapter 1). Social scientists and scholars of the humanities generally accept that the Great Acceleration during the last 70 years of the post-WWII period has changed the human–nature relationship and the relation between time and space. Most of these scholars also agree that human actions have caused unprecedented ecological and socioecological

DOI: 10.4324/9781003319672-16

challenges, and that the future of socially organized human life has been put at risk. However, as we shall highlight in this chapter, they also disagree on several issues, including how the period should be designated. Within the social sciences and the humanities, the new development characterized by the Anthropocene has been constructed by existing and competing paradigms. Simpson (2020: 54) argues that the concept of the Anthropocene derives meaning from other established concepts and frames of analysis, and that the notion of the Anthropocene should be received as a bundle, knit together from already established languages and frameworks of understanding. In some ways, it challenges and extends the limits of existing discourse; in other ways, it reinforces the thinking that precedes it (see also Moore, 2016: 1).

Against this background, first, we present core characteristics of the Anthropocene concept as proposed by natural scientists. We then turn to conceptualizations of the notion within the social sciences and the humanities. Our aim is to critically reflect important differences between positions and to analyze how they may legitimize different political paradigms regarding how to cope with socioecological challenges in the Anthropocene. We have chosen to focus on three selected themes: (1) the human–nature relationship; (2) the unified notion of the "Anthropos"; and (3) alternative understandings of what is driving the Anthropocene. In presenting these themes, the chapter covers different notions of the epoch such as "Multiple Anthropocenes," the "Capitalocene," and the "Plantationocene," and different scholarly paradigms such as neo-materialist, post-human, postmodern, critical reflexive, eco-Marxist, and degrowth.

The Anthropocene in the natural sciences

The concept of the Anthropocene originally arose from the field of Earth system science (ESS). ESS looks at the entire Earth system and includes human as well as natural forces (Biermann, 2021: 62f; Toivanen et al., 2017: 2). The scientific history of ESS builds on advances in climatology, geoscience, and ecosystem ecology and can be traced back several decades. It has evolved through numerous international scientific programs and projects that were based on a drive for a more holistic and transdisciplinary approach on the state of planetary ecosystems (see also Chapter 13). However, it was not until the 1990s that scientists gained proper technological tools to understand the operation of complex Earth systems as a whole and the pervasive human impact on them (Toivanen et al., 2017: 3). By coupling graphs showing socioeconomic trends with graphs showing trends pertaining to the geosphere and the biosphere, ESS scientists detected how both trends have been exponentially accelerating from the mid-1970s onwards. This intertwined development gave birth to the notions of the Great Acceleration (see also Chapter 1). Looking back in time, it became apparent that, coupled with human activities, the rise in CO_2 emissions and global warming and the extinction rate of species have been unprecedented through thousands of years. Looking forward, Earth system scientists started to forecast that the Earth system might turn into a hothouse state and that the degradation of biological life might continue to a degree that will lead to a sixth mass species extinction (see also Chapter 1).

In 2000, Paul Crutzen and Eugene Stoermer proposed that human activities had so profoundly altered the planet as to constitute a new geological epoch different from the Holocene (Crutzen & Stormer, 2000, see also Chapter 1). They suggested that this new epoch should be termed the Anthropocene and that it should be formally acknowledged by the International Commission on Stratigraphy. Concerned with the study of rock layers (strata) and layering (stratification), this Commission has the competence to decide on new geological epochs. As response to the suggestion, the Commission decided to establish the Anthropocene Working Group. In May 2019, the Working Group voted in favor of submitting a formal proposal to the Commission to define the Anthropocene as an epoch in the geologic timescale. In this proposal, stratigraphic markers were located to the mid-20th century at the start of the "Great Acceleration." However, as at mid-2022, the International Commission on Stratigraphy has not approved the term.

Within the natural sciences there have been debates about when the Anthropocene began. Baskin (2015: 11f) refers to three views on dating the Anthropocene: (1) The "Early Anthropocene" view associates the proposed shift in epoch with the emergence of human settlement and agriculture; (2) the "Contemporary Anthropocene" view links the beginning of the Anthropocene to the commencement of the industrial revolution; and (3) the proponents of the "Great Acceleration Anthropocene" date the commencement of the epoch to around 1950, linking it to the Great Acceleration and the radioactive global residues of nuclear-weapons testing regarded as the physical "golden spike" that needs be identified when geologically dating an epoch. A fourth proposal is concerned with the dramatic transformation of biota on Earth caused by the activities of humankind. Historically, it has been suggested that human biota impacts on a global scale began as early as the Age of Exploration, from the 15th to the 18th centuries (Toivanen et al., 2017: 7).

The Anthropocene in the social sciences and the humanities

Simpson (2020: 61ff) traces the predecessors of the Anthropocene back to earlier scholars starting with Buffon in 1778 and continuing with Stoppani, March, Vernadsky, Le Roy, and Teilhard de Chardin. He argues that the early theorists of the Anthropocene hold three "modernist" ideas in common: (1) the narrative about the gradual progression of human cultures through different stages of advancement and development; (2) the idea that, at some stage along this trajectory of human development, human cultures step out of a state of nature or savagery and into a state of civilization; and (3) the idea that the progressive advancement of cultures from a state of nature to one of civilization and modernity is the unfolding of an internal human drive toward a higher state of consciousness, rationality, and enlightenment. The ESS concept of the Anthropocene represents a break with many aspects of these modernist ideas and especially with the idea of civilization and nature-independency portrayed as a linear progress.

Within the social sciences and the humanities, critique of this modernist idea is not a new phenomenon. According to Bhatasara (2015: 219), the first and second generations of classic sociological authors such as Max Weber, John Dewey, Herbert Mead, Emile Durkheim, Georg Simmel, and many others provided conceptual models for developing sociological perspectives on ecological and socioecological issues. Dewey, for example, talked about American capitalism compounding the potential "extinction of natural resources." Furthermore, Zehr (2015: 131) mentions Marx's concept of "the metabolic rift" that occurs when capitalist agriculture depletes rural soils of nutrients by transferring them from rural lands to the city to feed a growing army of urban industrial workers. Attempts to solve the rift through artificial fertilizers deplete other resources.

Among these scholars, Weber was the most pessimistic. In his seminal work from 1904 on the genesis and diffusion of European modernity, he gave a diagnosis of the immense environmental pressures the world population faces today. According to Weber, the agents of modernity in the 16th century turned the invention of a new spirituality into a set of rules that ordinary people in the Global North gradually started to turn into codes of life; this happened to such a degree that no one alive even today can avoid acting in accordance with the logics of the modern capitalist order. In this framework, lifestyles today are, first, bound to the capitalist order, and the capitalist order itself is bound to an economic, political, cultural, and epistemological framework of modernity that shapes all aspects of the way that we look at the world and how we interact with each other. In the words of Weber:

> This order is now bound to the technical and economic conditions of machine production which to-day determine the lives of all the individuals who are born into this mechanism, not only those directly concerned with economic acquisition, with irresistible force. Perhaps it will so determine them until the last ton of fossilized coal is burnt.
>
> (Weber, 2005: 123)

Weber here presents a fundamentally European perspective, and it is worth remembering that he contemplated European modernity from an outlook in the late 19th-century decades before Planetary Boundaries appeared as a phenomenon in Western science and politics. For a reader concerned with the extreme challenges of climate change, biodiversity loss, and resource depletion, as well as the ever-expanding capitalist framework dominating even more spheres today than at the time when Weber made his observations, his final statement leaves no other option than disillusion. First, because it presents a deterministic perception of human life. All people born within the realms of capitalism and European modernity are deemed to follow not only the rules dictated by economic acquisition but, even more importantly, the larger framework of cultural and political codes of conduct. Second, because he anticipated that this "iron cage" of modernity would remain in order until resource depletion had presented its consequences to humanity. Further, he predicted that the peoples of Europe, when finally discovering their depletion of natural resources, would not be able to act due to the epistemological limitations of their positions. In the conclusion of his book, he contemplates the quality of the people inhabiting the world in his near future by indicating that, at the end of European modernity, a "mechanized petrification" would be inhabited by "specialists without spirit, sensualists without heart; this nullity imagines that it has attained a level of civilization never before achieved" (Weber, 2005: 124).

Weber was a European, his outlook was European, and the context of his writings was the ever-expanding project of European modernity. However, he was always on the lookout for sustainable projects able to open the iron cage in terms of changing the lanes of modernity away from extinction. That said, in the foreword to his book, in one sentence, he accepted that the European outlook might not be the only one "of universal importance and validity"; he just did not know how to identify such "cultural phenomena" that could transcend the limitations of modernity, the limitations of the iron cage.

In many ways, the notion of the Anthropocene radicalizes Weber's critique of modernity as a conceptual framework for understanding the present development of societies and human–nature relations. His notion of modernity is primarily a human-centered way of studying the evolution of contemporary societies under the influence of structural social changes caused by secularization, industrialization, enlightenment, and rationalization. According to Grove and Chandler (2017), Chernilo (2021), and Chakrabarty (2019), the notion of the Anthropocene imaginary radicalizes earlier criticisms of modernity and questions different interconnected categories that provide new orientations for human action:

1 Acknowledging human-enforced all-encompassing planetary processes
  First, it breaks down modernist understandings of space as fixed, bounded, and quantifiably determined by mobilizing a global imaginary of all-encompassing planetary processes, implying that geological changes can only be adequately described at a planetary scale, rather than just locally or regionally (Chernilo, 2021: 16f; Grove & Chandler, 2017: 82).
2 Destabilizing linear time
  Second, it runs counter to a modernist sense of time as quantifiable, ordered, and predictable. In the Anthropocene, complex interconnections and feedback loops generate nonlinear changes (tipping points) that cannot be predicted from past experiences, and time itself is constituted in the interplay between very long-term planetary geological processes, long-term processes creating biological Life on Earth, and the

relatively short time span of human history making (Chakrabarty, 2019: 1; Chernilo, 2021: 16f; Grove & Chandler, 2017: 82). Chakrabarty highlights that even the everyday distinction between renewable and nonrenewable sources of energy makes a constant reference to human as well as biological scales of time. He quotes Langmuir and Broecker in arguing that biodiversity is perhaps the most precious planetary resource, and one for which the timescale of replenishment, known from past mass extinctions, is tens of millions of years (Chakrabarty, 2019: 22ff).

3   Destabilizing the division between nature and society
    Third, it destabilizes the modernist division between nature and society. On one hand, it posits humans as a geological force capable of making and remaking the entire planet leaving altered the "normal" cycles of nature. On the other hand, if humans are to be conceived as a geological force, then human and nonhuman worlds are inextricably intertwined (Chernilo, 2021: 16f; Grove & Chandler, 2017: 83f). Baskin (2015) differs between two different accounts of the Anthropocene within the natural and the applied sciences. Those of a "Promethean" persuasion see the Anthropocene as something to be embraced and further managed for human purposes, while those of the "Aidosean" persuasion stress the existence of biophysical limits and argue that the planet should return to the Holocene (Baskin, 2015: 14).

4   Presenting the Earth as radically unstable and unsafe
    Fourth, it presents Earth as radically unstable and dynamic and abandons the possibility of a safe, confined, predictable interior space that can be shielded from a threatening, unknown, and unpredictable outside (Grove & Chandler, 2017: 84). The enemy is within – it is us, *Homo sapiens*.

As mentioned, within the social sciences and the humanities, it is generally accepted that human activities are increasingly threatening life on Earth. According to Verburgt (2021: 4), since the year 2000, the Anthropocene concept has moved to center stage in the social sciences and the humanities. Within several disciplines, it has developed into a rapidly growing interdisciplinary object of research that has given rise to entirely new fields and to several academic controversies (see also Chapter 13). In the following we have chosen to highlight three different perspectives on the Anthropocene: (1) the human–nature relationship; (2) the unified notion of the Anthropos; and (3) alternative notions to the Anthropocene.

The human–nature relation

Fremaux and Barry (2019: 1) highlight that, in Anthropocene debates, we find promotion of techno-hybrid ontologies by neo-materialists, techno-optimistic talk of a good Anthropocene from ecomodernists as well as postmodern thinkers, and eco-managerial aspirations of Earth system stewardship and governance. They argue that, based on very different ontological and epistemological grounds, these paradigms offer a techno-nature monism (Fremaux & Barry, 2019: 3). Dobson (2022: 132) notes that, in some accounts, the gap between the human and the natural realms has been closed as nature has been humanized and that this leaves only turbo-charged geo-engineering as a solution to the socioecological crisis. Fremaux and Barry (2019: 9) highlight that, for ecomodernists, the concept of the Anthropocene supports the urgency and legitimacy of their program: that is, the call for more technology, more capitalism, more technological innovation, more expertise, less politics, less contestation, more top-down governance, and less nature (see also Chapter 11).

In post-humanist theory, Earth's agency is that of a counter-power specifically counteracting human action (Latour & Chakrabarty, 2020: 14). From a socioecological post-human point of view, this is echoed by Burke and Biermann (2019: 1), who state that nowhere on Earth does "nature" exist outside of human social impacts or human society exist separate from "nature." Ontologically, this implies that we should see humans no longer as a distinct unit surrounded by a nonhuman "natural environment" but as an integral part of complex socioecological systems at various scales, from local systems up to the Earth system. These authors portray nonhuman systems and ecologies as behaving and acting and exercising power in ways that profoundly cross the barrier between society and nature (Burke & Biermann, 2019: 2ff). They argue for a model of power that conceptualizes it working across large and complex systems, where power and effects are created across vast distances and connected institutions, technologies, substances, ecologies, and communities through the ways they are caught up in larger processes and systems. At the same time, however, they argue that although nonhuman actants exercise power, moral and political responsibility must be taken up by human actors and institutions acknowledging that it is humans who possess the self-reflexive and interrogatory capacity for complex moral reasoning and self-consciousness (Burke & Biermann, 2019: 10).

Burke and Biermann (2019: 10) argue that the Anthropocene should be addressed by a cosmopolitics pursued at multiple scales and locales, practices of governance and subversion, of regulation and resistance, and carried by an intent to amplify marginalized voices and create new forms of solidarity and governance to confront the power of big energy, big farming, big finance, and fossil fuel capitalism. According to these authors (2019: 11), in an ethic of entanglement, cosmopolitics must honor the fundamental moral worth of ecosystems and nonhuman life and make the preservation of the Earth system and ecosystems a priority. The authors highlight that in the Anthropocene, the hierarchy between a wealthy and powerful core dominating a poor and powerless periphery and a refusal to accept limits are no longer viable. Thus, questions of global social and environmental justice must be addressed together. They propose that states must interiorize an understanding of humans' social entanglement with ecologies and the Earth system and make it central to their approach to international relations. This implies that a strongly eco-centric ethos should infuse environmental governance at every level, and that nonhuman animals and ecosystems should increasingly have representation in political assemblies and governance institutions based on innovative models of cross-national and ecosystem-centered deliberative democracy (Burke & Biermann, 2019: 13).

Dobson, however, criticizes concepts of identity between humans and nature. To Dobson (2022: 124), dialectics is about an interacting relationship between two entities, where neither entity remains the same as it was before the encounter. He argues that the dialectical relationship between humanity and nature has now got to the historical point at which both are irrevocably different from what they were before that moment. Following Critical Realism, Chernilo (2021: 16f) highlights that dialectics has a historical dimension, as no action takes place in a vacuum, and that actions of past agents become the structures of the present, which both constrain and enable the options that are available to current actors. In turn, contemporary actions are to become the social structures of the future. Fremaux and Barry (2019: 7) also apply the concept of dialectics and criticize post-humanist thinkers who have tried to show how much nature and culture are entangled and how much our world is made up of "nature-cultures" and hybrids. They argue that it is possible to acknowledge the increasing intertwinement of nature and society around us – and inside us – without abandoning the analytic (and ethically significant) distinction between human societies and nature's "non-identity" (otherness). They claim that postmodern "identity thinking," which proclaims that "nature is dead," is an attempt to reduce the other to the self (Fremaux & Barry, 2019: 1f). Instead, they take the dialectical approach according to which nature is identical (a product of human action) as well as non-identical (a process that escapes human power and knowledge) (Fremaux & Barry, 2019: 10). To Fremaux and Barry (2019: 11), the concept of nature's non-identity (Adorno) defines what in nature is ungraspable and unknowable by concepts and therefore escapes the process of domination, and they criticize the fact that instrumental reason has attempted to override non-identity. They argue that the idea of the control of nature fails in the face of the non-identity of nature, implying that nature can never be totally subsumed under social practices and that its own logic must be respected to avoid negative and tragic feedback loops or consequences. These authors state that, on the one hand, nature is a discursive and practical social construction, but that, on the other hand, it produces society and remains a principle of production on its own that displays processes that societies cannot control, know, or manage (Fremaux & Barry 2019: 11). To Fremaux and Barry (2019: 13), the shift to the Anthropocene should be an invitation to rethink politics in a more democratic way, taking into account the necessity to limit ourselves, to repair what is repairable, or to withdraw as much as possible when necessary for sustainability and/or ethical reasons. Such a moral conception of politics would need to replace the individualistic ethos of liberal democracies with concern for the common good, and to replace the current "destruction of nature as usual" scenario with new philosophical and political narratives that call for the respect of the ecological communities to which we all belong.

Other scholars argue that human reason and enlightenment have created the challenges of the Anthropocene. At the same time, they argue that it is only human reason and enlightenment that can bring humanity back on track. The historian Chakrabarty (2019: 30) indicates that any theory of politics that is adequate for dealing with the planetary crisis humans face today would have to begin from the premise of securing human life, grounding itself in a new philosophical anthropology, that is, in a new understanding of the changing place of humans in the "web of life." Chakrabarty argues that the Anthropocene might best be seen as an unintended consequence of human choices and activities, whether political or scientific, and that, in the era of the Anthropocene, we need enlightenment, reason, and reflexive knowledge even more than in the past (Verburgt, 2021: 5).

Alongside Chakrabarty, Chernilo (2021) argues that a continuously reflexive form of modernization is to be preferred rather than "throwing out the modern baby with the bathwater" (Chernilo, 2021: 23). To Chernilo, the idea of reflexive modernization allows us to explicitly articulate our normative goals and then think through what are the implications of their (im)possible implementation. Referring to philosopher Hans Jonas, Chernilo (2021: 24) develops an idea of humanity for whom the stewardship of the planet's natural resources, environments, and different forms of life to secure the continuation of human life in the future ought to be its most important moral duty. To Chernilo, present generations bear a moral obligation to leave the planet in a habitable state, to allow future human beings to lead a fully human life.

The unified notion of the Anthropos

Several scholars criticize the notion of the Anthropocene for being too little concerned with differences in the world between the Global North and the Global South, the poor and the rich, the powerful and the disempowered. Many of these scholars question the narrative of an undifferentiated world where everybody everywhere carries the same responsibility for the life-threatening development. They argue that this undifferentiated narrative might overshadow the fact that the responsibility for many previous as well as present challenges cannot be attributed equally to humans all over the world but must be laid primarily at the door of a few people who are dominating many other people (see also Chapters 3 and 4).

Dobson (2022: 128) argues that in the dominant account of the Anthropocene, the "battle" between humans and nature takes precedence over the social struggles within the Anthropos. The concept of the Anthropocene thus plays an ideological role by obscuring the relative roles of rich and poor in bringing about environmental and social problems. Following the same line of argument, Lövbrand et al. (2015: 9) state that, when linking environmental change to social categories such as class, race, gender, power, and capital, it becomes clear that the challenges of the Anthropocene are far from universal. Rather, they emerge from different sociopolitical settings, produce different kinds of exposure and vulnerability, and will therefore most likely generate different kinds of political response. They further argue that to resist unified accounts of "the human," it is important to situate people and social groups in patterns of cultural and historical diversity (Lövbrand et al., 2015: 14). Somewhat similarly, Biermann et al. (2016: 342) indicate that, while the Anthropocene concept can be powerful in raising awareness of the overall human impacts on our planet, it risks being framed in a way that is too "global" and monolithic, neglecting persistent social inequalities and regional differences. According to these authors, the vast human inequality that characterizes the 21st century should be recognized within the conceptual frame of the Anthropocene if the concept is to be operationalized in research practice and policy development.

Amoureux and Reddy (2021: 2) argue for a project of "Multiple Anthropocenes" that acknowledges ongoing extinctions and exterminations of biological life-forms, epistemologies, histories, relationships, and values or ways of life, as well as different agencies and responses. Likewise, Hoelle and Kawa (2021: 658) argue for applying the notion of the "Pluriverse" as a broad transcultural compilation of concepts, worldviews, and practices from around the world, challenging the modernist ontology of universalism in favor of a multiplicity of possible worlds. These types of idea are implied in criticisms of the Anthropocene discourse for overlooking the ecological impacts of the misrecognition of different vulnerable groups. Hoelle and Kawa further indicate that perspectives from ecofeminism, environmental racism, and environmental justice argue that reconnection requires confronting the linkages between capitalism, racism, and sexism that result in environmental degradation and disproportionately affect the poor, women, and people of color. These types of idea are reiterated by proponents of Global South perspectives. Different aspects of the current understandings of the Anthropocene, such as the ontological split between nature and society, the assumption of the centrality and individuality of the human, and the framing of environmental discourse in largely scientific terms, have been criticized by scholars applying concepts rooted in the criticism of colonialism and postcolonialism. Arguing from a "Global South" perspective, Simpson (2020: 65) saw the underpinnings of the Anthropocene as reinforcing the colonial separation of nature and culture and the associated narratives of enlightenment as man's progressive mastery of nature. This means that the Anthropocene narrative could be deployed to suggest that further modernist interventions are necessary to carry us out of a state of environmental crises. Simpson further argues that epistemological critique of the Anthropocene should question the procedures of knowledge creation that the natural sciences privilege, such as have been produced in the white intellectual space of the Euro-Western academy, where not all humans equally are invited to participate. This implies that other narratives related to environmental change and possible responses struggle to be heard.

To substantiate their notion of the Multiple Anthropocenes, Amoureux and Reddy (2021: 10) describe how indigenous communities, relationships, and knowledge practices have been disrupted by colonialism, capitalism, and industrialization, featuring the loss not just of people but also of land and relationships extending to nonhuman agents with their own agency and spiritual and material significance. In a similar vein, also focusing on indigenous knowledge systems and indigenous conceptions of nature, Inoue and Moreira (2016: 2) argue that the recognition of "many worlds" implies that there are many knowledge systems and different notions of nature that guide and engage agents toward the global environment. Instead of a "post nature" world, they propose that there are many nature(s). They highlight that indigenous peoples' conceptions of nature can be rather differentiated. Generally, however, indigenous knowledge can be characterized by being holistic, embedded, and bounded in the local, and by the importance of the community and moral values. There is no separation between nature and culture, or between subject and object. Also, there is no separation among the physical, spiritual, emotional, and intellectual dimensions. Thus, epistemological parity among knowledge systems could be seen as a fundamental part of indigenous peoples' struggles (Inoue & Moreira, 2016: 13). Inoue and Moira (2016: 15) further argue that the uniqueness of indigenous peoples' knowledge regarding their homelands and ecosystems would also be an important pragmatic reason to consider including it in global environmental governance.

Alternative understandings of what is driving the Anthropocene

Some scholars criticize the notion of the Anthropocene for being too unaware of the indirect drivers that are producing the ecological and socioecological challenges that are facing the planet. Critical conceptions of these drivers vary widely.

Scholars such as the sociologist Jason Moore have suggested naming the epoch the "Capitalocene." This implies that capitalism is the fundamental reason for the ecological crisis, rather than just humans in general (Hoelle & Kawa, 2021: 659). According to Moore (2016: 6f), the Capitalocene does not stand for capitalism as an economic and social system; rather, it signifies capitalism as a way of organizing nature as a multispecies, situated, monist "capitalist world-ecology." The term captures the basic historical pattern of world history as the "Age of Capital" – and the era of capitalism as an integrated world-ecology of power, capital, and nature that has been developed in successive historical configurations. Jansen and Jongerden (2021: 639) highlight that crucial to Moore's understanding of capitalism as a world-ecology is the relationship between Marx's "law of value" and Moore's "law of Cheap Nature." Following Marx, Moore defines a "law" as a "durable pattern of power and production" and "value" as abstract social labor determined by socially necessary labor time. However, Moore argues that for capital to accumulate, it ceaselessly searches for a rising stream of low-cost

(1) food; (2) labor power; (3) energy; and (4) raw materials to reduce socially necessary labor time. Capitalism, in Moore's perspective, is centered on the Cartesian separation of humanity and nature, enabling the separation of direct producers and the means of production (Reichel & Perey, 2018: 243). Moore suggests that capitalism has entered an era of epochal crisis (Reichel & Perey, 2018: 298) as the options for finding new frontiers have been reduced (Jansen & Jongerden, 2021: 639). In Moore's monist view, which he refers to using the term "singular metabolism," capital and nature cannot be separated even by abstraction.

To Jansen and Jongerden (2021: 645), Moore's analysis tends to obscure: (1) contradictions between capital and its antagonists; (2) social struggles around these contradictions; and (3) the possibility of change. They argue that his monism runs the risk of reducing everything to the singular. Instead, they apply the notion of dialectics as a process in which social change occurs as a result of contradictions between the parts from which the whole emerges; some parts, such as elements of nature, should be distinguished analytically and not fully turned social. They state that a dialectical approach necessitates a language in which one distinguishes nature and society, labor, and capital, etc.

To act collectively to protect the people and the planet, Jansen and Jongerden (2021: 642) argue, it will be necessary to find new ways of conceptualizing intersections between class relationships and other social relationships, tensions, contradictions, and forms of power such as gender, ethnicity, and identity and, furthermore, to lean toward practice, looking at ruptures and resistance, hegemony, and autonomy. They state that a worrying effect of representing capitalism as a unitary substance is the emphasis on its self-sustaining character. This may have the performative effect of underscoring its strength while rendering invisible the cracks, while agency and imaginations of alternatives turn irrelevant and unrealizable. Instead of a capitalism that is beyond any control and for which we must just wait until it destroys itself, the authors argue for conceptualizing capitalism as constituted by a set of rules and practices that are produced and reproduced, as well as distorted and disrupted through enactments. Furthermore, they highlight that the notion of the Capitalocene seems to have only one kind of capitalist. They argue that raw material suppliers, energy companies, large food producers, and service firms that organize the supply of labor do not necessarily benefit from going cheap. Therefore, they find it important not to presume a unified capitalist going-cheap strategy but to study how different groups try to make the commodities they sell expensive: creating monopolies by pushing for certain state regulations (e.g., quality criteria, import barriers), demanding stricter law enforcement that excludes price-reducing competitors, reducing production through cartels, and so on (Jansen & Jongerden, 2021: 644). As an alternative to Moore's unified capital–nature system, Jansen and Jongerden (2021: 644f) suggest distinguishing between capital and capitalism. While capital is value in motion, capitalism is a social formation in which capital accumulation is hegemonic in shaping the material basis of social life. However, this social formation encompasses various contradictions and inequalities, among them gender, ethnicity, and (cultural) identity, co-determining outcomes.

In line with the arguments of Jansen and Jongerden, representing, however, an institutional approach to analyzing the history of capitalism, Görg et al. (2020: 44) view history not as a linear unfolding of underlying economic drivers but as a sequence of discrete growth models stabilized by political and cultural institutions. To these authors, as the driver of the Anthropocene, capitalism, and its history represents an interplay between the continuity of the structural conditions of capitalism and the discontinuity of specific institutional constellations that stabilizes certain phases. Structural conditions mean primarily the accumulation imperative shaped by underlying tensions and contradictions that cause periodic crises. The institutional patterns that respond to these crises within a certain mode of regulation represent economic and political institutions as well as cultural standards and technical innovations (accumulation regimes). These institutional patterns stabilize capitalism for a while but without resolving the underlying contradictions (Görg et al., 2020: 51).

Highlighted by Jansen and Jongerden, Foster argues that the notion of the "Capitalocene" eliminates the very possibility for an ecological critique of the relation between capitalism and the Anthropocene. By reducing capitalism and nature to one substance, the contradictions between capitalism and nature are dissolved. Foster also expresses concern about Moore attacking both the green movement and ecological Marxists for worrying about the growing rifts in the planetary boundaries of the Earth system and for excluding the perspectives of the ecological movements. Whereas Moore expects a transition of capitalism in the near future, since the end of Cheap Nature is arriving at high speed, Foster emphasizes the political project of socialism as the source for change (Jansen & Jongerden 2021: 641; see also Chapter 11).

Linking an understanding of the fundamental drivers to the need to identify sources of change, Haraway (2015: 160) adds the responsibility for all types of species. Focusing on the plantation processes ("Plantationocene"), she states that it is important to take into consideration the networks of sugar, precious metals, plantations, indigenous genocides, and slavery, with their labor innovations and relocations sweeping up both human and nonhuman workers of all kinds. She argues that since the Earth is full of human and nonhuman refugees without a refuge, the job is "to make the Anthropocene as short/thin as possible and to cultivate with each other in every way imaginable Epochs to come that can replenish refuge." Her phrase "making kin" is a metaphor for multispecies ecojustice that embraces diverse human and nonhuman species. Haraway writes within a strong discourse in the humanities and social sciences that is present in such fields and disciplines as design thinking, urban planning, social innovation and intervention, postcolonial studies, and heterodox economy. Such articulations of conviviality and interspecies coexistence are also becoming influential in political agenda-setting.

Thus, the United Nations Development Programme (UNDP) (2020: 89) highlights that "rethinking of our humanity can include its co-construction with nonhuman natures. This recognizes the intimate interconnectedness of human lives with all living things, their dynamism and agency." This includes an understanding of the interrelationships between humans and nonhumans, which are often intimate, affective, emotional, and embodied. In the end "these perspectives redefine humanity as part of nature" to avoid processes of "othering" (UNDP, 2020: 89). Finally, the UNDP depicts how this ultimately questions the Cartesian divide between the human and the nonhuman and calls for an approach that is more embedded in the knowledge tradition of many so-called indigenous societies.

Davis et al. (2018: 3), however, criticize the multispecies framing of the Plantationocene for minimizing the role of racial politics, arguing that this framing leads to a flattened notion of "making kin" that is inadequate for the creation of more just ecologies. In a broader perspective, they criticize that even critical Anthropocene scholars only mention the chasm between rich and poor, or developed and developing, countries as if the geography of wealth and power was nonracial. These authors emphasize that the preconditions for the development of global capitalism were shaped through processes of settler colonialism and enslavement, organized and rationalized by racism, and they track the ideology and practice of "the plantation" toward the prison and the impoverished and destroyed city sectors as an ongoing locus of anti-Black violence and death. According to Davis et al. (2018: 4), in Haraway's account, human labor only receives brief attention and the matters of Black embodiment and the disciplinary regimes of slavery remain obscured together with the deep history of Black struggle.

Following Escobar (2018: 139), multidimensional design represents a hope with respect to the "increasingly devastating anthropogenic forces." To Escobar (2017: 45), as a very broad term, critical design studies is a way of bridging critical approaches stemming from the Global North and the Global South as a pathway to design for autonomy that includes a responsibility for conviviality as well as a "practice of inter-existence and inter-being." While, historically, design has been embedded in global historical relations of power and domination, there is a growing interest for "novel framings of design praxis, such as those going under the rubrics of decolonial design" and other typologies that are parts of a trend across the scientific disciplines questioning "the modern/colonial matrix of power, the geopolitics of knowledge (eurocentrism), racism, and patriarchal capitalist colonial modernity" (Escobar, 2018: 140).

While acknowledging that capitalism is an important driver of development in the Anthropocene, Reichel and Perey (2018: 243f) regard it as a problem substituting the notion of the Anthropocene by applying the notion of the Capitalocene because capitalism is not the only but one of many ideologies framing economic activities. Thus, the notion of the Capitalocene lacks the more inclusive character of the Anthropocene. They argue that previously existing economic systems such as communism may have applied a different sociopolitical rationale to organizing economics and yet share with capitalism a foundational belief in growth. They further argue that hierarchical and "growth-addicted" societies existed long before the emergence of capitalism and criticize that, for example, Marxist analysis is biased toward economic explanations for political injustices and distortions. They state that such bias ignores political interests and larger cultural currents that influence economic behavior, which jointly shape our societies (Reichel & Perey, 2018: 244). Instead of only focusing on capital and capitalism, they apply a degrowth perspective and propose a radical reimagination of what it means to live well within present and future societies. The political consequence inherent in this perspective is the need to dematerialize consumer society, demanding new societal and economic models (Reichel & Perey, 2018: 245). To Reichel and Perey (2018: 246), degrowth requires a fundamental change in the underlying political-economic-cultural mindset and the abandoning of growth as a conceptual and practical ideal and norm. It also requires new types of global governance, such as Frank Biermann's proposals for a UN Sustainable Development Council as an enforcer of the UN Sustainable Development Goals, a World Environment Organization along the lines of the World Trade Organization, and a Global Environmental Assessment Commission to evaluate global and national policymaking for its impact on the natural environment (Reichel & Perey, 2018: 247). Reichel and Perey (2018: 247) argue that their perspective positions degrowth as an important social-ecological transition discourse that complements alternatives to development, rights of nature, and social justice discourses across both the developed and the developing worlds and that it could dissolve the binary distinction between the Global North and the Global South (see also Chapters 4 and 11).

Summary

In this chapter we have taken our departure in the notion of the Anthropocene. Although the Anthropocene epoch has not yet been accepted by the International Commission of Stratigraphy, the notion is widely applied in scientific reports and publications. The notion changes modernist ideas of space and time and divisions between nature and society, and presents the Earth as being radically destabilized by human activities, especially during the last 70 years. We have presented a discussion of the notion within the natural sciences and expanded our view to encompass conceptualizations of the notion within the social sciences and the humanities, focusing on the human–nature relation, the unified notion of the Anthropos, and different understandings of what is driving the Anthropocene.

Some social scientists and scholars of the humanities argue that, in the Anthropocene, nowhere does nature exist outside of human impact, and nowhere do human societies exist outside nature. This implies that nature is completely transformed by humans to the extent that the barrier between humans and nature has been crossed and there is no longer a viable road back from this trajectory. Other scholars criticize this concept of identity between humans and nature, arguing that even if the relationship between humans and nature has been changed and mutually intertwined, what is at play is identity as well as non-identity. From their dialectical point of view, it is important to understand the evolutionary logics and working operations of nature that created the Earth as a livable planet long before humans came on the scene. To their view, it is important to acknowledge that human reflectivity and collective learning processes represent another "mode of production" than the evolutionary processes of nature. Therefore, on the one hand, humans must acknowledge that their actions are destroying nature and their own future; on the other hand, through the means of critical reflection and collective learning, they must recognize nature's intrinsic values and prevent the destruction of its life-sustaining operations.

The natural science conceptualization of the Anthropocene is criticized for creating a picture of a single connected humanity being responsible for global climate change and the environmental challenges. Critical scholars argue against this construction of a unitary subject because it hides who are the most responsible for creating the challenges and who will suffer the most. Some authors argue for the concepts of "Multiple Anthropocenes," "Multiple Natures," or the "Pluriverse" to highlight different responsibilities and to recognize different worldviews that should be respected to promote ecological and socioecological transformation. The notion of "Multiple Anthropocenes" also includes the recognition of indigenous worldviews, ontologies, and epistemologies that contain no separation between nature and culture or between the physical, the spiritual, the emotional, and the intellectual realms of life. This pluralistic notion is very different from the unitary notions that present the human–nature identity in the Anthropocene as a global phenomenon.

The theoretical dialog between proponents of unitary or monist views and supporters of dialectical views is reiterated in Marxist debates on the character and drivers of the present epoch. However, in this debate, the discussion between proponents of the "single subject" and those of "dialectical processes" has a very different character. In the notion of the "Capitalocene," nature is totally subsumed by the logic of capital to one single "World Ecology." According to this concept, because capital is dependent on the continuous stream of low-cost resources and because these resources are getting scarce, capital will soon destruct itself. Eco-Marxists question this monist model, arguing that societal development is shaped by more complex combinations of "capital-logics" and path- and power-dependent institutionalized societal formations, alongside cracks, multiple types of contradiction, and antagonisms. To these authors, the Capitalocene conceptualization of the epoch is at risk of inhibiting collective human action from transforming the ecological and socioecological trajectory toward sustainable development. Other authors argue that seeing capital as the only driver of climate change, environment degradation, and social challenges neglects the fact that dependency on and extraction of a limited resource base characterize different societal models, including premodern and "communist" models. This is not conceived as an argument against being critical of capital; rather, it is seen as putting a stronger emphasis on the general problem of resource extraction, arguing for degrowth. The concept of the "Plantationocene" emphasizes colonialism and postcolonialism as important drivers underlying the present condition. Multispecies justice recognizes the interconnectedness of human lives with all living things. In such articulations of conviviality and interspecies coexistence, the job is to make kin as a metaphor for multispecies ecojustice, to avoid processes of "othering," Critical design studies have expanded this focus on interspecies justice by questioning the overall modern/colonial matrix of power, the geopolitics of knowledge (eurocentrism), racism, and patriarchal, capitalist, colonial modernity.

In the next chapter of the book, we will turn our attention to the question of knowledge creation and interdisciplinary research. Why do we need new forms of knowledge creation and interdisciplinary research to address ecological and socioecological challenges in the Anthropocene; which barriers are confronting this kind of knowledge creation and research efforts; which traditions are there to build on; and which new pathways could be followed?

References

Amoureux, J. and Reddy, V. (2021). Multiple Anthropocenes: Pluralizing space–time as a response to "the Anthropocene." *Globalizations*, 18(6), 929–946. DOI: 10.1080/14747731.2020.1864178

Baskin, J. (2015). Paradigm dressed as epoch: The ideology of the Anthropocene. *Environmental Values*, 24, 9–29. DOI: 10.3197/096327115X141831823537

Bhatasara, S. (2015). Debating sociology and climate change. *Journal of Integrative Environmental Sciences*, 12(3), 217–233. DOI: 10.1080/1943815X.2015.1108342

Biermann, F. (2021). The future of "environmental" policy in the Anthropocene: Time for a paradigm shift. *Environmental Politics*, 30(1–2), 61–80. DOI:10.1080/09644016.2020.1846958

Biermann, F., Baic, X., Bondred, N., Broadgatee, W., Chenf, C.-T. A., Dubeg, O. P., Erismanh, J. W., Glaser, M., van der Helk, S., Lemos, M. C., Seitzingerm, S. and Seton, K. C. (2016). Down to earth: Contextualizing the Anthropocene. *Global Environmental Change*, 39, 241–350. DOI: 10.1016/j.gloenvcha.2015.11.004

Burke, A., and Bierman, S. F. (2019). Power, world politics and thing-systems in the Anthropocene. In F. Biermann & E. Lövbrand (eds.), *Anthropocene encounters: New directions in green political thinking*, 1–27. Cambridge University Press.

Chakrabarty, D. (2019). The planet: An emergent humanist category. *Critical Inquiry*, 46(1), 1–31.

Chernilo, D. (2021). One globalisation or many? Risk society in the age of the Anthropocene. *Journal of Sociology*, 57(1), 12–26. DOI: 10.1177/1440783321997563

Crutzen, P. J. and Stoermer, E. F. (2000). The "Anthropocene." *Global Change Newsletter*, 41, 17–18.

Davis, J., Moulton, A. A., Van Sant, L. and Wil, B. (2018). Anthropocene, Capitalocene,... Plantationocene? A manifesto for ecological justice in an age of global crises. *Geography Compass*, 13, 1–15. DOI: 10.1111/gec3.12438

Dobson, A. (2022). Emancipation in the Anthropocene: Taking the dialectic seriously. *European Journal of Social Theory*, 25(1), 118–135. DOI: 10.1177/13684310211028148

Escobar, A. (2017). Response: Design for/by (and from) the 'global South'. *Design Philosophy Papers*, 15(1), 39–49. DOI: 10.1080/14487136.2017.1301016

Escobar, A. (2018). Autonomous design and the emergent transanational critical design studies. *Strategic design Research Journal*, 11(2), 139–146 May-August 2018. Unisinos – DOI: 10.4013/sdrj.2018.112.10

Folke, C., Polasky, S. Rockström, J., Galaz, V., Westley, F., Lamont, M., Scheffer, M., Österblom, H., Carpenter, S. R., Chapin III, F. S., Seto, K. C., Weber, E. U., Crona, B. I., Daily, G. C., Dasgupta, P., Gaffney, O., Gordon, L. J., Hoff, H., Levin, S. A., Lubchenco, J., Steffen, W., and Walker, B. H. (2021). Our future in the Anthropocene biosphere. *Ambio*, 50, 834–869. DOI: 10.1007/s13280-021-01544-8

Fremaux, A., and Barry, J. (2019). The "Good Anthropocene" and green political theory: Rethinking environmentalism, resisting ecomodernism. In: F. Biermann & E. Lövbrand (eds.), *Anthropocene encounters: New directions in green political thinking*, 171–190. Cambridge University Press. Retrieved from https://www.researchgate.net/publication/330762459_The_Good_Anthropocene_and_Green_Political_Theory_Rethinking_Environmentalism_Resisting_Eco-modernism

Görg, C., Plank, C., Wiedenhofer, D., Mayer, A., Pichler, M., Schaffartzik, A. and Krausmann, F. (2020). Scrutinizing the great acceleration: The Anthropocene and its analytic challenges for social-ecological transformations. *The Anthropocene Review*, 7(1), 42–61. DOI: 10.1177/2053019619895034

Grove, K. and Chandler, D. (2017). Introduction: Resilience and the Anthropocene: The stakes of "renaturalising" politics. *Resilience*, 5(2), 79–91. DOI: 10.1080/21693293.2016.1241476

Haraway, D. (2015). Anthropocene, capitalocene, plantationocene, chthulucene: Making kin. *Environmental Humanities*, 6, 159–165.

Hoelle, J. and Kawa, N. C. (2021). Placing the anthropos in Anthropocene. *Annals of the American Association of Geographers*, 111(3), 655–662. DOI: 10.1080/24694452.2020.1842171

Inoue, C. Y. A. and Moreira, P. F. (2016). Many worlds, many nature(s), one planet: Indigenous knowledge in the Anthropocene. *Revista Brasileira de Política Internacional*, 59(2). DOI: 10.1590/0034-7329201600209

Jansen, K., and Jongerden, J. (2021). The capitalocene response to the Anthropocene. In: H. Akram-Lodhi, K. Dietz, B. Engels & B. McKay (eds.), *The Edward Elgar handbook of critical Agrarian studies*, 637–647. Edward Elgar. DOI: 10.4337/9781788972468

Latour, B. and Chakrabarty, D. (2020). Conflicts of planetary proportion: A conversation. *Journal of the Philosophy of History*, 14, 1–36. DOI: 10.1163/18722636-12341450

Lövbrand, E., Beck, S., Chilvers, J., Forsyth, T., Hedrén, J., Hulme, M., Lidskog, R. and Vasileiadou, E. (2015). Who speaks for the future of Earth? How critical social science can extend the conversation on the Anthropocene. *Global Environmental Change*, 32(211–218), 1–24. Retrieved from: http://eprints.lse.ac.uk/61703/

Moore, J. W. (2016). *Anthropocene or capitalocene? Nature, history, and the crisis of capitalism*. Sociology Faculty Scholarship. Retrieved from: https://orb.binghamton.edu/sociology_fac/1

Reichel, A. and Perey, R. (2018). Moving beyond growth in the Anthropocene. *The Anthropocene Review*, 5(3), 242–249. DOI: 10.1177/2053019618799104

Simpson, M. (2020). The Anthropocene as colonial discourse. *EPD: Society and Space*, 38(1), 53–71. DOI: 10.1177/0263775818764679

Toivanen, T., Lummaa, K., Majava, A., Järvensivu, P., Lähde, V., Vaden, T. and Eronen, J. T. (2017). The many Anthropocenes: A transdisciplinary challenge for the Anthropocene research. *The Anthropocene Review*, 1–16. DOI: 10.1 177/2053019617738099

UNDP Human Development Report (2020). The next frontier: Human development and the Anthropocene, 412 pages. Retrieved from: http://hdr.undp.org/sites/default/files/hdr2020.pdf

Verburgt, L. M. (2021). History, scientific ignorance, and the Anthropocene. *Journal for the History of Knowledge*, 2(1), 1–12. DOI: 10.5334/jhk.46

Weber, M. (2005). *The protestant ethic and the spirit of capitalism*. New York: Routledge.

Zehr, S. (2015). The sociology of global climate change. *WIREs Climate Change*, 6, 129–150. DOI: 10.1002/wcc.328

13 Interdisciplinary research and knowledge creation

Anders Siig Andersen, Henrik Hauggaard-Nielsen, Thomas Budde Christen, and Lars Hulgaard

> We cultivate a project and problem-oriented approach to knowledge creation, because we believe that the most relevant results are obtained by solving real problems in collaboration with others. We employ interdisciplinary approaches because no major problems are ever resolved on the basis of any single academic discipline alone. We also cultivate transparency, because we passionately believe that participation and knowledge-sharing are prerequisites for freedom of thought, democracy, tolerance, and development.
>
> Roskilde University, Denmark

Introduction

The recognition that the Anthropocene confronts humanity with unprecedented ecological and socioecological challenges has questioned several taken-for-granted viewpoints in science and academic scholarship and initiated a multifaceted endeavor to understand and find solutions to new and wicked problems. One reaction by scientists as well as politicians has been a call for increased interdisciplinarity. In this chapter we start by presenting the background for this call and continue by defining interdisciplinarity and by highlighting some of the barriers to implementing the concept. Focusing on ecological and socioecological challenges—and acknowledging that we primarily deal indirectly with the formal sciences (mathematics and computer science) and the applied sciences (e.g., engineering)—we outline some aspects of the history of interdisciplinarity within the natural and social sciences and the humanities, to consider how each of these has adapted to the call. Looking across the three areas, we look at the advances in interdisciplinary research efforts and reflect on possible pathways to lead science and academic scholarship forwards—including the question of how such approaches can translate into private and public practices. We conclude the chapter with some examples from our own multi-actor and participatory action research funded by the EU. These examples cover the areas urban circularity, agroecological food systems, and nature-based solutions.

The call for interdisciplinarity

In recent decades, scientists have provided interdisciplinary knowledge demonstrating that human activities are pushing planetary boundaries toward cascading points of no return and that the current responses to the intertwined character of ecological, social, and economic challenges must be improved to secure a just and fair development. The natural sciences have taken a lead position in analyzing direct drivers, pressures, impacts, and states pertaining to human-enforced changes in the natural environment and the consequences of these changes for the biosphere and embedded humanity. The social sciences and the humanities have contributed significantly to our understanding of socioecological challenges and to critically reflecting on possible solutions. The social sciences have provided insights into the great variety of challenges—from the local to the global scale; the social, political, and economic indirect drivers that are affecting direct drivers, impacts, pressures, and states; and possible solutions regarding economy, technology, governance, innovation, and organization. The humanities have provided knowledge on how ecological and socioecological challenges are perceived by people, and treated in dominant political and counter discourses, and how these challenges are embedded in the meaning making and practices of everyday life. The concept of the Anthropocene has affected existing ideas within most branches of science and academic scholarship. For example, it is no longer viable to keep up the strict division between humans and nature. Today, human history cannot be understood as an upward linear process, spreading the promises of modernization globally, and the dominant idea that human well-being can be secured by continuous growth in gross domestic product (GDP) has become increasingly dubious.

In the context of the Anthropocene (see also Chapter 12), many scientists and academic scholars conceive disciplinary approaches—as well as interdisciplinary approaches between the individual disciplines within faculty boundaries—as necessary and yet problematic. Because human activities are the root cause of the present and future environment and climate challenges, the intertwined character of drivers, challenges, and solutions calls for interdisciplinary knowledge that integrates theory and methods from the natural and the social sciences to the humanities. Brondizio et al. (2016: 319) argue that the concept of the Anthropocene calls for new ways of understanding the interactions between the biophysical system of the planet; the world of social, economic, and political systems and processes; and sensemaking and motivation—in order to move toward a sustainable and socially fair future (see also Chapter 12). Kelly et al. (2019: 150) highlight that disentangling modern ecological and socioecological challenges demands knowledge creation on complex, multi-scale interactions between ecosystems and society as an interdisciplinary endeavor that recognizes the intertwined character of society and the biosphere. Snick (2020) emphasizes that the many current man-made crises challenge specialist paradigms because "yesterday's solutions have turned out to be today's problem" (Snick, 2020: 76). Furthermore, Brondizio et al. (2016: 318f) indicate that the concept of the Anthropocene motivates ethical questions about the politics and economics of global change, including diverse interpretations of past causes and future possibilities (see also the Introduction to this book). For research communities, the call for interdisciplinarity implies a willingness to recognize and appreciate strengths and limitations as well as the dissolving of barriers between knowledge systems.

Brondizio et al. (2016) and Toivanen et al. (2017) argue that possible antagonisms between disciplines should not be neglected, but rather, discussed and researched as fruitful tensions for future scientific understanding (Brondizio et al., 2016: 319; Toivanen et al., 2017: 2). Palsson et al. (2012: 4f) add that such research should go beyond the sterile polarization characteristic of the 1990s' "science wars" and that the social sciences and the humanities should take up the "meta-responsibility" of analyzing the nature of global ecological and socioecological research in general. They state that this call for involvement is both a "call to arms" to the mainstream social sciences and humanities and a call for intensive cooperation with natural scientists in this endeavor, starting with joint framings of key research questions.

Types of interdisciplinarity

To highlight variations within the broad field of interdisciplinary research, we apply a conceptual taxonomy. Distinctions are often made between three forms of interdisciplinarity: (1) "multi-/pluridisciplinarity," (2) "cross-/interdisciplinarity," and (3) "transdisciplinarity," where the degree of conceptual and methodological merging increases from the separation of diverse disciplines working together toward the most integrated type of research, operating with questions, concepts, and methods that do not clearly originate from any specific existing discipline (Andersen & Kjeldsen, 2015: 19f; Toivanen et al., 2017: 2).

Multi-/pluridisciplinary approaches: Multi-/pluridisciplinary approaches feature an additive approach to the disciplines. In these approaches, the collaborating researchers draw on knowledge, theories, and methods from different disciplines, without modifying their disciplinary approaches. The researchers each contribute with their own disciplinary traditions, working in parallel to address a problem defined by a coordinated work process. The goal of multi-/pluridisciplinary approaches is to facilitate a multi-perspective view on research projects. This may be a crucial point for scientific collaboration, as the researchers are being trained in the mutual understanding of their different academic "homelands." This may raise awareness and insights across disciplines to counteract the negative effects of specialization (Andersen & Kjeldsen, 2015: 19; Holzer et al., 2018: 809).

Cross-/interdisciplinary approaches: Cross-/interdisciplinary approaches develop research on the same issues in collaboration and mutual influence across the disciplines. To create holistic knowledge, issues and problems are addressed from many disciplinary perspectives, as theories developed within one discipline affect theories in other disciplines, or as methods developed within one discipline affect the methods of other disciplines. The purpose of these approaches is to integrate knowledge or modes of thinking in two or more disciplines or established areas of expertise. Through cross-/interdisciplinary approaches, researchers from different disciplines create a common academic undertaking and adopt relevant theories and methods from each other, while still retaining their disciplinary independence within the collaboration (Andersen & Kjeldsen, 2015: 19).

Transdisciplinary approaches: The concept of transdisciplinarity signifies that the disciplines needed to explain a problem should work together, subordinating their scientific axioms, theories, and methods to the common research enterprise. Transdisciplinary approaches transcend disciplinary boundaries and transform the disciplines into something new that becomes greater than the sum of its parts; such approaches raise new questions that could not have been raised by a single discipline, nor by a cross-/interdisciplinary effort lacking integration in a problem-solving context (Holzer et al., 2018: 809).

These approaches can be purely academic, or they may involve a collaboration between researchers and a variety of practitioners through a transgression of the boundaries between academic and non-academic knowledge. Wohlgezogen et al. (2020: 1049) argue that by integrating, synthesizing, and reconciling multiple disciplinary problem diagnoses and conceptualizations, transdisciplinary scholarship can support the dialog between researchers and practitioners and develop a shared understanding of the problem and potential solutions. Transdisciplinary research can also assist practitioners in conducting more robust and comprehensive assessments of the likely efficacy and efficiency of alternative pathways. According to Holzer et al. (2018: 809), this type of transdisciplinary research connotes an inclusive team, high standards of knowledge integration, and cooperation with non-academic stakeholders, thereby requiring sophisticated team communication and knowledge-sharing.

As suggested by Andersen and Kjeldsen (2015: 20), transdisciplinary approaches may be divided into two types and four subtypes.

- The transgression of boundaries between scientific disciplines: (A) Transdisciplinary approaches may supplement disciplinary approaches in the study of a research field, or they may be gradually converted into new monodisciplinary fields, as, for instance, in disciplines such as environmental science, mathematical economics, environmental sociology, and human ecology. These examples represent efforts to integrate disciplines to create new specialized disciplines in the intersection of two or more existing disciplines. (B) Transdisciplinarity may be the main approach of research and may prove useful in the study of ecological and socioecological problems as the contributions from single disciplines could be viewed as insufficient to grasp the intertwined complexity. In this instance, the

integration of disciplines is determined by the practical research problem, and transdisciplinarity is seen as the adequate answer to the need for scientific problem solving.
- The transgression of boundaries between scientific and non-scientific knowledge: (A) Transdisciplinary approaches may be practice-oriented and involve external participants, stakeholders, and other participants who are affected by the issues being investigated. On the academic side, this kind of transdisciplinary research may range from multi- to cross-, and transdisciplinary, approaches. The involved academic disciplines, however, undergo different degrees of modifications by linking with non-academic forms of knowledge. This kind of research has generally been defined as Mode 2. Mode 2 research is characterized by a focus on problems as they arise outside an academic context, by including external parties as producers of knowledge, and by knowledge being produced in the context of use. It is socially distributed and accountable to multiple actors. The primary aim of Mode 2 research is, pragmatically speaking, to generate knowledge that is socially robust. Problems are formulated in dialog with researchers and stakeholders, who use a range of heterogeneous skills and expertise to elicit knowledge, and they develop research projects via the interaction between science and application. (B) Transdisciplinary approaches may also have a more emancipatory focus, aimed at helping non-scientific local participants to change their situation and enhance their power to control their own lives. This type of research is often termed "participatory action research" based on principles of collaboration, such as collaborative problem identification and formulation, co-diagnosis, co-design, co-implementation, co-governance, co-monitoring, co-creation, and co-production. Local participants formulate the problems to be understood and solved and involve researchers in this knowledge creation and problem solving. Researchers may support the local participants by helping formulate their needs for research and by providing expert assistance for developing solutions, keeping in mind that the local participants should "own their projects" (see also Holzer et al., 2018: 808).

According to Wohlgezogen et al. (2020: 1050), another distinction can be made between narrow interdisciplinarity and broad interdisciplinarity. Narrow interdisciplinarity connects disciplines with similar epistemologies. This means that two or more fields that share similar theoretical, methodological, and terminological basis engage in interdisciplinary research and coexist. For example, Earth system sciences is a combination of geology, meteorology, oceanography, and astronomy that all share similar epistemological backgrounds. Broad interdisciplinarity connects disciplines with dissimilar epistemologies (e.g., physics and sociology; for examples, see below in this chapter). Connecting the natural and social sciences and the humanities is the most distinct example of broad interdisciplinarity.

In institutional settings such as research projects, power relations between disciplines may be asymmetric. This may be the case when natural and social scientists collaborate on large projects funded by external institutions. In this mode, social scientists are expected to adopt the "correct" natural science definition of an environmental problem and to devise relevant solution strategies or strategies to support the involvement of institutional or civil actors. In many instances, social science aspects of these projects function as an "add on" to the main project. Kelly et al. (2019: 150) highlight that sometimes narrowly focused research programs are conducted under the banner of interdisciplinarity. Here, a commonly voiced issue is the late inclusion of a "token" researcher from a different discipline (often, from the social sciences) after a research program has been designed, rather than integrating all disciplinary perspectives from the beginning. Alternatives to these kinds of projects would be interdisciplinary projects that are developed in close collaboration with different disciplines and characterized by mutual recognition and symmetric power relations (for examples, see below).

Barriers to interdisciplinarity

Snick (2020: 78) argues that the division of sciences into separate silos makes it very difficult for the single sciences to contribute to the co-creation of pathways for sustainability. If sustainability is integrated into academia, it is often "neutralized" by transforming it into a new discipline or specialism, and not taken as a paradigm for all science—one that requires it to break out of its silos and redefine its aim from one of "increasing competitiveness" to "reinforcing societal and natural wisdom and peace." The idea and practice of interdisciplinary research is challenged by a set of dilemmas that are visible in research institutions, communities, and policy. On the one hand, it is emphasized that the understanding of real-life problems cannot be limited to a single academic discipline; so-called "wicked problems" call for interdisciplinary research and require researchers who integrate knowledge, methods, and ways of thinking from different disciplines. On the other hand, academic specialization seems to be an embedded norm that persists with respect to research included in institutional procedures for promotions that threaten to undermine any attempt to rethink research and practices. For example, Kelly et al. (2019: 150) claim that research that successfully integrates social, human, health, and natural science realms is a rarity because the culture, structures, and practices necessary to facilitate interdisciplinary research are lacking. The barriers to interdisciplinary research can be categorized as detailed below.

a   It is a persistent norm that good science is produced within the academic disciplines. Norms governing the success of interdisciplinary research are less codified than those of disciplinary work.
b   It is a widespread belief that high-quality research is disseminated in scientific journals, which are aligned with the academic disciplines.

Specialization requires similarly specialized audiences who are qualified to evaluate the quality of research. This compartmentalization implies self-referential subcultures.

c   Disciplinarity remains a core element of the social order of modern science. Universities and professional associations continue to be organized mainly along disciplinary lines.

d   Institutional features of funding structures make interdisciplinary research harder to initiate. Funding proposals that straddle these lines (i.e., falling between natural and social sciences) are largely judged from single disciplinary perspectives, which lack the expertise necessary to assess research proposals outside their core disciplines.

e   Despite increasing job opportunities in temporary interdisciplinary research centers and networks, most permanent academic positions are still located within disciplinary contexts. As such, academics seeking permanent positions will largely be judged by disciplinary standards (Andersen & Kjeldsen, 2015: 22f; Inkpen & DesRoches, 2019: 4; Kelly et al., 2019: 150; Koehrsen et al., 2019: 10).

From the point of view of researchers, many scientists and scholars in academia consider that they are under pressure and exposed to hard competition. They respond by acting in accordance with the rules of the scientific disciplines, which are assessed by the application of internal disciplinary standards. This may be seen as a means of meeting academic standards as well as publishing requirements that can be best achieved through publishing in journals that align with the academic disciplines (Andersen & Kjeldsen, 2015: 32). Researchers may be reluctant to engage with interdisciplinary research because they do not receive recognition for their efforts in their home disciplines and because academic organization and culture often penalize interdisciplinary research. Ultimately, there is a risk that this defensive position will lead to the conclusion that the boundaries between disciplines should not be transgressed and that researchers should not engage in direct collaboration with the outside world (Olesen & Andersen, 2015: 277).

Bhatasara (2015: 228) exemplifies the tension field of disciplinarity and interdisciplinarity by highlighting the development within sociology. Sociology comprises a range of subfields, many of which do not combine on a day-to-day basis. Environmental sociology, which has its roots in the environmental movement of the 1970s, suits into, for example, climate change research. According to Bhatsara, however, environmental sociologists are isolated from the discipline's mainstream, featuring sparsely at the bigger conferences, and publishing in different journals. He indicates that dominant coalitions and their status hierarchy within the field of sociology persist, and that there are no signs to suggest any radical change. Bhatsara also argues that the standard evaluation procedures undervalue any interdisciplinary cooperation as not useful for the advancement of core sociological theory and methodology.

In addition to institutional and cultural barriers, different epistemologies play an important role as a barrier to interdisciplinarity. Toivanen et al. (2017: 9) highlight that the divide between the natural sciences (that seek to explain nature) and the humanities (that seek to understand human life) originates from the 19th century—as, for example, articulated by C. P. Snow in his analysis of the "Two Cultures." Whereas the natural sciences rely on empiricism and verifiability, the humanities build their body of knowledge through interpretative and critical modes of inspection. Palsson et al. (2012: 4) state that when the general awareness of our ecological predicament started to emerge in the early 20th century, the human sciences contributed significantly. In line with modernist theories about technology and progress, however, the postwar framing of the environment reduced it to an object of natural science. The "eternal truth of mathematics" nurtured the idea that science reveals objective truths about reality. This means that scientific progress has been widely associated with quantitative methodologies, while qualitative aspects of life were dismissed as "subjective," belonging to the domains of arts and religion. After World War II, in the social sciences and the humanities, the tendency toward the use of quantitative methods to process "data" has also been gradually growing.

Urry (2015: 46) argues that, because economics got into the field of climate change first and because most major studies of climate change issues involve economic analysis, economics monopolized the framing of humans in their understanding of, and debate around, climate change. This led to a focus on human practices as individualistic, market-based, and calculative, and thus generated responses to climate change based on individual calculation to modify behavior, new technologies to fix the problem, and developing markets for novel "green products" (see also Chapter 11). According to Urry (2015: 47), the economist approach misrecognizes that most of the time people do not behave as individually rational economic consumers, maximizing their utility from the basket of goods and services they purchase and use. People are also creatures of social routine and habit that stem from the many ways that they are locked into social practices and social institutions, including families, households, friendship groups, social classes, genders, work groups, businesses, schools, ethnicities, age, and cohorts.

During the 1980s, certain branches of the humanities and the social sciences paid growing critical attention to the natural sciences, interpreting their societal role and knowledge production as cultural constructions. Among the empirically oriented natural scientists, these ideas were perceived as a direct assault, resulting in the "science wars" during the 1990s (Toivanen et al., 2017: 11). Social constructivists reject the notion that there is anything self-evident to be found out there. As such, constructionists tend to frame climate change as a political and social issue. According to Bhatasara (2015: 220), this framing has raised alarm particularly within the scientific and modeling community. According to Toivanen et al. (2017: 11), the science wars have resulted in a paralyzing stalemate where the epistemological and methodological differences prevail.

Brondizio et al. (2016: 321f) highlights that, at present, epistemologies range from positivist and materialist understandings of reality to more interpretivist, constructivist, and post-structuralist approaches emphasizing meaning, perceptions, and intentionality influencing action. Furthermore, more individualistic approaches tend to regard social structures as the properties and interactions of individual agents, whereas structural approaches view individuals as relatively powerless. Brondizio et al. argue that, at least implicitly, those holding a more positivist and materialist orientation tend to downplay epistemological differences between the traditional natural and social sciences, while those holding a more constructivist or critical-studies orientation tend to highlight ontological and epistemological differences. Both "sides" hold quite different views about the potential for the integration of approaches. Positivist approaches may aim toward a "total systems" view of science, while post-structuralist and constructivist approaches tend to argue for a position of pluralism. In practice, it has proven quite difficult to engage with the potentially radical implications of bringing in the social. When doing so, one brings in values, social systems, institutions, contestations, and so on—including contestations of "facts," or at least of which "facts" might count. This approach also involves recognizing that it is problematic to frame the environment as an object largely comprising of natural science (Baskin 2015: 24). According to Brondizio et al. (2016: 325), debates around the Anthropocene concept have brought forward deep epistemological rifts between disciplines, but also collaborative research agendas for global change and sustainability.

Interdisciplinary traditions and developments

Toivanen et al. (2017: 5 and 10) argue that the three main branches of science build on three different notions of the Anthropocene. (1) The natural sciences focus on the "geological" as well as the "biological" Anthropocene. The geological Anthropocene analyzes the physical realization of the Anthropocene phenomena, whereas the biological Anthropocene analyzes the long-term anthropogenic changes in the biosphere and observes the ecological effects of human activities. (2) The "social" Anthropocene intertwines the geological and biological Anthropocene in social, societal, and historical processes and puts emphasis on structural social causes and effects. (3) The "cultural" Anthropocene refers to the cultural understanding of various creative and speculative reactions and representations of the geological, biological, and social Anthropocene and focuses on human-experienced and represented effects. The authors state that, currently, these approaches are mostly disciplinarily divided: the geological and biological Anthropocene are studied in the natural sciences, the social Anthropocene in the social sciences, and the cultural Anthropocene in the humanities (Toivanen et al., 2017: 5).

In the following, we apply this triple division to account for some historical and current perspectives on the development of interdisciplinarity within the natural and social sciences and the humanities. At the same time, we highlight ambitions to cross and transcend these academic boundaries.

Interdisciplinarity and the natural sciences

As accounted for in Part I of this book, the content of different UN reports reflects an increase in the interdisciplinary scientific understanding of the interplay between processes in the biosphere, atmosphere, lithosphere, and hydrosphere, and a correspondingly expanded knowledge of the impact of human activities on these processes as well as the significance of impacts to biological life on Earth and human opportunities. Until approximately 50 years ago, the majority of natural and social scientists and scholars from the humanities, as well as politicians, regarded nature as an inexhaustible source of human prosperity and well-being. Since then, it has become increasingly clear that nature sets limits to exploitation and that exceeding these limits can threaten biological as well as interconnected human life. In the following, we will highlight developments within the natural sciences by presenting advanced scientific work and knowledge integration within the field of environment and climate change. We have chosen to focus on the development of Earth system science (ESS) and the work of the International Panel on Climate Change (IPCC). Originating in the natural sciences, ESS and the IPCC have been increasingly focused on integrating the social sciences and the humanities in terms of modeling, understanding, and predicting ecological and socioecological risks and challenges and in the recommendation of solutions.

Earth system science

In general, Earth system science (ESS) attempts to understand the structure and functioning of the Earth as a single complex adaptive system driven by the diverse interactions among energy, matter, and organisms. The Earth system is driven by a primarily external energy source as a single closed system within which the biosphere is an active essential component (see also Chapter 1). The major dynamic components of the Earth system are a suite of interlinked physical, chemical, and biological processes that cycle (transport and transform) materials and energy in complex, dynamic ways within the system. Human activities are an integral part of this and affect the Earth system at a global, regional, and local scale in complex, interactive, and accelerating ways (Angus, 2016: 31). Some researchers regard the discovery of the Earth system as a revolutionary scientific shift—as a second 'Copernican' revolution (Angus, 2016: 32). Copernicus (and Galileo) decentered Earth as part of the solar system (heliocentrism). Science has now revealed that we are in a closed, very precarious, system that we need to stabilize. Following primarily Steffen et al. (2020) and Angus (2016), we will trace the development of the ESS paradigm from the 1980s until today and present some critical considerations.

ESS emerged in the 1980s. Since then, it has generated new insights, concepts, and frameworks, such as the Anthropocene, the Great Acceleration, tipping elements, tipping cascades, and planetary boundaries. As precursors to the contemporary understanding of the Earth system, Steffen et al. (2020) recognize Hutton (1788), Humboldtian science in the 19th century, and especially the Russian mineralogist and geochemist Vladimir Vernadsky (1926). For different reasons, the research undertaken by these scientists had little influence on their contemporaries. The development of the Earth system science paradigm only gained widespread and global influence among the scientific communities from the 1980s.

Steffen et al. (2020: 4) follow the origin of ESS from the modern climatology, plate tectonics, and ecosystem ecology that provided the basis for understanding the role of the biosphere in the functioning of the Earth system as a whole. The same authors underline that during the 1960s and 1970s, ecological awareness on a planetary scale increased among scientists and the general public—with, for example, the publication of R. Carson's *Silent Spring* (1962), the UN's "Only One Earth" discourse (1972), and the Club of Rome's publication of *The Limits to Growth* (1972). At the same time, the "Blue Marble" image was recorded by the crew of the Apollo 17 spacecraft (1972). The National Aeronautics and Space Administration in the USA (NASA) established an Earth System Science Committee in 1983, aimed at supporting the Earth observation satellite system and associated research. Steffen et al. (2020) highlight that NASA's interest in the Earth system occurred to prevent massive cuts in funding promised by the Reagan administration. Therefore, the space agency redirected its focus from space toward the Earth by developing a program of new satellites. NASA built on the outcomes of Cold War geophysics that paved the way for the realization that the Earth system comprises physical, chemical, biological, and human components (Steffen et al., 2020: 253).

In the 1980s, triggered by human-driven ozone depletion and climatic change, several conference reports called for a new scientific endeavor based on the recognition of an integrated Earth system (Steffen et al., 2020: 5). In 1986, the International Council of Scientific Unions (ICSU) initiated the International Geosphere-Biosphere Program (IGBP), which joined the World Climate Research Program (WCRP)—formed in 1980 to study the physical climate components of the Earth system (Steffen et al., 2020: 5). The aim of the IGBP program was to describe and understand the interactive physical, chemical, and biological processes that regulate the total Earth system; the unique environment that this system provides for life; the changes that are occurring in that system; and the manner in which these changes are influenced by human actions (Angus, 2016: 30f; see also Steffen et al., 2020: 254). Created in 1991, the international research program DIVERSITAS was developed to examine change in global biodiversity, thus complementing IGBP's research into terrestrial and marine ecosystems (Steffen et al., 2020: 6).

In 1996, the international research programs were accompanied by the International Human Dimensions Programme on Global Environmental Change (IHDP), which provided a global platform for social sciences to explore the consequences of a rapidly changing Earth system in relation to human and societal well-being (Steffen et al., 2020: 6).

In the late 1990s, German climatologist Hans Joachim Schellnhuber introduced concepts centered around the dynamic, co-evolutionary relationship between nature and human civilization at the planetary scale, and the possibility of catastrophe domains in the co-evolutionary space of the Earth system (Steffen et al., 2020: 7). Schellnhuber called for a deep integration of human activities into ESS and for greater emphasis on nonlinear dynamics in the Earth system. The 2001 conference "Challenges of a Changing Earth" triggered the formation of the Earth System Science Partnership (ESSP), which aimed to connect fundamental ESS with issues of central importance for human well-being and led to the integration of the ESS and global sustainability communities (Steffen et al., 2020: 7). Research centers—such as the Potsdam Institute for Climate Impact Research (PIK), the US National Center for Atmospheric Research (NCAR), the Stockholm Resilience Center, and the International Institute for Applied System Analysis—now directed their research toward ESS and global sustainability (Steffen et al., 2020: 8).

Steffen et al. (2020: 8) cite three interrelated foci that drove science forward: (1) observations of changing Earth systems; (2) computer simulations of system dynamics into the future; and (3) high-level assessments and synthesis that initiated the development of new concepts. The most influential concept of ESS is the Anthropocene, building the foundation for a deeper integration of the natural sciences, social sciences, and humanities (Steffen et al., 2020: 11; see also Angus, 2016: 33). From 2001 to 2005, several studies examined human impacts on nature by applying the word "Anthropocene," confirming the main results of the IGBP: humans are fundamentally, and to a significant extent irreversibly, changing the ecosystems and the diversity of life on Earth (Angus, 2016: 40f). In 2005, Steffen et al. termed the period after World War II "the Great Acceleration," as a direct homage to Karl Polanyi's book *The Great Transformation* (Angus, 2016: 43).

In 2007, initiated by the Stockholm Resilience Center, and headed by environmental scientist Johan Rockström, a project began to identify which processes are the most important to maintaining the stability of the planet as we know it. This project led to a new key-concept: planetary boundaries (Angus, 2016: 71; see also Chapter 1). Planetary boundaries research on tipping elements, tipping points, and tipping cascades highlights the severe risks of climate change, biosphere degradation, and the destabilization of the Earth system as a whole (Steffen et al., 2020: 12). The present framework, however, considers the planetary boundaries in isolation. The ambition is to simulate interactions among individual boundaries, integrating the dynamics of the Earth system into the planetary boundaries framework (Steffen et al., 2020: 12).

Through the development of Gaia theory, biologists have supplemented ESS with theoretical considerations on Life on Earth (Latour & Lenton, 2019:

676). Contemporary Gaia theory has further developed the work of Lovelock and Margulis initiated in the 1970s. Lovelock and Margulis proposed that living organisms interact with their inorganic surroundings on Earth to form a synergistic and self-regulating complex system that helps to maintain and perpetuate the conditions for life on the planet (Latour & Lenton, 2019: 668). One important challenge to Gaia theory, however, is that there is no valid theory on how Gaia works. The main hypothesis is that systems that find self-stabilizing configurations tend to persist, and systems that persist have a greater likelihood of acquiring further persistence-enhancing properties. Through these cruder selection mechanisms, Earth may have acquired and accumulated stabilizing feedback mechanisms involving life.

Steffen et al. (2020: 12) argue that ESS has to answer two critical questions: (1) How stable is the Earth system? and (2) What can ESS contribute to understanding and steering the integrated geosphere-biosphere-anthroposphere trajectory of the Anthropocene? The second question underscores that ESS has gradually been expanding its perspective from an understanding of Earth system dynamics that includes the role of humanity, incorporating solutions to the ecological and socioecological challenges and possible tools for steering the Earth system in a safer direction. The future aim of the ESS community would be to model and forecast the intertwined and complex linkages between ecological, social, and economic drivers and trajectories. As presented in Chapter 3 of this book, the ambition to create one model "telling it all" has proven difficult to fulfill (see also Randers et al., 2018).

From a social sciences and humanities point of view, ESS modeling shapes complex social and human issues in the picture of the natural sciences and applies GDP as the most important proxy for human well-being. Furthermore, Toivanen et al. (2017: 4) are critical of the fact that the internal consistency of ESS—in terms of ontology (systems, cycles, thermodynamics, feedback, deep time, etc.) and epistemology (data standardization, remote sensing, methods of reconstructing the past, computer models, visual grammar of timelines, etc.)—might prevent the integration of other disciplines on their own terms. They argue that contemporary Earth system analysis does not adequately incorporate the human systems (demographics, inequality, economic growth, migration, etc.) into its models. Instead, the knowledge of human systems is brought to Earth system analysis as exogenous estimates. Baskin (2015) notes that there has been only partial progress in attempts to incorporate the social into models of Earth systems; to date, these still seem "to assume an autonomous, reified social world, with inputs and outputs, whose causal mechanisms can be understood from outside, much as the natural sciences might represent natural systems" (Baskin, 2015: 24).

The international panel on climate change

The Intergovernmental Panel on Climate Change (IPCC) is the world's largest-ever scientific endeavor and one remaining relatively open to industry experts, outsiders, and non-governmental organizations (NGOs)

(Urry, 2015: 49). Similar smaller organizations funded by the UN exist within the areas of biodiversity (the Intergovernmental Science-Policy Platform on Biodiversity and Ecosystem Services/IPBES) and resources (the International Resource Panel/IRP). IPCC reports are based on reviews, assessments, and synthesis of a great number of disciplinary and interdisciplinary research publications. Each finding in IPCC reports is grounded in an evaluation of underlying evidence and agreement. A level of confidence is expressed using five qualifiers: very low, low, medium, high, and very high confidence (IPCC, 2022a: 5, note 4). Summaries for policymakers in IPCC assessment and special reports are subjected to line-by-line approval by IPCC member countries together with the scientists responsible for drafting the reports. When the summaries have been approved, the underlying reports are modified to ensure consistency with the summaries for policymakers. Synthesis reports represent the integrated results from assessment and special reports. Synthesis reports are adopted by a section-by-section discussion leading to agreement among participating governments in consultation with the authors. On the one hand, this means that IPCC analysis and recommendations represent a common negotiated voice, and on the other, that they pass through a political filter.

A recent example of the characteristics as well as the scientific development of IPCC is the 3056-page report "Climate Change 2022: Impacts, Adaptation and Vulnerability. Contribution of Working Group II to the Sixth Assessment Report of the Intergovernmental Panel on Climate Change" (IPCC, 2022a). This report is the result of combined efforts of hundreds of experts in the scientific, technological, and socioeconomic fields of climate science. The team consisted of 231 coordinating lead authors and lead authors and 39 review editors. In addition, more than 675 contributing authors provided draft text and information to the author teams. Drafts prepared by the authors were subject to two rounds of formal review and revision. A total of 62,418 written review comments were submitted by more than 1,600 individual expert reviewers and 51 governments. The review editors for each chapter have monitored the review process to ensure that all substantive review comments received appropriate consideration (IPCC, 2022b: IXf).

This IPCC report covers several interdisciplinary perspectives, structured in five main parts: (1) the introduction frames and contextualize the report and highlights key concepts; (2) seven sectoral chapters cover risks, adaptation, and sustainability for natural and human systems impacted by climate change; (3) seven regional chapters assess the observed impacts and projected risks at regional and sub-regional levels; (4) seven cross-chapters consider additional regionalization—including polar regions, tropical forests, deserts, mountains, and the Mediterranean—and highlight the topics of biodiversity hotspots and cities by the sea; and (5) three synthesis chapters assess key risks across sectors and regions, decision-making options for managing risk, and the ways in which climate impacts and risks hinder climate-resilient development in different sectoral and regional contexts, as well as pathways to achieving climate-resilient development (IPCC, 2022b: IX).

The IPCC highlights four areas where the work of the organization has expanded in new interdisciplinary directions. First, the report has an increased focus on risk- and solutions frameworks. The risk framing includes risks from global and regional responses to climate change and considers dynamic and cascading consequences. The focus on solutions encompasses the interconnections among climate responses, sustainable development, and transformation, and the implications for governance across scales within the public and private sectors. The assessment therefore includes climate-related decision making and risk management, climate-resilient development pathways, implementation, and evaluations of adaptation and loss and damage. Second, emphasis on social justice and different forms of expertise have emerged. As climate change impacts and implemented responses increasingly occur, there is heightened awareness of the ways that climate responses interact with issues of justice and social progress. In the report, there is expanded attention to inequity in climate vulnerability and responses, and to the role of power and participation in processes of implementation, unequal and differential impacts, and climate justice. The focus on scientific literature has also been increasingly accompanied by attention to, and the incorporation of, Indigenous knowledge, local knowledge, and associated scholars. Third, the report has a more extensive focus on the role of transformation in meeting societal goals. The underlying literature increasingly evaluates the lived experiences of climate change—the physical changes underway, the impacts for people and ecosystems, the perceptions of the risks, and adaptation and mitigation responses that are planned and implemented. Fourth, interdisciplinarity has increased, combining experts across natural and social sciences, engineering, humanities, law, and business administration. Furthermore, best practices are being adopted from applied decision and policy analysis, decision support, and co-production.

Important aspects of the IPCC's increasing emphasis on equality and justice are demonstrated in the following text example from the IPCC 2022 report, focusing on climate resilience, social justice, equality, and participation:

> *Climate resilient development is advanced when actors work in equitable, just and enabling ways to reconcile divergent interests, values, and worldviews, toward equitable and just outcomes (high confidence). These practices build on diverse knowledges about climate risk and chosen development pathways account for local, regional, and global climate impacts, risks, barriers, and opportunities (high confidence). Structural vulnerabilities to climate change can be reduced through carefully designed and implemented legal, policy, and process interventions from the local to global that address inequities based on gender, ethnicity, disability, age, location, and income (very high confidence). This includes rights-based approaches that focus on capacity-building, meaningful participation of the most vulnerable groups, and their access to key resources, including financing, to reduce risk and adapt (high confidence). Evidence shows that climate resilient development processes link scientific, Indigenous, local, practitioner and other forms of knowledge, and are more*

effective and sustainable because they are locally appropriate and lead to more legitimate, relevant, and effective actions (high confidence).

(IPCC, 2022a: 29).

Although IPCC acknowledges the intertwined character of ecological, social, and ecological challenges, and also that, to an increasing degree, the IPCC seems to be critical to the actions taken at the global, regional, national, and local level, the origin of the IPCC efforts in the epistemologies, ontologies, and methodologies of the natural sciences makes it somewhat difficult to establish a symmetric relationship with the social sciences and the humanities. Furthermore, the inherent political and negotiated character of the IPCC reports, may also function as a barrier toward more widespread interdisciplinary collaboration. For example, Bhatasara (2015: 220) indicates that the lack of interest in climate change among, for example, sociologists is driven by a widespread suspicion of naturalistic explanations, teleological arguments, and environmental determinism. The same author highlights the methodological divergences between the natural and social sciences, stating that few sociologists would subscribe to the notion that social processes can be modeled. The overly political nature of climate change may also have caused some cautiousness among social scientists.

Interdisciplinarity and the social sciences

Toivanen et al. (2017: 8) define the social Anthropocene as a socioenvironmental approach in which the evolution of human–nature relations is investigated within historical social structures. This perspective generates knowledge on how changes in the biosphere are connected to both global as well as national and regional social hierarchies, power and economic structures, or political interests. It searches the causes and indirect drivers of environmental problems from human social behavior, economic development, technological solutions, or political institutions adapted. Additionally, it opens the question of difference within and between distinct social groups (nation, class, race, gender) and how they relate, cause, or are affected by environmental crisis. The social sciences have a longstanding research-interest in social justice and equality issues. Apart from being a major environmental problem, global climate change is a highly significant global environmental justice or human rights issue in at least four ways: (1) wealthy industrialized countries of the Northern hemisphere contribute highly disproportionately to the pollution of the common global airshed; (2) low-lying geography and weaker infrastructure mean that the consequences of global climate change will be worse in the poorer nations of the Southern hemisphere; (3) climate treaty negotiations have favored industrialized nations in terms of outcome and process; and (4) intergenerational equity—those alive today are negatively altering the Earth's atmosphere and climate, reducing its capacity to sustain life for generations to come (Bhatasara, 2015: 218; see also Chapters 3 and 4).

The social Anthropocene often focuses on the eco-social histories of the 500 years of the modern era following the Columbian exchange (the beginning colonization of South America) marking the birth, growth, and expansion of the European-led world capitalism, which simultaneously intensified anthropogenic environmental problems around the globe. The Industrial Revolution marked a novel step in productivity, resource use, and the accumulation of greenhouse gases originating from the use of fossil fuels (Toivanen et al., 2017: 8). The social Anthropocene also contributes to the possible solutions on how the planet is steered toward the "safe operating space for humanity," because it can identify and problematize the economic, political, and ideological barriers that stand in front of sustainable pathways. The social Anthropocene can contribute to innovating, establishing, and reordering the institutional arrangements that structure the economy, social life, and environmental relations while representing an orientation to identify social, economic, and cultural life forms that are already "sustainable" in order to learn, support, and expand them (Toivanen et al., 2017: 9).

Holzer et al. (2018: 810) highlight how past research strands originating from ecology, economics and engineering, land use studies, geography, anthropology, sociology, and history gave rise to four current-day socioecological research themes: environment and development, global environmental change, sustainability, and socioecological systems. They conceptualize social ecology as an archipelago situated between two "continents"—the natural sciences and engineering on one side and the social sciences and humanities on the other (Holzer et al., 2018: 810). They use the term "socioecological research" to refer to research that explores aspects of coupled socioecological systems—integrated systems in which humans and nature interact. According to Dick et al. (2018), there are several characteristics intrinsic to socioecological research: (1) its focus on knowledge production useful for addressing and solving sustainability challenges; (2) the promotion of interdisciplinary collaborations between ecologists and social scientists, and transdisciplinary collaborations between scientists and non-scientist stakeholders; (3) its focus on interaction processes between social and natural systems and the integration of socioeconomic concerns with ecological monitoring and analysis; (4) its application to multiple spatial, temporal, and organizational scales, with interactions between scales; and (5) the investigation of general themes of socioecological metabolism, land use and landscapes, governance, and communication.

Brondizio et al. (2016: 323) claim that many advances have been made in understanding socioecological systems that bring together diverse segments of Earth system sciences, the social and ecological sciences, and the humanities. These efforts are leading to new conceptual syntheses and forms of analytics that are pushing the boundaries of disciplinary and interdisciplinary research and pushing the knowledge production enterprise beyond science to include both concerns with its usability by decision-makers and various sectors of society, as well as synergies with other knowledge systems (e.g., Indigenous, traditional, and local). As mentioned, however, looking at sociology, Bhatasara (2015: 220) highlights that new interdisciplinary developments based on the discipline have been marginalized. He states that environmental sociologists have been writing on climate change and other socioecological issues for some time, using quantitative and qualitative methods to research the social and cultural processes that configure attitudes, discourses, and ideological dimensions of climate change in public debates and policy processes, whereas mainstream sociologists have largely not.

Interdisciplinarity and the humanities

The cultural Anthropocene approaches comprise the creative and cultural-critical reactions to, and representations of, the geological-biological Anthropocene and its social aspects. As such, the cultural aspects of the Anthropocene are important to acknowledge and study in order to understand the ideas, beliefs, and narratives behind human actions. Moreover, the cultural perspective is important when we are interested in the experiential and psychological effects of the large-scale environmental changes taking place in the Anthropocene.

According to Palsson et al. (2012: 5), within the humanities, organized disciplinary, and interdisciplinary research focusing on environmental issues started to emerge from the 1950s onward. These approaches include cultural ecology (1950s), environmental history, environmental philosophy (particularly ethics and esthetics), and literary ecocriticism—all emerging in the 1970s—and historical ecology in the 1990s. Recently, the more inclusive term "environmental humanities" has been gaining ground, i.e., a set of multidisciplinary approaches that focus on human–nature relations. Based on a multitude of theoretical paradigms and methodologies, and analyzing a wide range of materials and texts, the field of environmental humanities is characterized by its engagement with environmental issues. It understands cultural phenomena as always intertwined with natural (physical, material) beings, places, and processes. Pertaining to environmental problems or problems in human–nature relations, the most fundamental idea is that all these problems and issues are based on certain ideas, beliefs, attitudes, habits, and practices that are cultural.

The humanities also include art and art-science. Toivanen et al. (2017: 10) argue that art and art-science may contribute significantly to the understanding of the Anthropocene and possible futures. Artists experiment with concepts and materials to open alternative perspectives or to create fictional worlds, and arts scholars and philosophers focus on understanding human conceptualizations, representations, interpretations, and experiences of both actual and imaginative realities. Angeler et al. (2020: 99) suggest that a starting point for collaboration can be the development of creative and intuitive scenarios of potential unknowns. Refining such scenarios or creating alternative scenarios through the introduction of unplanned elements may lead to surprises that may ultimately help identify novel pathways toward a desirable future. Pragmatically, such scenarios may help to reduce the risk of worst-case outcomes resulting from change becoming real. The authors highlight that such a strategy is already pursued by the French army, which is recruiting science fiction writers to help military strategists anticipate future threats to national security.

Toivanen et al. (2017: 10) argue that the cultural approach to the Anthropocene can have a double role in future research practices. This approach would not only help in creating more discerning models for understanding human involvement in the Earth's processes (and the Earth's involvement in human processes) but would also point to the diverse social and cultural phenomena resistant to modeling and help develop alternative methods to researching such phenomena. These could include, for example, repressed or denied beliefs and ideological commitments, narratives of individual or collective identity or destiny, ideas about rights and responsibilities, and other forms of individual and collective thought that underlie human action.

Examples of new interdisciplinary research agendas

To understand the intertwined ecological, social, and economic challenges, the need for new interdisciplinary research agendas is vast. According to Toivanen et al. (2017: 13), some of the key research questions invoked by the general notion of the Anthropocene are as follows: what are the specific global human-induced changes we are currently looking at? When and where did they originate? How did they spread? What were the prime driving factors and what kind of dynamism exists between these factors? Do we focus on the point of origin, or some key dynamic of change, or what? Additionally, the authors argue (1) that in order to implement effective science-based solutions, natural scientists need to collaborate with social scientists and non-scientific actors to achieve greater and faster impact in the political sphere, and (2) that the social sciences and the humanities should contribute increasingly to the solving of contemporary anthropogenic environmental problems (Toivanen et al., 2017: 12).

These questions and research ideas, however, do not cover all research agendas pertaining to the present and future ecological and socioecological conditions. In the following we present a selected variety of different suggestions to pursue interdisciplinary research agendas, acknowledging, however, that they are just examples and that many other agendas would be needed to address complex drivers and possible futures as well as wicked challenges and sustainable solutions.

According to Palsson et al. (2012: 66ff), five main challenges for the social sciences and the humanities can be outlined, thus: (1) the environment must be understood as a social category, and efforts must be made to integrate the humanities and social sciences more fully into our understanding of the environmental; (2) the notions of planetary limits and boundaries need to be sensitive to human experience and the nature constructed by humans, embedded in a scientific framework that includes issues of distribution, geography, and equity as well as environmental effects on humans; (3) the culture of emerging Anthropocene societies should be articulated by drawing upon natural scientists, humanities scholars, and social scientists asking how the contemporary syndromes of anxiety, drift, and self-delusion can be transformed into a more positive task of building a culture of sustainability; (4) the new "human condition" characterized by rapidly growing human impact in both the environment and life itself represents calls for concerted social science and humanities efforts to analyze the complexities of the real world and the different institutions and social arrangements involved, and to explore alternatives and potential avenues for mobilization; and (5) it is essential to enhance and intensify the work of social sciences and humanities on how directionality could be articulated, democratically anchored, and implemented.

Brondizio et al. (2016: 319), argue that there has been little advancement in analytical frameworks that are able to deal with the complex interactions between historical and current political economies as processes that are patterned and specific to different contexts. They argue that there is a need to increase focus on the social drivers of global change, including changes in technology, resource consumption, population and settlement patterns, mobility, cultures and ideas, communication, and trade, as well as civil and military conflicts. Furthermore, the authors state that inequalities in power and political and resource control have become as significant within as they are across regions, and are connected across scales, from the local to the global. On this background, they question how the social sciences and the humanities can contribute to the analysis of complexities pertaining to the intertwined ecological, social, and economic challenges. Their point of departure is that the Anthropocene reflects the cumulative history of local and regional social changes operating in various and evolving forms of connections to global processes. They highlight that these changes have been intertwined with evolving extractive commodity chains, resource use systems, urbanization and industrialization, infrastructure, and flows of technological diffusion, all which exhibit some level of path dependency as well as different types of emergent patterns manifested in regional land- and seascapes. At the same time, the simultaneity and/or synchronicity of an increasingly connected world means that new technologies, financial systems, and ideas have the potential to be adopted almost simultaneously around the globe. Such synchronicity and simultaneity indicate that small actions at a local scale can add up to positive or negative impacts at a regional or global scale that affect distant areas at an increasingly rapid pace (Brondizio et al., 2016: 323). As the authors conceive these drivers and complexities as not well understood, they posit several research questions (Brondizio et al., 2016: 322ff):

1 In what ways can new conceptual frameworks help to advance models of coupled socioecological systems that are able to account for intertwined drivers and path dependency, complex networks, and emergent phenomena that are all occurring within multiple and increasingly connected biophysical constraints and risks?
2 To what extent are global changes reaching or surpassing potential biophysical boundaries at regional and planetary scales? How are these changes linked with social, economic, or cultural processes? And what are possible alternatives to prevent and respond to the cascading effects of socioecological regime shifts at different scales?
3 How are political economies linking local and transnational processes connecting extractive systems, production, consumption, industrial transformations, and pollution affecting the biosphere? How is increasing mobility and communication interacting with global economic and politic processes? And what are the outcomes of interactions in mobility, social reorganizations, economic networks, and policy?
4 How do we understand the tele-coupled interactions across resources and the connections between distant drivers affecting demand for agricultural land and terrestrial, mineral, marine, water, and energy resources? And how do these nexuses place burdens on different regions and sectors of society?
5 How can we understand the social and environmental trade-offs relating to policy choices, institutional arrangements, and economic incentives, and their local and distant outcomes?
6 How do we conceptualize and analyze interactions between historically rooted inequalities (within and between societies) and contemporary globalized economic networks influencing regional and global environmental change?
7 When do local-level actions dampen out to have no appreciable effects at larger levels, and when do they amplify to drive significant impacts at larger levels—even the global?

Methodologically, Brondizio et al. (2016: 324f) place special emphasis on the importance of interdisciplinary work between data-science, the social sciences, and the humanities, as this will provide significant opportunities across a wide array of questions—including the opportunity to collaborate on new analytics for integrating qualitative and survey data with Big Data and Earth observations.

Focusing on adaption, Bhatasara (2015: 226) indicates that research should concentrate more on (1) the factors that underpin the vulnerability and resilience of various social groups and scales to effectively inform policies on climate change adaption, particularly at local scales; (2) the changing structures, processes, and conditions underpinning adaption specifically in local contexts; (3) the social organization of adaption practices; how these practices are formed and reproduced, negotiated, and contested between social groups; and how they become institutionalized; (4) the constraints and opportunities to institute shifts in practices toward sustainable adaption; and (5) the questions about the role and limits of individual human agency in adapting to climate change and in providing practical knowledge by identifying the social structures and dimensions of human agency that will facilitate transitional pathways, as well as adapting to the impacts of socioecological changes already occurring.

Brondizio et al. (2016: 324f) complement the focus on adaption by suggesting that early warning systems are needed to reduce the impacts of crises before and after their occurrence. These early warning systems should increasingly compensate for accelerated changes, from market shifts to disease outbreaks, to climate events. This includes widening their detection range to capture connections, emergences, and weak signals, and their cascading consequences. The authors state that advancing collaborative and interdisciplinary research on these issues could make a difference to a significant portion of the population in many regions confronting environmental stresses and risks at unprecedented scales.

As alternatives to GDP, within the field of economics, more than three dozen new, multidimensional indexes and indicators have been proposed in the last decades (e.g., the Human Development Index, Happy Planet Index, Global Innovation Index, and Genuine Progress Indicator). According to Palsson et al. (2012), these indexes are more salient, credible, and legitimate than GDP because they relate to the social and environmental pillars of sustainable development. To date, however, none of these has received widespread attention. Therefore, interdisciplinary research is needed in order to stop using evaluation and reward systems that are counter-incentives for sustainability. As GDP is deeply ingrained in governmental and intergovernmental action, changes will require a transformation of the core axioms of economics as well as interdisciplinary research into the complex barriers. Some new inventions within the field of economy itself are pointing in this direction, such as heterodox economics, doughnut economics, and feminist economics (see also Chapters 4 and 11).

As an answer to the divide between the Global North and the Global South, Newel et al. (2020) focus on southern-led research into climate justice. They suggest new research agendas pertaining to three main areas: (1) governance for climate justice from a global perspective, (2) inclusive climate justice, and (3) deepening climate justice.

Governance for climate justice from a Global perspective

Under this headline, Newell et al. (2020: 8ff) suggest (1) building networks of researchers and practitioners working at the frontier of legal innovations for accountability, justice, and redress in relation to climate change; (2) involving research in strengthening democracy for climate justice in different contexts; (3) thinking more clearly, systematically, and strategically about who bears rights and responsibilities and for what in the climate arena and in which ways to go beyond the state; and (4) looking at how responses to conflict situations—through cooperation, sharing of resources, and new governance mechanisms—could be designed in new ways to address climate injustices and embed more fair outcomes.

Inclusive climate justice

To enhance inclusive climate justice, Newell at al. (2020) propose that (1) research and support are required pertaining to new international alliances of climate justice; (2) research should investigate under what conditions climate justice concerns could be the basis for broader social mobilizations and how activism can be supported through engagement activities, research, and toolkits for advocacy and legal activism; (3) comparative studies should be conducted on the meanings and practices of climate justice, to understand which framings resonate in which contexts; (4) research is required to examine the intersectional effects of climate change adaption as well as mitigation such as nuanced gendered analysis, to assess low-carbon pathways at the global and local levels in order to understand the costs of these transitions; and (5) comparative research should be conducted that builds on areas such as traditions of citizen climate science, indigenous environmentalism, and alternative cosmologies.

Deepening climate justice

To deepen climate justice, Newel et al. (2020) suggest that (1) there is a need both to innovate participatory scenario-building exercises about climate futures and to include deliberative development of scenarios for change; (2) research projects should analyze the possibilities and challenges of developing supply-side international law, to develop a global legal framework for equitably agreeing on how to leave remaining reserves of fossil fuels in the ground; (3) in the area of climate-related disasters, research should analyze what has worked well and less well and what might be learned from related crises to help inform concrete strategies required in the face of climate change; and (4) research should consider not just inter-human and intergenerational, but also inter-species, perspectives when building the foundations for climate justice.

Many of these different suggestions build on the hope that interdisciplinary research involving the natural sciences, the social sciences, and the humanities will increase. This means that the natural sciences would have to be more open to the critical and speculative modes of knowledge production fostered in social sciences, arts, and humanities. It also means that the social sciences and the humanities should be open about the limitations and possibilities of their concepts and methods and listen closely to what kind of questions natural scientists are asking about the connection between society, culture, and material planetary conditions (Toivanen et al., 2017: 11).

Brondizio et al. (2016: 325) highlight that debates surrounding the Anthropocene concept have already proven fertile in opening a conversation around fundamental issues underlying global change and pathways to sustainability. They argue that, instead of remaking historical bifurcations between and within the natural and social sciences and the humanities, it would be more productive to concentrate on ideas and approaches that make collaboration successful and meaningful to broader society. They invest their hope in the idea that creative (and constructive) tensions around the concept of interdisciplinarity can help the research community to move toward new conceptual syntheses and integrative methodologies that are needed to understand the complexities of the Earth system, and which are commensurable with the social and environmental challenges ahead.

To Palsson et al. (2012: 11), transdisciplinary research demands rigorous discussions on the deep-seated differences between natural sciences, social sciences, and humanities, and it is therefore important to address the question of disciplinary differences and antagonisms. They call for research that must go beyond the sterile polarization characteristic of the 1990s' "science wars," and they highlight the difference between characterizing the Anthropocene "by means of quantitative data" on the one hand and understanding "how it perceives human interaction, culture, institutions, and societies" on the other. Toivanen et al. (2017: 11) argue that the Anthropocene clamors for both attentive measuring and careful interpretation, thus challenging the sciences and the humanities at their classic point of demarcation.

Examples of multi-actor and participatory action research

To finalize this chapter, we have chosen to present three examples of EU-funded interdisciplinary research—involving editors of this book—that can be characterized by the notions of "multi-stakeholder-based" and "participatory-action-research-based" collaboration between the natural, social, and applied sciences and that builds on cooperation with external stakeholders and participants. The general aims of these projects are to contribute to interdisciplinary scientific knowledge generation as well as pragmatic and scalable solutions regarding different intertwined ecological and socioecological challenges covering circular economy, agroecology, and nature-based solutions.

CityLoops

Closing the loop for urban material flows (CityLoops) is a multi-stakeholder project financed by Horizon 2020 (grant agreement no. 821033). The project received a grant of €9.99 million and runs for four years, from 2019 to 2023. The overarching objective of CityLoops is to develop, implement, and replicate a series of urban planning approaches and instruments, helping to close the loops of urban material and resource flows and promote the transition to a circular economy, thereby reducing the environmental footprint, increasing regenerative capacities, and stimulating new business opportunities and job creation in European cities. CityLoops specifically focuses on two of the most significant urban material flows: construction and demolition waste (including soil), and organic waste. The project brings together six European cities to demonstrate a series of tools and urban planning approaches, with the aim of closing the loops of urban material flows and increasing their regenerative capacities. The six cities are Apeldoorn/Netherlands; Bodø/Norway; Mikkeli/Finland; Porto/Portugal; Seville/Spain; and Roskilde and Høje-Taastrup/Denmark.

The CityLoops cities are committed to embedding circularity within their decision making and planning procedures over the long term. To this end, CityLoops seeks to embed actions within a support framework, consisting of the following elements:

Stakeholder engagement—to support the active involvement of key stakeholders at every stage of the project, from planning, through demonstration, evaluation, and replication. In each city, a local stakeholder partnership has been established at the project outset, involving civil society, the business community, academia, and public authority stakeholders. The aim of these partnerships is to promote stakeholder buy-in and cooperation; identify and promote business opportunities; develop coherent and flexible regulatory and policy frameworks, along with innovative governance structures; and establish stakeholder networks.

Urban circularity assessment—to develop and implement a methodology for the purpose of analyzing circularity within the urban context, and feed this into decision-making processes. During the inception phase, a circular city scan methodology and indicators are developed and implemented in each city—to include context-specific data and challenges, to adjust planned demonstration actions, and to provide an evaluation framework for the measures and monitor their progress toward a circular economy. A series of further decision support tools are developed for specific demonstration actions.

Circular procurement—to exploit the huge potential of public sector purchases in order to create markets for circular economy products and solutions. In each case, public procurement actions are analyzed to assess potential supportive measures.

The tools, approaches, and solutions demonstrated will be replicable in a large number of cities across Europe and embedded throughout the project. At a city level, all demonstration cities prepare scale-up plans. At a regional level, collaborative learning networks are established—consisting of other municipalities, public bodies, and other relevant regional institutions—to help with the preparation of regional upscaling plans. At a European level, a series of replication zones are recruited over the course of the project, to assist the preparation of replication plans. Guidance on replication will also be issued.

Agroecology-TRANSECT

The Agroecology-TRANSECT project is an interdisciplinary project with the overall objective of unfolding the full potential of agroecology principles within the EU (Wezel et al., 2009: 2018); it receives a grant of €7 million by Horizon Europe (grant agreement no. 101060816), which runs from 2022 to 2026. The Agroecology-TRANSECT project is a continuation of the past 8–12 years' EU projects and consortia building and is generally aimed at fighting decades of serious environmental impacts and supporting public expectations toward healthier diets. In that perspective, two recent projects worthy of mention are ReMIX and DiverIMPACTS (HORIZON 2020, 2017–2022), which were involved in the formation of the Crop Diversification Cluster in 2017 (www.cropdiversification.eu)—operating in countries across Europe to encourage uptake of diversification measures by European farmers and agri-value chain actors.

Unlocking the predominant industrial agricultural systems to include more diversity, synergies, efficiency, and recycling while substituting synthetic chemical inputs by ecosystem functions requires the adoption of a radical holistic and transdisciplinary approach. Action at the production-system level is not sufficient to ensure a lasting and sustainable transition. Systemic departure and transdisciplinary approaches are applied all along the Agroecology-TRANSECT project timeline, involving key agri-food value chain actors while mobilizing agronomy, ecology, economics, and social sciences.

The project consortium consists of ten academic partners and nine non-profit organizations and private companies from 12 European countries. Co-innovation strategies (Rossing et al., 2021) govern the project, closely accompanied by the local knowledge development of contextualized agroecology innovators embedded in situated Innovation Hubs (IHs). Ten of the 12 countries host an already-running IH used to track demand-driven challenges, recording data over time for sharing across other IHs. In order to secure a high level of diversity across the IHs, a few national characteristics can be highlighted: (1) South of Spain and Slovenia—with their extreme heat and drought conditions leading to water scarcity; (2) French West Indies—with its increased occurrence of hurricanes; (3) Hungary and Romania—where the lack of cooperation among agricultural actors contributes to increasing inequality and vulnerability along the value chain; (4) Bulgaria—where the majority of small farms are below the threshold for CAP support; (5) Denmark, Belgium, and the Netherlands—where the development of low-tillage strategies is encouraged to improve ecosystem services and resilience; and (6) France and Switzerland—where their citizens are encouraged to assist in developing ethical and sustainable market-ready produce from their grassland systems. The IHs incorporate a variety of actors representing different forms of knowledge (implicit, explicit, experiential, formal), who are integrated by facilitators that negotiate missions and associated innovation activities. In this way, the project aims to generate new knowledge that is both scientifically credible and socially valuable. This implies sometimes rather complex adaptive system perspectives that foster social learning as a basis for new insights, along with learning-oriented history monitoring and evaluation to explore and analyze its efficacy in bringing about the aspirations of the IH actors and the project participants at large.

The focus of the actor-driven IHs exemplify agroecology as a contextualized social and political movement that maintains and promotes diversity and socio-ecological/technical/economic and cultural multifunctionality within agri-food systems. The Farm to Fork Strategy (see Chapter 8) supports agroecology as a lever to a fair, healthy, and resilient EU agriculture (Pe'er et al., 2019) in accordance with the European Green Deal (see Chapter 5) and the Biodiversity Strategy for 2030, thereby influencing nature conservation policies (see Chapter 9). However, agroecology, like every other agri-food system, has a dedicated local origin (Compagnone et al., 2018), requiring local biophysical, socioeconomic, and political understanding before successful implementations can be achieved (López-García et al., 2021).

Previous research has shown that actors throughout the agricultural innovation system need to change their actions in order to move from the predominant industrial, external, input-based systems to agroecological systems. In the spirit of the project, improving know-what and know-how capacities is best acquired on the job, as agroecological farming methods are deeply context dependent. With this entry point, the expected impact of the project is a better understanding of how to enhance the resilience and mitigation potential of natural and managed ecosystems, water and soil systems, and economic sectors in the context of the changing climate, including a reduction in greenhouse gas emissions, the maintenance of natural carbon sinks, and an enhancement of the sequestration and storage of carbon in ecosystems. This is linked to improved decision making and expectations that actors will positively influence the integration of adaption measures in relevant EU policies.

TRANS-lighthouses

The TRANS-lighthouses project is funded by the EU's Horizon 2020 research and innovation program under grant agreement no. 776783. It has received a grant of €5.99 million. Starting in 2022, the project brings together researchers from Portugal, Denmark, Germany, Cyprus, France, Belgium, Italy, Greece, Spain, Belgium, and Sweden. It integrates a network of nature-based solutions (NBSs) for (1) urban, (2) rural, (3) coastal, and (4) forested areas, and aims to establish the conditions needed for a scientific renewal regarding the co-creation of NBSs—thereby generating new transdisciplinary articulations between science and alternative knowledge(s) in a more egalitarian relationship supporting social emancipation and recognizing community voices and actions that can contribute to improving nature-based solutions. This means that the project will not only focus on how to use nature to improve environmental sustainability and climate resilience, but also on how to do this with justice at its core: prioritizing the voices, experiences, and needs of marginalized sectors in the design, implementation, and evaluation of NBSs. The project will consider distributional, procedural, and recognitional justice and also adopt a "society-focused" approach to just transitions, taking into account the claims of workers and communities in contributing to transformative socioenvironmental change. Intertwining issues are jointly addressed to promote social change—namely, the human–nature relationship, the plural concept of the everyday economy (valuing the householding as well as reciprocity and redistribution mechanisms), Just Transitions, innovative co-governance, and rural/urban social innovation.

The TRANS-lighthouses project is a direct follow-up on the previous URBINAT project, which was aimed at building innovative NBSs for social inclusion in urban areas. The project generated an interdisciplinary tool and methodology for a territorial, technological, and participatory approach to the design of NBSs, with a strong reference to the social and solidarity economy. Many ideas were implemented—such as the Healthy Green Corridors initiative—that have become drivers in more inclusive social housing neighborhoods. In the TRANS-lighthouses project, the interdisciplinary frameworks are developed further by including the epistemologies of the South framework, which questions the hegemony of Northern science by inviting a dialog between European-oriented approaches to NBSs and approaches that builds upon the epistemologies of the South and intersectional analysis.

The TRANS-lighthouses project uses the concept of collaborative governance to guide the assessment and design of governance interventions. This concept attempts to overcome a series of dualisms between representation and democratic practices, between politics and policy, between state and civil society, and between normative and empirical concerns. Measuring the meaning and value of participatory processes requires analysis of the participating actors—the relationships between them, and between them and the context in which they are integrated—as much as the content under discussion. Co-governance processes have several criteria that inform their scope: (1) processes that "seek to enable cooperation and co-production between citizens, public authorities, and stakeholders"; (2) the self-selection or intentional selection of participants; (3) their mode of participation, which is fundamentally based on discursive expression; and (4) the seeking of consensus building articulated through either bargaining/negotiation or deliberation. It is a way of co-producing a diversity of basic needs and services between communities, governments, and private organizations from a variety of sectors, and across multiple scales, from the local community and municipality to the national and international governance arenas.

The co-creation methodology aims to engage all in the regeneration process from the first moment—to map the needs and dreams (co-diagnostic), to ideate and design solutions (co-design), to build products and develop processes (co-implementation), and to evaluate the impact on people's life (co-monitoring). The following criteria guide the introduction of co-governance and co-creation approaches: (1) the inclusion of a diversity of participants; (2) the continued expansion of opportunities for discursive interaction as generated during the co-diagnostic and co-design of the participatory process, in which all the actors involved have been mobilized to experiment, widen, and expand ways of making, based on increased levels of dialog, debate, and discussion of options and opinions, between participants and municipal actors; (3) cooperation and co-production between citizens, public authorities, and stakeholders; (4) the building of consensus through opportunities to influence, negotiate, and deliberate on decisions; and (5) the integration and successful handling of emerging conflicts, dissensus, and disagreement.

The TRANS-lighthouses project gathers and combines diverse and complementary expertise/knowledge(s) based on the inter-sectorial composition of consortium, including NGOs, public authorities, and universities. The contributions of the various disciplines are integrated into a "cross-fertilization process" to provide systemic outcomes, acknowledging that all technical-scientific knowledge is also socio-political knowledge. Collaboration with engaged researchers is viewed as significant for translating and bridging citizens' knowledge of marginalized communities and scientific and policy spaces. The TRANS-lighthouses project brings together academic institutions from the social sciences in collaborative work with technological institutions.

These three projects are all quite large-scale EU projects involving several EU countries. They are all oriented toward creating, monitoring, evaluating, and upscaling solutions, and they are all transdisciplinary, transcending the boundaries between academia and other actors. Furthermore, they all promote politically decided solutions in the EU—circular economy, agroecology, and nature-based solutions—and they all represent ideals of the "catalytic state" and "polycentric governance" (see also Chapter 11). Each of the projects, however, has its own distinct goals and interdisciplinary methodologies:

CityLoops is a multi-stakeholder project aimed at strengthening the interplay between urban planning and the circular economy, with a focus on construction and demolition waste and organic waste. The project promotes lasting stakeholder engagement and the development of regulatory and policy frameworks, as well as increased public procurement and new business opportunities.

The *Agroecology-TRANSECT* project is based on broad interdisciplinarity and the collaboration between researcher and non-profit organizations, private companies, and local farmers. The project aims to create new scientific and socially valuable knowledge that can support transformations in the agricultural sector—from industrial, external, input-based systems to agroecological systems that enhance the resilience and mitigation potential of naturally managed ecosystems.

The *TRANS-lighthouses* project is based on the principles of participatory action research and aims to co-create nature-based solutions through processes of co-governance, with a special focus on consensus-building and the ability to cope with emergent conflicts. The project emphasizes distributional, procedural, and recognitional justice by prioritizing the voices, needs, and experiences of communities, including a focus on Just Transition and epistemologies of the South. Though it further develops nature-based solutions, the primary aim of the project is to enhance the social emancipation of local participants.

Regarding types of interdisciplinarity, the CityLoops project can be regarded as a typical Modus 2, multi-stakeholder project, aiming to improve governance, technical solutions, and new business models. The Agroecology-TRANSECT project combines a multi-stakeholder with a participatory action research approach, especially regarding the involvement of local farmers and the development of their agroecological practices. The TRANS-lighthouses project emphasizes the participatory action research perspective by prioritizing social outcomes pertaining to equality and democratic participation.

Summary

As accounted for in this chapter, in the Anthropocene, the ecological and socioecological challenges are intertwined at all levels. Throughout the book, we have focused on the biodiversity–climate change–resource nexus; the nexus between ecological, economic, and social challenges; the interplay between indirect and direct drivers, pressures, impacts, and states; the intertwined character of local and global challenges; the connected and contested character of challenges and solutions; and the very different conceptualizations of the entangled human–nature history and the future of everything alive on Earth. Furthermore, we have highlighted the significant contributions of the natural as well as the social sciences and the humanities to conceptualize and understand these complexities.

In this chapter, we have presented arguments pointing at the need for increased interdisciplinary collaboration within and between the different branches of science. For example, from a past-present-future perspective, climate change may be understood from an interdisciplinary natural science perspective. However, important drivers, socially differentiated impacts, possible solutions, and the consequences of chosen solutions cannot be fully understood without engaging the social sciences and the humanities in a close collaboration with the natural sciences. In the chapter, we have listed some of the arguments for interdisciplinarity, we have described different types of interdisciplinarity, and we have analyzed institutional as well as paradigmatic barriers to interdisciplinarity pertaining to theory-of-science, theories, and methodologies.

To present state-of-the-art examples regarding interdisciplinarity, we have highlighted some aspects of the interdisciplinary development within the natural sciences, the social sciences, and the humanities; furthermore, we have focused on how each of these scientific 'camps' has attempted to transcend the boundaries between them. Within the natural sciences, Earth system science is working on how to engage the social sciences and the humanities in more complete and differentiated understandings of the human–nature relation, and the International Panel on Climate Change (IPCC) is increasingly integrating contributions from the social sciences and the humanities in its reports. Transcending the boundaries between the social sciences and the natural sciences, broad interdisciplinarity in the social sciences has primarily developed as specializations such as social ecology, socioenvironmental approaches, and socioecological research, whereas the mainstream social sciences have been more reluctant to engage in this kind of complex cooperation. Within the humanities, interest in the human–nature relation has developed and expanded during the last 70 years. Today, this type of research interest is pursued under the headings of ecological or environmental humanities, understanding cultural phenomena as always intertwined with natural beings, states, and processes. Within the humanities, art and art-science have also provided new ways to understand the Anthropocene and the possible futures of nature and humanity.

To highlight possible future pathways that may strengthen broad interdisciplinarity, we presented contributions concerning overall research questions about the Anthropocene and future human–nature conditions; the complex and accelerating systemic interactions between global and local contexts; socioecological adaption processes; possible reconfigurations of economic theory and praxis; and climate justice from a Global South perspective.

In concluding the chapter, we presented three examples of interdisciplinary EU-funded research projects that focus on circular economy, agroecology, and nature-based solutions. All three projects include external stakeholders/participants but prioritize the relation between ecological, economic, and social outcomes somewhat differently.

To understand ecological and socioecological challenges and to recommend sustainable solutions, interdisciplinary research is required at all levels and all scales. Much more research needs to be developed through a variety of interdisciplinary projects. The ambition to conduct broad transdisciplinary research between the natural and social sciences and the humanities will not be met in all projects. Since, however, in the Anthropocene, most of the problems facing the world can only be understood and acted upon by employing the full range of scientific disciplines, the most important task will be to establish new types of collaboration based on mutual recognition between the disciplines, collaborative definitions of the problems to be investigated, and a willingness to always try to understand, respect, and learn from each other. In many instances, to provide strong and sustainable solutions and to pursue social goals while respecting the planetary boundaries, it will be important to transgress the boundaries between academia, institutional, and private actors, and civil society

References

Andersen, A. S., and Kjeldsen, T. H. (2015). A critical review of key concepts in PPL. In: A. S. Andersen & S. B. Heilesen (eds.), *The roskilde model: Problem-oriented learning and project Work*. Heidelberg, New York, Dordrecht, London: Springer, 17–35 (Innovation and Change in Professional Education, Bind 12).

Angeler, D. G., Allen, C. R. and Carnaval, A. (2020). Convergence science in the Anthropocene: Navigating the known and unknown. *People and Nature*, 2(96), 96–102. DOI: 10.1002/pan3.10069

Angus, I. (2016). *Facing the Anthropocene: Fossil capitalism and the crisis of the Earth system*. New York: Monthly Review Press.

Baskin, J. (2015). Paradigm dressed as epoch: The ideology of the Anthropocene. *Environmental Values*, 24, 9–29. DOI: 10.3197/096327115X141831823537

Bhatasara, S. (2015). Debating sociology and climate change. *Journal of Integrative Environmental Sciences*, 12(3), 217–233. DOI: 10.1080/1943815X.2015.1108342

Brondizio, E. S., O'Brien, K., Bai, X., Biermann, F., Steffen, W., Berkhout, F., Cudennec, C., Lemos, M. C., Wolfe, A., Palma-Oliveira, J. and Chen, C.-T. A. (2016). Re-conceptualizing the Anthropocene: A call for collaboration. *Global Environmental Change*, 39, 318–327. DOI: 10.1016/j.gloenvcha.2016.02.006

Compagnone, C., Lamine, C., and Dupré, L. (2018). The production and circulation of agricultural knowledge as interrogated by agroecology. *Revue D'anthropologie des Connaissances [En ligne]*, 12–2|, mis en ligne le 01 juin 2018, consulté le 06 septembre 2022. http://journals.openedition.org/rac/815

Dick, J., Orenstein, D. E., Holzer, J. M., Wohner, C., Achard, A.-L., Andrews, C., Avriel-Avni, N., Beja, P., Blond, N. and Cabello, J. (2018). What is socio-ecological research delivering? A literature survey across 25 international LTSER platforms. *Science of the Total Environment*, 622–623, 1225–1240. DOI: 10.1016/j.scitotenv.2017.11.324

Holzer, J. M., Carmon, N. and Orenstein, D. E. (2018). A methodology for evaluating transdisciplinary research on coupled socio-ecological systems. *Ecological Indicators*, 85, 808–819. DOI: 10.1016/j.ecolind.2017.10.074

Inkpen, S. A. and DesRoches, C. T. (2019). Revamping the image of science of the Anthropocene. *Philosophy, Theory, and Practice in Biology*, 11(3), 1–7. DOI: 10.3998/ptpbio.16039257.0011.003

IPCC (2022a). Summary for policymakers. In: H.-O. Pörtner, D. C. Roberts, E. S. Poloczanska, K. Mintenbeck, M. Tignor, A. Alegría, M. Craig, S. Langsdorf, S. Löschke, V. Möller & A. Okem (eds.), *Climate change 2022: Impacts, adaptation and vulnerability. Contribution of working group II to the sixth assessment report of the intergovernmental panel on climate change*. Cambridge and New York: Cambridge University Press, 3–33. DOI: 10.1017/9781009325844.001.

IPCC (2022b). *Climate change 2022: Impacts, adaptation and vulnerability. Contribution of Working Group II to the sixth assessment report of the intergovernmental panel on climate change*. H.-O. Pörtner, D. C. Roberts, M. Tignor, E. S. Poloczanska, K. Mintenbeck, A. Alegría, M. Craig, S. Langsdorf, S. Löschke, V. Möller, A. Okem & B. Rama (eds.). Cambridge and New York: Cambridge University Press. DOI: 10.1017/9781009325844.001.

Kelly, R., Mackay, M., Nash, K. L., Cvitanovic, C., Allison, E. H., Armitage, D., Bonn, A., Cooke, S. J., Frusher, S., Fulton, E. A., Halpern, B. S., Lopes, P. F. M., Milner-Gulland, E. J., Peck, M. A., Peci, G. T., Stephenson, R. L. and Werner,

F. (2019). Ten tips for developing interdisciplinary socio-ecological researchers. *Socio-Ecological Practice Research,* 1, 149–161. DOI: 10.1007/s42532-019-00018-2

Koehrsen, J., Dickel, S., Pfister, T., Rödder, S., Böschen, S., Wendt, B., Block, K. and Henkel, A. (2019). Climate change in sociology: Still silent or resonating, 1–47. Draft version to be published in *Current Sociology,* 68(6), 738–760. Retrieved from: https://scholar.google.com/scholar?lookup=0&q=koehrsen+climate+change+in+sociology&hl=da&as_sdt=0,5

Latour, B. and Lenton T. M. (2019). Extending the domain of freedom, or why Gaia is so hard to understand. *Critical Inquiry,* 45(3), 659–680. DOI: 10.1086/702611

López-García, D., Cuéllar-Padilla, M., de Azevedo Olival, A., Laranjeira, N. P., Méndez, V. E., Peredo y Parada, S., Barbosa, C. A., Barrera Salas, C., Caswell, M., Cohen, R., Correro-Humanes, A., García-García, V., Gliessman, S., Pomar-León, A., Sastre-Morató, A. and Tendero-Acín, G. (2021). Building agroecology with people: Challenges of participatory methods to deepen on the agroecological transition in different contexts. *Journal of Rural Studies,* 83, 257–267. DOI: 10.1016/j.jrurstud.2021.02.003

Newell, P., Srivastava, S., Naess, L. O., Contreras, G. A. T., and Price, R. (2020). *Towards transformative climate justice: Key challenges and future directions for research.* Working Paper, Volume 2020, No. 540. The Institute of Development Studies, pp. 151. Retrieved from: https://opendocs.ids.ac.uk/opendocs/bitstream/handle/20.500.12413/15497/Wp540_Towards_Transformative_Climate_Justice.pdf?sequence=1&isAllowed=y

Olesen, H. S., and Andersen, A. S. (2015). The Roskilde model and the challenges for universities in the future. In: A. S. Andersen & S. B. Heilesen (eds.), *The roskilde model: Problem-oriented learning and project work.* Heidelberg, New York, Dordrecht, London: Springer, 17–35 (Innovation and Change in Professional Education, Bind 12).

Palsson, G., Szerszynski, B., Sörlin, S., Marks, J., Avril, B., Crumley, C., Hackmann, H., Holm, P., Ingram, J., Kirman, A., Buendía, M. P. and Weehuizen, R. (2012). Reconceptualizing the 'Anthropos' in the Anthropocene: Integrating the social sciences and humanities in global environmental change research. *Environmental Science & Policy,* 28, 3–13. DOI: 10.1016/j.envsci.2012.11.004.

Pe'er, G., Zinngrebe, Y., Moreira, F., Sirami, C., Schindler, S., Müller, R., Bontzorlos, V. A., Clough, D., Bezák, P., Bonn, A., Hansjürgens, B., Lomba, Â., Möckel, S., Passoni, G., Schleyer, C., Schmidt, J. and Lakner, S. (2019). A greener path for the EU Common Agricultural Policy. *Science,* 365, 449–451. DOI: 10.1126/science.aax3146

Randers, J., Rockström, J., Stoknes, P. E., Golüke, U., Collste, D., and Cornell, S. (2018). *Transformation is feasible. How to achieve the sustainable development goals within planetary boundaries.* A report to the Club of Rome, for its 50 years anniversary 17 October 2018. Stockholm Resilience Centre, p. 60. Retrieved from: https://www.stockholmresilience.org/download/18.51d83659166367a9a16353/1539675518425/Report_Achieving%20the%20Sustainable%20Development%20Goals_WEB.pdf

Rossing, W. A. H., Albicette, M. M., Aguerre, V., Leoni, C., Ruggia, A. and Dogliotti, S. (2021). Crafting actionable knowledge on ecological intensification: Lessons from co-innoovation approaches in Uruguay and Europe. *Agricultural Systems,* 190. DOI: 10.1016/j.agsy.2021.103103

Snick, A. (2020). Wiser than the vikings? Redefining sustainability in the Anthropocene. SAPIRR – Systems Approach to Public Innovation and Responsible Research Club of Rome – EU Chapter

Steffen, W., Richardson, K., Rockström, J., Schellnhuber, H.-J., Dube, O. P., Dutreuil, S., Lenton, T. M. and Lubchenco, J. (2020). The emergence and evolution of Earth System Science. *Nature Reviews Earth & Environment*, 1, 54–63. http://hdl.handle.net/10871/4041 6

Toivanen, T., Lummaa, K., Majava, A., Järvensivu, P., Lähde, V., Vaden, T. and Eronen, J. T. (2017). The many Anthropocenes: A transdisciplinary challenge for the Anthropocene research. *The Anthropocene Review*, 4. DOI: 10.1 177/2053019617738099.

Urry, J. (2015). Climate change and society. In: Michie, J., and Cooper, C. L. (eds.), *Why the social sciences matter*, 45–59. London: Palgrave Macmillan.

Wezel, A., Bellon, S., Doré, T., Francis, C., Vallod, D. and David, C. (2009). Agroecology as a science, a movement and a practice: A review. *Agronomy for Sustainable Development*, 29, 503–515. DOI: 10.1051/agro/2009004

Wezel, A., Goette, J., Lagneaux, E., Passuello, G., Reisman, E., Rodier, C. and Turpin, G. (2018). Agroecology in Europe: Research, education, collective action networks, and alternative food systems. *Sustainability*, 10, 1214. DOI: 10.3390/su10041214

Wohlgezogen, F., McCabe, A., Osegowitsch, T. and Mol, J. (2020). The wicked problem of climate change and interdisciplinary research: Tracking management scholarship's contribution. *Journal of Management & Organization*, 26, 1048–1072. DOI: 10.1017/jmo.2020.14

Index

Note: **Bold** page numbers refer to tables and *italic* page numbers refer to figures.

accountability: government climate action 70; and human rights advocates 108; lack of 52; legal innovations for 341; in non-government/private sector climate action 70
action research: multi-actor 343–349; participatory 343–349
active inequality reduction 80
adaptation 69; climate 107; climate change 53–54, 119, 200, 334; in climate finance 38; and ecological challenges 33; in human systems 33, 71; in SDGs 101
adaption: technology-based adaption strategies 285; unequal consequences of 67–69
Adelman, S. 105, 285
affirmative views: on 2030 Agenda 94–97; on SDGs 94–97
African Union (AU) 268
"After Capital" (Venn) 292
Age of Capital 311
Age of Exploration 303
agriculture: capitalist 304; climate-smart 68–69, 79; food system and 194–211; -related goals, and power relations 101; -related goals and structures 101; slash-and-burn 225
agriculture, forestry, and other land use (AFOLU) 146, *147*
agri-food systems 198; decentralized 10, 196; development and governance of 202; diversified 204; economic profitability in 196; European 195, 200; global 201, 211; sustainable 195, 198, 201, 204; sustainable transition of 208–209
agroecological food systems 13, 320
agroecology 200–201, 281, 343, 345–346, 348, 350
Agroecology-TRANSECT project 345–346, 348
Aichi Biodiversity Targets (SPB) 43, 72, 267
Alexander C. 286–288
Allan, J. R. 223
Alternative Food Networks (AFN) 202
ambition mechanism 37, 268
American capitalism 304
Amoureux, J. 310, 311
Angeler, D. G. 337
Angus, I. 20, 329
Annual Progress Reports 76, 268
Anthropocene 3, 4, 7, 11–13, 16, 18, 28, 65, 112, 264, 301–302; alternative understandings of what is driving 311–315; in humanities 303–315; human–nature relation 306–309; in natural sciences 302–303; in social sciences 303–315; unified notion of Anthropos 309–311
Anthropocene Working Group 303
Anthropos 12, 65, 302; unified notion of 309–311
anti-capitalism approaches 292–295
Arnott, D. 224
Association of Southeast Asian Nations (ASEAN) 268
Attenborough, D. Sir. 301

356 Index

Barca, S. 108
barriers to interdisciplinarity 325–328
Barry, J. 306–308
Baskin, J. 303, 306, 332
Bayer 202
Beltran-Pena, A. A. 195
Bennett, N. J. 230
Bhatasara, S. 304, 326, 327, 335, 337, 340
Bierman, S. F. 307
Biermann, F. 310, 315
biochar 51
biodiversity 22–25, 221; and 2030 Agenda 43–44; global stocktaking of plans and actions 44–45; loss, drivers of 223–225; and nature's contributions to people 218–232; preserving and restoring 122–123; protection of 226–231; and SDGs 43–44; UN governance structure regarding 33–34; valuation 221–223
biodiversity protection 226–227; and climate change mitigation 49–50; data-based considerations for 227–231; reciprocity between climate change mitigation and 50–52
Biodiversity Strategy for 2030 218, 232
bioeconomy 134
biofuels 68, 152, 154, 160, 162–163
biomass 10, 25, 28, 51, 130, 146, 149, 151, 160, 174, 186, 218, 228; of domestic poultry 24; free-standing 85; increased consumption of 183; pyrolysis of 51; wild mammal 24
BirdLife 203
Blondet, M. 227
"blue carbon" biological sinks 51
"Blue Marble" image 330
Blueprint for Just Transition 289–290; companies 290; decent and democratic jobs 290; finance 289–290; global trade 290; public ownership 290; taxation 290
box schemes 202
Brexit 242–243
Brodie, J. F. 225
Brondizio, E. S. 321, 322, 328, 336, 339, 340, 341, 343
"brown" capitalism 292
"brown" jobs 11, 259
Brundtland Report 32
bureaucratic state 265
Burke, A. 307
Burton, M. H. 104, 109

capitalism 108, 294, 295, 305, 307, 310–315, 336; "brown" 292; "green" 292
capitalist agriculture 304
"capitalist world-ecology" 311
Capitalocene 12, 302, 311, 312
Carbon Border Adjustment Mechanism (CBAM) 119, 127, 275, 276–277, 296
Carbon Dioxide Removal (CDR) 285
carbon leakage 126–127, 158, 227
carbon market 36, 68, 98, 275, 277, 294
carbon pricing and Just Transition 246–247
Carrasco, L. R. 222
Carson, R. 330
Cartagena Protocol on Biosafety 42
certified emission reductions (CERs) 36
Chakrabarty, D. 305–306, 309
"Challenges of a Changing Earth" conference 331
Chandler, D. 305
de Chardin, T. 303
Chaudhary, A. 224
Chernilo, D. 305, 308, 309
circular economic policies: circular economy action plan **179,** 179–180; circular economy monitoring framework 181; as decoupling strategy 187–190; in Europe 178–182; and European Green Deal 181–182; evaluating 187–190
circular economy 10, 131–132, 134, 175–178; circular economic policies in Europe 178–182; circular economy policies as decoupling strategy 187–190; as decoupling agenda 177, 177–178; defining 176; and economic growth 188–190; mobilizing industry for 119–120; monitoring framework 181; overview 174–175; patterns of resource consumption 182–187; and sustainable development 188–190
"Circular Economy Promotion Law of the Republic of China" 175
citizens' assemblies 248–249, 260
CityLoops 343–345, 348; circular procurement 344; stakeholder engagement 344; urban circularity assessment 344
Claeys, G. 246
Clean Development Mechanism (CDM) 36, 38, 153, 154
clean economy, mobilizing industry for 119–120

Index

climate: and environmental progress in the EU 131–134; hazards 66; manipulation 285; systems 19, 23
climate change 3, 19–22; and 2030 Agenda 38–39; adaptation 53–54, 119, 200, 334; inequalities pertaining to 241–242; market-based approach to 271–273; and SDGs 38–39; UN governance structure regarding 33–34
"Climate Change 2022: Impacts, Adaptation and Vulnerability. Contribution of Working Group II to the Sixth Assessment Report of the Intergovernmental Panel on Climate Change" report 333
climate change–biodiversity nexus 48–49
climate change–biodiversity–resource nexus 4
climate change mitigation: and biodiversity protection 49–50; reciprocity between biodiversity protection and 50–52
"Climate endgame: Exploring catastrophic climate change scenarios" (Kemp) 1
climate justice 72; deepening 342–343; governance from global perspective 341–342; inclusive 342
Climate Justice Movement 98–99
climate-neutral economy 134, 244
Climate Pact 250
Climate Pact Ambassadors 249
climate-smart agriculture 68–69, 79
Club of Rome 32, 78, 330
Coad, L. 226
cobalt mining 68
Coen, D. 268
Cold War geophysics 330
Colli, F. 248–250
Collins, L. B. 98
colonial "heritage" 293
colonialism 295, 310, 317
Columbian exchange 336
community projects 253, 255
Community Supported Agriculture (CSA) 202
Conference of the Parties (COP) 22, 35, 42, 153
consumerism 136, 282, 291
consumption systems 129, 134–136, 140, 151, 174–175, 187, 189, 291
"Contemporary Anthropocene" 303
Convention on Biological Diversity (CBD) 22, 34, 40–41, 43, 267

cooperative farming 202
cooperatives 253–255
COP15 in Copenhagen 36, 154–155
Copenhagen Accord 36–38, 155
'Copernican' revolution 329
Copernicus 329
COVID-19 pandemic 11, 20, 21, 39, 40, 64, 209, 240, 241, 243, 245, 259, 269, 279, 286
critical raw materials 186–187
Critical Realism 308
critical views: on 2030 Agenda 97–108; general framings of 108–111; on goal-based governance 75–81; Nationally Determined Contributions 75–81; on SDGs 97–108
Crop diversity strategies 230
Crutzen, P. 303
Curtis, P. G. 225

data-based considerations for biodiversity protection 227–231
Davis, J. 314
decentering humanity 301–317
decent work: 2030 Agenda 107–108; SDGs 107–108
decoupling: 2030 Agenda 102–105; agenda, circular economy as 177, 177–178; SDGs 102–105; strategy, circular economy policies as 187–190
degrowth 290–292; 2030 Agenda 102–105; SDGs 102–105
Democracy in Europe Movement 297
Dewey, J. 304
digital technologies 69
"direct drivers" 5, **5**, 52
distributional equity 61–62
distributional justice 61–62
DiverIMPACTS project 345
diversification strategies 229
DIVERSITAS (international research program) 330
Divestment Movement 99
Dobson, A. 307–309
Domestic Material Consumption (DMC) 178, 187–188
"Doughnut Economics" 59, 341
drivers: affecting wildlife and ecosystems 102; of biodiversity loss 223–225; direct 5, 52; indirect 4, 5–6, 52; structural 67, 101
Drivers-Pressures-States-Impacts-Responses (DPSIR) framework 108–109

Durkheim, E. 304
Dynamic Integrated Model of Climate Change and Economy (DICE) 271, 276

"Early Anthropocene" 303
Earth3 model 78–81, 89
Earth Summit 32, 34
Earth system 3, 7, 17, 18, 20, 22, 23, 26, 27, 307; as revolutionary scientific shift 329
Earth system science (ESS) 329–332
Earth System Science Committee 330
Earth System Science Partnership (ESSP) 331
EAT-Lancet Commission Report 210
Eberle, C. 258
ecological challenges: socially differentiated consequences of 65–67; socially differentiated contributions to 64–65
ecological depth and loss & damages 107
ecological devastation 295
ecological governance: in EU 264–297; in UN 264–297
ecological modernization 12, 264, 270, 278–279; in the EU 279–280
ecological sustainability 56, 60, 61, 67, 71–72
eco-Marxist debates 316
"eco-nationalism" 287
economic growth: and circular economy 188–190; and sustainable development 188–190
economy: circular (see circular economy); climate-neutral 134, 244; low-carbon 131–132; resource-efficient 131–132; solidarity 258, 289, 295, 347
ecosystems: preserving 122–123; restoring 122–123
EEA report: circular economy 131–132; environmental risks to health and well-being 132; low-carbon economy 131–132; protecting, conserving, and enhancing natural capital 131; resource-efficient 131–132
Egmose, J. 210, 221
Ellen MacArthur Foundation 175
emission reduction units (ERU) 36
empowerment 61–62, 72, 75, 255; legal 70
energy: accelerated renewables growth 79; consumption, and societal development 147–150; supplying clean, affordable, and secure 119
energy infrastructure 159, 254
Energy Justice Movement 99–100
energy production: and climate crisis 146–147; energy consumption and societal development 147–150; energy-prerequisites and capabilities 150–151; European Union climate action policies 152–160; impact/justice/fairness 165–170; twenty-first-century developments in 160–165
Energy Return on Energy Investment (EROI) 149, 170
Energy Taxation Directive 119
Enhanced Transparency Framework (ETF) 267
environment: in europe 128–138; policies 138; zero-pollution ambition for toxic-free 123
environmental justice 97
Environmental Justice Commission (EJC) 252, 256, 289
Environmental Justice Movement 97–98
environmental risks 132
environmental sociology 326
environmental solutions: inequalities pertaining to 241–242
Environmental Union (EnU) 252, 256
epistemicide 258
equality 7, 22, 59, 65, 239, 246; and dignity 73; gender 80; intergenerational 267; social 102, 260, 279
equity 61–63
Escobar, A. 314
ETS system 153–154, 275
EU Commission 224, 245, 257, 269
EU Critical Raw Materials Program 186–187
EU Emissions Trading System (ETC) 119, 121, 275
EU Forest Strategy 225, 226
EU Joint Research Center 187
Eurofound 240, 241
Europe: circular economic policies in 178–182; development of food system in 208–211; economic policy 269; emissions from a local perspective 169–170; environment in 128–138; income inequalities in 240–241; inequalities in 240–242; terrestrial biodiversity 10; transformative change across 137; wealth inequalities in 240–241; in the world 129–131
European Carbon Transfer (ECT) system 276

Index 359

European Central Bank 269, 289
European climate action: from a global perspective 167–168; from a regional perspective 168–169
European Climate Change Programme 153
European Climate Law 157, 270
European Climate Pact 128
European colonialism 293
European Commission (EC) 10, 116, 201, 219, 269, 275; Anthropocene Working Group 303; "Farm-to-Fork" strategy 122; "Roadmap for a Resource-Efficient Europe" 175; State of Nature Report 219
European Common Agricultural Policy (CAP) 10, 194, 196–198, 203–204, 206–207, 223, 224, 232
European Council 269; strategic agenda for 2019–2024 117
European Court of Justice 269
European economy: consumption in 184–186, *185*; resource flows in 184–186, *185*
European environment: climate progress in EU 131–134; environmental pressures from systems perspective 134; environmental progress in EU 131–134; Europe in the world 129–131; insights across systems 135–137; mobility system 134–135; politics and governance 137–138; state of 128–138
European Environment Agency (EEA) 8–9, 116, 182, 194, 219, 220, 243, 248, 291, 297; DPSIR framework 108–109; environmental policies 138; financial markets and sustainability transitions 138; knowledge and skills fit for 21st century 138; private investments 138; public budgets 138; and SDGs 137–138; systemic policy frameworks with binding targets 138; transformative change across Europe 137
European Environmental Bureau (EEB) 203
European Environment Information and Observation Network (Eionet) 128
European Green Deal 8, 9, 10, 11, 116, 219, 220, 232, 239, 240, 241, 242–243, 245, 246, 248, 249, 250, 251, 252, 253, 257, 258, 259, 260, 269; accelerating shift to sustainable/smart mobility 121–122; areas of intervention of 119–128; background 117; climate ambitions 119; ecosystems and biodiversity 122–123; energy-and resource-efficient way 120–121; EU and global sustainable transformation 125–127; European Union climate action policies 156–157; farm to fork 122; finance, investments, and economic incentives 124–125; global cooperation 142; inclusion and citizen participation 127–128; and Just Transition 127, 141, 242–247; levers in sustainable transformation 141–142; mobilizing industry for clean/circular economy 119–120; mobilizing research and fostering innovation 125; overall characterization of 117–119; overview 116–117; policy objectives 138–143; procedural justice and 247–251; and revised circular economy action plan 181–182; scientific recommendations 138–143; state of the environment in Europe 128–138; supplying clean, affordable, and secure energy 119; supporting innovations of society 142–143; and toxic-free environment 123
European imperialism 293
European Innovation Council 125
European Investment Bank (EIB) Group 124, 244, 253
European modernity 304–305
European Natura 2000 network 226
European Parliament 117, 118, 269
European Pillar of Social Rights 118, 246, 253; Just Transition Mechanism 243
European political thinking 278
European security crisis 13
European Semester 269; Country Reports 245
European Single Act 269
European Trade Union Confederation 239
European Union (EU) 4, 9, 11, 12, 34, 116, 220, 221, 223, 224, 227, 241, 244, 246, 248, 250, 260, 264–265, 268, 269, 273; 2030 Biodiversity Strategy 222; Border Adjustment Mechanism 277; circular economy and sustainable development in 188–190; Climate Action Pact 169; climate and environmental progress in 131–134; Climate Pact 249; critical raw materials for 186–187; ecological governance in 264–297; economic growth and sustainable development in 188–190;

economic incentives in 124–125; finance incentives in 124–125; Green Deal 10; greenhouse gas emission reductions in 166, *167*; International Platform on Sustainable Finance 126; investment incentives in 124–125; Just Transition and 239–261; as leader of global sustainable transformation 125–127; market-based solutions in 275, 276–277; political and theoretical paradigms underlying solutions 270–284; Seventh Environment Action Program (7th EAP) 129; socioecological governance in 264–297; socioecological modernization in 279–280; version of socioecological modernization paradigm 282–284; and the world 208–211

European Union climate action policies: 2020 Climate Action Package 154; COP15 in Copenhagen 154–155; ETS 153–154; European Climate Change Programme 153; European Green Deal 156–157; financial crisis 155; Fit for 55 157–158; launch of 152–160; overview of 159–160; Paris Agreement 155–156; Renewable Energy Directive2 (RED2) 156; Russian invasion of Ukraine 158–159

EU's energy sector: temporal scale 163–165; twenty-first-century developments in 160–165

exposure 33

family planning 80
Farmland Bird Index 207
Farm-to-Fork Strategy 10, 122, 198, 210, 224, 232, 270
financial crises in 2008 155, 240
financial markets 138
financing: 2030 Agenda 105–107; and free trade 105; and the multinationals 105; SDGs 105–107
Fit for 55 157–158
Fleming, R. C. 244–245
Flouros, F. 168
Food Policy Councils 208
food system: and agriculture 194–211; basis of food grown 198–201; defined 194; environmental impact of CAP 201–206; fair, healthy, and environmentally friendly 122; fundamental theoretical/political questions concerning 208–211; necessary interventions to transform 206–208; overview 194–198

Fordist model 106
Foster, J. B. 294–295, 313
Frazer, N. 62
freedom 60–61
free trade: 2030 Agenda 105–107; SDGs 105–107
Fremaux, A. 306, 307–308
"Fridays for Future" 117
Friends of the Earth Europe 203
Fronteddu, B. 245
Fukuda-Parr, S. 95–96
The Future is Now: Science for Achieving Sustainable Development 82

G7 countries 125, 293
G20 (Group of Twenty) 40, 125, 293
G20 Development Finance Institutions (DFIs) 40
Gaia theory 331–332
Galileo 329
Geissdoerfer, M. 176
Geldmann, J. 226
gender equality 80
general inequality 64
genetically modified organism (GMO) 42
geoengineering 285
Ghoddousi, A. 228
Gibson, K. 295
Gilbert, N. 102
Global Biodiversity Outlook 5 (2020) 48
global cooperation, and European Green Deal 142
global ecological risks: biodiversity 22–25; climate change 19–22; natural evolution and human development 17–18; overview 16; planetary boundaries 26–27; resources 25–26
Global Environmental Assessment Commission 315
Global Environment Facility (GEF) 35, 41
global food crisis 13
global health crisis 13
global inequality 64
globalization 109, 136, 240, 282, 288
Global North 3, 37, 89, 97, 98, 104, 107, 111, 220, 258, 260, 293, 304, 309, 315
Global Partnership for Sustainable Development 73

Global South 2, 3, 8, 11, 28, 37, 69, 70, 89, 93, 95–96, 97, 98, 104, 107, 220, 226, 239, 257, 258, 260, 293, 309, 315; and Europe's Just Transition 257–259; perspectives 111
global stocktaking: of biodiversity plans and actions 44–45; of national climate change plans and actions 39–40
Global Sustainability Report 8, 81–88, 90, 268, 280; bottom-up innovation 281; first 81–88; fossil fuels 281; GDP 281; global commons 281; movements and activists 281; structures 281; technological solutions 281
Global Sustainable Development Reports (UN) 76, 83, 268; economy and finance 87–88; energy decarbonization with universal access 85; food systems and nutrition patterns 84–85; global environmental commons 86; governance 87; human wellbeing and capabilities 83–84; individual and collective action 88; science and technology 88; sustainable and just economies 84; urban and peri-urban development 85–86
global sustainable transformation 125–127
goal-based governance 8, 53–54; critical views on 75–81; and Nationally Determined Contributions 75–81
governance 4, 11–13, 265–266; for climate justice from global perspective 341–342; European environment 137–138; goal-based 53–54, 75–81; procedures of 265–266; structures and procedures in EU 269–270; structures and procedures in UN 266–268
government 265–266; and governance structures 265; procedures of 265–266; structures and procedures in EU 269–270; structures and procedures in UN 266–268
Great Acceleration 6, 16, 18, 28, 102, 301, 303, 330, 331
"Great Acceleration Anthropocene" 303
"Great Divergence" 65
Great Oxidation Event 6, 16
Great Oxygenation Event 17
The Great Transformation (Polanyi) 331
"green" capitalism 292
Green Climate Fund 38
Green Deal for Europe 251, 289–290
"Green Deal Missions" 125

"green economy" 175, 278
"green growth" 175, 278
greenhouse gases (GHGs) 20, 21, 23, 26, 28, 34, 35, 36, 268; emission reductions 166, *167*
"green" jobs 11
Green New Deal 239, 252, 255
Green New Deal for Europa Coalition 11, 260
Greenpeace 203
Green Public Works (GPW) 252–255, 256; cooperatives and community projects 255; energy infrastructure 254; housing and energy poverty 254; mobility 254–255; reproductive and care work 255; rural communities 255; workers' rights 255
Gro Harlem Brundtland 82
Gross State Output (GSP) 274
Grove, K. 305
growth paradigm: 2030 Agenda 102–105; SDGs 102–105
Guterres, A. 1, 39, 48, 82, 183

Haraway, D. 313–314
Hawking, S. 16
health 80, 132
Heikkurinen, P. 103–105, 292
Heyen, D. A. 241–242, 247
Hickel, J. 183
High-Level Political Forum on Sustainable Development 81
Holocene 7, 16, 17, 18, 303, 306
Holzer, J. M. 323, 336
Homo sapiens 17, 27, 306
Horizon 2020 program 203, 251, 343
Horizon Europe 125, 203
human development 17; natural evolution and 17–18
Human Development Index (HDI) (UNDP) 81
humanities: Anthropocene in 303–315; decentering 301–317
human–nature relation 12, 306–309
human rights perspectives 94–95
human settlement planning 75

IBM 202
Ideas to Postpone the End of the World (Krenak) 257
IMF 293
impacts, defined 5, **5**
imperialism 295

362 Index

inclusion and citizen participation 127–128
inclusive climate justice 342
income inequalities 240–241
indirect drivers 4, 5–6, 52
individualism 136
Industrial Revolution 336
inequalities 4, 239; in Europe 240–242; general 64; households and consumers 242; income 240–241; jobs, workers, and regions 242; pertaining to climate change and environmental solutions 241–242; procedural 69–70; wealth 240–241
innovation, fostering 125
Innovation Hubs (IHs) 345–346
Inoue, C.Y.A. 311
Integrated Assessment Models 274
interdisciplinarity: barriers to 325–328; call for 321–322; cross-/interdisciplinary approaches 322–323; and humanities 337–338; multi-/pluridisciplinary approaches 322; and the natural sciences 329–332; and social sciences 335–337; transdisciplinary approaches 323; types of 322–325
interdisciplinary knowledge 4
interdisciplinary research 11–13; barriers to interdisciplinarity 325–328; call for interdisciplinarity 321–322; interdisciplinary traditions and developments 328–338; and knowledge creation 320–350; multi-actor and participatory action research 343–349; new interdisciplinary research agendas 338–343; types of interdisciplinarity 322–325
intergenerational: equity 62; justice 5, 62, 253, 256
Intergovernmental Panel on Climate Change (IPCC) 1, 7, 19, 20, 21, 22, 25, 28, 33, 82, 105, 152, 272, 276, 329, 332–335, 350; "enabling conditions" 71
Intergovernmental Science-Policy Platform on Biodiversity and Ecosystem Services (IPBES) 7, 10–11, 19, 22, 23, 24, 25, 28, 33, 82, 218, 220, 221, 222, 225, 232, 276
International Commission on Stratigraphy 303, 315
International Council of Scientific Unions (ICSU) 330

International Geosphere-Biosphere Program (IGBP) 330
International Human Dimensions Programme on Global Environmental Change (IHDP) 331
International Institute for Applied System Analysis 331
International Labor Organization (ILO) 96–97, 111
International Resource Panel (IRP) 7, 19, 25, 26, 28, 33, 45–46, 104, 182
International Union for Conservation (IUCN) 223
InvestEU 124, 243
IPES-Food & ETC Group 202, 206–207

Jansen, K. 311–313
Jessop, B. 102
John Deere 202
Joint Implementation (JI) 36
Jongerden, J. 311–313
justice 61–63, 100–101; 2030 Agenda 100–102; distributional 61–62; energy production 165–170; intergenerational 5, 62, 253, 256; multispecies 317; SDGs 100–102
Just Transition 72, 96, 116, 240, 246, 247, 249, 252, 253, 256, 257, 258, 279; 2030 Agenda 107–108; blueprint for 252–257; carbon pricing and 246–247; and decent work 96–97; and EU 239–261; European Green Deal 141, 247–251; Global South perspective 257–259; inequalities in Europe 240–242; leaving no one behind 127; overview 239; procedural justice 247–251; promoting 127; SDGs 107–108
Just Transition Fund 141, 243, 244, 259
Just Transition Mechanism (JTM) 157, 243–246, 249, 259, 270, 283; European Investment Bank (EIB) 244–245; Just Transition Fund 243–244; Just Transition Scheme 244
Just Transition Platform 249
Just Transition Scheme 259; Just Transition Mechanism 244

Kagan, C. 104, 109
Kastner, T. 224
Katowice package 37
Keen, S. 273, 274, 275
Kelly, R. 321, 325
Kennedy, R. 264
Keynesianism 102

Keynesian welfare state 102
Kirchherr, J. 176
knowledge: creation 320–350; interdisciplinary 4; scientific 2; and skills fit for 21st century 138
Koehler, G. 94, 95, 100, 104, 105
Krenak, A. 257–258
Kyoto Agreement 296
Kyoto Protocol 35–36, 37, 38, 97, 153–154, 165, 272, 275

Least Developed Countries (LDCs) 35, 38
legal empowerment and use of rights 70
The Limits to Growth (Meadows) 32, 330
living modified organisms (LMOs) 42
loss and damages 107
Lovbrand, E. 309
low-carbon economy 131–132
low-carbon transitions 67

Mair, S. 76
Major Economic Forum (MEF) 268
maladaptation 33
Maris, G. 168
market-based approach to climate change 271–273
market-based solutions 296; criticism of empirical 273–275; criticism of theoretical 273–275; in EU 275; in UN 275
Marx, K. 304, 311
Marxism 289
material consumption 64–65
Mauger, R. 244–245
Mazor, T. 223
McPhee, C. 230
Mead, H. 304
Menton, M. 69, 100, 101, 103, 105, 106, 107
Metaverse 284–285
migration crisis 13
mileurista 241
Millennium Development Goals (MDGs) 8, 32, 93, 94
mineral weathering 51, 285
mitigation: climate change (*see* climate change mitigation); unequal consequences of 67–69
mobility system 134–135
modernity: European 304–305; "iron cage" of 305
monocentric (or centralist) government 265

mono-culturality 110
Monsanto 202
Montreal Protocol on Substances that Deplete the Ozone Layer 34–35
Moore, J. 311–313
Moreira, P. F. 311
Muchhala, B. 95–96
multi-actor action research 343–349
Multiannual Financial Framework (MMF) 244
Multilateral Development Banks (MDBs) 40
multinationals: 2030 Agenda 105–107; SDGs 105–107
Multiple Anthropocenes 12, 302, 310, 311, 316
"Multiple Natures" 316
multispecies justice 317

Nagoya Protocol 43–44, 55
National Aeronautics and Space Administration (NASA) 330
National Biodiversity Strategies and Action Plans (NBSAPs) 41, 43, 267
national climate change plans and actions 39–40
National Determined Contributions (NDCs) 8, 36, 37, 38, 39, 75–81, 89, 90, 266, 267
National Energy and Climate Plans (NECPs) 156, 165, 168
national governments 82, 86, 241, 253, 269, 271, 286
nationalism, defined 286
nationalist strategies 286–288, 297
National Recovery and Resilience Investments Plans 246
National Recovery and Resilience Programs 246
Natura 2000 areas 11, 219
Natura 2000 network 122, 226, 227
natural capital: conserving 131; enhancing 131; protecting 131
natural evolution and human development 17–18
natural sciences: Anthropocene in 302–303; interdisciplinarity and 329–332
natural scientists 12, 65, 301
nature-based solutions (NBSs) 13, 23, 346–347
Net Energy Output (NEO) 149, 170
Netherlands Enterprise Agency (RVO) 160
Newell, P. 61, 67, 69, 98, 341–342

New Green Deal 256
new interdisciplinary research agendas 338–343
Next Generation EU 244, 259
NIMBY 169
Nobre, C. A. 227
non-governmental actors 265–268
non-governmental organizations (NGOs) 8, 93, 100, 110, 128, 203, 208, 212, 276, 283, 296, 332, 348
Non-State Actor Zone for Climate Action (NAZCA) platform 38
Nordhaus, W. 270–273, 274, 275
Norwegian Business School 8, 78

Ocasio-Cortez, A. 289
OECD 175, 278
OECD Green Growth Indicator Report 178
official development assistance (ODA) 87
One Planet Network 34, 45–47, 267
One-World doctrine 258
Open Working Group (OWG) 94
orchestration 227, 266
"The Outlook 5" report (Secretariat of the Convention on Biological Diversity, 2020) 44
Oxfam 108

Paloniemi, R. 231
Palsson, G. 322, 337, 338, 341, 343
pan-European Mobility Cohesion Fund 254
Paris Agreement 1, 9, 36–38, 53, 72, 85, 103, 266, 267, 268, 272, 275; European Union climate action policies 155–156
participation 5, 9, 36, 42, 55, 61–62, 69, 72–75, 95–97, 111, 116, 204, 206, 208, 227, 229, 240, 247–256, 259–260; inclusion and citizen 127–128
participatory action research 343–349
Perey, R. 314, 315
Perry, K. P. 105, 107
Piketty, T. 13, 258
planetary boundaries 8, 26–27, 79, 80, 304, 331; framework 26; reaching SDGs within 78–81
Plantationocene 12, 302, 317
plural knowledges 70
"Pluriverse" 316
Polanyi, K. 98, 331
political/theoretical paradigms: underlying alternative solutions 284–289; underlying UN and EU solutions 270–284
politics: European environment 137–138; pro-poor and gender sensitive 75
polluter pays principle 98
poor countries, and new development models 80
postcolonialism 310, 317
Potsdam Institute for Climate Impact Research (PIK) 331
poverty 72, 73, 95
poverty reduction: 2030 Agenda 100; SDGs 100
"poverty traps" 66
power: density 67; of transformative decision-making 10; wind 79
precautionary principle 42
pressures: Drivers-Pressures-States-Impacts-Responses (DPSIR) framework 108–109; environmental 134; from systems perspective 134
primacy of exploitation 110
private investments 138
procedural equity 62
procedural inequalities 69–70
procedural justice 62, 247, 283; citizens' assemblies 248–249; and European Green Deal 247–251; local projects 249; public consultations 248
procedural Just Transition 251
Proceedings of the National Academy of Sciences 1
Production Gap Report 39, 280
production systems 98, 149, 174, 194, 199, 211–212, 345
pro-poor and gender sensitive politics 75
protection of biodiversity 226–231
public budgets, and sustainability transitions 138
public consultations 248
public-loans facility 243, 244, 259

Qie, S. 104–105

racism 295, 314, 317; environmental 310
Raworth, K. 59
Randers, J. 78–80
recognition 5, 7, 13, 32, 62, 70, 75, 97, 107–108, 111, 133, 210, 212, 221, 226, 239, 256, 266, 311, 316, 320, 325–326, 350; and equity 62; and justice 62
recognitional equity 62
recognitional justice 62
Reddy, V. 310, 311

Red List of threatened species 223
Reed, J. 231
Rega, C. 207
Reichel, A. 314, 315
ReMIX project 345
renewable energy 67, 102, 131, 147, 149, 152–154, 156–157, 162, 187, 190, 204, 286–287
Renewable Energy Directive2 (RED2) 156
REPowerEU plan 159
reproductive and care work 255
research, mobilizing 125
resilience 33, 37–38, 63, 69, 71, 74, 83–86, 118, 126–127, 139, 195, 201, 209, 219, 225, 230, 246, 285, 340, 345–348
resource consumption: circular economy 182–187; critical raw materials for EU 186–187; patterns of 182–187; resource flows and consumption in European economy 184–186, *185*
resource-efficient economy 131–132
"resource nexus" 282–283
resources 25–26; the 2030 Agenda 47–48; decoupling 177; and Sustainable Development Goals 47–48; UN governance structure regarding 33–34
responses 108–109; biodiversity 53; Drivers-Pressures-States-Impacts-Responses (DPSIR) framework 108–109; flexible 53; policy 118, 131, 133, 136, 137, 144, 186–187; political 3, 11
rhythmic "breathing" 20
Rio Declaration on the Environment and Development 41, 71
Robra, B. 103–105, 292
Rockstrom, J. 331
rural communities 255
Russian invasion of Ukraine 158–159

Sabato, S. 245
safety 60–61
Sampaio, G. 227
SCAR 209
Schaller, S. 286–288
Schellnhuber, H. J. 331
Schleicher, J. 78, 106
Schlosberg, D. 98
Schumpeterian workfare state 102
"science wars" 322
scientific analysis 27
scientific knowledge 2, 14

Searchinger, T. 194
Secretariat of the Convention of Biological Diversity 44
sector- and system-oriented strategies 9
semi-permanent settlements 17
share farming 202
short-termism 136
Siddiqi, A. 258
Silent Spring (Carson) 330
Simmel, G. 304
Simpson, M. 302, 303, 310
slash-and-burn agriculture 225
Snick, A. 321, 325
Snow, C. P. 327
Social Climate Fund 283
Social Climate Plans 158
social development 4, 94; energy consumption driving 147–150
social inequalities 2, 3
social legitimacy 99
socially differentiated consequences of ecological challenges 65–67
social sciences: Anthropocene in 303–315; interdisciplinarity and 335–337
social scientists 12, 301
society: fundamental innovations of 142–143
socioecological challenges: and differentiated human consequences 63–70
socioecological challenges/UN policies: and differentiated human consequences 63–70; first Global Sustainability Report 81–88; goal-based governance 75–81; Nationally Determined Contributions 75–81; overview 59–60; SDG outcomes 81–88; socioecological governance within the UN 70–75; socioecological sustainable transformation 60–63
socioecological governance: in EU 264–297; in UN 264–297; within the UN 70–75
socioecological modernization 278–279, 296; in EU 279–280; EU version of 282–284; UN version of 280–282
socioecological sustainable transformation: key concepts about 60–63; notions of equity and justice 61–63; notions of freedom and safety 60–61; UN decisions on ecological sustainability 71–72
socioecological transformation strategies 288–289

Index

solar PV technologies 68
Solar Radiation Management (SRM) 285
solar radiation management techniques 285
solidarity economy 258, 289, 295, 347
de Sousa Santos, B. 258
Spangenberg, J. H. 109, 111
"Specific Actions for Vigorous Energy Efficiency" (SAVE) program 152
"states" 5, **5**
Steffen, W. 27, 176, 329, 330, 331, 332
Stiglitz, J. 258
Stockholm Environmental Institute's Climate Equity Reference Calculator 168
Stockholm Resilience Center 8, 26, 78, 331
stocktaking: of biodiversity plans and actions 44–45; of national climate change plans and actions 39–40; UN ecological risk governance 48
Stoermer, E. 303
Strategic Plan for Biodiversity 2011-2020 43, 267
structure, defined 109
Supiot 106
sustainability transitions: financial markets toward promoting 138; and private investments 138; and public budgets 138
"Sustainable Community Movement Organizations" (SCMOs) 295
sustainable development: and circular economy 188–190; and economic growth 188–190
Sustainable Development Goals (SDGs) 6, 7, 8, 47–48, 72, 73, 74, 75, 77, 78, 80, 81, 82, 85, 87, 89, 93, 94, 103, 104, 106, 267, 268; and 2030 Agenda 47–48; adaptation in 101; affirmative views on 94–97; and biodiversity 43–44; and climate change 38–39; Climate Justice Movement 98–99; critical views on 97–108; decent work and Just Transition 107–108; ecological depth and loss & damages 107; Energy Justice Movement 99–100; Environmental Justice Movement 97–98; financing, free trade, and multinationals 105–107; first Global Sustainability Report 81–88; as framework for policy-making and implementation 137–138; Global South 95–96; growth paradigm, decoupling, and degrowth 102–105; human rights perspectives 94–95; justice 100–102; Just Transition and decent work 96–97; main themes in 100–108; outcomes and proposing ways forward 81–88; and planetary boundaries 78–81; poverty reduction 100; success score 78, 79, 80
sustainable food chains 79
sustainable local planning 75
sustainable/smart mobility 121–122

taming natures 110
technology-based and quick fix strategies 284–286
10-Year Framework of Programs on Sustainable Consumption and Production (10YFP) 34, 45–47, 72, 89, 94, 267
territorial Just Transition plans 245
"the metabolic rift" 304
3D Google Metaverse 284
Tilman, D. 222
Timmermans, F. 117
Toivanen, T. 322, 328, 335, 337, 338, 343
TRANS-lighthouses project 346–349
transnational movement and people's assemblies 256–257
Treaty of Maastricht 269
2020 Climate Action Package 154–155
2030 Agenda for Sustainable Development 6, 8, 32, 72, 76, 93, 94, 95, 100, 105, 267, 268; affirmative views on 94–97; and biodiversity 43–44; climate change 38–39; Climate Justice Movement 98–99; critical views on 97–108; decent work and Just Transition 107–108; ecological depth and loss & damages 107; Energy Justice Movement 99–100; Environmental Justice Movement 97–98; financing, free trade, and multinationals 105–107; general framings of critical views 108–111; Global South 95–96; growth paradigm, decoupling, and degrowth 102–105; human rights perspectives 94–95; indicators in 72–75; justice 100–102; Just Transition and decent work 96–97; main themes in critical discussion of 100–108; overview 93–94; poverty reduction 100; and resources 47–48; and SDGs 47–48; socioecological goals of 72–75; socioecological targets of 72–75

Index 367

Ukraine, Russian invasion of 158–159
UN Climate Conferences (COPs) 19, 37
UN Conventions on Biodiversity 94
UN Conventions on Climate Change 94
under development 77, **77**
UN ecological risk governance: Aichi targets 43; biodiversity, 2030 Agenda, and SDGs 43–44; biodiversity plans and actions 44–45; biodiversity protection and climate change mitigation 49–52; Cartagena Protocol on Biosafety 42; climate change, 2030 Agenda, and SDGs 38–39; climate change–biodiversity nexus 48–49; Copenhagen Accord 36–38; goal-based governance 53–54; Kyoto Protocol 35–36; Nagoya Protocol 43; national climate change plans and actions 39–40; overview 32–33; Paris Agreement 36–38; resources, 2030 agenda, and SDGs 47–48; stocktaking 48; UN biodiversity governance 40–42; UN climate change governance 34; United Nations Framework Convention on Climate Change 34–35; UN resource governance 45–47; wicked problems and flexible solutions 52–53
UN Environment Program's Emission Gap Report 182
UN Framework Convention on Climate Change (UNFCCC) 35, 36, 37, 38, 182, 272
United Nations (UN) 4, 6, 7, 11, 12, 16, 18, 19, 25, 32, 82, 89, 96, 98, 220, 239, 264; agreements 34, 93, 268; biodiversity governance 40–42; climate change governance 34; decisions on ecological sustainability 71–72; ecological governance in 264–297; Enhanced Transparency Framework (ETF) 37; governance structures 33–34; market-based solutions in 275, 276–277; "Only One Earth" discourse 330; Our Common Future 32; policies 89; political/theoretical paradigms underlying solutions 270–284; reports 19, 26; resource governance 45–47; socioecological governance in 264–297; socioecological governance within 70–75; version of socioecological modernization paradigm 280–282
United Nations Development Programme (UNDP) 7, 17, 18, 27, 33, 59, 65, 151, 290–291, 314
United Nations Environment Program (UNEP) 19, 22, 25, 175, 278
United Nations Framework Convention on Climate Change (UNFCCC) 9, 34–35, 54, 72, 98, 152, 275
United Nations Framework Convention on on Biological Diversity 72
United Nations General Assembly 34
United Nations Member States 32, 81
universal access 75, 85
Universal Declaration of Human Rights (UN) 60, 72
unsustainable development 3, 6, 111
UN Sustainable Development Council 315
urban circularity 13, 320, 344
Urry, J. 327
US National Center for Atmospheric Research (NCAR) 331

Velicu, I. 108
Venn, C. 292–293
Venter, O. 227
Verburgt, L. M. 306
Vernadsky, V. 303, 330
Voet, L. 239
Voluntary Carbon Offsets (VCO) 36, 275, 276, 296
von der Leyen, U. 117, 218
vulnerability 33, 61–62, 66–67, 71, 84, 159, 187, 310, 333–334, 340, 345
vulnerable cropping system 230
vulnerable groups 102

Waste Framework Directive (WFD) 178–179
wealth inequalities 240–241
Weber, M. 304–305
weight-based assessments 186
well-being 21, 24, 27, 46–47, 100, 104, 118, 132, 138, 144, 218, 269, 321, 329, 331
Wennersten, R. 104–105
Western civilization 110
Wezel, A. 200
wicked problems 52–53, 325
Williams, C. 94, 107, 225
Winkler, I. T. 94, 107, 225
Wohlgezogen, F. 323, 324

workers' rights 255
World Bank 64, 293
World Climate Research Program (WCRP) 330
World Environment Organization 315
World Meteorological Organization (WMO) 19, 20, 28, 66; 2021 report 39; State of the Climate Report 20
World Soil Day 200–201
World Trade Organization (WTO) 97, 106, 127, 290, 315

World War II 10, 63, 102, 195, 327, 331
World Wide Fund for Nature (WWF) 203

Yara 202
Yellow Vest Movement in France 169, 247
"Youth Strike for Climate" 117

Zafra-Calvo, N. 226
Zehr, S. 304
zero-pollution ambition for toxic-free environment 123

Printed in the United States
by Baker & Taylor Publisher Services